STUDIES IN MODERNITY AND NATIONAL IDENTITY
Sibel Bozdoğan and Reşat Kasaba, Series Editors

Studies in Modernity and National Identity examine the relationships among modernity, the nation-state, and nationalism as these have evolved in the nineteenth and twentieth centuries. Titles in this interdisciplinary and transregional series also illuminate how the nation-state is being undermined by the forces of globalization, international migration, and electronic information flows, as well as resurgent ethnic and religious affiliations. These books highlight historical parallels and continuities while documenting the social, cultural, and spatial expressions through which modern national identities have been constructed, contested, and reinvented.

Modernism and Nation Building: Turkish Architectural Culture in the Early Republic by Sibel Bozdoğan

Chandigarh's Le Corbusier: The Struggle for Modernity in Postcolonial India by Vikramaditya Prakash

Islamist Mobilization in Turkey: A Study in Vernacular Politics by Jenny B. White

The Landscape of Stalinism: The Art and Ideology of Soviet Space, edited by Evgeny Dobrenko and Eric Naiman

Architecture and Tourism in Italian Colonial Libya: An Ambivalent Modernism by Brian L. McLaren

Everyday Modernity in China, edited by Madeleine Yue Dong and Joshua L. Goldstein

Nationalizing Iran: Culture, Power, and the State, 1870–1940 by Afshin Marashi

Empire, Architecture, and the City: French-Ottoman Encounters (1830–1914), by Zeynep Çelik

Modernism and the Middle East: Architecture and Politics in the Twentieth Century, edited by Sandy Isenstadt and Kishwar Rizvi

MODERNISM AND THE MIDDLE EAST

Architecture and Politics in the Twentieth Century

EDITED BY SANDY ISENSTADT AND KISHWAR RIZVI

UNIVERSITY OF WASHINGTON PRESS | SEATTLE AND LONDON

Publication of *Modernism and the Middle East* was supported by a grant from the Graham Foundation for Advanced Studies in the Fine Arts. Additional assistance came from the Frederick W. Hilles Publication Fund and the Edward J. and Dorothy Clarke Kempf Memorial Fund, both of Yale University.

© 2008 by the University of Washington Press
Printed in the United States of America
12 11 10 09 08   5 4 3 2 1

All rights reserved. No part of this publication may be reproduced or transmitted in any form or by any means, electronic or mechanical, including photocopy, recording, or any information storage or retrieval system, without permission in writing from the publisher.

University of Washington Press
P.O. Box 50096, Seattle, WA 98145 U.S.A.
www.washington.edu/uwpress

Library of Congress Cataloging-in-Publication Data

Modernism and the Middle East : architecture and politics in the twentieth century / edited by Sandy Isenstadt and Kishwar Rizvi. — 1st ed.
  p. cm. — (Studies in modernity and national identity)
Includes bibliographical references and index.
ISBN 978-0-295-98821-4 (hardback : alk. paper)
ISBN 978-0-295-98794-1 (pbk. : alk. paper)
1. Architecture and society—Middle East—History—20th century. 2. Modernism (Aesthetics)—Middle East—History—20th century. I. Isenstadt, Sandy, 1957–
II. Rizvi, Kishwar.
NA2543.S6M58 2008
720.1'030956 0904—dc22   2007051765

The paper used in this publication meets the minimum requirements of American National Standard for Information Sciences—Permanence of Paper for Printed Library Materials, ANSI Z39.48–1984.

Contents

Preface vii

Acknowledgments ix

Introduction: Modern Architecture and the Middle East:
The Burden of Representation 3
SANDY ISENSTADT AND KISHWAR RIZVI

PART I *Colonial Constructions*

1   Jerusalem Remade 39
    ANNABEL WHARTON

2   Modern Architecture, Preservation, and the Discourse on Local
    Culture in Italian Colonial Libya 61
    BRIAN L. McLAREN

PART II *Building the Nation*

3   Visions of Iraq: Modernizing the Past in 1950s Baghdad 81
    MAGNUS T. BERNHARDSSON

4   Baghdad's Urban Restructuring, 1958: Aesthetics and the Politics
    of Nation Building 97
    PANAYIOTA I. PYLA

5   Democracy, Development, and the Americanization of Turkish
    Architectural Culture in the 1950s 116
    SIBEL BOZDOĞAN

6   Temporal States of Architecture: Mass Immigration and
    Provisional Housing in Israel 139
    ROY KOZLOVSKY

7   Modernisms in Conflict: Architecture and Cultural Politics
    in Post-1967 Jerusalem 161
    ALONA NITZAN-SHIFTAN

8   Palestinian Remembrance Days and Plans: Kafr Qasim,
    Fact and Echo 186
    WALEED KHLEIF AND SUSAN SLYOMOVICS

PART III *Overviews and Openings*

9   Global Ambition and Local Knowledge 221
    GWENDOLYN WRIGHT

10 From Modernism to Globalization: The Middle East in Context 255
    NEZAR ALSAYYAD

Bibliography 267

Contributors 289

Index 293

Preface

This book emerged from the symposium "Local Sites of Global Practice: Modernism and the Middle East," held at Yale University's School of Architecture, April 4–5, 2003.[1] The symposium was organized to address a pressing issue in architecture today: the emerging friction between increasingly globalized economic and cultural relationships and an increasingly heightened sense of local identity. As symbols of indigenous character and political sovereignty continue to stream through the global media, architecture has become a powerful icon for the performance of local, regional, and national identities. Many architects find themselves choosing one side or the other, either promoting regional specificity or professing the international validity of modernism. Even as they strive to synthesize local building traditions with modern construction technologies, practitioners may inadvertently reinforce stereotypes or serve only the interests of a narrow stratum of the local population. Around the world, architects are absorbing and responding to local concerns with construction methods and materials that are by now familiar in any major city on earth.

The symposium brought together architects and scholars from a range of backgrounds to present papers and debate issues that proved to be more conflictive than the planners originally imagined: American-led troops had marched into Iraq just two weeks before, and the symposium opened to the news that American tanks were rolling into Baghdad. Many participants were impassioned and eloquent as they spoke about these events, unfolding at a distance but very close to their scholarly interests. At the same time, a number of participants expressed their sense of frustration and the fear that any debates about Iraq, at the very moment that the country was erupting into flames, threatened to make their concerns irrelevant. But the looting of the National Museum of Iraq one week later reinvigorated some participants' convictions that cultural understandings and misunderstandings had contributed to processes that had led to military action. With these essays, we illustrate how the long history of the built environment in the modern Middle East can both reinforce and subvert more explicit—and more catastrophic—governmental and institutional policies.

NOTE

1. The "Local Sites of Global Practice" symposium was sponsored by Yale University's School of Architecture and the Department of the History of Art, and was co-chaired by Sandy Isenstadt and Kishwar Rizvi, the editors of this volume, along with Eeva-Liisa Pelkonen of the School of Architecture.

Acknowledgments

We are indebted to Yale University's School of Architecture, under the leadership of Dean Robert A. M. Stern, for the sponsorship of "Local Sites of Global Practice: Modernism and the Middle East," the symposium in which many of these essays were first presented. We are grateful as well for financial support from the Edward J. and Dorothy Clarke Kempf Memorial Fund at the Yale Center for International and Area Studies (YCIAS); and the David W. Roth and Robert H. Symonds Memorial Lecture Fund, and the Department of the History of Art, Yale University. In this regard, we thank Robert Stern; Abbas Amanat, former chair of the Council on Middle East Studies; Gustav Ronis, former director of the YCIAS; and Edward Cooke Jr., former chair of the Department of the History of Art. Eeva-Liisa Pelkonen, our friend and colleague, was likewise instrumental in guaranteeing the success of the symposium.

Additionally, we would like to acknowledge those colleagues who contributed to the symposium but chose not to have their papers included in this volume: Gulsum Baydar, Layla Diba, Ijlal Muzaffar, Hashim Sarkis, and Hasan Uddin Khan. We greatly appreciate the participation and insights of our colleagues Keller Easterling and Alan Plattus, and of our keynote speaker, Arjun Appadurai. We are also grateful to Richard Kane, John Jacobson, and Jennifer Castellon for their "local" support.

Many of these same individuals and organizations were unstinting in their generosity as we worked to transform the symposium papers into this volume of essays. Barbara Shailor, Robert Stern, and Ian Shapiro, director of the MacMillan Center (formerly the YCIAS), drawing again on its Edward J. and Dorothy Clarke Kempf Memorial Fund, marshaled considerable resources on behalf of this project, and we thank them. We are honored to have received support from Yale University's Hilles Publication Fund and from the Graham Foundation for Advanced Studies in the Fine Arts.

The primary motivation for compiling this book was the students in our classes on "Global Modernism" and "Modernism in the Middle East," whose curiosity and interest encouraged us to undertake the project. Additionally, we are grateful for the provocative comments of colleagues and students at Columbia University in New York and Zayed University in Dubai, where material from the introductory essay was presented. In particular, we thank Nasser Rabbat for his perceptive comments on the essay. For the assistance they lent to this volume, we also thank Zachary Heineman and Brad Walters. Finally, we would like to thank Michael Duckworth, Sibel Bozdoğan, Reşat Kasaba, and Beth Fuget, in their various roles at the University of Washington Press, for their tireless efforts to develop and advance *Modernism and the Middle East*.

Modernism and the Middle East

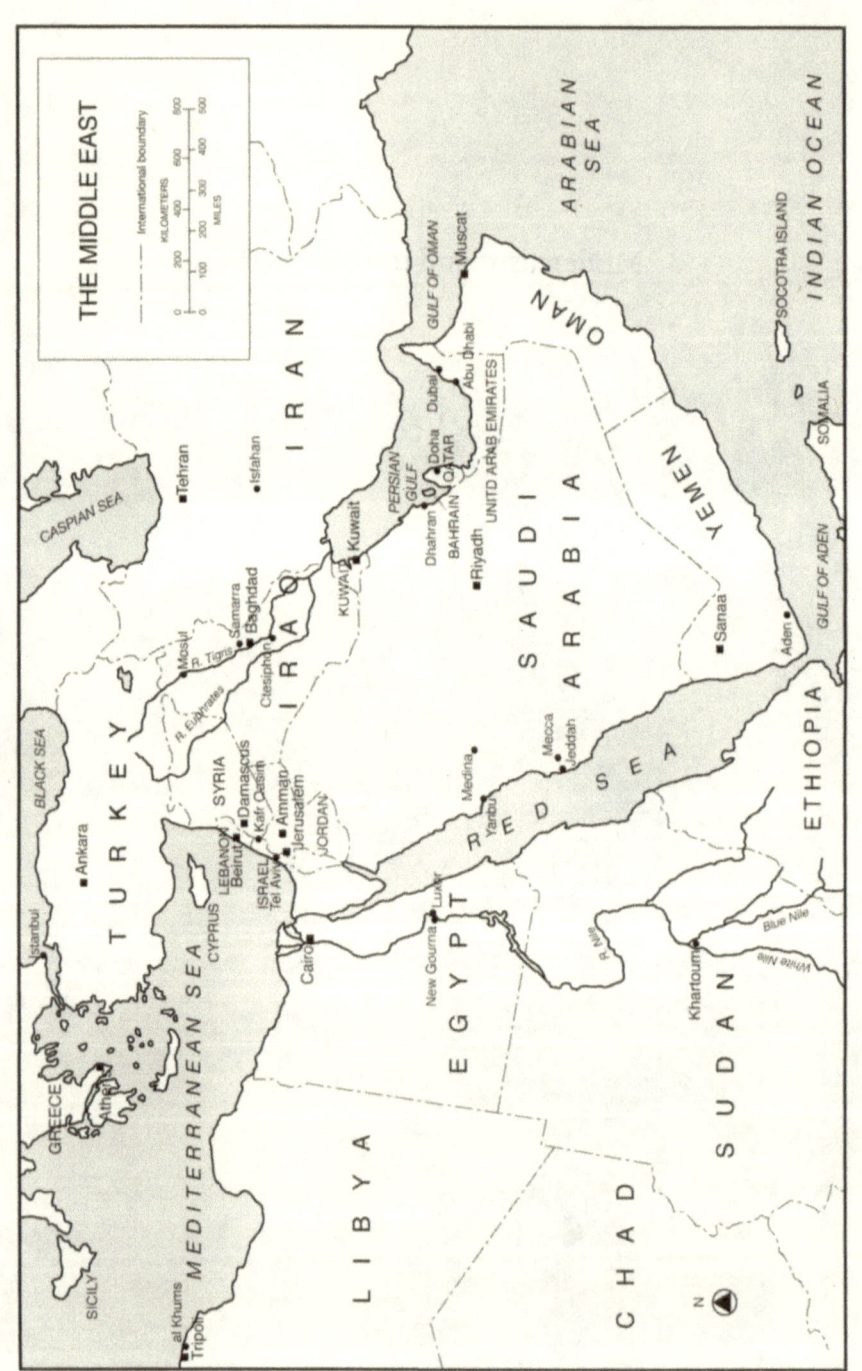

FIG. 1.1. *Map of the Middle East*

Introduction

Modern Architecture and the Middle East: The Burden of Representation

SANDY ISENSTADT AND KISHWAR RIZVI

The essays in this volume investigate the contribution that local Middle Eastern contexts make to discourses in international modernism. The essayists define modernization not only as the extension of industrialized building processes and urban infrastructure, but also as the spread of ideals of progress and standards of comfort—which is to say, modernization is the ideology as well as the built framework for the administration of industrial societies. Architecture can help consolidate identity by providing both a degree of social cohesion and iconic forms that can become a source of pride for communities. Yet, for others, such architectural forms can become stereotypes that flatten culture into a mere sign. Throughout these essays, one discerns an abiding concern for questions of representation, for how buildings and monuments—or in some cases, the lack of them—acquire meaning, harden conviction, and set the spatial infrastructure for subsequent generations.

The Middle East, with its diverse social, religious, and national histories, has often been seen by architects and academics as rich in traditional architecture but poor as a resource for understanding the Modern period. Europeans have idealized the Middle East as an almost timeless place, a region that stands in distinct and didactic contrast with the disruptive displacement and disillusionment that has resulted from its own industrialization.[1] These essays describe the unique ways by which Middle Eastern countries have invented their own versions of modernism, sometimes aligned and sometimes at odds with more familiar European versions, and in varying relations with larger patterns of imperialism and colonialism. When individual designers and decision makers crossed national borders to build or to learn, to provide aid or extract resources, as architects, teachers, or tourists, the dichotomies of modern-traditional or Western-Eastern did not truly hold.

Our goal here is to build into the study of transnational architectural exchange the widest consideration of constituencies and the most extended opportunities for input. Contributors examine a wide range of cultural encounters in terms of institutionalization of relationships, dynamic interactions of bureaucratic structures, and patterns of patronage amid debates over design and urban planning. Even local histories are multiple, often disputed in their formation, and inevitably shifting over time. Taken together, they illustrate the various strategies that set national policies and decide who is housed and who goes wanting, who is remembered and who is forgotten, and who is empowered to remake the built landscape.

Several essays profile the individuals who helped realize certain specifically Middle Eastern forms of modernity. Some of them, such as European art historians and expatriate architects and archeologists, positioned themselves as the arbiters of Western knowledge, while others were seen as importing Western ideals and technologies to the Middle East. In other cases, institutions, such as governments or development agencies, assumed these roles. In many instances, however, cultural authority was as much a matter of dynamic transitions in political or architectural sympathies as it was the result of official credentials. These essays call attention to circuits of intention and response, which inflamed allegedly objective depictions of technological progress into heated debates regarding the nature of modernity itself.

Modernism and the Middle East contextualizes the challenges facing building efforts today by placing them within a larger historical trajectory stretching from colonialism and the rise of nation-states to the present postcolonial search for local identity. By detailing how architecture has been integral to complex political ambitions and economic programs, the contributors make evident the historical roles played by competing visions of the built environment, as forms of representation and as a means of directing capital and labor flows. With such attention to its deep traditions and rapid modernization, the Middle East emerges as a rich setting for the study of modern architecture.

Modernism and the Middle East begins at the cusp of the twentieth century amid the decline of colonialism and the rise of independent nation-states in regions once ruled by the Ottomans (r. 1290–1924) in present-day Turkey and

North Africa, and the Qajars (r. 1779–1924) in Iran (see fig. I.1).² Under the dynastic leadership of the Sultan, overseer of the holy sites of Mecca and Medina and the supreme ruler of the Sunni Islamic world, the relatively stable and unified Ottoman Empire had administered much of today's Middle East. But this administrative unity and geographic cohesion was eroded greatly during the nineteenth century, and it dissolved completely in the twentieth.³ Beyond the actual loss of land, Ottoman rule was disrupted by major infrastructure developments, most notably the Suez Canal (1854–69), which brought French and, later, English capital and technology to Egypt.⁴

By the twilight of World War I, in 1918, Istanbul had itself come under Allied control, and the six-hundred-year-old Ottoman Empire came to an end, its former lands divided into areas administered by the French (Syria and Lebanon) and the British (Iraq and Palestine).⁵ Even as new nations emerged with at least nominal sovereignty from the Mandate period, the idea of a coherent, if not exactly cohesive, Middle East was reinforced. The Mandates carved new political entities, such as Palestine and Iraq, out of former Ottoman administrative zones, but it kept these nations from being fully independent, and left them wanting in terms of industrial development. At the same time, European occupation sparked nationalist movements in neighboring Turkey and Iran, resulting in the overthrow of puppet monarchies and the rise of charismatic military leaders, who threw off centuries of imperial rule and modernized in the name of national progress. The advent of Mustafa Kemal in Turkey (1919) and Riza Khan in Iran (1921) brought new modes of judicial and educational reforms (often based on European models), in an effort to forge homogeneous, if fictive, native identities.⁶ The characterization of entire peoples by their positions along the trajectory of history and modernization was as much embraced by regional leaders as it was imposed by European power and ideology.

Oil came to be written into this idea of a cohesive Middle East as much by its discovery there as by the increasing industrial thirst for sources of fuel. The image of Arab states unified by oceans of oil lying unseen beneath their soil emerged in the nineteenth century with the advent of a British-controlled Anglo-Persian oil company. It was extended as new fields were discovered, such as those in Iraq in the 1930s and those in Kuwait and Saudi Arabia by 1945. With the institution of the American's Marshall Plan (1948–52), the European economy was reconfigured according to American precepts, resulting in an emphasis on continued growth in productivity and an even greater dependence on oil. The Middle East thus moved to the center of foreign-policy strategies for a number of Western nations, becoming also a site of contentious ideological positioning between the Soviet Union and the United States, with both nations acting out their political differences through technical aid and development projects as well as cultural exports. Although some small Persian Gulf monarchies enjoyed considerable advantages over their oil-poor neighbors, to Westerners the region maintained its conceptual integrity as a site of superpower struggle and vast economic opportunity.[7]

The creation of the state of Israel, on May 14, 1948, also helped consolidate an idea of the Middle East, albeit in a way unanticipated by most Western politicians. Although Jewish immigration to the area in the first half of the twentieth century had profoundly affected the economic and demographic character of Mandate Palestine, the United Nations' 1947 plan to partition the area into Jewish and Arab states, which was rejected by the Arab League, formed in 1945, seemed only to reassert Western colonialism at the very moment it was breaking apart elsewhere.

Within this context, the Middle East must be historically situated as a place defined both by European colonial interests and by the specific imperial configurations that had existed in the region. Just as the specter of essentialism hovers over the term "Middle East," one may argue that it also haunts the idea of a homogeneous "Europe"; nonetheless, as Dipesh Chakrabarty has argued in another context, these terms highlight, rather than obfuscate, the problematic of domination and intellectual dependency that permeates any discussion of these two entities.[8] The interdependency of Europe and the Middle East can be seen in the unfolding of an "Oriental" supplement to European identity: what was understood by nineteenth-century policymakers as the "Eastern question" had to do less with the inhabitants of these regions than with the raw currency of human labor and material wealth promised through imperialism.

Along with unabashed military power, European systems of social organization also marched across the region. By the end of the nineteenth century, in Istanbul as well as Tehran, there were two primary modes of thinking about Islamic government. On the one hand, an indigenous intelligentsia, educated at European institutions, subscribed to the idea of nations organized to uphold individual rights, and so demanded constitutional government. On the other hand, reformers, who interpreted Islamic law and rule as being consistent with individual freedom, called for an Islamic revival from within these very institutions. These tensions resulted in a series of experiments with European legal institutions and, in the early twentieth century, fully developed, albeit short-lived constitutions in Turkey and Iran.

In the early years of the twentieth century, intellectuals in both Europe and the Middle East looked to an idea of the "East" in search of alternative modes of living, an expression of their dissatisfaction and disillusionment with the artifacts of modernity. The political fragmentation of great empires, rapid industrialization, and an expanding urban malaise and the alienation it produced were all motivating factors for a renewed interest in Eastern art and religion. This interest was filtered through notions of racial and cultural superiority, however, and the lands of the Middle East became subject to orientalist interpretations, both by natives and by their European counterparts. The orientalist interpretation was very different from the lived experience of those in the Middle East: independence movements, increasing autonomy for the arts, and the growth of a middle class were all phenomena that the residents of cities as diverse as Cairo, Tehran, and Algiers experienced. This shared experience of modernity, seldom implemented on the basis of parity, demands closer scrutiny.

WRITING A MIDDLE EAST

Several sites in the Middle East were of particular interest to European and American archeologists, who since the late nineteenth century had focused almost obsessively on the search for biblical and classical origins of mankind. When their attention turned toward the Islamic period, it too was centered on questions of origins. Excavations were begun at Ummayad palaces and mosques in Syria, and at the Abbasid capitals of Baghdad and Samarra in Iraq, while monuments built during the six-hundred-year reign of the Ottomans were ignored.[9] From as early as the seventeenth century, documentation and description by travelers, such as Adam Olearius and Engelbert Kaempfer in Iran, had made certain cities and monuments familiar to Europeans, although whole-scale architectural documentation emerged only later through diplomatic commissions, such as those undertaken in the nineteenth century by Charles Texier (1802–1871) and Pascale Coste (1787–1879). Coste's two significant works, *Monuments modernes de la Perse, mesurés, dessinés et décrits* (1867) and the monumental *Architecture Arabe; ou, Monuments du Kaire: Mesurés et dessinés, de 1818 à 1826* (1839), were milestones in the manner in which architecture was disassembled and presented to the viewer in an academic, Beaux-Arts style. The documentation already undertaken by the French, in the *Description de l'Egypt* (1828), for example, on the occasion of Napoleon's conquest of Egypt, and by the British in India (e.g., *Annals and Antiquities of Rajasthan* [1829] by General James Tod), would fall into the category of colonial ethnography. By contrast, Coste's works were valued primarily for the architectural information they contained, although they too were arguably still within the colonial frame.[10] The travel documentary would be the precursor to the more academic survey, which would provide an intellectual and art historical interpretation for the works catalogued.

European museums and their local counterparts played a significant role in constructing a visual and architectural documentary of the Middle East. Among the earliest museum collections of Near Eastern art were those in Istanbul, London, Berlin, and Vienna. These museums were advised and supplied by a series of scholars influential in the study of Islamic art. Friedrich Sarre (1865–1945), for instance, served as a director of the Berlin Museum and was an influential collector of Islamic art. He had traveled extensively in the Middle East and made valuable contributions to the study of Iranian architecture in the form of publications and documentary photographs. Sarre worked closely with his protégé, Ernst Herzfeld (1879–1948), who had been educated in the classics and trained as an architect. Together they curated the influential 1910 Munich exhibition of Islamic art, which was a milestone in its scope and execution.[11] Exhibitions like these were spectacles of European fantasies of the Middle East, and their catalogues would become important guides for the collecting and dissemination of the artifacts displayed.

Europeans saw proof of their superior stewardship of cultural artifacts when they compared their own concern for national treasures to the relative lack of interest in and disrepair of historic sites in the Middle East. Not only were viewpoints about the art and architectural history of the region skewed to European preoccupations, but the very artifacts under study were often removed and sometimes destroyed in the process of radical decontextualization.[12] Although the Europeans were primarily focused on the ancient Babylonian and Pharaonic period, they did include Islamic art in their collections, although typically the art was represented with easily transported objects like textiles and ceramics. When they did transport entire buildings or large fragments, these heroic feats only added to the sense of authority which legitimated the dismemberment and expatriation of the region's architectural heritage (see fig. I.2). The fate of these objects shifted according to what was in vogue among European and nationalist scholars, highlighting the close association of academic research with political rivalry and self-definition. It is important to note here the close affinity that would form between orientalist interests in the region and the later co-opting of rhetoric by the newly formed states of the Middle East.[13]

Institutions that claimed authority over cultural heritage came to wield

FIG. I.2. *Mshatta Palace façade. Photo by Kishwar Rizvi.*

significant political influence in the remaining colonies, as well as in the new states. In the Middle East, directors and officials were appointed from among European scholars and administrators to head museums and other institutions charged with the study and conservation of Islamic monuments.[14] In Egypt, for example, although the Committee for the Conservation of Monuments of Arab Art, convened in 1881, included three Europeans and five Arabs, decision making was controlled by European officials. With the founding of the Museum of Arab Art the cultural authority of the British in Cairo was secure for the next fifty years, as all decisions regarding the collection and display of Arab art were filtered through colonial authorities. In a similar vein, in 1881 Osman Hamdi was put in charge of the Imperial Ottoman Museum in Istanbul. This museum, however, housed artifacts from classical antiquity (a Museum of Islamic Art would open, in the Suleymaniyye Mosque complex, only in 1914).[15] In Iran, even before Riza Khan declared himself Shah and initiated programs for education, industrialization, and a liberal government, the Society for National Heritage was charged with overseeing the restoration and conservation, and thus the very identification, of that nation's "national heritage." The society undertook not only to restore

Introduction 9

old monuments, but to "invent" new ones: for example, in 1926, the grave of the famous eleventh-century poet Firdawsi was dug up and a new, "authentic," structure, designed by André Godard, was erected in its place (it was completed in 1934).[16] Riza Shah invited Ernst Herzfeld to come to Iran in 1925 to explain to the nation's citizenry the importance of the nation's legacy of Persian art. Herzfeld was also invited to survey crucial Persian monuments and make recommendations for their preservation and possible reconstruction.[17] The result was *A Brief Inventory of the Historical Heritage and Edifices of Iran* (1925), a founding document in the Iranians' understanding of their architectural history. The document's bias was toward the pre-Islamic past of the Achaemenid and Sasanian periods; their immediate precedent, the Qajar reign, was deemed by the Pahlavi nationalists as having been a dishonorable and deviant moment in Iranian art and history. The ensuing cultural knowledge was mobilized by political forces in Iran to bolster claims to power and to legitimate policies and directions of development. Architecture was in the forefront of the imagining of an Iranian heritage—real and fictional.[18]

Perhaps the most influential figure writing about Islamic architecture was Keppel Archibald Creswell (1869–1974).[19] Trained at the Technical College in Finsbury (England) in electrical engineering, Creswell was an accomplished draftsman. Although his early employment was at Siemens and the London branch of Deutsche Bank, his real passion was, as he noted, early Muslim architecture. He trained himself in the architectural history of the Middle East—in particular, Iran. By 1920, Creswell found himself in Egypt, employed by the British army, and he took advantage of his appointment to study the local monuments. At the end of World War I, Creswell requested and received the help of King Fuʿad I of Egypt to assist in funding his magnum opus, *Early Muslim Architecture* (1932–40). The project, as Creswell described it, would catalogue "one of the greatest and most interesting branches of Muslim architecture, which will make known in all parts of the world the glorious achievements, as well as the history and evolution, of modern architecture in Egypt."[20] The statement is valuable in pointing to the mixed goals increasingly common to students of Islamic architecture in the early twentieth century: to both locate and describe a glorious past, and, as Creswell wrote to King Fuʿad, to inspire the future.

The relationship of the architectural and artistic past, present, and future of Iran was explored by Creswell's contemporary, the American scholar-turned-purveyor, Arthur Upham Pope (1881–1969).[21] In a 1925 speech given in the presence of Riza Khan, Pope had advocated the study and preservation of Iran's artistic heritage. According to him, the arts (architecture was included as the most "formal of visual arts") were the nation's greatest assets, and proof of its place as a great world civilization. In later publications, most notably the six-volume *Survey of Persian Art* (1938–39), Pope and the various contributors delved deep into the past to find inspiration for Iran's future.[22] As the dedications of *Early Muslim Architecture* (to King Fuʿad) and *The Survey of Persian Art* (to Riza Shah Pahlavi) make explicit, these books were written not only to satisfy academe, but also to assist in the goal of creating a nationalist ideology.[23] In contrast with many of their Western counterparts, who in seeking a modern architecture for Europe and the United States were beginning at this moment to advocate a decisive break from historical references, Creswell and Pope advanced the idea that the past might itself be recovered in service to the task of nation-building.

Travel literature, catalogues of exhibitions and fairs, and architectural surveys all served to provide a rich and comprehensive documentation of architecture in the Middle East. Their audiences were as varied as the styles of representations they employed. Books like these provoked an interest that resulted in the inclusion of the "non-West" into the canon of Western architecture as well. From James Fergusson's *History of Architecture in All Countries, from the Earliest Times to the Present Day* (1887) to Banister Fletcher's *A History of Architecture for the Student, Craftsman, and Amateur, Being a Comparative View of the Historical Styles from the Earliest Period* (1896), architectural history was conceived as a meta-discipline charged with linking forms and meanings. The "marginal" architecture of the Middle East was presented in purely formal terms—metonymic, fragmentary representations in two-dimensional and decontextualized settings.

In Sir Bannister Fletcher's *History of Architecture*, architectural history is a tree with the great monuments of the non-Western nations apparent on its lower branches, but unable to grow further (fig. I.3).[24] The tree's trunk rises out of the Greek and Roman world, and its youngest branches contain the newest and most dramatic building type, the skyscraper. How then, in Fletcher's model, could a nation in the Middle East establish its legitimacy in architectural terms that would be meaningful to local populations and at the same time position itself along the main trunk of progress and development? How could one be both rooted and modern when civilization required an inheritance from the past but modernity was seen as a conscious distancing from one's roots? The questions unfolded in two directions, toward a legitimizing past and toward a promising future, both of which were reciprocally

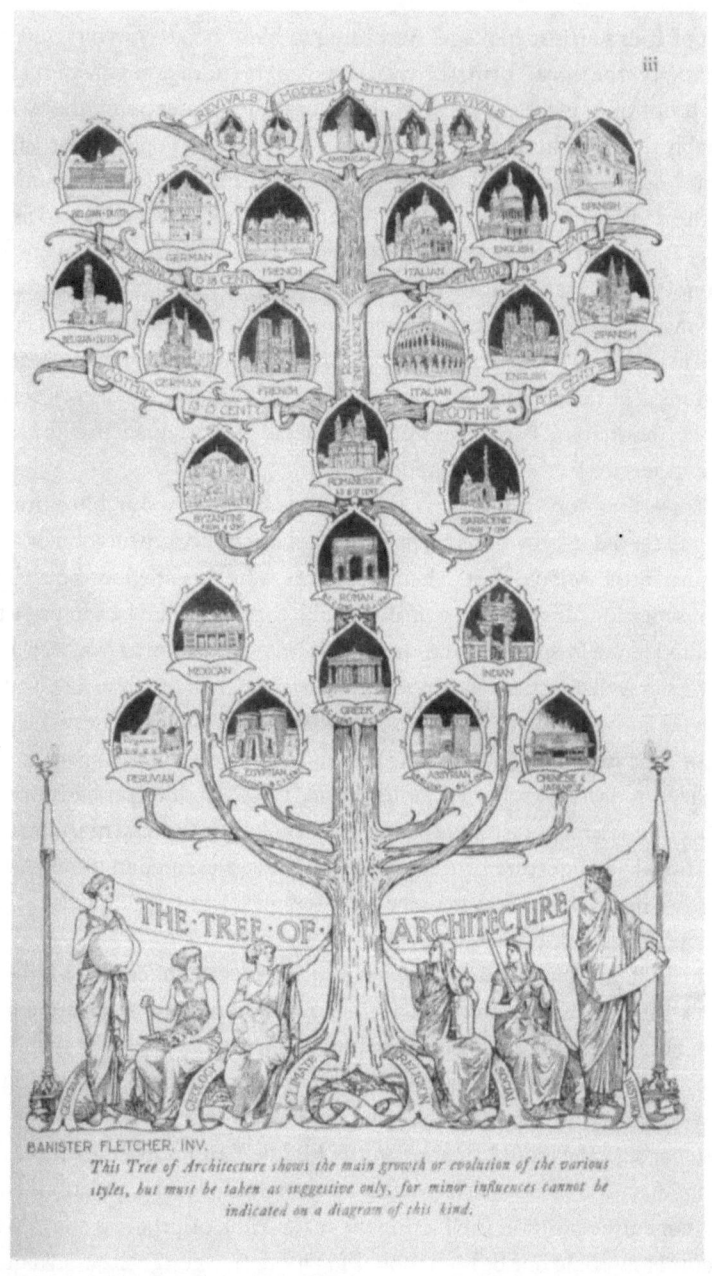

FIG. I.3. *"The Tree of Architecture,"* frontispiece from Sir Bannister Fletcher, History of Architecture *(London, B.T. Batsford; New York, C. Scribner's Sons, 1896).*

constructed. The past and its corresponding future were determined by the exigencies and particularities of each country and its self-representation at different moments in time.

BUILDING A MIDDLE EAST

In 1883, the Fine Arts Academy was established in Istanbul, under the directorship of Osman Hamdi Bey (1842–1910), an artist trained in Paris in the studio of Jean-Léon Gérôme. The academy was the first of its kind there to teach architecture, a subject traditionally offered only to engineering students, as part of a curriculum that included painting and sculpture. One result of this was fresh attention given to historicism and the role of the past in constructing contemporary architecture, such that architects attempted to revive Ottoman architecture by applying its formal motifs to new functional programs such as banks and post offices.[25] Architects such as Vedat Bey (1873–1942) were among the first generation of professionals sent abroad to study. Like his Iranian contemporaries, he was trained at the École des Beaux-Arts in Paris, while his compatriot, Kemallettin Bey (1870–1927) was trained at the Charlottenburg Technische Hochschule in Berlin. Both believed in reviving older Ottoman architecture as a symbol of the reemergence of Ottoman political authority. The exigencies of a new secular Republic after 1923, however, forced the issue, and led to a rejection of Ottoman forms in favor of greater architectural abstraction.[26]

Similar revivals could be witnessed in Iran and Egypt; however, in each case the architectural history worthy of revival was markedly different. Qajar architects were selective in their borrowing of symbols from Achaemenid (559–350 BCE) and Sasanian (224–461) architecture, in opposition to the great monuments of Islamic dynasties. Although European-style palaces and decorative motifs were also employed, imperial iconography—in the form of large sculptural programs as well as tile embellishments—was taken from pre-Islamic architecture.[27] Similarly, architects writing and building in Egypt—in particular, Cairo—distanced themselves from the immediate history of Ottoman architecture to seek indigenous solutions from the Mamluk era (1250–1517). The "medieval" representations of contemporary architecture were certainly curious choices given the ideas of progress and reform that often accompanied them.[28] "Modern" architecture, in contrast, was equated with the West and thus beyond the reach of local architectural expression, an attitude that would change from the 1930s onward.

During the Qajar and Ottoman periods, schools of architecture were typically led by foreigners or local elite educated in Europe. The Frenchman André Godard (1881–1965) is representative. A graduate of the École des Beaux-Arts, he worked in Iraq, Egypt, and Afghanistan before arriving in Iran. In 1928 he was appointed to the post of director of the first museum of antiquities in Tehran, the Iran Bastan Museum.[29] Along with being placed in charge of archeological and preservation projects, he was also the first Dean of the Faculty of Fine Arts at Tehran University, directing the education of future architects. Like other foreign architects of the time, Godard found inspiration for Iran's future in its past. For the design of the Iran Bastan Museum project, for instance, Godard collaborated with another expatriate French archeologist turned architect, Maxime Siroux (see fig. I.4). The monumental arch at the building's entrance did not simply emulate the Sasanian remnants at Ctesiphon, its designers believed that it improved the original with more refined details. In adapting antique forms to new building types and new political programs, Godard borrowed motifs from a range of sources and invented quasi-historical forms for new projects, much as archaeological artifacts were decontextualized to fit vitrines and historical timelines in the museums he directed. In many ways, Godard's designs were congruent with the larger contours of eclecticism. Other architects, in Europe and the United States as well as in the Middle East, made use of historical form in an attempt to adapt to modern circumstances.[30]

Mohsen Forughi (1907–1982) is representative of those architects originally from the Middle East but trained in Europe and dedicated to bringing Western practices to their homelands. He studied at the École des Beaux-Arts in Paris and returned to Iran soon afterward to launch his architectural career. Although having little practical experience, he had acquired the École's signature sensitivity to historical form and compositional virtuosity, and so was immediately welcomed into government service and soon won important commissions, such as the Faculty of Technology at Tehran University, built with Maxime Siroux (see fig. I.5). Forughi's rationalist approach to design and his use of more abstract forms contrasted with the work of older colleagues. His buildings are adorned with a minimum of ornament, and the historical references are restrained—evident, for example, in the limited use of glazed tiles at the entrance to his Iranian Senate building in Tehran. Unlike Godard's Iran Bastan Museum, built in brick, Forughi turned to reinforced concrete for his public commissions, which included hospitals, ministries, and bank buildings.[31] The use of concrete may be seen as an important deviation from the use of the traditional material, one that pointed to the iconic role of modern architecture in the nationalist ideology.

FIG. I.4. *Iran Bastan Museum, Tehran, André Godard and Maxime Siroux. Photo by Talinn Grigor.*

In Turkey, the early proponents of a new style that based its progressive posture partly on a rejection of historical form were imported from Europe. Rather than romanticizing local cultural heritage, like the previous generation, they brought with them the functionalist emphasis of a developing modern movement spurred by industrialization and rapid urbanization, as well as the background of European classicism and its long-standing values of symmetry and monumentality. The German planner Hermann Jansen (1869–1947) was invited to design and implement the master plan for the new capital, Ankara. He was followed by the Swiss Ernst Egli (1893–1974), who was brought in as the head of the Academy of Fine Arts. Egli's designs were self-consciously abstract and aloof from any local context, embodying a kind of architectural self-determination—that is, form generated from function and methods of construction—that would mirror Ataturk's ideals of a nation free from Ottoman malfeasance.[32] Subsequent Turkish architects incorporated this official nationalist aesthetic into their "new architecture," which featured cubic forms and a fondness for grids: a language of rationalized form evoked the clarity and single-mindedness of the new government.[33]

Much of these architects' cultural authority resided in their international experience, either as émigrés and foreign experts, or as professionals trained in foreign schools. Their education enabled them to import the motifs and

Introduction 15

FIG. I.5. *Tehran University, Faculty of Technology, Mohsen Forughi. From Mina Marefat, "The Protagonists Who Shaped Modern Tehran," in* Téhéran, capitale bicentenaire, *ed. C. Adle (Paris–Tehran, 1992).*

methods of Western Europe, thereby helping to make the dominant political force in the region the cultural standard as well. Although such figures were channels to Western practices, their expertise seemed to be self-contained and therefore transportable, and their choice of locale in which to practice appeared to demonstrate self-determination and to personify global citizenship. The émigré or foreign expert was thus a representative figure of modernity, with transnational experience a prerequisite to regional inflections within a larger modernism, and with local rootings of modern architecture vindicating its universal ambitions.[34] The Turkish architect Sedad Eldem stands out in this context for working out his modernist designs through an idealized Turkish house that he conceptualized after encountering in Germany publications of Frank Lloyd Wright's prairie houses in Illinois.[35] The heightened status of émigré or foreign-trained architects would continue after World War II, although such figures were often engaged with larger-scale planning efforts, such as Constantinos Doxiades, and in many instances evinced an overriding concern for technological solutions based on universal physical facts, such as strength of materials, without explicit cultural references. Ultimately, the émigré or foreign-trained architect turned out to be a figure with limited historical appeal and only one of a number of ways to represent or embody international mobility.

As the preceding examples suggest, two design approaches prevailed in the early-twentieth-century Middle East: selective adaptation of historical forms to suit new building programs, and experimentation with the abstracting tendencies then emerging internationally. In many instances, combining these approaches resulted in designs that could recapitulate an ideal of nationhood rooted in cultural heritage, yet progressive and growing. Alongside the cultural constructions of archeologists and art historians, the conceptual spectrum of these approaches helped direct and frame the building of nations.

The World War II ascendance of an international style of modern architecture was characterized by cubic massing and elemental, unornamented forms, along with a present-tense commitment to the most advanced materials and methods of construction. As the editors of *Progressive Architecture* insisted in 1948: "Modern design—design of our time—is not a style. It is a solution to modern problems in modern terms."[36] In other words, modernism was intimately related to the vital spirit of the industrial age. It was the logical outcome, in aesthetic terms, both of modernization—a network of infrastructures that underpinned an advanced material civilization that included mass sanitation, mass housing, and mass transportation; and of modernity—the acceptance of systemic societal change triggered not simply by technological developments, but by the embrace of change itself as a constituent factor of everyday life. Nations that had become politically independent if not exactly free of foreign influence typically intensified their modernization program in an effort to keep pace with neighboring countries and with world opinion. This international style of modern architecture contributed in several ways to the continuing construction of a cultural concept of the Middle East: through its claims to a universal applicability that cast the Middle East as one in a series of successful instances of modernism taking root in distinct locales;

by repositioning historical motifs in relation to modern practice; and by focusing design attention on generalized, supposedly regional themes, such as a hot climate, which could be mitigated by a modern approach.

The dissemination of values held to be both Western and universal was a keynote of international politics after World War II, with the United Nations emblematic of such aspirations. The Universal Declaration of Human Rights, for example, approved in 1948 by the United Nations' General Assembly, which included some seven Middle Eastern countries, stressed rights such as personal privacy, private property, leisure, access to social services, freedom of speech, free choice in marriage, and free choice in nationality. The United Nations approved a "symbolic figure" for the teaching of its universal ideals, a deracinated everyman standing atop a globe that is likewise featureless but for its gridded surface (see fig. I.6). In terms drawn directly from the Declaration, this figure "represents all of us, everyone on earth, whoever we are, without distinction of any kind such as race, color, sex, language, religion, political or other opinion, national or social origin, property, birth or any other status."[37] The power of this unmarked monad is its presumption of a universal humanity underlying cultural differences, which become then mere circumstance. As an anticipation of impending individuation and a cipher for pure possibility, it stands as well for another, related ideal, namely, that of economic development. Indeed, an unquestioned faith in the goodness of development, in terms of both new goods and markets for global capital and material and social benefits for local populations, is an often overlooked but nonetheless fundamental aspect of modernism. International institutions such as the United Nations were crucial in helping to articulate and promulgate such beliefs. Of course, declaring universal rights and implementing them turned out to be entirely different matters.

An architectural accord with such ideals was evident in the design of the United Nations' Secretariat building itself, begun in 1947. As Sibel Bozdoğan notes in her essay, the elegant glass-walled slab was the leading symbol of a "new supranational aesthetic of bureaucratic and technocratic efficiency" that evoked a prosperous future precisely by forgoing cultural references. The abstracted forms of modern architecture seemed to herald wider participation in society by sponsoring a symbolic franchise accessible to all social strata, in contrast with, say, the ornate and costly ornament of traditional elites. It signified traits common to an economic class, rather than to kin or ethnic origin. In terms of actual construction programs in the Middle East, corollaries to the Declaration include an emphasis on mass housing and attempts to visualize the city in its entirety and to plan for future urban growth.

THIS SYMBOLIC FIGURE represents all of us, everyone on earth, whoever we are, without distinction of any kind such as race, color, sex, language, religion, political or other opinion, national or social origin, property, birth or any other status

FIG. I.6. *"Symbolic Figure," from Stephen Fenichell and Phillip Andrews,* The United Nations: Blueprint for Peace *(Philadelphia: John C. Winston Publishing, 1951).*

Also evident is the use of a common language of stripped cubic forms and greater attention to questions of building type, along with a new role for the architect, who shifted from providing custom designs for the elite to a more socially central role of accommodating the larger polity.

In the Middle East particularly, a central tenet of postwar modernism—the irrelevance of the past for the problems of the present—swiftly came into conflict with an earlier ideal of nationhood rooted in ethnic genealogy but growing toward material progress. The "flying carpet" entry canopy at the 1955 Istanbul Hilton Hotel, by the American architectural firm of Skidmore, Owings and Merrill in collaboration with Sedad Eldem, for instance, evoked an orientalist fantasy, but it was an ancillary flourish to a grid of rooms and a sequence of pools, lawns, and lounges serving burgers and soda that was, as Bozdoğan notes, "the paradigm of benevolent and democratic capitalist society."[38] In such ways, traditional forms were reintroduced by modernism itself; the immediately recognizable motifs could appear as proof of their persistence, however denatured. Thus, modern architecture, when it took up some notion of local heritage, could represent itself as the healing praxis for that which it had injured.

A "burden of representation"—a term we feel aptly describes this situation—strained both tendencies, as all architects in service to new nations tried to find forms that would make sense of the novel configurations of land marshaled under new flags and the varied combinations of ethnic groups that were expected to cohere under new systems of law. It was a task that occupied twentieth-century architects and builders in the Middle East in ways profoundly different than before, and despite important similarities, in ways strikingly different from those of their contemporaries in Europe. Although similar questions regarding a modern architecture—that is, an architecture aesthetically commensurate with modern society—likewise troubled European architecture, in the Middle East they seem to refract and turn in upon themselves. Among the questions that can be asked and that continue to be relevant to students and practitioners today are these: How does one build for a culture that is grounded in rich history and in strong continuing traditions and also trying to establish a distance with that history? How might one represent a culture to itself as a means of establishing what that culture might become? And how can one make use of an architectural paradigm that has already marked a culture as unequal, or at least lagging behind on an evolutionary track, to now represent that culture as a political equal among others like it?

Greater emphasis after World War II on technological solutions is evident in the attention architects gave to finding ways to mitigate the climate. Climate had been growing in importance in Western universities as an academic subject related to human welfare. But its adoption as a primary design problem helped to consolidate a sense of the unity of the Middle East at the same time that modernism could be represented as being indifferent to political boundaries, much like the climate itself.[39] Although always subject to local conditions, climate is both global and trans-historical. As Josep Lluis Sert, architect of the 1955 American Embassy in Baghdad, suggested, climate is one of several "eternal factors" most deserving of the architect's attention. Modern architecture could appear as a technical response to facts of nature, rather than as a displacement of more traditional accommodations to patterns of weather. However sensible, long-standing customs, such as adapting activities to the daily and seasonal path of the sun, could be seen as un-self-reflective responses to weather, in contrast to modernism's rational analyses and all-encompassing solutions.[40] In the long run, however, design rationales based on an appeal to climate failed to distinguish one political entity from another.

A postwar emphasis on technological approaches to design also meant that architects would tend to focus on specifically modern issues, such as accommodating automobiles, or on distinctly architectural problems, such as the physical properties and aesthetic implications of new materials. With a mandate to be modern driving them, many architects were predisposed to the use of those materials that served their professional agenda. At times this could lead to rather strained assertions. In support of his embassy design, for instance, Sert claimed he had used concrete because it was a local material, although it had not been made in Baghdad until 1952 and was in any case in short supply, as was the timber needed for formwork. His decision to use steel for the Embassy's window sash, he said, was in response to the local problem of termites. In 1957, looking back on a decade of building in Iraq, Ellen Jawdat, an architect and the wife of Iraqi architect Nizar Jawdat, whom she met when both studied at Harvard, wrote that modernism had forced a divide between an architecture "which is technically possible and that which can economically be achieved under local building conditions." An architect could be modern only by choosing the former. Concrete, for example, was important for iconographic as well as functional reasons, whereas brick bore no significance for modernism. For architects, this mindset would favor one sort of material over another, such as concrete (modern) over brick (traditional), even when the use of brick would have been the most efficient use of existing materials and existing skilled labor.

The effect of what seem at first to have been merely aesthetic decisions

Introduction 21

turned out to be enormous. In Iraq, local officials and foreign observers worried about a shortage of skilled labor that would hobble or at least slow modernization. But even Lord Salter, a distinguished British politician and former minister for economic affairs, acting in the early 1950s as consultant to the Iraq Development Board, noted that labor could only be said to be in short supply in relation to planned development. In Iraq, he said, politicians were beholden to a Western model of industrial development that emphasized ways to "utilize fully the country's potential physical resources rather than to increase the welfare of its people."[41] Decisions by architects channel the use of physical resources, sometimes, as Salter suggests, to the disadvantage of other issues, such as full employment.

At the same time that these developments helped to reinforce modernism's core principles, they also redefined them: attention to climate led to an often monumental emphasis on technique, which, being ill-suited for the range of building tasks necessary to modernization, began to strain its underlying technological determinism. Questions of architectural representation remained inescapable in the Middle East because the primary issue was to make modernity and independence manifest, to visibly demonstrate with material form claims of political parity with former colonial and hegemonic Western powers. Modernist flirtations with vernacular architecture in the West were extended to a much more explicit concern for questions of historical and regional context, matters that were paramount to nations attempting to articulate their legitimacy and importance.[42] Preserving tradition and modernization were posited as oppositional goals that could not be resolved. Although much of this effort would involve new infrastructural projects like roads and railways, shipping facilities, airports, urban water and sanitation systems, and so on, the most visible portions nearly always involved architecture. Whether providing housing for immigrants streaming into cities, or a monumental government center, new buildings were both the means and the very symbol of participation in Western ideals of progress and development promoted to foreign investors and aggressive neighbors.

Issues regarding representation also came to the fore through the work of the Egyptian architect Hassan Fathy. Like many of his colleagues, Fathy explored Beaux-Arts-inspired designs through much of the 1930s, but later he turned his attention to housing for the rural poor, the use of traditional materials such as mud brick, and vernacular traditions. Even his evident interest in addressing issues of climate was pursued through careful manipulation of orientation and the size and location of openings, the use of shading devices, and generous courtyards that would be at least partially shaded throughout the day. Although his 1948 project for New Gourna was criticized in terms of its economic viability, it was richly imagined and led to a series of important positions for Fathy advising the Egyptian government, as well as consulting with other architects across the Middle East. The Iraqi architect Rifat Chadirji, to take another example, studied architecture in London, but upon his return to Baghdad in 1952 he became involved with preserving the urban fabric that was often threatened by modernization projects. In the following years, he worked to incorporate vernacular motifs with new materials and a larger scale of modern architecture. Iraq Consult, the firm he established, became one of the region's most important architectural practices.[43]

Issues of representation were only sharpened with the rising power of the United States in the years following World War II. In the American Embassy building program, for instance, a number of architects, many of whom were not American by birth, were asked to represent the United States to the non-American audience of the host country as a powerful industrialized nation that was nonetheless sensitive to the local interests of its host country. Embassy architects were asked to express "such qualities as dignity, strength, and neighborly sympathy." Issues of representation were explicit and internally contradictory, and architects struggled to protect core modernist principles of subordinating representation to practical matters of function and structure even as they added ornamental flourishes to indicate "neighborly sympathy."[44] What one author called "Ornamented Modern," had, he wrote in 1959, "crystallized, in large measure, as the result of a U.S. State Department policy regarding the construction of embassies abroad."[45] Questions of ornament and representation in modern architecture were triggered not by the 1960s postmodern critique of modernism, but emerged in the context of decolonization and nationalism, in an optimistic if ambiguous confidence in modern architecture to simultaneously represent the rooted particularities of a given place and population as well as their progress toward future prospects.

Narratives of modernism in the Middle East have by and large relied upon categories based on Western experience. Temporal divisions such as "prewar" or "postwar" reflect systemic changes that took place in the West following World War II, such as Europe's enormous reconstruction effort and the transformation of the American economy from military to consumer goods and its emergence upon the global stage. Such labels also reflect an implicit belief in the homogeneity of temporal experience. That is to say, the present is itself defined by the rapid and incessant changes wrought by modernity; therefore, to participate in the present means to embrace change and to demonstrate that embrace with cultural signs and material forms.

Although affected by World War II, the experience of the Middle East was different, attesting to the tenuous coherence of the very idea of a Middle East. Iran and Turkey were already independent nations in the 1920s, whereas a number of North African nations remained colonies into the 1950s. Somewhere in between was Iraq—autonomous after World War I, officially independent in 1932 but still effectively under British influence, occupied by the British throughout the Second World War, re-independent in 1947, and only freed from British authority in 1958 after a coup led by Abdul Karim Qassim. With many such changes of administration, grand modernization projects were initiated, redirected, or shut down. With each iteration of national identity, different actors appeared in an altered context, and newly independent governments made as much or as little use of new technologies and cultural heritage as did their colonial predecessors. Considered across the wide range of the Middle East, such a pattern amounts to a kind of punctuated development: rather than being explained by a gradual or even a fitful assimilation of Western practices, modernism in the Middle East evolved in a geographically and temporally disjointed manner.[46] New symbols were brandished and old ones recycled; various modernisms were accepted, amended, rejected.

Perhaps the most important development since the 1970s has been the resurgence of Islam as a touchstone of nationalist discourse. This is best exemplified in Iran, but is also evident throughout the Middle East and South Asia. In countries as distinct as Turkey and Algeria, Islam has been an increasingly galvanizing form of socio-political expression. Religious identity has re-emerged in political and civic discourse and has thus joined individual status and national or ethnic origin as a major factor in the production and study of architecture. Religious identification has lead to a new, hybrid type of modern architecture, evident not only in the Middle East but in other global contexts from India to the United States.

New patrons promoting religious ideology as a source of political agency have sponsored wholesale reinterpretations of traditional building types. This trend is unlike earlier ones involving the application of traditional motifs onto contemporary structures and state patronage in service to modernization. It is also unlike the token ornamentalism and corporate sponsorship evident in buildings like the Istanbul Hilton. Two examples can begin to illustrate this new development. The first is the tomb of the patriarch of the Iranian revolution, Ayatollah Khomeini (d. 1988), whose body is interred in an enormous

FIG. I.7. *Tomb of Ayatollah Khomeini, Tehran, Iran. Photo by Kishwar Rizvi.*

structure on the outskirts of Tehran. The building is in the form of a traditional Shi'i shrine, but it is built entirely of contemporary materials such as concrete and prefabricated metal, with a space-frame interior (see fig. I.7). The state-sponsored tomb was overseen by Khomeini's son, Ahmad, and designed by the architect Mohammed Tehrani. It functions simultaneously as a religious edifice and a state monument, frequented as often by pilgrims as by diplomats.[47]

A similar bridging of temporal and formal boundaries is seen in the Kocatepe Mosque in Ankara (1967–87).[48] The massive mosque, with a parking garage and shopping mall in its lower levels, is similar to the tomb of Khomeini in evoking a traditional style (see fig. I.8). But unlike the case of the imperial patrons who built Ottoman mosques in previous centuries, the Kocatepe Mosque was financed by the populist Welfare Party (Refa Partesi). In both these cases, that of the Khomeini tomb and that of the Kocatepe Mosque, religion, as co-opted by the state, is the driving factor in the architectural program. Similarly, traditional rather than modern form is the starting, if not exactly the concluding, point for design.

Critics of the populist architecture these buildings represent consider them reactionary and anti-modern. But these same critics can laud the translation of traditional motifs into modern terms evident in a building such as

Introduction 25

FIG. I.8. *Kocatepe Mosque, Ankara, Turkey.* Photo by Sibel Bozdoğan.

Jean Nouvel's 1988 Insitut du Monde Arabe, an institution founded by elite Gulf Arabs and U.N. diplomats to refine the image of the Arab world in the West. Whatever such attitudes say about the architectural practices in question, they also point to the limits of modernist discourse. Architects and historians of modernism are mute or often vituperative regarding buildings like the Kocatepe Mosque, since they lack the evaluative categories to weigh the cultural significance, if not the aesthetic merit, of populist architecture.

Recently, the actual rather than just symbolic presence of Muslim communities throughout the West has only made the situation more complex. Diasporic communities are growing rapidly throughout the northern hemisphere, remaking urban districts in cities such as Paris and New York with new religious and cultural institutions, shops catering to varied ethnicities, unfamiliar forms of dress, and even different patterns of occupying the street. Identity in the Muslim diaspora draws from notions of Middle Eastern nationality and religious affiliation, but is addressed to its various Western contexts. Whereas the forms, materials, practices, and cultural values of modern architecture had migrated to the Middle East throughout the twentieth century, the Middle East—its people, its architecture, its culture—

is now migrating to the West. The hybrid buildings that result from this process in cities all over the world require a sharpened focus on the present and provide a fresh opportunity to rethink the future of modernism and architecture.

STRUCTURE OF THE BOOK

The central ambition of *Modernism and the Middle East* is to serve as a set of detailed case studies that contextualize architectural form and practice within the discourses of national and postcolonial identity as they have developed in the Middle East. But if the strength of an edited volume of essays when taken as a whole is the variety of perspectives that respond to a common set of questions, then the editors' charge will inevitably be to emphasize the areas of congruency without compromising the range and depth of individual points of view. To achieve this balancing act, we have set thematic and geographic boundaries that focus this volume as well as limit it. As a whole, some degree of temporal breadth is reached by including essays that touch upon every decade of the twentieth century. Similarly, nations from Libya to Iraq come up for discussion, and thus offer geographic breadth. Four essays focus on Mandate Palestine, Israel, and the Occupied Territories, which reflects not only the current high level of scholarship on these places, but also their political—and perhaps, as mentioned above, conceptual—importance to the region. They also demonstrate how a single physical location is subject to conflicting political claims and historical narratives generated to legitimate those claims. In other words, the geographic coordinates may remain more or the less the same for these four essays, but the "place" is in every instance quite different. While the tension between regional relevance and international validity structures many of the individual essays, *Modernism and the Middle East* as a whole aims to transcend that dichotomy to arrive at a richer and more dynamic way to understand a region that is the site both of deep traditions and of rapid modernization. The collected essays vividly demonstrate the political dimensions of creating the built environment, of subsequently inhabiting it, and, finally, of deploying it for symbolic ends.

Modernism and the Middle East begins with a section entitled "Colonial Constructions," in which the politics of domination are situated within the interaction between Europe and the Middle East. The two essays presented here question the balance between tradition and modernity that in the 1930s was seen by many to be the goal of European colonial patronage in the Middle East. Annabel Wharton, in her essay "Jerusalem Remade," shows how the region was reconfigured as a haven of traditional architecture, in contrast with the new building campaigns of Jewish settlers and in preparation for European pilgrims who would expect modern comforts along with the historic and holy urban fabric. Wharton makes evident the crucial role of representation in the modern-day shaping of Jerusalem as an ancient city with a visible architectural heritage serving as an analog of religious insight. Jerusalem, in other words, was remade in the 1930s so that Protestant pilgrims, in particular, could bear witness to their own religious sentiments.

Brian McLaren's essay, "Modern Architecture, Preservation and the Discourse on Local Culture in Italian Colonial Libya," describes Italian appropriation of Libyan architecture from the late 1920s to the late 1930s, as Italians attempted to legitimate their occupation of Libya through architecture. McLaren reveals the racial underpinnings of the sophisticated and self-conscious rationalist discourse of Italian architects that guided architectural policy in Libya, and then traces those policies as they shifted from scholarly and preservation-minded modes to an increasingly didactic and eclectic use of Libyan formal motifs. Whereas earlier designs had been abstract and in keeping with developments in Italy, later designs were more traditional in form and conceived largely for Italian tourists, who were proving to be an increasingly important part of the colony's economy.

The second section, "Building the Nation," takes as its premise that the primary agenda for twentieth-century architects and builders in the Middle East was to construct an architectural vocabulary for nations newly liberated either from European colonial or local imperial regimes. In all, the underlying theme is one of representation: political, architectural, and ideological. The first two essays focus on the role of architects and institutions in mediating the various encounters of modernism with older ways of building. As Magnus Bernhardsson argues in "1001 Fantasies: Development, Architecture, and Modernizing the Past in Baghdad, 1950–1958," institutions are devices that embody these contradictions, as they are simultaneously predicated on programs of modernization and development and embedded in the society and place that is going to be developed. Bernhardsson reveals that the individual architects' proposals for the greater Baghdad plan, sponsored by the Iraqi Development Board (IDB), were secondary to the plan itself, with a mandate for Western-styled development the common underpinning of any specific proposal. The IDB programs emphasized the government's ambivalence toward its own cultural inheritance, as well as the perils of elite sponsorship of a conspicuous building program aimed at a weakly defined citizenry that may not comprehend or approve of the government's ambitions. As Bernhardsson shows, the majority of Iraqis were unaware of the IDB's activities or of its mandate for change. Panayiota Pyla's essay, "Baghdad's Urban Restructuring, 1958: Constantinos Doxiades, Aesthetics, and the Politics of Nation Building," examines the IDB plan for Baghdad in greater detail, focusing in particular on the work of the Greek architect and planner Constantinos Doxiadis. Pyla shows how Doxiadis's simultaneous claims of technocratic objectivity and cultural sensitivity meshed with those of the IDB. She reads the Baghdad plan closely to trace the various transformations by which specific cultural traits were isolated by the planners and then accommodated in fixed urban forms. In "Democracy, Development, and the Americanization of Turkish Architectural Culture in the 1950s," Sibel Bozdoğan surveys the shift in Turkey in the 1950s from Europe to the United States as a reference point for modern architectural practices that became a progressive counterpoint to vestigial orientalist ideas, a hopeful amalgam that evaporated in 1960 following a military coup. She follows individual designers and signal projects, most notably Sedad Eldem and his work on the Hilton Hotel in Istanbul, to argue that there were as many modernisms as there were modern architects.

The following three essays sharpen the book's focus by examining the case of Israel and Palestine, a region that, in terms of the premises of *Modernism and the Middle East*, is founded on a tension between its historic past and its promising future. Roy Kozlovsky's essay, "Temporal States of Architecture: The Provisional Infrastructure of Immigration in Israel," argues that the new Israeli government managed the rapid immigration of the late 1940s and 1950s by appropriating modernist tenets of transitoriness and ephemerality. Kozlovsky shows how government agencies were able to abrogate private property rights in the name of the state's larger transition to stability. With modernism decisively established as the visible vocabulary of progress and material development, professional debate in the 1960s regarding landmark projects in Jerusalem began to shift toward a revived interest in traditional forms and a picturesque sensibility, as described by Alona Nitzan-Shiftan in her essay, "Modernisms in Conflict: Architecture and Cultural Politics in Post-1967 Jerusalem." An international advisory committee, relying on a modernist posture of objective disinterest, argued for greater use of historical references, while an Israeli team of designers called for an unabashed modernism to represent the capital of a progressive nation that was focused unblinkingly on the future. Finally, by looking at the ways Palestinians have memorialized the 1956 massacre at Kufr Qasim, which was at first denied by Israel and then summarily rushed through its military court, Waleed Khleif and Susan Slyomovics, in their essay "Palestinian Remembrance Days and Practices," move well beyond the use of built form as a kind of civic representation to reach an ideal of "historical justice" that nonetheless centers on the importance of place and cultural memory. Rather than recognize the tragedy with a memorial that would, in any case, have been compromised, even if it had been allowed, the making and reciting of poetry became a ritual practice of memorialization. Memory, the authors imply, can become monumental even in the absence of any built monuments.

The concluding section, "Overviews and Openings," reestablishes a broader outlook. In "Global Ambition and Local Knowledge," Gwendolyn Wright emphasizes the tension between the modern and the traditional in Beirut, Cairo, and Riyadh, mostly in the period of the 1950s and 1960s. As she sheds light on the intellectual constructs and effects of modernism, Wright also lays out essential questions of global processes and local agency—the essence of postcolonial tensions—that remain pressing in our own day. Nezar AlSayyad's essay, "From Modernism to Globalization: The Middle East in Context," brings issues discussed in the preceding essays to the present day. He retraces how the idea of a cohesive Middle East was articulated and reinforced in the twentieth century, even as he shows through varied examples how tenuous this geopolitical entity truly is. Pointing toward greater rather than less cultural differentiation in the process of globalization, AlSayyad confirms the need to look beyond formal similarities to comprehend the many unique articulations of cultural identity in the place that is called the "Middle East."

NOTES

1. On orientalism, the seminal text is that of Edward Said (*Orientalism* [New York: Vintage, 1978]). For a critique of Said's work, see Aijaz Ahmad, "Orientalism and After: Ambivalence and Metropolitan Location in the Work of Edward Said," in *In Theory: Classes, Nations, Literatures* (London: Verso, 1992).

2. For a collection of essays that deal with various aspects of modernization and the Middle East, see Albert Hourani, Philip S. Khoury, and Mary C. Wilson, eds., *The Modern Middle East: A Reader* (Berkeley: University of California Press, 1993).

3. Crimea, e.g., was taken in 1774 by the Russians, while Egypt was occupied by Napoleon's army in 1798. In 1828 the Russians further asserted their military strength by absorbing Georgia and parts of Iranian Azerbaijan.

4. On the "modernization" of Cairo, see Doris Behrens-Abouseif, *Azbakiyya*

and Its Environs (Le Caire: Institut Français d'Archéologie Orientale, 1985); and Nezar AlSayyad, Irene A. Bierman, and Nasser Rabbat, eds., *Making Cairo Medieval* (Lanham, Md.: Lexington Books, 2005).

5. Libya was occupied by the Italians in 1911, and in 1914 Egypt became a protectorate of Britain. In addition, the kingdom of Morocco became a protectorate of France.

6. The seminal texts on the subject of nationalism are Eric Hobsbawm and Terrence Ranger, eds., *The Invention of Tradition* (New York: Cambridge University Press, 1992); and Benedict R. O'G. Anderson, *Imagined Communities* (London: Verso, 1983).

7. A recent overview is Paul Stevens, "Oil and Development," in *A Companion to the History of the Middle East*, ed. Youssef M. Choveiri (Malden, Mass.: Blackwell, 2005).

8. Dipesh Chakrabarty, "Postcoloniality and the Artifice of History," in *Unpacking Europe*, ed. Salah Hassan and Iftikhar Dadi (Rotterdam: NAi Publishers, 2001).

9. Archeology is discussed by Stephen Vernoit in "The Rise of Islamic Archeology" (*Muqarnas* 14 [1997]: 1–10). Usually, for these scholars, Ottoman artifacts were emblems of a corrupt and impotent rule. On travelers to Iran, see Jennifer Scarce, "Persian Art through the Eyes of Nineteenth-Century British Travelers," *Bulletin of British Society for Middle Eastern Studies* 8, no. 1 (1981): 38–50.

10. The primary task for European colonialists was to inventory their newly procured assets, for which they used scholarly tools such as more-or-less standardized survey formats, with their structuring biological metaphors of stylistic birth, flowering, and decay, and the catalogue, a format generally understood to be authoritative for fitting specific fragments of past art into grand narratives of cultural progress. The aesthetic categories and intellectual preoccupations of European scholars determined both the merit and the historical value of the entire field of Islamic art and architecture. Grand imperial projects, such as palace complexes and mosques, attracted the most attention, while sites of what would now be termed "popular culture," such as local shrines and bazaars, received little notice, except in discussions about the mythical "Islamic City." At that time, some monuments were destroyed only to be rebuilt in what were deemed more authentic ways, while others were fabricated anew on the basis of the nationalist rediscovery of their importance. In Iran, Susa and other pre-Islamic sites were studied from as early as 1884, but it was not until the beginning of the twentieth century that much attention was given to Islamic sites.

11. Herzfeld subsequently joined the German dig at Assur and completed a dissertation on the Achaemenid palace at Pasargade, in Iran. Still a young man,

Herzfeld had also completed a survey of the monuments of the province of Luristan in Iran, as well as a preliminary report on the great Abbasid city of Samarra. With permission from local authorities to conduct excavations in Iraq, he defined the physical contours and set the temporal limits of Samarra. This latter project was to be Herzfeld's masterwork, and he returned to Iraq to conduct two seasons of excavations, in 1911 and 1912–13. With the changed political climate of Iraq under British rule and in the wake of World War I, Herzfeld, along with other Germans throughout the Middle East, was expelled, and so forced to shift his scholarly focus. On Sarre, Herzfeld, and their contemporaries, see Alaister Northedge, "Creswell, Herzfeld, and Samarra," *Muqarnas* 8 (1991): 74–93; Robert Hillenbrand, "Creswell and Contemporary Central European Scholarship," *Muqarnas* 8 (1991): 23–35; and Yuri Bregel, "Barthold and Modern Oriental Studies," *IJMES* 12 (1980): 385–403. For more comprehensive analysis, see the collection in Ann C. Gunter and Stefan R. Hauser, eds., *Ernst Herzfeld and the Development of Near Eastern Studies, 1900–1950* (Leiden: Brill, 2005). A partial overview of early exhibitions, limited primarily to European contexts, is provided in D. Roxburgh, "Au Bonheur des Amateurs: Collecting and Exhibiting Islamic Art, ca. 1880–1910," *Ars Orientalis* 30 (2000): 9–38, in which he discusses the modes of display in light of contemporary taste.

12. The Mshatta palace façade was removed to Berlin in the early twentieth century, as a presentation to Kaiser Wilhelm II. Objects from the Middle East, like carpets, might be valued for their appearance in European paintings, as were Holbein or Polonaise carpets. An example of the complete dismemberment of ceramics from their original sites is seen in the wholesale removal of the mihrab from a fourteenth-century mosque in Isfahan, which was purchased by the Metropolitan Museum of Art in 1939.

13. On the profound complicity between orientalist scholarship and nationalism, see Edmund Burke III, "Orientalism and World History: Representing Middle Eastern Nationalism and Islamism in the Twentieth Century," *Theory and Society* 27, no. 4 (August 1998): 489–507.

14. As has been noted, "The Europeans were not just Europeans, but citizens of powers that were endlessly maneuvering for advantage in Egypt" (Donald Malcolm Reid, "Cultural Imperialism and Nationalism: The Struggle to Define and Control the Heritage of Arab Art in Egypt," *IJMES* 29 [1992]: 63).

15. Many museum administrators were also interested in surveying the built landscape, a task shared by other colonial officials, such as geographers, census-takers, and urban planners. Their task was to preserve those sites considered to be part of the long and evolutionary narrative of world history.

16. In an attempt to assert the Aryan claims of the Pahlavi dynasty, the remains of Firdawsi and others were then examined and subjected to racial examination.

This material has been explored by Talin Grigor in "Cultivat(ing) Modernities: The Society for National Heritage, Political Propaganda, and Public Architecture in Twentieth-Century Iran," Ph.D. diss., MIT, 2005.

17. See Talin Grigor, "Recultivating 'Good Taste': The Early Pahlavi Modernists and Their Society for National Heritage," *Iranian Studies* 37, no. 1 (March 2004): 17–45.

18. See Kishwar Rizvi, "Art History and the Nation: Arthur Upham Pope and the Discourse on 'Persian Art' in the Early Twentieth Century," *Muqarnas: Journal of Islamic Art and Architecture* 24 (2007).

19. *Muqarnas* 8 (1990) is a special issue dedicated to the life and legacy of K. A. C. Creswell.

20. Quoted in R. W. Hamilton, "Keppel Archibald Cameron Creswell, 1879–1974," *Proceedings of the British Academy* (1974): 1–20.

21. Detailed archival information about Pope's life is contained in Jay Gluck and Noel Siver, eds., *Surveyors of Persian Art: A Documentary Biography of Arthur Upham Pope and Phyllis Ackerman* (Costa Mesa, CA: Mazda Publishers, 1996). See also Arthur Upham Pope, "The Past and Future of Persian Art," in Gluck and Silver, *Surveyors of Persian Art*, 93.

22. Arthur Upham Pope and Phyllis Ackerman, *A Survey of Persian Art, from Prehistoric Times to the Present* (New York: Oxford University Press, 1938–39).

23. The dedication to King Fuʿad on the original 1932 manuscript of *Early Muslim Architecture*, is edited out of the 1969 reprint.

24. See the discussion in Gulsum Baydar, "Toward Postcolonial Openings: Rereading Sir Banister Fletcher's History of Architecture," *Assemblage* 35 (1998): 6–17.

25. In Tehran, the Dār al-Funūn, or Academy of Arts and Sciences, had already been established in 1851, but by 1861 fine arts and painting were included in the curriculum.

26. For more on modern architecture in Turkey, see Renata Holod and Ahmet Evin, *Modern Turkish Architecture* (Philadelphia: University of Pennsylvania Press, 1984); and Sibel Bozdoğan, *Modernism and Nation Building* (Seattle: University of Washington Press, 2001).

27. For more on Qajar architecture, see Jennifer Scarce, "Ancestral Themes in the Art of Qajar Iran, 1785–1925," in *Islamic Art in the Nineteenth Century*, ed. Doris Behrens-Abouseif and Stephen Vernoit (Leiden: Brill, 2006).

28. A case study is provided by Nasser Rabbat, "The Formation of the Neo-Mamluk Style in Modern Egypt," in *The Education of the Architect: Historiography, Urbanism, and the Growth of Architectural Knowledge*, ed. Martha Pollak (Cambridge, MA: MIT Press, 1997). See also Mercedes Volait, "Appropriating Orientalism?

Saer Sabri's Mamluk Revivals in Late-Nineteenth-Century Cairo," in *Islamic Art in the Nineteenth Century: Tradition, Innovation, and Eclecticism,* ed. Doris Behrens-Abouseif and Stephen Vernoit (Leiden: Brill, 2006). The term "medieval," in the context of Victorian Europe and Egypt, is discussed in Paula Sanders, "The Victorian Invention of Medieval Cairo: A Case Study of Medievalism and the Construction of the East," *MESA Bulletin* 37, no. 2 (2003): 179–98.

29. A museum was already established in the Academy of Arts and Sciences in 1915, but it was deemed inadequate for the purposes of a national institution. For a further introduction to Godard, see Ève Gran-Aymerich and Mina Marefat, "Godard, André," *Encyclopædia Iranica* Web site, www.iranica.com.

30. Well-known examples would include the Woolworth Tower (1913), Cass Gilbert's Gothic Revival skyscraper in New York, and McKim, Mead, and White's Classical Municipal Building (1915), also in New York.

31. Mina Marefat, "The Protagonists Who Shaped Modern Tehran," in *Téhéran, capitale bicentenaire,* ed. C. Adle and B. Hourcade (Paris and Tehran: Bibliothèque Iranienne, 1992), 110.

32. For more on Jansen, Egli, and others, see Bernd Nicolai, *Moderne und Exil: Deutschsprachige Architekten in der Türkei, 1925–1955* (Berlin: Verlag für Bauwesen, 1998); as well as Sibel Bozdoğan, *Modernism and Nation Building.*

33. When a native architectural intelligence was discovered, it was not in the built legacy of centuries of Ottoman rule, but in the more ancient cultures of Anatolia, such as the Hittites. A good example is the Anit Kabir mausoleum of Mutstafa Kemal Ataturk, built by Emin Onat and Orhan Arda, and completed in 1953.

34. The "outsider as insider," as Peter Gay put it, was a common trope. The role of German émigrés in twentieth-century cultural production generally, and in relation to architecture, is discussed in Gay, "Weimar Culture: The Outsider as Insider," and William Jordy, "The Aftermath of the Bauhaus in America: Gropius, Mies, and Breuer," in *The Intellectual Migration: Europe and America, 1930–1960,* ed. Donald Fleming and Bernard Bailyn (Cambridge, MA: Harvard University Press, 1969). More contemporary sources would include Talcott Parsons, *Structure and Process in Modern Societies* (Glencoe, IL: Free Press, 1960); and K. W. Deutsch, "Social Mobilization and Political Development," *American Political Science Review* 55 (September 1961): 494–95.

35. See Sibel Bozdoğan, *Sedad Hakki Eldem: Architect in Turkey* (Singapore and New York: Concept Media, Aperture, 1987).

36. "Architecture—Not Style," *Progressive Architecture* (December 1948), 49.

37. Stephen S. Fenichell and Phillip Andrews, *The United Nations: Blueprint For Peace* (Philadelphia: John C. Winston, 1951); the quotation also appears in UNESCO. *Teaching about the United Nations and the Specialized Agencies: A Selected*

Bibliography, Educational Studies and Documents, no. 29 (UNESCO: Paris, 1958), 31. Original members of the United Nations were Egypt, Iran, Iraq, Lebanon, Saudi Arabia, Syria, and Turkey.

38. See also Annabel Jane Wharton, *Building the Cold War: Hilton International Hotels and Modern Architecture* (Chicago: University of Chicago Press, 2001).

39. For some context for Western ideas of climate, see Matthias Gross, "Human Geography and Ecological Sociology: The Unfolding of a Human Ecology, 1890 to 1930—and Beyond," *Social Science History* 28, no. 4 (2004): 575–605.

40. Discussed in Samuel Isenstadt, "'Faith in a Better Future': Josep Lluis Sert's American Embassy in Baghdad," *Journal of Architectural Education* 50 (February 1997): 172–88.

41. Ellen Jawdat, "The New Architecture in Iraq," *Architectural Design* 27 (March 1957): 79–80; Lord Salter [Arthur Salter], *The Development of Iraq: A Plan of Action* (London: n.p., 1955), 31, 159, and passim. Both are discussed in Isenstadt, "Faith in a Better Future." See also Alexander Melamid, "Economic Development in the Middle East," *Annals of the Association of American Geographers* 48, no. 3 (1958): 308.

42. See, e.g., Richard J. Neutra, "Regionalism in Architecture," *Plus,* no. 2 (February 1939): 22–23; James Stirling, "Regionalism in Modern Architecture," *Architect's Year Book* 7 (1957): 62–68; Sibyl Moholy-Nagy, *Native Genius in Anonymous Architecture* (New York: Horizon Press, 1957).

43. For more on Fathy, see Hassan Fathy, *Gourna: A Tale of Two Villages* (Cairo: Ministry of Culture, 1969); H. Fathy, *Architecture for the Poor: An Experiment in Rural Egypt* (Chicago: University of Chicago Press, 1973); and James Steele, *An Architecture for People: The Complete Works of Hassan Fathy* (New York: Whitney Library of Design, 1997). As influential as Fathy's work was, and remains, it has been criticized for its own version of orientalism. On Chadirji, see Rifat Chadirji, *Concepts and Influences: Towards a Regionalized International Architecture* (New York: Routledge and Paul Kegan, 1986); and "Chairman's Award," in *Space for Freedom: Aga Khan Award Monograph,* ed. Ismail Serageldin (London: Butterworth Architecture, 1989).

44. National Research Council (U.S.), Committee on Research for the Security of Future U.S. Embassy Buildings, *The Embassy of the Future: Recommendations for the Design of Future U.S. Embassy Buildings* (Washington, D.C.: National Academy Press, 1986), 27. Since the 1970s, security has been the overwhelming issue for embassy design.

45. Jules Langaner, "Neo-classicism? Ornamented Modern? The Quest for Ornament in American Architecture," *Zodiac* 4 (April 1959): 68–72. On the American Embassy program, see Ron Robin, *Enclaves of America: The Rhetoric of American Political Architecture Abroad, 1900–1965* (Princeton, NJ: Princeton Univer-

sity Press, 1992); and Jane Loeffler, *Architecture of Diplomacy: Building America's Embassies* (New York: Princeton Architectural Press, 1998).

46. "The mega-rhetoric of developmental modernization," as Arjun Appadurai put it, is crosscut synchronically by media narratives and diachronically by the fitful implementation of actual modernization projects (see Arjun Appadurai, "Here and Now," in *Modernity at Large: Cultural Dimensions of Globalization* [Minneapolis: University of Minnesota Press, 1996], 9–10).

47. Mohammed Tehrani is criticized by local Iranian architects for "selling out" to the Islamist regime. This criticism is similar to the one directed at the Turkish architect Vedat Dalokay, the architect of such buildings as the mosque of Shah Faisal in Islamabad, Pakistan (see Kishwar Rizvi, "Religious Icon and National Symbol: The Tomb of Ayatollah Khomeini in Iran," *Muqarnas* 20 [2003]).

48. An interesting anthropological analysis of this site, especially in the context of nationalism, is provided in M. Meeker, "Once There Was, Once There Wasn't: National Monuments and Interpersonal Exchange," in *Rethinking Modernity and National Identity in Turkey*, ed. Sibel Bozdoğan and Reşat Kasaba (Seattle: University of Washington Press, 1997).

PART I *Colonial Constructions*

1 Jerusalem Remade

ANNABEL WHARTON

In the nineteenth century the Old City of Jerusalem was a rich historical mix: a Roman grid obscured by nearly two millennia of later construction. Monuments to different political hegemonies survived: the Herodian retaining-wall of al-Haram al-Sharif, the Constantinian and Crusader Church of the Holy Sepulchre, the Umayyad Dome of the Rock, the Mamluk fountains, all sheltered from a rugged landscape by the great sixteenth-century walls of Süleyman the Magnificent and set in the sympathetic Ottoman matrix of vernacular domestic and commercial construction in Jerusalem stone. Before 1850, Western travelers were still able to see Jerusalem as the ideal ancient walled city, at least from a distance. The French poet and traveler, Alphonse de Lamartine, described the view of Jerusalem from the Mount of Olives in October 1832:

> The whole of Jerusalem is stretched before us, like the plan of a town in relief, spread by an artist upon a table. . . . This city is not, as it has been represented, an unshapely and confused mass of ruins and ashes, over which a few Arab cottages are thrown, or a few Bedouin tents pitched; neither is it, like Athens, a chaos of dust and crumbling walls, where the traveler seeks in vain the shadow of edifices, the trace of streets, the phantom of a city;— but it is a city shining in light and color; presenting nobly to view her intact and battlemented walls, her blue mosque with its white colonnades, her thousand resplendent domes, from which the rays of the autumnal sun

FIG. 1.1. *David Roberts,* Jerusalem from the Mount of Olives, *in* The Holy Land: Syria, Idumea, Arabia, Egypt & Nubia, *vol. 1, plate 17. This volume is in the collection of the Nasher Museum of Art at Duke University; museum purchase.*

are reflected in a dazzling vapor; the facades of her houses, tinted by time and heat, of the yellow and golden hue of the edifices of Paestum or of Rome; her old towers, the guardians of her walls, to which neither one stone, one loophole, nor one battlement is wanting; and above all, amidst that ocean of houses, that cloud of little domes which cover them, it is a dark elliptical dome, larger than the others, overlooked by another and a white one. These are the churches of the Holy Sepulchre and of Calvary. . . . The view is the most splendid that can be presented to the eye, of a city that is no more.[1]

Lamartine's rapturous image of the city was a literary convention with an equally stereotypical visual counterpart. Western prints and paintings of Jerusalem similarly rendered it as a mythical fortified city set in an alien wilderness. Many of those renderings, despite claims of authenticity, were utterly fanciful.[2] Among the more convincing were those of the Scottish artist David Roberts (fig. 1.1). Roberts's master work, *The Holy Land: Syria, Idumea, Arabia, Egypt & Nubia,* published in London between 1840 and 1845, was one of the most lavish lithographic art-print collections ever manufactured; its images were reproduced in multiple editions, both legal and pirated.[3]

Jerusalem was transformed during the second half of the nineteenth century. Economic and political stability under the enlightened despot, Muhammad Ali, viceroy and pasha of Egypt (1805–49), as well as increasingly affordable travel with the extension of railroads and steamship lines, contributed to a revival of pilgrimage and the advent of tourism. Süleyman's great walls, built in the sixteenth century to protect Jerusalem from an anticipated Christian Crusade, had long separated the city from a hostile hinterland; by the end of the nineteenth century, those walls divided the Old City from its rapidly developing suburbs. The earlier, sublime Jerusalem was, however, the Jerusalem still sought by the city's Western visitors. High-art representations of the city, like Frederick Edwin Church's *Jerusalem* of 1871, as well as popular renderings, like the persuasively illusionistic versions of *Jerusalem on the Day of the Crucifixion* displayed in the great panoramas of the end of the nineteenth century, perpetuated notions of Jerusalem as an ancient walled city.[4] Images also whetted the Western appetite for the Holy City.

The desire for a particular view of Jerusalem might appear benign, but it was part of the drive for a more literal form of possession. European and American travelers of the nineteenth and early twentieth century, experiencing the East under control of the Turks, willed Western domination of the old Ottoman Empire. The travel writer Edwin de Leon gave characteristic expression to this sentiment: "The Turcoman came as a scourge from his far wilds, to chastise the vices of an effete and decaying civilization. Those vices he has aggravated and perpetuated. . . . The Turk cannot stay much longer, nor will he make more than a feeble resistance against his expulsion."[5] Another travel writer, John Stoddard, commented, "Whether it be Russia, Austria, Germany, England or a joint protectorate of nations, some Christian power must ere long occupy this site, and lift it to the rank designed for it by destiny."[6]

The "destiny" that de Leon predicted seemed to come to fulfillment during World War I when, in 1917, British and allied troops under General Allenby entered Jerusalem.[7] A speech by Lord Northcliffe exemplifies the spiritual charge of Jerusalem as Christian. The redemptive mission of restoring to the city its true spiritual inheritance, begun by Christian Crusaders, would finally be accomplished by Great Britain:

> Jerusalem is a small city among the cities of the earth; in its great period it was never more than chief town, almost the only town, of a small and pastoral people: yet there is no city in the world's history that has made a longer or a stronger appeal to the spiritual and romantic sense of the human

soul.... Jerusalem has remained the City of Cities to millions who have never entered her gates, the capital of the ideal State, the goal of the unending pilgrimage.... Throughout England, as throughout Europe, generation after generation sent its sons in thousands across unknown lands and seas, through dangers undreamed of, on the mystical quest of the Crusaders, eternal and unsatisfied for the Holy City of Jerusalem.... Jerusalem has dominated the minds and spirits of men throughout the centuries, until that great day ... when it was peacefully conquered by a British Army, and it became our privilege to restore Jerusalem and Palestine to their place among the nations. (Cheers.)[8]

John H. Finley, head of the American Red Cross in Palestine at the onset of the British occupation, even more ecstatically expressed the spiritual fervor of the West's delirious optimism that the British would finally put Jerusalem right. The distant view of the Holy City is apocalyptic; the British will cleanse the city of the cultural pollution that has dimmed its spiritual brilliance:

But even as I looked toward the place of the ancient and holy city, the gray curtain of mist or fog parted as if drawn aside by invisible hands. A golden rift immediately over the city—over the Church of the Holy Sepulchre itself—slowly widened, till in a few minutes there stood as in an Apocalypse before me, a city shut away from the outer city, and from all about, as if rebuilded in the golden and jeweled image of itself.... This sight of Jerusalem given to me in such a dramatic way will always remain as an intimation of that which Americans, in common with all who are fighting for justice in the earth, must help to bring into this Holy City. Many that make abominations and lies in the world have entered in the past, but under the British Government it is being cleansed, and prepared for the genius of the nations, and especially of those whose religions found a cradle here—Moslem, Jewish, and Christian—to adorn it, make it the most beautiful city on the planet and give it most fit setting amid the mountains round about it—"as the stars of a crown glistening upon his land."[9]

Ronald Storrs, the British governor of the city from the beginning of the mandate in 1917 until 1927, was perfectly suited to the job of remaking Jerusalem. Storrs, born in Bury St. Edmunds in 1881, was the eldest son of the Reverend John Storrs, a vicar who became Dean of Rochester. Storrs was educated at Charterhouse and Pembroke College, Cambridge. At Cambridge he received a first-class degree in the Classical Tripos of 1903. There he was also elected to the elite Decemviri, whose ten at his time included Charles Tennyson, J. M. Keynes, and Lytton Strachey.¹⁰ Storrs moved directly from Cambridge into the Egyptian Civil Service in 1904.¹¹ In Cairo he served as Oriental Secretary under Sir Eldon Gorst, Lord Kitchener, and Sir Henry McMahon. During the early years of World War I, Storrs was involved with such figures as Sherif Hussein, later King Hussein, and T. E. Lawrence, better known as Lawrence of Arabia. Lawrence described Storrs, in his *Seven Pillars of Wisdom*:

> The first of us was Ronald Storrs, Oriental Secretary of the Residency, the most brilliant Englishman in the Near East, and subtly efficient, despite his diversion of energy in love of music and letters, of sculpture, painting, of whatever was beautiful in the world's fruit. None the less, Storrs sowed what we reaped, and was always first, and the great man among us. His shadow would have covered our work and British policy in the East like a cloak, had he been able to deny himself the world, and to prepare his mind and body with the sternness of an athlete for a great fight.¹²

As Lawrence suggests, Storrs was never willing to abstain from the arts, whatever his military and administrative obligations. Another of Lawrence's anecdotes, describing their shipboard passage to Jidda to meet with Sharif Hussein's representative, Abdullah, to help plan the Arab Legion's war against the Turks, suggests something of Storrs's sophistication:

> Storrs' intolerant brain seldom stooped to company. But today he was more abrupt than usual. He turned twice around the decks, sniffed, "No one worth talking to," and sat down in one of the two comfortable armchairs, to begin a discussion of Debussy with Aziz el Masri. Aziz, the Arab-Circassian ex-colonel in the Turkish Army, now general of the Sherifian Army, was on his way to discuss with the Emir of Mecca the equipment and standing of the Arab regulars he was forming at Rabegh. A few minutes later they had left Debussy, and were depreciating Wagner: Aziz in fluent German, and Storrs in German, French and Arabic. The ship's officers found the whole conversation unnecessary.¹³

Emblematic of Storrs's close connections with those in the arts was his intimate friendship with Bernard Berenson, the well-known art connoisseur, and his wife Mary.¹⁴ His administrative posts were always extended to include both music and the fine arts. In Cairo he was a member of the Comité pour la Conservation des Monuments Arabes. He was also central to the establishment of the Coptic Museum in Cairo. But Storrs's most notable contribution to the arts and to preservation was made in Jerusalem after his appointment there as governor of the city.

RESTITUTION: REFUSING THE MODERN

Storrs became governor of Jerusalem on December 28, 1917, in the aftermath of the Turkish evacuation of the city and its occupation by the British army. He was confronted with a population that had been on starvation rations for three years and had been left by the Turkish withdrawal entirely without provisions.[15] Foodstuffs and movables had been confiscated by the retreating army. Water supplies were contaminated. Roads were impassable and the rails of the Jaffa-Jerusalem train line had been dismantled. Despite having to address the enormous fiscal pressures on the civil order of the city, Storrs did not neglect his commitment to archeology and the preservation of Jerusalem. He willed Jerusalem to remain

> a city unparalleled in the world, with an appeal to the imagination that not Rome, nor even Athens, could rival. Even in its appearance . . . there was an impression of something strange and moving. The austere gray walls and battlements, stone-built on hills of stone, commanded and dominated the gaunt Judean plateau. Travelers . . . would pass the ancient walls, whose stones were hewn from the quarries of Solomon, and climb the Mount of Olives, from whose summit they could look over the city, of which, though its towers, pinnacles, and minarets wore the work of more recent ages, the general appearance was, and he hoped would be allowed to remain, very much what it was 2,000 years ago.[16]

In order to realize his vision, within four months of the British seizure of the city, Storrs had published in English, French, Arabic and Hebrew—all languages in which he was reasonably adept—a proclamation concerning construction:

> No person shall demolish, erect, alter, or repair the structure of any building in the city of Jerusalem or its environs within a radius of 2,500 metres from the Damascus Gate (Bab al Amud) until he has obtained a written permit from the Military Governor. Any person contravening the orders contained in this proclamation, or any term or terms contained in a license issued to him under this proclamation, will be liable upon convic-

tion to a fine not exceeding £E.200 [Egyptian pounds]. R. Storrs, Colonel, Military Governor, Jerusalem, April 8th, 1918.[17]

Another decree of about the same time prohibited the use of stucco and corrugated iron within the city walls. Red tiles were also forbidden.[18] The banning of stucco, corrugated iron, and red tiles stood at the core of Storrs's commitment to the local and historic and his opposition to the modern and Western. Stucco and iron were suspect as imported technologies; red tiles were mistrusted on ideological grounds. Red roof tiles were then and remain politically loaded indices of an alien European presence in Palestine. As Arthur Ruppin, a Zionist administrator of the Jewish National Fund, reported to the Jewish Colonization Society of Vienna in 1908, "In contrast with the pitiful Arab villages, with their huts of baked clay, the Jewish colonies, with their wide streets, their strong stone houses and their red-tiled roofs, look like veritable oases of culture."[19] The continued ideological power of "red roofs" is indicated by the use of that epithet in the political struggles over Jewish settlements in the occupied territories.[20] For Storrs, Jerusalem was no place for red tiles. He mandated the use of Jerusalem stone; the tradition of stone vaulting was maintained, thus salvaging "the heritage in Jerusalem of an immemorial and a hallowed past."[21]

Storrs's opposition to the modern went beyond current construction technologies: "Replying to a request for a tram line (from Jerusalem) to Bethlehem, I said that the first rail laid would be laid over the dead body of the Military Governor. The cars did seem so wholly out of keeping with the surroundings that I forbade them throughout the province of Judea."[22] Advertising, except minimally on shop fronts, was also proscribed: "Stricter measures are being enforced for the preservation of the traditional building style of Jerusalem, offensive and unsuitable materials are being prohibited or removed, and an effective control of new buildings and town planning sections has been instituted. The size of shop signs, which had become of recent years a serious disfigurement to the city, has been regulated by Municipal By-laws, under which also the posting of bills, placards, and advertisements is restricted to moderate-sized notice boards displayed in specially chosen localities."[23] Storrs also closed bars within his jurisdiction that served alcoholic beverages.

RESTITUTION: RETRIEVING THE ANCIENT

Not allowing the introduction of the modern was part of Storrs's strategy for producing old Jerusalem; restoring the city was a second component. The vehicle for Storrs's project of remaking was the Pro-Jerusalem Society. Storrs established the Pro-Jerusalem Society as an independent, non-governmental association of distinguished representatives of the various ethnic communities in the city. Members included the Grand Mufti, the most powerful religious representative of the Muslim community; the mayor of Jerusalem; the Orthodox Patriarch; the Latin Patriarch; the head of the Armenian Convent in Jerusalem; the Custode di Terra Santa; and the head of the Jewish community. Storrs served on the committee for the duration of its eight years of existence. As Secretary to this Society, as well as Civic Advisor, Storrs appointed C. R. Ashbee, a friend and follower of William Morris and a committed Arts and Crafts advocate.[24] In a city tense with ethnic and religious hostility, project decisions made within this group might escape charges of preference or prejudice. Indeed, this committee, made up of individuals whose only shared commitment was to the physical well-being of the city, seems to have been the one setting in which representatives of the different factions regularly worked productively together. Ashbee described the British project in a press interview:

> "There is the old Jerusalem, the city within the walls, to preserve," he said, "and there is the growth and development of the new city to regulate. All the work is under the control of Sir Arthur Money, the head of the Occupied Enemy Territories Administration, and it is the special charge of General Ronald Storrs, the Governor of Jerusalem. A number of us are busy on different branches of the work. Mr. Ernest Richmond, for instance, is Director-General of Public Monuments; Mr. Maclean is in charge of town-planning in the new city; and Dr. Betts has come from Egypt to help in the work of the municipality. We have to deal with the consequences of the years of Turkish misrule and with the results of the bitter jealousies of the nations. Where there has not been actual ill-treatment of the buildings there has been neglect. At the same time, we have to work very tenderly and carefully. Do not think of that alarming word 'restoration' in connection with what we are doing. Our aim is rather to discover and preserve all that remains of the past and to undo so far as we can the evil that has been done. We are getting ready, for instance, to fill up the gap that was made in the wall to enable the Kaiser to make his triumphal entry into Jerusalem, and the terrible clock-tower that was put up to celebrate that event will be pulled down. And we have to get rid of the jealousies of the nations. During the past fifteen or twenty years the peoples of the earth seem to have chosen Jerusalem as the right place to advertise their bitter-

est and their most extreme discrimination. Moslems, Jews, Armenians, Greeks, Latins—all these took a bit of Jerusalem and put a wall round it to keep off all the others. The Germans, of course, got possession of the best military position they could find, and practically fortified it. We English, for our part, put up a bad imitation of an Oxford College. Well, we want to get all these bits out of their prisons and to set them free. . . . In conclusion, you must remember that what we are doing in Jerusalem is being done not for any one nation, but for all the world. For, after all, it belongs to the world."[25]

Restoration is, however, expensive. The public funds available to Storrs for the improvements that he sought to make were extremely limited. The British Empire was not a charity. The "Cromer System" of colonial order was designed to produce wealth rather than give it away. As Gideon Bigger described it, the "Cromer System"

> emphasized the importance of low taxation, efficient fiscal administration, careful expenditure on remunerative public work, and a minimal interference in the internal and external traffic of goods (of colonial territories). This system was most effective in countries with a clear-cut native ruling class. . . . Development programs and services in the colonies were funded by local tax revenues, British government loans, and public or private investment. . . . Since tax revenues were much lower than in Britain, the services provided in the colonies were obviously more limited.[26]

The British government was unwilling to divert its resources to Palestine. Indeed, as the British exacted loads on the province's revenue, not even all local income was devoted to local infrastructure. Notably, the British treasury insisted that Palestine contribute to the repayment of the Ottoman debt, which of course involved British creditors. Further, concessions granted by the Ottomans before the war were deemed valid after it. Standard Oil had a concession for oil development; a French company for the operation of various railroads and cargo and passenger ships; and there were also foreign monopolies on water and power and tobacco growing. Finally, the British government refused to guarantee a loan that was repeatedly requested by Herbert Samuel, the first High Commissioner of Palestine because Palestine was never intended to be part of the Empire. The British were willing to pay only for military expenditures—and when they proved too costly, in 1948, they withdrew.[27]

Storrs finally extracted an annual subsidy of between £500 and £2,000 from Samuel, through the threat of a tourist tax.[28] All other monies had to be raised privately. His trip to the United States in 1923—designed to exploit connections to the very wealthy—represents his most notable effort in fundraising. The Pro-Palestine Society's yearbooks, which provide the most useful documentation of its activities, were actually published by Ashbee and privately circulated as part of Storrs's fundraising efforts. In his autobiography, he describes himself as a well-practiced beggar:

> Many of the leading merchants, realizing how greatly the future prosperity of Jerusalem depended upon its preservation as Jerusalem (and not an inferior Kiev, Manchester or Baltimore), subscribed liberally to our funds; and in Egypt, England and America, Moslems, Christians and Jews, suspicious of any creed, culture or policy other than their own, gave gladly to a Jerusalem which represented all three. I realized then the power of the name of Jerusalem; I realized it even more afterwards when appealing for other countries or causes; I became, I am happy to believe, a convincing and successful *Schnorrer* (Yiddish for professional beggar). My subscription list, of cheques ranging from £3 to £600, included from Cairo the names of Smouha and Btesh, the Syrian Community, and the editor of the *Mokattam;* in Jerusalem the Anglo-Egyptian Bank, Sir Abbas Effendi Abd al-Bahá, the Mufti, several Jewish firms, the Imperial Ottoman Bank, the Crédit Lyonnais, the Anglo-Palestine Bank, the Banco di Roma, the 51st Sikh Regiment, the Zionist Commission, the Municipality, and the Administration; in Europe and America, Lord Milner, Sir Basil Zaharoff, Lord Northcliffe, Sir Alred Mond, Mrs. Holman Hunt, Mrs. Carnegie, Messrs Pierpont Morgan, and Messrs Keun Loeb. I found institutions more generous than individuals, and (especially in America) men than women.[29]

Storrs also requested financial support for the Pro-Jerusalem Society from King George V, but was sharply rebuffed for his impertinence.[30] Despite limited funds, during the first years of British occupation a number of important repairs were made to the fabric of Jerusalem under the aegis of the Pro-Jerusalem Society.[31] The Dome of the Rock, the architectural icon of the city, received desperately needed attention:

> The supervision of this important work has been since the outset in the hands of Mr. Ernest Richmond, the advisor architect of the Wakf, from

FIG. 1.2. *Ceramic street sign, Mandate period, now in the Christian Information Center at Jaffa Gate. Author's photograph.*

whose report of March 1919 the following extract is given: "To ensure complete immunity from decay, especially in the case of the more modern tiles, is impossible. The surface of this kind of tile . . . is bound to disappear much sooner than that of the earlier tiles, thereby seriously increasing the denuded areas. . . . Is the method adopted in the sixteenth century of decorating the outer walls of this building with glazed tiles to be continued . . . or abandoned? . . . All skin decays, but so long as there is life in the body which it covers its tissues are continually renewed. So long as the Dome of the Rock remains a live building—a building that is to say which is an integral part in the life that surrounds it—so long as it fulfils the functions it has fulfilled for 1,200 years, so long must its skin be continually renewed."[32]

The medieval kilns were restored and tile makers brought from Turkey to provide the high-quality tiles essential to a credible restoration of the structure.[33] Those tile makers also produced beautiful street signs for the city that have since been replaced (see figs. 1.2 and 1.3).

The Dome of the Rock is the most familiar sign of Jerusalem, but its Islamic identity makes it an ambiguous one for Western viewers. Even in the descriptions of the city quoted above, the Dome of the Rock's prominence is oddly elided. The religious affiliations of the walls of the city are, in contrast, illeg-

Jerusalem Remade 49

FIG. 1.3. *Ceramic street sign, Jewish Quarter, 2005. Author's photograph.*

ible. Their Ottoman origins were ignored; they were represented as timeless. Fisher Howe, an evangelical amateur archaeologist writing in the mid-nineteenth century, for example, described the walls as unchanged by time: "Our first impressions on walking about Jerusalem were an agreeable disappointment to find it, as compared with other eastern cities, so well built, and surrounded with walls and battlements so imposing. . . . Its ancient topographical features are marked and mainly unchanged."[34] The British effort to repair the wall made this reading of the walls as transparently ancient even easier. The walls' Turkish associations were purged.[35] The Turkish fortress, guard-rooms, and offices of the Citadel were cleared away. Storrs oversaw the elimination of encumbrances from the walls themselves and from the sentry walk at their summit, which was subsequently opened to tourists. Guardhouses at the gates, functioning in their decrepit state as hovels for the dispossessed, or, in one case, as a latrine, were demolished or redeemed. The great gates into the city—Damascus Gate, St. Stephen's Gate, Herod's Gate, and Jaffa Gate—were also restored.

Storrs also supervised the elimination of the more modern reminders of Jerusalem's connection to Britain's Axis enemies: "The clock tower erected by the loyal burgesses of Jerusalem, in a style midway between that of the Eddystone lighthouse and a jubilee memorial to commemorate the thirty-third year of the auspicious reign of the late Sultan Abdul Hamid, has been bodily removed from the north side of the Jaffa Gate, which it too long disfigured"[36] (see fig. 1.4). As described in the popular press,

> The famous Clock Tower at the Jaffa Gate, in Jerusalem, has been taken down on the grounds that it was ugly and not in keeping with the ancient wall. It was put up in 1907, and boasted of a fine timepiece, giving both European and Arabic times. . . . The tower was removed at the instigation of the Pro-Jerusalem Society, which was founded by Sir Ronald Storrs, the Present Governor of the Holy City, some eighteen months ago, and whose object is "to preserve the ancient monuments, encourage technical education, plant trees, and in general beautify the ancient and historic city of Jerusalem."[37]

The breach in the wall at the Jaffa Gate, opened for Kaiser Wilhelm II's triumphal visit to Jerusalem in 1898, was also repaired.

Restoration of the walls of the city was not enough. Those walls also had to be framed so that they might be properly seen. In addition to forbidding the construction of the new and promoting the reconstruction of the old, Storrs sought to re-create the view of Jerusalem as isolated in the landscape. Patrick Geddes, the well-known Scottish town planner, embraced Storrs's project in his report on the expansion Jerusalem. He proposed that Jerusalem's ancient ruggedness be re-created:

> On the east side of the Valley there is too little soil . . . while on the opposite side of the old City of David, the Tyropean Valley and the slope of the Christian Zion are all buried deep under the accumulated rubbish of centuries, the present gardens being thus many feet above the normal surface

FIG. 1.4. *Jerusalem, Jaffa Gate with the Turkish clock tower, and Jaffa Gate after its removal.* The Graphic, April 19, 1924, 577.

of historic times. . . . It would be an easy matter to remove this earth and rubbish further downhill, and lay it on both sides of the valley below Siloah, with large new garden terraces. . . . In this way may be laid out and kept permanently open the early biblical Jerusalem, of which the present old City is but a later development. . . . On the economic gain to Jerusalem as a pilgrim and tourist city by this operation I need not expatiate. It is obvious that its attractions would be increased.[38]

Geddes's reference to the (Western) pilgrim suggests his focal interest in Jerusalem as a view. Elsewhere in the same document he is explicit: "No symptom of the modern decay of Jerusalem can be more serious than the recent and continued filling up of the fosse of the castle with concealment of its impressive slope of wall. . . . [An effort should be made] to restore this valley to its normal [sic] park condition. The whole will then particularly correspond to that of the central panorama of Edinburgh, with its Valley Gardens and Castle above."[39] A green zone around the city was mandated: the suburbs were to be separated from the city by parklands. The disciplined space of a garden city was designed to contrast with the undisciplined, nomadic setting of the nostalgically desired medieval town.[40] Appropriately, Geddes named Jerusalem "the most extensive Sacred Park in the world."[41] A photograph of Jaffa Gate juxtaposed to Ashbee's drawing of how the same scene should appear perfectly represents Storrs's vision of Jerusalem (see fig. 1.5).

The Jaffa Gate reconstruction as at present, looking towards the city.   No. 44.

The same, as suggested when the unsightly obstructions that hide the wall   No. 45.
line are cleared away.

FIG. 1.5. *Plates 44 and 45 (1921), as they appeared in Pro-Jerusalem Society Council, Jerusalem, 1918–1920. The drawing is by C. R. Ashbee.*

EFFORT AND EFFECT

Storrs worked to realize a vision of Jerusalem not unlike that described by John Finley. The *New York Globe* quoted Storrs: "We must preserve the character of the Holy City. The repose of its sacred sites, the colorful beauty of its vaulted streets, must not be disturbed. The sentiment that brings thousands of pilgrims here is our trust, the force by which Jerusalem attracts the homage of the whole world. We can have a sound and yet an ancient city."[42] Ashbee articulated the task set by Storrs for the Pro-Jerusalem Society:

> The disaster of the Great War has forced upon all men and women the necessity of preserving all that is possible of the beauty and purpose, in actual

Jerusalem Remade 53

form, of the civilizations that have passed before. We have come to see, moreover, that this is not a mere matter of archaeology or the protection of ancient buildings. In the blind mechanical order with which we are threatened everything that we associate with our sense of beauty is alike in danger. Landscape, the unities of streets and sites, the embodied vision of the men that set the great whole together, the sense of color which in any oriental city is still a living sense—all these things have to be considered practically; they must, to put it plainly, be protected against the incursions of the grasping trader, the ignorant workman, the self-interested property owner, the well-intentioned Government Department. In Jerusalem, perhaps more than in any other city, these facts are brought home to us.[43]

In July 1918, Storrs wrote to his mother, "I only regret that I was not here 50 years ago when Jerusalem would have been in practice, as it is in effect, an absolutely unique City in the world surrounded by its medieval walls (which are quite perfect) and without houses or monasteries concealing any part of them."[44]

The Western popular press embraced Storrs's mission—that is, that the means of renewing Jerusalem lay not only in revealing its antiquity, but also in eliminating its modernity. The *Aberdeen Free Press* reported:

> The only "new Jerusalem" is the old one. The gray, austere, ancient, rock-built Palestinian capital, which has for ages appealed to the imagination of the world as no other city has done, . . . is experiencing the greatest transformation it has undergone since its destruction by Titus. . . . It is gratifying to find that the British Administration is setting its face against forms of modernization which would interfere with the traditional appearance of the city, and, if it had its way, would macadamize Gethsemane and rebuild Solomon's Temple with corrugated iron.[45]

Storrs salvaged the old Jerusalem and opposed the external modernization of the new Jerusalem for a purpose. His object was not intentionally the historical packaging of Jerusalem for sale to tourists. It might, of course, be argued that British Jerusalem was a precursor of the familiar Italian urban shopping mall, the *centro storico*, an invention of the 1960s.[46] It could equally be represented as a prototype for Colonial Williamsburg, America's most successful construction of history for the market, or even as a distant antecedent of Celebration, the pseudo–New England 1930s town reconstructed in Orlando as a theme park for daily living. But Storrs did not plan Jerusalem as a means of putting history to commercial use. His strategy for the city was less venal, but in the end, more dangerous. Jerusalem was intended to serve as an appropriate vessel of aesthetic or religious experience. His commitment to the aestheticization of Jerusalem is apparent from his diary entry of December 25, 1917:

> So far as I can recall them, my impressions, though aesthetically and architecturally better founded, resume what we felt seven years ago: firstly, that the faking of the sites and the indignity with which even when authentic they are now mispresented, is an irritation, an imposition, and an affront to the intelligence; secondly, that the pathos, grandeur and nobility of the ancient City of the Heart easily countervails these very real annoyances:
>
> "How beautiful, if sorrow had not made
> Sorrow more beautiful than beauty's self."
> Aesthetic death is swallowed up in spiritual victory.[47]

For Storrs, Jerusalem transcended time and existed outside history:[48] "not the hopeless beauty of Venice, the embalmed majesty of Thebes, the abandon of Ferrara, or the melancholy of Ravenna; but some past yet unalloyed and throbbing, that seems to confound ancient and modern, and to undate recorded history."[49]

The apparent historical transcendence of Jerusalem—a transcendence to which Storrs fundamentally contributed—provided no resistance to the observer's desire to see in it the material proof of a particular religious past. Like its walls, most of the vernacular buildings in the Old City date from the period of Ottoman rule or later, but the ramparts, streets, buildings, and gardens are still treated by travelers from the West as surviving witnesses to the city's remote and sacred past. In 2006, Discovery Ministries advertised its tours of the Holy Land as a return to Jesus's Jerusalem: "Join us as we travel to the land of the Bible and share a life-changing spiritual journey. *You will walk where Jesus walked,* and experience Bible teaching. . . . Make this a Trip of a Lifetime!"[50]

Storrs was not a Christian pilgrim. Although his conception of Jerusalem was deeply informed by his own spiritual idealization of the city and its idealized Western images, he did not have to impose on the city a particularly Christian form. Rather, Storrs confirmed the city's metaphysical affect by consolidating its antiquity and denying its present. He treated the city as the embodiment of the peculiarly Western, Hegelian notion of religion and art as elevated above life. Jerusalem, thus preserved, was confirmed as the authorization of ominously tendentious religious anxieties and historical claims, as Daniel Monk has demonstrated.[51]

Storrs assumed that his own obsession with Jerusalem as the physical embodiment of a transcendent history was shared by the contentious population he governed. He supposed that a common concern with the preservation of their city would establish a communal ground for the belligerent ethnic groups of Jerusalem—Arabs, Christians, and Jews. His expectations were frustrated. All parties involved cared passionately for Jerusalem, but their Jerusalems were not the same. Most particularly, the historical Jerusalem that Storrs imagined and struggled with some success to realize was not the city as it had become for Muslims, Jews, and Orthodox Christians by the early twentieth century.

Storrs's governorship of Jerusalem and the work of the Pro-Jerusalem Society collapsed under the pressure of rising ethnic and religious antagonisms in 1927. The optimism with which many in the West had viewed the British control of Palestine at the occupation's origins was unfounded. The interests of the various factions engaged in Palestine proved irreconcilable. The Mandate government's attempt to create a peaceful multiethnic state failed; Storrs's attempt to produce ancient Jerusalem was, in contrast, perhaps too successful. Storrs's presentation of Jerusalem and its buildings as aesthetic and authentic, above the ideological and political, allows them to do dangerous ideological and political work. His effort to re-create the ancient city, for example, could be understood as authorizing tendentious plans for further projects of restoration—namely, the reconstruction the Jewish Temple on the site of the Dome of the Rock. The apparently benign Western spirituality of British Mandate officials has been displaced by the truly dangerous religiosity of Jewish and Christian evangelical extremists who seek the destruction of the Islamic other as essential to their own apocalyptic redemption.

NOTES

I am indebted to Kishwar Rizvi and Sandy Isenstadt for inviting me to participate in the Conference on the West in the East, held at Yale University in April 2003. The research and argument developed for this paper was subsequently used in my book, *Selling Jerusalem* (University of Chicago Press, 2006). A grant from the Graham Foundation and fellowships from the American Council of Learned Societies and the National Humanities Center supported the work and writing involved in this project. I would also like to thank Professors Kalman Bland and Bernard Wasserstein for their critical readings of this essay.

1. Alphonse de Lamartine, *A Pilgrimage to the Holy Land Comprising Recollections, Sketches and Reflections Made During a Tour in the East*, 2 vols. (New York: D. Appleton and Co., 1848), 1:267–68.

2. See, e.g., William Finden, Edward Francis Finden, and Thomas Hartwell Horne, *Landscape Illustrations of the Bible: Consisting of Views of the Most Remarkable Places Mentioned in the Old and New Testaments, From Original Sketches Taken on the Spot* (London: John Murray, 1836), fig. 3. A pretend image of Jerusalem, like that in Mel Gibson's film, *The Passion of the Christ*, is, even now, more convincing than the real thing.

3. For Roberts and for bibliographies of earlier studies, see Kenneth Paul Bendiner, "David Roberts in the Near East: Social and Religious Themes," *Art History* 6, no. 1 (1983): 67–81. For reproductions of the entire set, see Michael P. Mezzatesta, ed., *Jerusalem and the Holy Land Rediscovered: The Prints of David Roberts (1796–1846)* (Durham, NC: Duke University Museum of Art, 1996).

4. Annabel Jane Wharton, *Selling Jerusalem* (Chicago: University of Chicago Press, 2006), 162ff.

5. Edwin de Leon, *Thirty Years of My Life on Three Continents*, 2 vols. (London: Ward and Downey, 1890), 2:141–42.

6. This comment was inspired by Constantinople, but might also be applied to Jerusalem (see John L. Stoddard, *John L. Stoddard's Lectures*, vol. 2, *Constantinople, Jerusalem, Egypt* [Boston: Balch Brothers, 1897], 108).

7. For a general sense of the British relationship to Palestine, see Barbara W. Tuchman, *Bible and Sword* (New York: New York University Press, 1956). For a balanced history of the British governance of Palestine between 1917 and 1928, see Bernard Wasserstein, *The British in Palestine*, 2d ed. (Oxford: Basil Blackwell, 1991).

8. Northcliffe greeting to the governor of Jerusalem at a joint meeting in London of the Overseas Club and Patriotic League. Northcliffe was ill on the occasion; his speech was read in his absence. See *Times (London)*, December 30, 1920.

9. John H. Finley, *A Pilgrim in Palestine: Being an Account of Journeys on Foot by the First American Pilgrim after General Allenby's Recovery of the Holy Land* (New York: Scribner, 1919), 60–62.

10. Ronald Storrs, *Orientations* (London: Nicholson and Watson, 1937), 15.

11. Ibid., chaps. 2–12. A summary of Storrs's Egyptian service is provided in "Colonel R. Storrs, C.M.G.," *The Sphinx*, February 23, 1918, 164.

12. T. E. (Thomas Edward) Lawrence, *Seven Pillars of Wisdom* (1935; repr., Garden City, N.Y.: Doubleday, 1966), 30.

13. Ibid.

14. The Berensons acted as liaisons in Storrs's unsuccessful courtship of wealthy American Margaret Strong, the only daughter of Bessie and Charles A. Strong and granddaughter of J. D. Rockefeller (see "The Papers of Sir Ronald Storrs [1881–1956] from Pembroke College, Cambridge," box 3, folder 3, Jerusalem, 1922.

15. For an overview of the economic history of Jerusalem, see Alfred E. Lieber, "An Economic History of Jerusalem," in *Jerusalem: City of the Ages*, ed. Alice L. Eckhardt (New York: University Press of America, 1987).

16. Ronald Storrs speech to the Overseas Club and Patriotic League, *Times* (London), December 30, 1920.

17. Ronald Storrs, preface to *Jerusalem, 1918–1920*, ed. Charles Robert Ashbee (London: John Murray, for the Council of the Pro-Jerusalem Society, 1921), iv.

18. Ashbee, *Jerusalem, 1918–1920*, 37–38.

19. From Arthur Ruppin's address, delivered on February 27, 1908. Published as "The Picture in 1907," in Arthur Ruppin, *Three Decades of Palestine* (Jerusalem: Schocken, 1936), 9.

20. For an ideological assessment of "red roofs," see Daniel Bertrand Monk, review of *Bauhaus on the Carmel and the Crossroads of Empire*, by Gilbert Herbert and Silvina Sosnovsky, *AA Files* 28 (1994): 94–99. This article begins with Shim'on Peres's 1991 attack on Itzhak Shamir's Likud government and Jewish settlements on the West Bank through reference to their "red roofs."

21. See Storrs, preface to Ashbee, *Jerusalem, 1918–1920*, vi.

22. *Evening Standard (London)*, December 21, 1920.

23. Storrs, preface to Ashbee, *Jerusalem, 1918–1920*, iv.

24. Charles Robert Ashbee, *A Palestine Notebook, 1918–1923* (Garden City, N.Y.: Doubleday, 1923); Inbal Ben-Asher Gitler, "C. R. Ashbee's Jerusalem Years: Arts and Crafts, Orientalism, and British Regionalism," *Assaph: Studies in Art History* 5 (2000): 29–52; Alan Crawford, *C. R. Ashbee: Architect, Designer, and Romantic Socialist* (New Haven, Conn.: Yale University Press, 1985).

25. Newspaper clipping from the *Observer (London)*, dated 1919, in "The Papers of Sir Ronald Storrs," Box 3, Folder 1, 1919.

26. Biger, *An Empire in the Holy Land*, 20–21.

27. Ibid., 94–95.

28. "The Papers of Sir Ronald Storrs (1881–1956) from Pembroke College, Cambridge," box 3, folder 2: Jerusalem, 1920–21.

29. Storrs, *Orientations*, 364–65.

30. A letter from J. A. C. Dilley to Sir Herbert Samuel, dated August 30, 1920, indicates that Storrs's request to the king for the patronage of the Pro-Jerusalem Society was an "irregularity": "His Majesty does not as a rule give his patronage to new undertakings until they have become firmly established, both financially and otherwise, and he very rightly points out that such a communication should have reached him through you and through this Department" (Storrs, "The Papers of Sir Ronald Storrs," box 3, folder 2, 1920–1921).

31. An idea of the complexity involved in disbursing monies is conveyed by a letter from Ashbee to Storrs, dated December 4, 1920 (ibid.).

32. Ashbee, *A Palestine Notebook*, 9.

33. Pro-Jerusalem Society, Council, Jerusalem, 1920–1922; being the records of the Pro-Jerusalem council during the first two years of the civil administration, edited by the Council of the Pro-Jerusalem Society by C. R. Ashbee . . . with a Preface by Sir Ronald Storrs (London: J. Murray, for the Council of the Pro-Jerusalem Society, 1924), 32.

34. Howe also noted with satisfaction that "[the walls] afford an ample protection against assaults from the Arab tribes, but would be no obstruction to European arms and modern engines of war" (Fisher Howe, *Oriental and Sacred Scenes* [New York: M. W. Dodd, 1854], 246–48).

35. The moat was cleaned. The Turks had used the southern and eastern parts of the fosse as a dump; they had planned to fill its western section to serve as a roadbed and building site. It was suggested that the Turks had also intended to sell the ancient ramparts. Supposedly, the walls were to be leveled, with the fosse as a means of providing new construction space. This proposal was later repeated by David Ben-Gurion, who "called for 'the demolition of the walls of Jerusalem because they are not Jewish'" (see Meron Benvenisti, *City of Stone* [Berkeley: University of California Press, 1966], 136).

36. Storrs, preface to Ashbee, *Jerusalem, 1918–1920*, vi.

37. Harold J. Shepstone, "Restoring the Walls of Jerusalem," *The Graphic*, April 19, 1924.

38. Patrick Geddes, "Jerusalem Actual and Possible: A Preliminary Report to the Chief Administrator of Palestine and the Military Governor of Jerusalem on Town Planning and Improvements," file Z4/10.202 (1919), 18–19, Central Zionist Archives, Jerusalem.

39. Ibid., 11–12.

40. Jerusalem offers a perfect site for reading Deleuze's agonistic relation of smooth and striated spaces; see Gilles Deleuze and Félix Guattari, *A Thousand Plateaus*, trans. Brian Massumi (Minneapolis: University of Minnesota Press, 1987), 474–500.

41. See Geddes, "Jerusalem Actual and Possible..

42. "Jerusalem Now Basks in Rule That Is Tactful," *New York Globe*, March 12, 1919.

43. Pro-Jerusalem Society, Council, *Jerusalem, 1920–1922*, 4.

44. "The Papers of Sir Ronald Storrs (1881–1956) from Pembroke College, Cambridge," box 3, folder 1, Jerusalem, 1919.

45. "Jerusalem Transformed," *Aberdeen Free Press*, December 24, 1920.

46. See Roberto Maria Dainotto, "The Gubbio Papers: Historic Centers in the Age of the Economic Miracle," *Journal of Modern Italian Studies* 8, no. 1 (2003): 67–83.

47. Storrs, *Orientations*, 333.

48. Storrs had great disdain for those who were not able to experience the city's transcendental qualities: "Many were 'disappointed with Jerusalem' because 'it was so different to what they had expected.' The roads were even worse than the hotels and in place of the Holy City they found—a smell" (ibid., 361).

49. Ibid., 327.

50. Discovery Ministries, Inc., Web site, *Prophecy Tours and Cruises*, www.discoveryministries.com/ministry/israeltour.php (accessed March 19, 2006) (emphasis added).

51. Daniel Bertrand Monk, *An Aesthetic Occupation* (Durham, N.C.: Duke University Press, 2002).

2 Modern Architecture, Preservation, and the Discourse on Local Culture in Italian Colonial Libya

BRIAN L. MCLAREN

This essay examines the discourse on local culture in Italian colonial Libya and the related use of indigenous building forms by architects working in the region. During the course of the 1930s two distinct approaches to the appropriation of local forms emerged in architectural discourse. The earliest of these tendencies, which began with the work and writings of Carlo Enrico Rava, was a quintessentially modernist one that offered an abstract assimilation of native forms and typologies. In the latter part of the 1930s, architects like Florestano Di Fausto evinced the material qualities of indigenous buildings in projects that called for their direct reenactment. The full significance of this second means of appropriation—which has all the appearance of a regionalist practice—reaches well beyond the formal or linguistic dimensions of architecture. The racially motivated understanding of Libyan culture that dominated Italian colonial politics in the late 1930s—an understanding that was largely borrowed from scientific disciplines like anthropology—was in this case being applied to architecture.

Any apparent conflict between modernist and regionalist appropriations of indigenous forms, however, does not arise from an opposition between modernity and tradition. When looking at the Italian presence in Libya, it is quite clear that both of these terms—"the modern" and "the traditional"— were entirely constructed by the colonial authorities. In the first case, Libya was regarded as Italy's "fourth shore"—that is, as an extension of Italian soil on the southern shore of the Mediterranean. Indeed, one major component of Italian colonial politics was the incorporation of Libya into the metropole through, among other things, the creation of a modern system of roads and public institutions. In the second, under the auspices of an "indigenous politics," Libyan traditions were the subject of a highly operative preservation program that established their status as primitive and backward in relation to the West—a political strategy that implicitly justified Italy's position as a colonizing nation. The contrast between these political strategies is a reflection of the ambivalence of colonial discourse—an ambivalence in which Homi Bhabha argues the colonizer and colonized are not dialectically opposed, but rather linked in a relationship of repetition and difference.[1]

MODERN ARCHITECTURE AND INDIGENOUS POLITICS

The use of native forms by Italian architects in Libya was a relatively direct result of the political policies developed by the colonial authorities to deal with the local populations. Although these indigenous politics were employed beginning with the first Italian occupation in 1911, they were given a more precise direction by Governor Giuseppe Volpi (1921–25), who also initiated a program to improve the colony's agricultural economy.[2] Among the preservation policies was a program directed at the conservation of the Roman, Arab, and Ottoman historical patrimony, which had the aim of appeasing the local populations. This program began in 1921 with the creation of a commission to identify buildings of historic interest and supervise their restoration. This list eventually included two Roman monuments, the ancient castle and walls of Tripoli; thirteen Muslim religious buildings; and twenty-four private residences. The commitment of the Volpi administration to this program was demonstrated through legislative measures introduced in early 1922 that extended government regulations to cover the restoration of the Islamic heritage of Libya, and established a list of buildings to be conserved.[3]

One of the most important areas in which the Volpi administration intervened in Libyan culture was the local artisanal industries. The Government Office of Indigenous Applied Arts was founded in January 1925 to study these industries and make proposals for their improvement.[4] A major focus of this office was the production of local craftsmen, who were seen to be practicing an "unclear and impure" interpretation of Arab art. As a consequence, master craftsmen were brought in from the French colonies of Algeria, Tunisia, and Morocco in order to assist the local workers to develop "more perfect techniques."[5] It should be noted, however, that these new methods were a return to practices that corresponded with the Italian view of what was authentic. Moreover, at the same time, this office was active in improving the productivity of the indigenous craft industries. These initiatives included participating in fairs and exhibitions, such as the permanent display in Corso Vittorio Emanuele III in Tripoli. This presentation had the appearance of an Arabized version of a metropolitan storefront—a perfect expression of the interaction between modernization and preservation that marked the Italian intervention into the indigenous culture of Libya (see fig. 2.1).

It is important to recognize that Italian interest in the local culture of Libya was profoundly shaped by a parallel research program that emerged much earlier in the French colonies in North Africa. In addition to the cultural nationalism of the "civilizing mission" that was carried out in Algeria, Tunisia, and Morocco, the French colonial authorities initiated educational and research programs related to the indigenous language and culture. One of the leading experts on the Muslim arts of North Africa was Prosper Ricard, who published numerous essays and books on the subject.[6] Among Ricard's most significant collaborations was his work with Hachette publishers, the Paris-based company that produced tourist-oriented books. The most widely disseminated of these works, *Pour comprendre l'art musulman dans l'Afrique du Nord et en Espagne* (1924), catalogs Muslim arts according to a taxonomic system. The importance of this publication to the Italian discourse on indigenous culture lies in the fact that Ricard provided arguments about the Roman origins of North African culture that would later be taken up by Italian architects and scholars.[7]

The research of Prosper Ricard had an even more direct impact on the interpretation of Libyan culture. While he was director of indigenous arts in Morocco, Ricard was hired by Giuseppe Volpi to study the artisanal industries of Tripolitania. The results of this project were published in two works in 1926, an essay and a book, in which Ricard surveyed a range of artistic productions, including architecture, decoration, and regional craft traditions.[8] In the essay, Ricard called for a program of modernization that involved the systematic study of native practices for the purposes of improving their productivity and quality, at the same time that it recommended a return to more ancient, and thus more authentic, techniques.[9] Notably, Ricard's interest in the Berbers, a group that held a great attraction for the Italians as a "primitive" society whose culture preceded the Arab invasion of North Africa, can be understood as a not so subtle validation of the argument that Libyan culture was built upon Roman foundations.

The construction of Libyan "traditions" under the auspices of Italian colonial politics was only one factor in determining Italian architects' interest in

FIG. 2.1. *A window display in Corso Vittorio Emanuele III, Tripoli, 1925. Author's collection.*

local culture. A more specific influence was the construction of regional identity in architectural periodicals. This discourse appeared in the pages of *Architettura e Arti Decorative,* which began publication in 1921 under the guidance of its two editors, Gustavo Giovannoni and Marcello Piacentini.[10] This journal was a crucial reference point for contemporary debates within modern architecture and the decorative arts, arguing for an appreciation for the

FIG. 2.2. *Courtyard of the Qaramanli house (ca. 1790) in Tripoli.* From Architettura e Arti Decorative 3, no. 5 (January 1924): 194.

indigenous traditions of the various regions of Italy. Notably, at the same time that this journal was constructing a regional identity for modern Italian architecture, it presented the indigenous architecture of Libya as a particular manifestation of Italy's regional traditions.

One of the most important essays to appear in the journal was Pietro Romanelli's "Vecchie case arabe di Tripoli," which was published in January 1924. This research, which presented eleven of the twenty-four private residences that had been singled out for conservation in November 1921, was a direct product of the Volpi administration's preservation program.[11] Romanelli categorized these courtyard houses into three distinct groups, based upon their age and their architectural influences. He also overlaid a political agenda on this scholarly one by arguing that "the plan of the Tripolitanian house, in its simplicity, is closer than any other Eastern house to the Roman one."[12] In the end, Romanelli asserted that the Roman *domus* was the underlying basis for the Arab house, while at the same time observing that it had been modified to better correspond to the cultural practices of the local populations. The essay further linked the native architecture of this region to Italian influences by arguing that the decorative schemes of buildings like the Qaramanli house in Tripoli (ca. 1790) were related to seventeenth-century

Italian sources, and that the craftsmen who built these projects were "without a doubt Italian"[13] (see fig. 2.2). Romanelli's argument that the so-called Arab house in Tripolitania was based upon Roman precedents and related to Italian influences became the predominant view of Italian architects in the late 1920s and early 1930s, and thus provided a scholarly justification for their use of indigenous forms.

TOWARD A MODERN COLONIAL ARCHITECTURE

Italian architects practicing in Tripolitania during the Volpi administration showed little interest in referencing indigenous buildings, despite the existence of a scholarly discourse on this architecture. However, with the hiring of Alessandro Limongelli as art consultant to the city of Tripoli in 1928, this situation changed quite dramatically. He was responsible for opening up the architectural scene in Libya through invited commissions and open competitions. His own work was also a part of this transformation, since his self-conscious use of classicism was carefully integrated with the local architecture. The synthesis of modern (and Roman) and indigenous is clearly evident in the 1931 proposal for the restructuring of the Piazza Italia in Tripoli. Working with the existing walls of the old city alongside the castle and with an appreciation of the definition of its open spaces, Limongelli integrated a classicized urban image of Italian architecture with the materials and built landscape of North Africa (see fig. 2.3).

One of the important figures in opening architectural discourse in Tripolitania to the contemporary discourse in Italy was Maurizio Rava, general secretary of Tripolitania and father of the rationalist architect Carlo Enrico Rava. The elder Rava authored an influential report on the present and future development of Tripoli and the surrounding oasis, which was published in several colonial journals in 1929.[14] This essay called for the preservation of the local character of Tripoli through a careful program of conserving the most representative existing buildings and introducing new structures that harmonized with the colonial environment.

In addition to making suggestions for conserving the historic character of Tripoli and the surrounding oasis, the essay argued that the local architecture — and specifically the Arab house — offered a valid source for the creation of a contemporary colonial architecture. There were multiple bases for this appropriation, the first being the visual effect of the indigenous constructions. These qualities were evident in what Rava referred to as "the geometric and alternating play of volumes," and "the coloration of the vast smooth walls with

FIG. 2.3. *Proposal for the rearrangement of the Piazza Italia in Tripoli (1931), by Alessandro Limongelli. From* Rassegna di Architettura *5, no. 9 (September 1933): 397.*

lively and soft hues." Rava also argued that the Arab house, which was typically organized around an outdoor courtyard, was an appropriate source of ideas for contemporary architects, based on its typology. In a manner similar to Pietro Romanelli in his earlier essay, Rava asserted that "the Arab patio is . . . the ideal and most logical solution that is also *intimately ours,* since it goes back in its time to the classical house of ancient Rome."[15] These local constructions were seen to accommodate the climatic demands of North Africa through a combination of verandas and ample greenery within the courtyard, and the restricted use of openings in their relatively mute exterior walls. In concluding his essay, Rava made a clear connection between the modernity of the "simple linear and cubic combinations" and "smooth and bare walls" of the Arab house, and the problem of a contemporary architecture, stating, "It will be simple to fuse all of the technical specialization and practical comfort of the most modern European constructions with the local characteristics."[16]

The second and most significant attempt to theorize a modern colonial architecture based on indigenous sources was his son Carlo Enrico Rava's 1931 essay entitled "Di un'architettura coloniale moderna." The theoretical position it espoused was part of a "Panorama of Rationalism," in which the younger Rava argued that Italian architects should seek a more independent direction proper to their Latin cultural roots—a direction whose inspiration would be the indigenous architecture of the Mediterranean region. In the essay, he asserted that indigenous Libyan architecture provided a rational solution to the problem of building in the colonial context, due to the fact that it was designed according to the region's climate and geography. In his discussion, he noted that there were three main attributes that made these buildings an appropriate source for a modern colonial architecture. The first of these qualities, their Roman influence, was linked with "the practical and organizing spirit of Rome" that, according to Rava, was "still very vital in the scheme of the Arab-Turkish house."[17] The rationality of this indigenous source had to do both with its derivation from an ancient precedent and with its accommodation of functional and climatic demands.

A second quality that Carlo Enrico Rava found in indigenous architecture in Libya was what he described as "the impulse of a vigorous primitivism that . . . derives from its relations with the populations of the South."[18] This tendency was connected with its use of simple geometric forms in buildings like the mosque in Qasr al-Hajj, a structure whose cubic massing and spherical and pyramidal forms, it was argued, were analogous to the abstract works of Russian constructivism. The final characteristic Rava identified in the indigenous architecture of this region was what he described as its Mediterranean character—a quality he connected to "the composition of blank rhythms of cubes and parallelipeds" and to "the large superimposed and alternating verandahs and roof terraces."[19] In this context, he argued that the characteristic forms of the simplest Arab houses found in the oasis of Tripoli were similar to the indigenous architecture of the Italian Mediterranean (see fig. 2.4). However, in the process of defining the Mediterranean character of Libyan architecture, the Arab cultural identity was largely removed. Rava alluded to this when he stated: "We will not derive anything from the Arabs, but . . . we relate to the real, the great tradition of Rome, that admirably endured through the centuries, and today rejoins us."[20]

Carlo Enrico Rava's inquiry into indigenous Libyan architecture was not only closely tied to modern architectural discourse, its means of appropriation was also modern. His experience of the local architecture in Libya and the dissemination of its image were modern, tied as they were to the detached mode of encounter of the metropolitan traveler and the lens of the camera. The Mediterranean qualities of the Arab house in Libya were not so much present in the original buildings, as they were expressed in their image, which was profoundly shaped by a modern photographic aesthetic. In addition, terms like primitivism that were used to analyze the indigenous architecture were a product of modern modes of artistic and cultural analy-

FIG. 2.4. *An Arab house in the oasis of Tripoli (December 1929), by Carlo Enrico Rava. From* Domus *42 (June 1931): 33.*

sis. Indeed, the Libyan people were often treated as a primitive society that could be understood through a direct reading of their customs and their cultural artifacts. The seeming objectivity of this "scientific" appropriation of the indigenous culture of Libya was the almost universal basis by which it was examined by Italian architects and scholars.

Notably, the arguments presented by Rava were consistent with his own projects in the colonies, such as his design for the Hotel at the Excavations of Leptis Magna—a project executed in conjunction with Sebastiano Larco. The connection between the project and the principles of Italian rationalism is evident in the fact that its drawings were exhibited at the 1928 Exhibition of Rationalist Architecture in Rome. Upon its publication in *Architettura e Arti Decorative* in 1931, it was seen as a direct derivation of the "most sane and acceptable" rationalist principles—that is, as "pure architectonic constructivity and functionality" and "the total and exclusive response of the external expression to the internal organism."[21] At the same time, it was understood as "completely contextualized to a Mediterranean country," based upon the perception that it had "conserved in the voids the sense of proportion typical to the houses of Libya."[22] A second article published on the project recognizes this same acclimatization to the Libyan environment—a quality which

FIG. 2.5. *Seafront view of the Hotel at the Excavations of Leptis Magna, in al-Khums.* From Domus 44 (August 1931): 21.

the article associated with the large veranda that faced the Mediterranean (see fig. 2.5).[23]

Constructed to cater to tourist interest in the archeological site at Leptis Magna, the ground floor of the hotel was organized around a central covered courtyard that linked a series of large public rooms with the primary orientation of the building toward the Mediterranean. This area was dedicated to the residents, for whom this space connects to an upper level that contains all of the guest rooms.[24] On the opposite side of the building, a second entrance faced the oasis of Al-Khums and the archeological site. As well as providing a point of intersection between these two distinct faces of the building, the courtyard was intended to refer to the vernacular tradition of the Arab house. This indigenous source was, for Rava, both derived from Roman origins and reflective of modern exigencies, such that "the conditions of nature and climate are ... the generators of architectonic form."[25] The Hotel at the Excavations of Leptis Magna was a combination of the theoretical and formal concerns typical to Italian rationalism, with abstract typological and climatic references to the indigenous architecture of the region. Although attempting to contextualize the project with the local environment, these architects ignored the cultural significance of its indigenous sources. The Hotel at the Excavations of Leptis Magna was the product of an attempt to incorporate the local architecture into a broader Mediterranean expression—an expression that was, in its essence, already Italian.

REGIONALIST PRACTICES AND RACIST DISCOURSES

The discourse on the native architecture of Libya that was expressed in the writings and projects of Carlo Enrico Rava was subject to a number of transformations in the late 1930s, transformations that were largely the result of changing political demands. In part owing to the imperial rhetoric generated by the Italian conquest of Ethiopia, the indigenous politics of Libya—then governed by Italo Balbo (1934–40)—took on an authoritarian, and even racist, tone. The connection between Italian colonial politics and race is apparent in the legislation that eventually incorporated Libya into metropolitan Italy, in January of 1939. Arguing that there was a fundamental difference between the Arab-Berber populations of the coastal regions and the Negroid races of the southern military zone, Balbo decided that the former should become a province of Italy, but the latter would remain a colony.[26]

In this context, the views of Rava on the contemporary value of indigenous Libyan architecture gave way to several new tendencies. One of these theoretical positions was expressed in the work and writings of Giovanni Pellegrini. This Milanese architect relocated to Libya in the late 1920s to join the public works office in Tripoli. He became one of the most active architects during the Balbo era, constructing a wide range of projects, including public buildings, agricultural town centers, and private villas.[27] Pellegrini's contribution to the theoretical discourse on the use of indigenous forms was his "Manifesto dell'architettura coloniale." This 1936 essay built upon Rava's ideas in arguing for the utilization of indigenous elements like porticoes and pergolas in order to deal with the demands of the North African climate (see fig. 2.6). He also asserted that the urban aesthetic of colonial cities should be related to the indigenous architecture, recommending that new buildings be "modeled plastically" in order to attain the same "effect of mass and polychromy."[28]

A second aspect of this manifesto which linked it with the writings of Rava was its use of the Arab house as the basis for building in the colonial context. In contrast to the views of Rava, however, this "tradition" was rationalized as both the basis of typological models and the source of practical solutions. For Pellegrini, the Arab house was useful to Italian architects because it contained "the best architectural techniques and the best solution for the adaptation of life to the geographical and climatic conditions." One of the most important aspects of the Arab house was its central courtyard, which was enhanced through elements like loggias, galleries, and vegetation. The aesthetic of the exterior of these houses was linked to the "exaltation of the por-

FIG. 2.6. *An isolated house in Tripoli, 1936, photographed by Giovanni Pellegrini. From* Rassegna di Architettura *8, no. 10 (October 1936): 355.*

tal, the concealment of the interior of the house," and "the sense of austerity of family life."[29]

In using Libyan traditions as the basis for a contemporary colonial architecture, Pellegrini's "Manifesto" proposed a fusion of the examples provided by indigenous buildings with modern technical and aesthetic practices.[30] Although on the surface this would appear to be the same argument offered some five years earlier, there are some significant differences. In Rava's "Panorama of Rationalism," the Libyan vernacular was subjected to a historical scheme that theorized its Latin, African, and Mediterranean identity. In the "Manifesto dell'architettura coloniale," Pellegrini "selected" the indigenous building forms, according to a modern technical and visual sensibility, as the solution to the problem of climate and the basis for a contemporary aesthetic.[31]

Another key protagonist in the development of a modern colonial architecture was Florestano Di Fausto, an architect who was already well known for his work on the master plan and public buildings of the colony of Rhodes during the late 1920s.[32] The Mediterranean architecture of Di Fausto was a form of regionalism that attempted to absorb the characteristic forms and incorporate the building traditions of the local architecture. Although his work in Libya was wide-ranging, his most representative projects were a distillation of the Libyan building traditions. In some of the most direct examples of the adoption of local forms, like his 1938 proposal for a madrasa in Tripoli, Di Fausto worked in the ambiguous space between restoration and new construction.

The theoretical position of Di Fausto was expressed in a 1937 article entitled "Visione mediterranea della mia architettura." In this essay, he argued that an architecture for Italy's Mediterranean colonies had always been, and should continue to be, based upon a careful reading of the local architecture. In a presentation of the large body of work that he constructed throughout this region, he emphasized a deliberate and studied process that established a close relationship between these projects and their historical and environmental contexts.[33] This is an approach to colonial architecture that called for the direct incorporation of local references into a contemporary expression. As a result, the Arab identity of Libyan architecture was reenacted as part of an eclectic architectural vocabulary for the purpose of harmonizing what was built with the spirit of the place.[34]

This approach to colonial architecture is evident in Di Fausto's design for the 'Ain el-Fras Hotel in Ghadames in 1935. This project responded to the formal language of the city, which is a complex labyrinth of narrow passages, covered courtyards, and terraces shaped by dense, walled structures. Forming one edge of a large piazza in front of one of the main gates of the old city that is characterized by its luxuriant landscape, the project created a massive exterior wall behind which is a series of courtyard spaces. The 'Ain el-Fras Hotel establishes a direct relationship to its oasis setting, something that is clearly evident when looking at the arcaded wings that flank the central body of the building (see fig. 2.7). There is an unmistakable relationship between this courtyard and the Piazza of the Large Mulberry. This very intimate urban space in the old town of Ghadames was described in the tourist literature as an "intersection of gloomy caves, vaults, large niches that pierce the four white wall of the piazza with their shade."[35]

The mimetic relationship between the building and the town of Ghadames can also seen in the interior spaces of the hotel. The timber ceilings, rich wall coverings, and minimal use of furnishings in the 'Ain el-Fras were intended to suggest the experience of the indigenous houses. These buildings, which were largely inaccessible to tourists, were described as being like "jewel boxes," as they contained all of the family treasures.[36] While on the surface this may seem to be a fundamentally anti-modern approach, it is important to recognize that this is merely a different kind of modernity.

The writings and works of Di Fausto reveal that, under the weight of Italian imperial politics, an interest in the indigenous architecture of Libya had shifted from its modernist origins. An equally scientific interpretation of Libyan architecture to that advanced by Di Fausto was offered in Fabrizio Maria Apollonj's 1937 essay, "L'architettura araba della Libia." In arguing that "nothing is more suggestive than the bare and taciturn appearance of an Arab house," Apollonj drew an analogy between the indigenous architecture, which he described as having "a primitivism, frank and free of any real artistic consistency," and the people, whom he characterized as "a poor and static population."[37] The idea that architecture is the direct expression of a people and its culture is closely tied to the contemporary research of individuals like Professor Emilio Scarin of the University of Florence, for whom the Troglodyte houses of the Jabal Nafusah region (see fig. 2.8) were an authentic repository of the customs and practices of the local populations.[38] In the context of Fascist Italy in the latter part of the 1930s, this "scientific" reading of the Libyan people through their cultural artifacts must be understood as having quite serious political connotations. At the same time that the Fascist government instituted its "Provisions for the defense of the Italian race"—including a law that prevented intermarriage between different racial and religious groups in Italy—in the journal *Difesa della Razza*, a number of noted scholars on colonial matters theorized a racial science to support Fascist imperial politics.[39]

CONCLUSION

The projects of Rava and Di Fausto in Libya raise important questions about the ambivalent status of modern architecture in the Italian colonies. Through incorporating indigenous references as a means of creating a contemporary colonial architecture, these architects reflected the shifting direction of Italian colonial politics. Although both negotiated between the forces of modernization that saw Libya as Italy's fourth shore, and those that were involved in the preservation of the indigenous culture, each did so in a different way. In the case of the Hotel at the Excavations of Leptis Magna, by Rava, we have a work whose Arab identity has been suppressed in favor of the structural and aesthetic principles of modernity. The 'Ain el-Fras Hotel, of Di Fausto, which directly reproduces native forms, offers a modernity of historic preservation—

FIG. 2.7. *View of the courtyard of the Hotel 'Ain el-Fras in Ghadames, postcard, ca. 1937. Author's collection.*

FIG. 2.8. *Libya, Troglodyte house, Jabal Nafusah region, postcard, ca. 1937. Author's collection.*

a modernity that objectivizes and historicizes the native in the manner of contemporary science. In the end, both of these projects reveal certain fundamental problems that would have existed in any attempt to create an Italian identity for modern architecture in Libya through a recourse to indigenous sources. The architectural traditions of Libya were not only constructed by Italian architects as a repository of native culture, they were also the material bases from which an architectural identity was produced, an identity whose Mediterranean character disguised an oppressive politics of cultural dominance and racial superiority.

NOTES

1. Homi K. Bhabha, "Of Mimicry and Man: The Ambivalence of Colonial Discourse," in *The Location of Culture* (London: Routledge, 1994), 86.

2. Sergio Romano, *Giuseppe Volpi: Industria e finanza tra Giolitti e Mussolini* (Milan: Bompiani, 1979), 113–20.

3. Renato Bartoccini, "Gli edifici di interesse storico, artistico ed archeologico di Tripoli e dintorni," in *La rinascità della Tripolitania: Memorie e studi sui quattro anni di governo del Conte Giuseppe Volpi di Misurata* (Milan: Casa Editrice A. Mondadori, 1926), 350–52.

4. Francesco M. Rossi, "Le Piccole industrie indigene," in *La rinascità della Tripolitania*, 517.

5. Ibid., 518.

6. See Alfred Bel and Prosper Ricard, *Le travail de la laine a Tlemcen* (Alger: Typ. A. Jourdan, 1913); and Prosper Ricard, *Corpus de tapis marocains*, 8 vols. (Paris: Guenther, 1923).

7. Prosper Ricard, *Pour comprendre l'art musulman dans l'Afrique du Nord et en Espagne* (Paris: Hachette, 1924).

8. Prosper Ricard, "Les arts tripolitains, parte I," *Rivista della Tripolitania* 2 (January–February): 203–35; 4–5 (March–April 1926): 275–92; Prosper Ricard, *Les arts tripolitains* (Rome: Tipografia del Senato del Dott. G. Bardi, 1926).

9. Ricard, "Les arts tripolitains, parte I," no. 4–5, 286–87.

10. For a detailed analysis of the activities of Giovannoni and Piacentini, see Richard Etlin, *Modernism in Italian Architecture, 1890–1940* (Cambridge, Mass.: MIT Press, 1991), 101–61.

11. Pietro Romanelli, "Vecchie case arabe di Tripoli," *Architettura e Arti Decorative* 3, no. 5 (January 1924): 193–211.

12. Ibid., 195.

13. Ibid., 211.

14. Maurizio Rava, "Dobbiamo rispettare il carattere dell'edilizia tripolina," *L'Oltremare* 3, no. 11 (November 1929): 462.

15. Ibid., 462–63.

16. Ibid., 463–64.

17. Carlo Enrico Rava, "Di un'architettura coloniale moderna, parte prima," *Domus* 41 (May 1931): 89.

18. Ibid.

19. Ibid.

20. Carlo Enrico Rava, "Di un'architettura coloniale moderna—Parte seconda," *Domus* 42 (June 1931): 36.

21. "Architetture libiche degli Arch. Carlo Enrico Rava e Sebastiano Larco," *Architettura e Arti Decorative* 10, no. 13 (September 1931): 682.

22. Ibid.

23. "L'Albergo agli Scavi di Leptis Magna," *Domus* 44 (August 1931): 21–23.

24. Ibid., 21.

25. Rava, "Di un'architettura coloniale moderna—Parte seconda," 32.

26. Italo Balbo, "La politica sociale fascista verso gli arabi della Libia," in *Convegno di scienze morali e storiche, 4–11 ottobre 1938. Tema: L'Africa* (Rome: Reale Accademia d'Italia, 1939), 1:734.

27. See Gian Paolo Consoli, "The Protagonists," *Rassegna* 51 (September 1992): 58–59. See also Plinio Marconi, "L'architettura nella colonizzazione della Libia: Opere dell'Arch. Giovanni Pellegrini," *Architettura* 18, no. 12 (December 1939): 711–26.

28. Pellegrini, "Manifesto dell'architettura coloniale," *Rassegna di Architettura* 8, no. 10 (October 1936): 349–50.

29. Ibid.

30. Ibid., 349.

31. The "Manifesto" was followed by a series of fifty-one photographs, twenty-nine of which were taken by Pellegrini. The remaining photos were the kind produced by local studios for tourist consumption. Each image was accompanied by both a title and a brief commentary. This text provided a literal identification or a general geographic location, along with a description of the building's particular applicability to the task of creating a contemporary architecture (ibid., 355, 357).

32. See Michele Biancale, *Florestano Di Fausto* (Geneva: Editions "Les Archives Internationales," 1932).

33. Florestano Di Fausto, "Visione mediterranea della mia architettura," *Libia* 1, no. 9 (December 1937): 16.

34. Ibid., 18.

35. *Itinerario Tripoli-Gadames* (Milan: Tipo-Litografia Turati Lombardi, 1938), 66.

36. One of the few houses accessible to tourists was located near the 'Ain el-Fras, and was described as follows: "On the outside it does not differ a lot from the others. Crossing the threshold, a steep stair, with delightful decorations sculpted or etched in the walls, leads to the main floor and flows into the central room, that one can say is representative. No furniture. On the floor are mats and carpets. The richness is on the mantels of the walls where innumerable silver, pewter and brass vases are collected. This is the jewel box: this is the safe of the family" (ibid., 72).

37. Apollonj, "L'architettura araba della libia," *Rassegna di Architettura* 9, no. 12 (December 1937): 461.

38. See Scarin, *L'insediamento umano nella Libia occidentale* (Verona: A. Mondadori, 1940).

39. This provision, which was called the "Regio decreto—legge 17 novembre 1938—XVII, n. 1728, recante provvedimenti per la difesa della razza italiana," was presented at the Presidency of the Council of Ministers for passage into law on November 25, 1938.

PART II *Building the Nation*

3   Visions of Iraq

Modernizing the Past in 1950s Baghdad

MAGNUS T. BERNHARDSSON

On August 23, 1921, the citizens of Baghdad witnessed a hastily arranged, historic, and somewhat comical ceremony. In the courtyard of the Serai, a grand-looking 1861 Ottoman palace, British military and civil administrators stood solemnly during a symbolic transfer of power. The leader that the British had hand-picked to govern Iraq, Faysal ibn Husayn, sat on a throne hurriedly made from Indian beer cases. Flanked by the British officials, he listened to the formal proclamations declaring him king of the newly established Hashemite Kingdom of Iraq. He then stood up, uttered a few words, and tentatively stepped forward on a red Persian rug, while a British military band played the British national anthem, "God Save the King"—the Iraqi anthem had yet to be composed.[1]

This coronation was very much a British affair and hardly pregnant with Iraqi patriotism. From an international legal perspective, Iraq was a new entity on the world stage. In many ways, its initial existence was predicated on British geopolitical concerns.[2] But Iraq at this point was a state in search of a nation. As sociologist Sami Zubaida points out, it was the state that initially made the nation.[3]

The new national government inherited from the Ottoman Empire diverse urban and rural communities with different economic orientations and historical memories. Under the watchful eyes of British advisors, Faysal and his government proceeded to nurture relevant institutions befitting a modern country in the postcolonial era. The events of World War I, the British occupation, and the breakup of the Ottoman Empire had created fresh facts on the ground. The Iraqi nationalist challenge was to effectively respond to these new realities and develop a sense of belonging among the many Iraqi groups. The government had to compete in the marketplace of loyalties by defining and promoting a modern Iraqi sensibility. Given the fragility of the Iraqi economy, the context for this articulation was particularly difficult. Further, the British restricted the actions of the Iraqi government so that it would not imperil British imperial interests, especially in the areas of defense and economic development. For example, the Iraqi Petroleum Company had a monopoly on oil production in the country and was dominated by British and other Western concerns. Iraq had no shareholders in the company. During the first three decades of Iraq's existence, an insignificant amount of the oil revenue stayed in Iraq. This arrangement exploited Iraqi natural resources, with no material benefits to Iraqi society. The British also continued to maintain military bases in Iraq and thus restricted Iraqi sovereignty and control over its own defense. Despite these limitations, Iraqis did develop a multifaceted national identity. As in other countries, this was an intricate and convoluted process, constantly changing with political and cultural circumstances.

Iraqi national identity has always been fluid, based on many competing, even contradictory visions of what modern Iraq should be.[4] Is Iraq part of the pan-Arab nation whose destiny was largely shaped by its Islamic heritage, or is it a unique nation due to its Mesopotamian, pre-Islamic history? These notions were not viewed as mutually exclusive, but rather enjoined under the broad rubric of Iraqi nationalism. Iraqis have defined their national identity by appealing to a broad spectrum of images, memories, dynasties, and histories. The question—What is Iraq?—has many different answers persistently subject to change and interpretation.

This essay investigates this question in the realm of architecture and urban planning, showing how architects contributed to a vibrant cultural experiment that forged a distinct but multifaceted Iraqi voice and aesthetic in music, visual arts, and poetry. Focusing on the ambitious and fantastic plans to modernize Baghdad in the 1950s, we can see the roots of a nationalistic modern architecture predicated on a rereading and appreciation of the distant Iraqi past. For young and ambitious Iraqi architects, the Islamic and pre-Islamic past was modernized and ancient forms and motifs put to use for the contemporary Iraqi nation.

These efforts took on an interesting twist because some of the world's most famous architects, such as Walter Gropius and Frank Lloyd Wright, became part of the conversation during the 1950s. The activities during this decade laid the foundation for a modern Iraqi architecture in which Iraqi architects sought creative paradigms drawn from Iraq's near and distant history. Reflecting the local environment and local traditions, this architecture was intended to convey a distinctly nationalist political and cultural spirit, while also embracing universal elements influenced by foreign techniques and trends. When evaluating the architectural trends of the 1950s, the vitality of the very idea of Iraq becomes clearer. In recent years, many commentators have questioned whether there is such as a thing as an Iraqi nation. As this essay suggests, however, there are multiple interpretations of what constitutes Iraq. These notions are fluid and in a constant flux, indicating regeneration and renewal. Iraqi national identities are characterized by this fluctuation, which is represented also in modern Iraqi architecture.

In contrast to many nations whose common denominators are language or blood, Iraqi leaders stressed culture and history, making modern-day Iraqis the inheritors of ancient Mesopotamian culture and/or the Abbasid Caliphate. In a nationalism based on sometimes vague and shifting cultural paradigms, where appropriate themes and images are located in what has been constructed as the national linear historical narrative, the practice of archaeology was crucial in providing a scientific basis for the nationalistic rhetoric. In Iraq, this nationalism based on cultural paradigms proved to be an important and effective tool to inculcate a distinct Iraqi national identity.

Unlike nationalisms based on language or race, paradigmatic nationalism, inherently tied to the ideology of the government and changing with political winds, is more prone to vacillation and political manipulation. In Iraq, the official emphasis wavered from stressing Iraq's pan-Arab ties (especially during the first twenty years of the Hashemite monarch) and stressing an identity concentrated more on Iraq's Mesopotamian heritage (as during the years 1958–63 and during much of Saddam Hussein's presidency). The role of paradigmatic nationalism is particularly evident in the development of Iraqi architecture, offering a vernacular to develop the modern architecture of Iraq.

DEVELOPING BAGHDAD AS A MODERN CAPITAL

By the time that the British installed Faysal as king in 1921, Baghdad was not the city of imperial splendor and magnificence it had enjoyed during Abbasid times. Similar to the Abbasid caliphs who reigned in Baghdad centuries before him, Faysal had ambitious plans to reconstruct Baghdad and mold its physical layout to suit his political and strategic interests. An immediate concern for Faysal's government was to consolidate and centralize authority and thus weaken the power of the various tribal leaders in the countryside.[5] Baghdad, which in Ottoman times had been a provincial town on the margins of empire, once again became a center of political and cultural power, destined to be integral to the political future of Iraq.[6] In many ways, it was returning to its traditional role as a burgeoning metropole, brimming with tradition and legacy.

In the first decades of the government's existence, the emphasis was on developing the army, the educational system, and transportation and communication infrastructure.[7] In this era, most of government's expenditures went toward defense and irrigation. By the 1950s, however, the Iraqi government was moving beyond the building of institutional foundations and had embarked on the large-scale project of developing a "modern," more urbanized nation. Like politicians in Asia and the Americas, Iraqi officials were becoming more critical of the imperial legacy, and they now sought to renegotiate the 1928 oil agreement with the British-dominated Iraqi Petroleum Company (IPC)—which was "Iraqi" in name alone.[8] The new agreement, in 1951, had staggering results for the Iraqi economy, increasing governmental oil revenues from 5.3 million Iraqi dinars in 1950 to almost 50 million dinars in 1953.[9]

To help manage this newly acquired revenue, the government established the Iraq Development Board, with six members including a foreign advisor.[10] The IDB was responsible for allocating approximately 70 percent of the new revenue for "development." This seemingly far-sighted effort to utilize new oil wealth was initially focused on developing Iraq's agriculture and the natural environment. By the mid-1950s, the IDB had turned its attention to Baghdad.

The city of Baghdad had experienced considerable change in its architecture in the first part of the twentieth century. In earlier centuries most of the main administrative buildings, markets, shrines, and mosques had been on the west side of the Tigris, with a circular wall enclosing the city. Eventually, the city expanded beyond those walls, and even across the Tigris. As the city spread to both sides of the river, it was connected by a bridge made of boats. Around the time of World War I, Rusafa, on the eastern side of the Tigris, became more developed, and the now famous al-Rashid Street became a major commercial avenue. After World War II, the city experienced an incredible population explosion. By some accounts, the population in Baghdad increased by 90 percent between 1947 and 1957. The Iraqi government therefore had to respond to this new demographic reality and consider how Baghdad, with its now one million inhabitants, should be organized.

In the midst of this population explosion, the IDB decided, in 1955, to focus its attention on developing Baghdad.[11] British architects and planning consultants were engaged to submit a master plan for the city, including redevelopment of the city's old historic quarters.[12] The consultants' plan recommended a large-scale urban expansion, including the construction of a comprehensive road system and five new bridges over the Tigris River to aid in the removal of the slums that were rapidly expanding on the outskirts of the city.

The master plan addressed some of the growing urban problems of Baghdad, in part by opening up more space for automobiles, an increasingly visible feature in the streets of modern Iraq. The plan reorganized the city into a number of distinct parts, with areas designed for educational institutions, open space, industry, government offices, and royal estates. Many traditional quarters, with their inward-looking houses and often organized along ethnic or religious lines, were razed in favor of the new, outward-looking Baghdad.[13] These changes were intended to bring "order" to the city, to make it more legible for the governmental authorities so that they could better control and administer its citizens. Physically, these changes were expected to "open up" space in Baghdad; symbolically, it was thought that the city and its inhabitants would become more open to the world around them, incorporating influences from a variety of sources. This aspect of the plan was particularly evident in the vibrant and experimental architectural and art of the 1950s.

ARCHITECTURE AND THE VISUAL ARTS IN THE 1950s

During the 1950s, the work of the Baghdad Modern Art Group (Jamāt Baghdād lil Fann al-Ḥadīth) became quite prominent and dominant on the Iraqi scene, and the Institute of Fine Arts became a significant component of Iraqi intellectual life.[14] While the Institute spawned a contingent of artists working in various fields, perhaps the most conspicuous area of development was in the visual arts. During World War II, hundreds of allied soldiers from Europe and America had been based in Iraq. Within the small but remarkable Polish contingency, there happened to be a number of acclaimed painters. In their spare time these artists had sought out their Iraqi counterparts and had gotten to know the Iraqi cultural scene. Several important Iraqi painters studied with the Polish soldier-artists, including Faiq Hassan and Jewad Salim, who would later form the influential Iraqi art group Al-Ruwad (The Pioneers) in the 1950s. The Poles encouraged the Iraqi artists to reject their previously held artistic norms and to instead explore new horizons by working in an individualistic, expressionist manner.[15]

The Al-Ruwad group and other post–World War II artists developed a distinctly national style that depicted nature and traditional village life. Some artists, like Jewad Salim, made a deliberate attempt to incorporate Assyrian, Babylonian, and Abbasid motifs into their paintings and sculpture. Salim, who had studied in Paris (1938–39) and Rome (1939–40), had previously worked in the Department of Antiquities and was well aware of pre-Islamic and Islamic art forms. This innovative synthesis is evident in his masterpiece, *Nasb al-Hurriyah* (The Monument of Freedom), a gigantic bronze mural in downtown Baghdad. It contains twenty-five figures and combines Arabic characters with Sumerian and Babylonian forms that have been clearly influenced by prevailing Western styles.

In their "search for the features of the national personality in art," Salim and other Iraqi artists during this period thus sought out cultural and nationalistic connections to earlier civilizations.[16] In their works, ancient and medieval civilizations became "Iraqi," and thus highly relevant to the modern citizen of Iraq. Heritage or tradition became modernized, and modernity was perceived to be based on tradition.[17] As these bourgeois Baghdadi artists experimented with new vocabularies and forms, they often felt trapped between their social connections to the Westernized elite of Iraq and their romantic, nostalgic visions of the local people and places they painted in country scenes or who represented the plight of the working poor in their poetry.[18] These artists became quite prominent within Iraq, displaying their paintings and publishing journals that reproduced their artwork.

Iraqi architects were also influenced by this cultural scene. Hoshia Nooradin characterizes the 1950s as a new phase in Iraqi architecture, when the superficial imitation of foreign trends was no longer acceptable. Instead, architects developed what Nooradin terms "local architecture," which was based on a reflection and absorption of both foreign and domestic influences.[19] Spurring this trend was the return to Baghdad, after studies abroad, of three architects who would be among the most influential Iraqi architects of the twentieth century—Rifat Chadirji, Hisham Munir, and Muhammad Makiya.[20] The three architects began their careers in the charged cultural and political environment of Baghdad of the 1950s. It was a time of optimism and growth, and these young architects sought to instill a new, modern Iraqi aesthetic into their designs. Like the visual artists and poets of the time, they experimented with form and structure and they sought to incorporate traditional and cultural paradigms into a modern setting. They found themselves working in exciting times. They were young and fresh out of school, and their government, through the IDB, was about to invest considerable sums of money in rethinking and redesigning the urban landscape of Iraq.

All of the young architects in this period lobbied to ensure that their voices and their talents would be considered in this massive development plan. One of them, Nizar Ali Jawdat, happened to be the son of the influential politician Ali Jawdat Al-Ayubbi, who served as prime minister on several occasions, including during 1957. According to Louis McMillen, Nizar convinced his father that it would be more "advantageous to the country to engage some of the world's great architects to do their projects rather than the old line British engineering firms left over from the days of the British protectorate."[21]

The IDB's ambitious goals for a radical new urban design included a new soccer stadium, national museum, opera house, symphony hall, art gallery, and post and telegraph office. The IDB, flush with cash and boundless optimism, contacted many of the leading architects around the world, and Le Corbusier, Walter Gropius, Gio Ponti, Alvar Aalto, and Frank Lloyd Wright all agreed to undertake various projects in Baghdad. In the initial plans, Le Corbusier was to design a sports center and stadium, Gropius a new university campus, and Aalto an art museum and central post office.

The ideas proposed by these world-famous architects were exciting and, of course, on the architectural cutting-edge. For the new art museum, the Finnish architect Alvar Aalto designed a virtually square, three-story building with heavy, closed external walls clad with dark-blue ceramic tiles.[22] The outer walls were supported by a velum system of wedge-shaped columns, and the top floor included a cafeteria in a rooftop garden. It is a "typical" Aalto building, with a floor plan that included five asymmetrical galleries arranged in the same echelon formation that Aalto had designed for a museum in Tallin, Estonia, and for the Johnson Institute, in Avesta, Sweden (neither building was built), and closely related to his Aalborg (Denmark) Museum. The Aalto plan for the Baghdad Art Museum was not particularly "nationalistic," in that it did not reflect the aesthetics of local culture or architectural practice. It was a modern "international" building, fully comparable to other, similar buildings elsewhere in the world.

Plans for the new University campus were submitted by Walter Gropius and the Architecture Collaborative. Gropius's team, then at Harvard, conducted considerable research into traditional Iraqi architecture, seeking to build on past experience while using modern building methods and material. The environmental control issues created by Baghdad's blazing summer sun garnered significant attention. Gropius's team designed sun breakers for each building, resulting in deep structures with very strong shadows. The location of the campus, on a peninsula formed by a bend in the Tigris River, provided the team with abundant water to develop all kinds of vegetation, including trees and lawns.[23] Though Gropius did take into account the local climate, his drawings were also "international," in the sense that they were not meant to convey an "Iraqi" spirit or architecture.[24] The main auditorium on campus, for example, was a modified version of an earlier, failed proposal to build a Civic Center in Tallahassee, Florida.

FRANK LLOYD WRIGHT'S BAGHDAD FANTASY

The role of Frank Lloyd Wright in this period is particularly intriguing. His creative proposal to utilize Iraq's unique medieval legacy, especially the spirit of the classic tales and adventures of *A Thousand and One Nights*, was an unusual source of inspiration that ran counter to the IDB's vision of modernization. The architect Mina Marefat has eloquently chronicled Wright's plan for Baghdad and argues that it perhaps constitutes his "magnum opus."[25] Unlike his contemporaries, Wright took an entirely different approach. When he was originally contacted, Wright had been extremely enthusiastic about the project. His original response to the Iraqi government basically sums up his attitude and also reveals his naiveté. He wrote that he was "pleased to join IRAQ in a twentieth-century enterprise. To me this opportunity to assist Persia is like a story to a boy fascinated by the Arabian Nights Entertainment as I was."[26] (Wright obviously made no distinction between Iranians and Iraqis.) He explained, furthermore, that he had grown up reading the stories in *A Thousand and One Nights* and would therefore be thrilled to help build a new Baghdad, which had been the city of his childhood fantasies. Just like the Iraqi nationalists of the time, Wright sought new paradigms from Iraqi history in order to formulate a unique vision of the modern city.

Although his original commission, in 1957, was to design only a combined theater and opera house, Wright obviously felt that he could achieve more.[27] He visited Baghdad that year in order to convince the IDB that he had ambitious plans for Baghdad, and to persuade the board to allow him to design and develop those plans, which included a "Garden of Eden" theme-type park, an art gallery, a national museum, and an open-air bazaar.

Wright suggested to the planners in Iraq that they should utilize the spirit of Harun al-Rashid and of the Abbasid Caliphate, or, as he put it, the "spirit of the East," in their plans to develop Baghdad. Wright was adamant that the Iraqis not "join the Western procession" and mimic what he called the empty architecture of Western cities. He pleaded instead that "no architect should come here and put a Western cliché to work." In his meetings with the Iraqi planners he essentially went on a diatribe against the blind expansion of Western commercialism, and warned that if they followed that kind of plan, Baghdad would be facing the same problems of overpopulation and automobile congestion that Western cities were facing. Juxtaposing Iraq's spiritualism to the West's materialism, Wright urged the Iraqis to "preserve their own spiritual integrity according to great oriental philosophies which has inspired East and West." Wright's solution was a "scientific modern principle" for the urbanization of Baghdad, one that emphasized decentralization because it "was so inevitable to the survival of all great cities either West or East."[28]

After an apparently persuasive meeting with Wright, the young King Faysal II (the grandson of Faysal ibn Husayn) decided that Wright alone should be responsible for a large portion of the reconstruction of Baghdad. Within a few months, Wright had drawn up plans for the opera house, the theme park, and post and telegraph office, botanical gardens, parking garages, an art gallery, a national museum, and the university. On paper and as art, these plans were magnificent: in playful and creative ways, they offered an architectural interpretation of the many themes of Iraqi history. The ambitious grandeur of Wright's plans evoke the fantasies and imaginings of Orientalists through the ages. Yet Wright was attempting to create something new, a modern aesthetic in the historical setting of Baghdad.

In a reflective address to studio members at Taliesen West, Wright preached that the duty of the modern architect was not to imitate the past, but to interpret it creatively in order to link it with the present. Obviously delighted by his Baghdad project, Wright mused: "It is rather interesting, isn't it, to have the—I think they call me the Dean of the Moderns or something like that—going back to the origin of civilization, to show what civilization amounts to now."[29]

Wright's plans seemed futuristic, yet based on ancient themes. Wright's designs drew heavily on Persian and Arab architecture and were more Orientalist than the International Style advocated by the other architects working on Baghdad projects. His opera house complex was a reference to al-Mansur's circular plan of eighth-century Baghdad; it included a graded natural-earth mound that was designed to form the substructure of most of the buildings, as an homage to the architecture of ancient Mesopotamia. In many ways, Wright was experimenting with the various paradigms of Iraqi history, just as the Iraqi artists were doing with art and poetry. He developed plans that were clearly based on his own personal relation with medieval Iraqi history and on what his imagination envisioned Iraq would have looked like at that time. At the same time, he was very concerned with the needs of contemporary urban design, such as the development of leisure spaces and the limiting of traffic congestion.

Wright's fantasy of reconstructing the city in *A Thousand and One Nights* came to an abrupt end, however, in the summer of 1958. On July 14, a military coup, spearheaded by General Abd al-Karim Qasem, overthrew the Hashemite monarchy. Throngs of people took part in the violent mayhem, which resulted in the horrific death of the king and of some of his closest associates. The regime that had started rather unceremoniously with Faysal ibn Husayn's coronation in 1921 came to an even more abrupt end. And one year later, Wright himself passed away.

IRAQI NATIONAL ARCHITECTURE

Under Qasem, the new government in Iraq showed little interest in the grandiose plans of the IDB. Indeed, the agency was considered part and parcel of the corrupt and questionable nature of the Hashemite Kingdom. The Qasem regime had different ideas of what constituted the nation and how to define modernity. It did not consider the construction of flashy cultural buildings a pressing concern, especially when large segments of Iraqi society did not have access to sufficient education or health care. Wright's plans did not resonate with how the new government wanted to identify itself or with how it wanted to expend its revenue. Nevertheless, other architects, for example, Gropius and Le Corbusier, continued their work with the new regime. The University of Baghdad, which Gropius designed, was opened in 1961, after Gropius had met with Qasen and discussed his plans with him.

The overthrow of the Hashemites was a drastic change of affairs in Iraqi history, suggesting, somewhat contradictorily, both the fragile, yet firm foundations of Iraqi national identity and self-image. In subsequent years, Iraqi architects would have a greater role in defining the urban landscape of Baghdad.

In 1959, the first Iraqi school of architecture was founded by Muhammad Makiya at Baghdad University. The architecture school drastically changed the training of Iraqi architects and had a tremendous impact on how Iraqi architecture would be defined.[30] Similar to experiments that were also taking place in the visual arts and literature, under Makiya and other instructors the school sought to establish a modern Iraqi architecture that had roots in the country's history and traditions.[31] Stimulated by the vibrant cultural and political scene around them, they were inspired by the different paradigms of Iraqi history.

Makiya, for example, was committed to developing an Iraqi architecture that paid homage to Iraq's classical Islamic architecture. Unlike Wright's ornamental approach, Makiya viewed Iraqi historical traditions as functional aspects of the natural environment. His 1963 Khulafa Mosque is perhaps the best example of how he worked to conserve, celebrate, and expand classical Islamic architecture in a modern urban setting. Makiya located the new mosque in the vicinity of a ninth-century Abbasid site and a historic minaret from the thirteenth century. Instead of competing with the old structures, Makiya re-created their medieval ambience through the use of Kufic calligraphy and brickwork resembling the original minaret. Instead of being distinct parts, the structures blend together, creating a seamless whole. In his presentation, the modern and the traditional are not separate buildings, but part of the same continuum. Makiya was adamant that historic structures such as domes and minarets "are so much part of the natural setting that they stand beyond the label of 'traditional' or 'contemporary.'"[32] The modern, thus, did not stand in contrast to the ancient, but was part of the same environment, forming the same spatial organization. For Makiya, Iraq was a synthesis of its various pasts, and especially its Islamic past. In his role as a practitioner, educator, and critic, Makiya would have a tremendous impact on Iraqi architecture. In 1965 he would design the Museum of Antiquities in Mosul, and in 1967, the Ministry of Foreign Affairs in Baghdad.

Makiya's contemporary, Rifat Chadirji, took a different approach, seeking inspiration in Iraq's historical past. In 1952, having returning to Baghdad from graduate training in England, he began work on his architectural "experiments."[33] Chadirji was critical of the work of the Egyptian Hasan Fathy and that of Muhammad Makiya; he considered their work "either naive or simplistic attempts" to resolve very complex problems.[34] Although he did not entirely dismiss their efforts, Chadirji felt that Iraq exhibited a "cultural gap" with the West, which could be seen in the disparity in development between the two cultures, especially in technology.[35] Chadirji maintained that this "gap" could not be bridged by a policy of "narrow regionalism, vernacularism, or nationalism because of the characteristics of the internationalization of modern culture." Instead, he sought to "synthesize concepts gleaned from the international avant-garde with abstract forms derived from tradition."[36] He called his own approach a "regional, international architecture" that he claimed excluded replicas of traditional elements. Nevertheless, his buildings, particularly those from early in his career, do in fact incorporate some traditional features like archways. These early works were firmly grounded in Iraqi nationalist discourse, evoking various Iraqi pasts.

Chadirji's earliest works dealt largely with the restoration of old structures. In the mid-1950s, he served as the director of the Department of Endowments, the government agency responsible for the preservation of old mosques and buildings. In 1960, he was commissioned to design Baghdad's Monument for the Unknown Soldier. In an obvious homage to Iraq's pre-Islamic past, the monument evokes the parabolic arch of the Sassanid Palace of Ctesiphon. As far as Chadirji was concerned, this ancient structure had meaning for contemporary Iraqis. The Ctesiphon arch was thus nationalized and used to commemorate Iraqi soldiers, even though Ctesiphon had been the seat for the ancient Persian Empire in the sixth century. Such historical distinctions clearly did not matter, for Chadirji or for the population at large. For all intents and purposes, the Ctesiphon motif, despite its Persian origin, has become a part of the modern Iraqi vernacular.

The critic Kanan Makiya (son of Muhammad Makiya) claims that Chadirji was a modernist "at heart," and that his interest in Iraqi heritage and tradition was "superficial." But Chadirji would continue to employ historical motifs and forms in his architecture, incorporating elements from the Great Mosque of Samarra and the Palace of Ukhaidir.[37] For example, his 1966 office building for the Tobacco Monopoly, with its arched windows and column structures, has the outward appearance of traditional architecture. The interior of the building, however, is linear, with the office spaces organized along a corridor—a more international approach to office design. Like his Iraqi contemporaries, Chadirji was developing an Iraqi architectural aesthetic that did not have a singular feature and that was based on his relationship to and interpretation of Iraqi history. In inventive ways, Chadirji combined the newest technologies and the latest trends from abroad with local forms to fashion his Iraqi architecture.

Iraqi architects who came of age in the 1950s had the knowledge, independence, and self-confidence to articulate new visions and structures for their country. Inspired by national tradition and aesthetics as well as the ambitious fantasies and hopes of foreign architects such as Gropius and Wright, and given the opportunity to build and test new solutions to local problems and surroundings, the Iraqi architects expanded the notion of Iraqiness. In that way, they strengthened their belief in the nation and distilled greater pride in its long and varied history. Although today many people question the validity of Iraq as an entity or its potential to survive as a nation, these multiple visions of Iraq, to which Iraqi architects contributed, will sustain the nation in years to come—despite difficult circumstances.

EPILOGUE

It is ironic that one of Frank Lloyd Wright's designs did end up having a very indirect role in the political and cultural development of Iraq. In October 2004 the final presidential debate between George W. Bush and John Kerry was held in Gammage Auditorium on the campus of Arizona State University. The auditorium was designed by Wright, and is basically the national art gallery that he had proposed for Baghdad. When the IDB's tenure had come to an end, Wright submitted the slightly modified plans for this building to Arizona State, which had commissioned him to design a gallery and auditorium for its Art Department.

That October evening in 2004, in a building that was originally supposed to have housed Iraq's cultural treasures, two American politicians debated the American war in Iraq and discussed Iraq's future. Given America's dominant role in determining and defining Iraq's near-term future, an event similar to Faysal ibn Husayn's coronation in 1921 may take place. Instead of British advisers, however, this time, American officials will "assist" a nascent Iraqi government to take steps toward full independence and sovereignty. Once again, Baghdad will be subject to ambitious reconstruction plans and extensive rebuilding. The city that inspired the legend of Scheherazade and her repetitive rendition of new tales will once again undergo a period of modernization and new urban design to bolster the powers of the new government. This time around, however, the Iraqi collective memory and the negative experience of earlier such efforts will undoubtedly be a complicating factor, and will possibly derail any plans that do not take into account the aspirations and desires of the Iraqi people.

NOTES

I would like to thank Alan DeGooyer, Helga Druxes, Kenda Mutongi, and Kashia Pieprzak for their helpful comments. I am also grateful to Mina Marefat for all her help.

1. For the creation of Iraq, see Charles Tripp, *A History of Iraq* (Cambridge: Cambridge University Press, 2000); Reeva Spector Simon, *Iraq between the Two World Wars* (New York: Columbia University Press, 1986); Stephen Longrigg, *Iraq, 1900 to 1950*, (Oxford: Oxford University Press, 1953); Peter Sluglett, *Britain in Iraq, 1914–1932* (London: Ithaca Press, 1976); Samaira Haj, *The Making of Iraq, 1900–1963* (Albany: State University of New York Press, 1997); and 'Abd al-Razzaq al-Hasani, *Tarikh al-Wizarat al-'Iraqiyya*, 10 vols. (Sidon: al-Maktaba al-Asriya li al-Tiba'a wa al-Nashr, 1953–1961).

2. There are many works that focus on how Iraq benefited British imperialism, including Reeva Spector Simon and Elanor H. Tejirian, *The Creation of Iraq, 1914–1921* (New York: Columbia University Press, 2004).

3. Sami Zubaida, "The Fragments Imagine the Nation: The Case of Iraq," *International Journal of Middle East Studies* 34, no. 2 (2002): 206.

4. For an excellent study of these competing visions, see Eric Davis, *Memories of State* (Berkeley: University of California Press, 2004).

5. The most thorough study of the Hashemite period is by far Hanat Batatu, *The Old Social Classes and the Revolutionary Movements of Iraq* (Princeton, N.J.: Princeton University Press, 1978).

6. For an excellent study of the economic role of Baghdad in the nineteenth century, see Hala Fattah, *The Politics of Regional Trade in Iraq, Arabia, and the Gulf, 1745–1900* (Albany: State University of New York, 1997). See also Muhmmad Salman Hasan, *Al-tatawur al-iqtisadi fi al-Iraq* (Sidon: al-Maktaba al-Asriya li al-Tiba'a wa al-Nashr, 1965).

7. See Reeva Spector Simon, *Iraq between the Two World Wars* (New York: Columbia University Press, 1986); Mohammad Tarbush, *The Role of the Military in Politics* (London: Routledge, 1985). See also Matthew Elliot, *Independent Iraq* (London: I. B. Tauris, 1996).

8. See Mostafa Elm, *Oil, Power, and Principle* (Syracuse, NY: Syracuse University Press, 1992); and Irvine Anderson, *Aramco, the United States, and Saudi Arabia* (Princeton, N.J.: Princeton University Press, 1981). In the early 1950s, many countries, such as Venezuela and Iran, made plans to nationalize their major industries. Saudi Arabia had recently negotiated an agreement with Aramco, which introduced a 50–50 profit-sharing formula in the Middle East. In 1952, the IPC agreed to share profits on a 50–50 basis (see Ferhang Jalal, *The Role of Government in the Industrialization of Iraq, 1950–1965* [London: Frank Cass, c. 1972]).

9. Yusuf Sayigh, *The Economies of the Arab World* (London: Croom Helm, 1978), 37.

10. For the activities of the board, see Jalal, *The Role of Government in the Industrialization of Iraq* (New York: Praeger, 1967); and Kahdim al-'Eyd, *Oil Revenues and Accelerated Growth* (New York: Praeger, 1979).

11. The IDB sought foreign advice. See, e.g., Lord Salter [Arthur Salter], *The Development of Iraq* (London: n.p., 195); and World Bank, *The Economic Development of Iraq* (Baltimore: Johns Hopkins University Press, 1952).

12. A copy of the IDB's master plan, "The Master Plan for the City of Baghdad, 1956," can be found in the Frank Lloyd Wright Archives (FLWA 5733.001) at Taliesen West in Phoenix, Arizona.

13. See Samir Al-Khalil [Kanan Makiya], *The Monument: Art, Vulgarity, and Responsibility in Iraq* (Berkeley: University of California Press, 1991), 20.

14. See Ulrike al-Khamis, "An Historical Overview, 1900s–1990s," in *Strokes of*

Genius, ed. Maysaloun Faraj (London: Saqi Books, 2001), 22. See also Jabra Ibrahim Jabra, *Juthur al-Fann al-Iraqi* (Baghdad: Al-Dar al-Arabiyya, 1986).

15. See al-Khamis, "An Historical Overview," 23.

16. Dia al-Azzaw in *Al-Jumhuriyyah* (Baghdad), no. 1432 (1972): 164. A good example of this type of connection can be found in Rashid Salim, "Diaspora, Departure, and Remains," in *Strokes of Genius*, 55.

17. The books by the critic Jabra Ibrahim Jabra really emphasize this trend among Iraqi artists; see, e.g., his *Jewad Salim wa Nasb al-Hurriya* (Baghdad, 1974). See also Shakir Hasan al-Said, *Fusul min tarikh al-haraka al-tashkiliyah fi al-Iraq*, 2 vols. (Baghdad: Wizarat al-thaqafah wa al-ilam, 1983); and al-Khalil, *The Monument*, 79. This experimentation was not confined to the visual arts. In literature, the Iraqi free-verse movement (*al-shi'r al-hurr*) made its first appearance in the early 1950s. Poets such as Naziq al-Mala'ika, Badr Shakir al-Sayyab, and 'Abd al-Wahhab al-Bayyati "radically changed the form of Arabic poetry and constituted a direct and uncompromising challenge to the rules that had formed the traditional poetic canon" (Terri Deyoung, *Placing the Poet* [Albany: State University of New York Press, 1998], 192).

18. This sentiment is expressed in part 1 of Shakir Hasan al-Said, *Fusul min tarikh al-haraka al-tashkiliyah fi al-Iraq*, 2 vols. (Baghdad: Wizarat al-thaqafah wa al-ilam, 1983), 126.

19. See Hoshiar Nooradin, "Globalization and the Search for Modern Local Architecture: Learning from Baghdad," in *Planning Middle Eastern Cities*, ed. Yasser Elsheshtawy (London: Routledge, 2004), 3.

20. Makiya studied at Liverpool and Cambridge, Chadirji in London, and Munir at the University of Texas and the University of Southern California.

21. Louis McMillen, "The University of Baghdad, Baghdad, Iraq," in vol. 4 of *The Walter Gropius Archive*, ed. Alexander Tzonis (New York: Garland Publishing, 1991), 189.

22. Göran Schildt and Alvar Aalto, *The Complete Catalogue of Architecture, Design, and Art* (New York: Rizzoli, 1994), 122–23.

23. McMillen, "The University of Baghdad," 190–91.

24. At the same time that Gropius was planning the University, his successor as Dean of Harvard's School of Design, José Louis Sert, was designing the new American Embassy in Baghdad. On the architecture of the Embassy, see Samuel Isenstadt, "'Faith in a Better Future': Josep Lluis Sert's American Embassy in Baghdad," *Journal of Architectural Education* 50 (February 1997): 172–88.

25. Mina Marefat, "Wright's Baghdad," in *Frank Lloyd Wright: Europe and Beyond*, ed. Anthony Alofsin (Berkeley: University of California Press, 1999).

26. Wright to the Iraq Development Board, January 24, 1957, Frank Lloyd Wright Archives (FLWA) at Taliesen West, Phoenix, Arizona.

27. The standard account of Wright's plans for Iraq can be found in Neil Levine's monumental *The Architecture of Frank Lloyd Wright* (Princeton, N.J.: Princeton University Press, 1996), 383–404.

28. FLWA document no. 2401.379, EE, 3–4, Frank Lloyd Wright Archives at Taliesen West, Phoenix, Arizona.

29. Quoted in Marefat, "Wright's Baghdad," 195–96.

30. On the establishment of the School of Architecture, see Fuad A. Uthman, "Exporting Architectural Education to the Arab World," *Journal of Architectural Education* 31, no. 3 (1978): 26–30; and Udo Kultermann, "The Architects of Iraq," *Mimar* 5 (1982): 54–61.

31. This emphasis is clearly seen in some of Makiya's writings—see, e.g., *Baghdad* (Baghdad: Niqabat al-Muhandisin al-Iraqiyah, 1969).

32. Muhammad Makiya, "The Arab House: A Historical Overview," in *Proceedings of the 1984 Colloquium on the Arab House*, ed. A. D. C. Hyland and Ahmad al-Shahi (Newcastle: University of Newcastle upon Tyne, 1986), 12.

33. Rifat Chadirji, *Concepts and Influences: Towards a Regionalized International Architecture* (New York: Routledge and Paul Kegan, 1986), 39.

34. Ibid., 44.

35. Ibid., 41.

36. Ibid., 49.

37. al-Khalil, *The Monument*, 95

4 Baghdad's Urban Restructuring, 1958

Aesthetics and Politics of Nation Building

PANAYIOTA I. PYLA

In August 1955 the Iraq Development Board, a quasi-governmental body overseeing an accelerated program of national modernization in the young nation of Iraq, solicited the Greek architect and planner Constantinos A. Doxiadis to prepare an ambitious housing program for the entire country. Chaired by Iraq's premier and supported by Western consultants, the IDB had at its disposal the lion's share of the country's oil revenues (which increased dramatically in the early 1950s as foreign ownership of the Iraqi petroleum industry diminished), and it used them to fund the construction of dams, irrigation and drainage systems, power plants, bridges, roads, factories, schools, hospitals, and other buildings.[1] Doxiadis was brought on board at the point in time when the IDB had decided to increase its emphasis on housing and community facilities, in an effort to prevent social unrest by providing more visible signs of progress.[2] The need for popular gestures of social reform seemed urgent because the increasingly unpopular Iraqi government, ruled by the Hashimite dynasty installed by the British in 1921, saw "uncomfortably obvious" parallels between Iraq and Czarist Russia, and was nervously hoping to secure political stability in order to sustain itself. For similar reasons, British and American consultants also encouraged reform, hoping that Iraq, which was seen as an important Middle Eastern bastion against Communism, would not replicate the experience of Egypt, where a 1952 revolt had brought Gamal Abdel Nasser to power, along with his Soviet-allied policies.[3]

Doxiadis's initial charge was to create a comprehensive five-year plan for the improvement of housing conditions throughout the country, and his firm began with projects in Mosul, Kirkuk, Mussayib, and Baghdad. In 1958, while the firm was already engaged in the construction of various rural and urban housing schemes, it was also assigned the task of creating a new master plan for the rapidly expanding city of Baghdad. As the administrative capital of a new nation, Baghdad became the focus of the IDB's activities. An earlier master plan, developed jointly by the British firm Minoprio & Spencely and P. W. Macfarlane in 1956, had instituted zoning principles and proposed the development of a system of roads to connect Baghdad's premodern urban core to its new river bridges.[4] Doxiadis Associates' master plan aspired to provide a more comprehensive framework for modernization. By incorporating the pilot projects Doxiadis Associates had already launched in the capital beginning in 1955, the firm made a double promise that the new comprehensive restructuring would improve housing for all while providing the foundation for long-term urban and regional growth.[5]

This essay focuses on Doxiadis's 1958 master plan for Baghdad. Moving from a dicussion of the overall master plan to the design and construction of specific housing units and public squares, the essay demonstrates how Doxiadis's conceptions of social reform and regional particularity, along with his technocratic postures of neutrality, became intertwined with the Iraqi regime's aspirations to assert the young nation's modernity and to nurture pride among its citizens. The goal is twofold: (1) to uncover how Doxiadis's formal and social experiments were appropriated as vehicles for building a modern nation state, and (2) to simultaneously demonstrate that postcolonial Baghdad was a significant site in the larger rethinking of architectural modernism that characterized the post–World War II era. Since new visions for reconstructing Baghdad are once again becoming current, it is particularly important to put this recent history of the city in critical perspective.

DOXIADIS'S APPEAL

Doxiadis, who had been a Greek government official from 1945 to 1951, first as the coordinator of postwar reconstruction and then as the administrator of the Marshal Plan in Greece, was well known in American and international development circles, and he was recommended to the Iraq Development Board by the International Bank for Reconstruction and Development.[6] Doxiadis was at that time taking his very first steps in establishing a private practice, and even though he had little to show in terms of independent built works (he barely had any staff when the IDB solicited him in 1955), he succeeded in securing this commission, which would soon become the stepping stone for his prolific international practice.[7] What made Doxiadis appealing to the IDB was partly his Greek background that rendered him free of "imperialist stigma" and distinguished him from most of the other Western consultants, advisers, and technicians who were streaming into Iraq.[8] Doxiadis's appeal also stemmed from his planning approach, which he called "Ekistics"—an approach that emphasized a rational and scientific version of urbanism and that gave his proposals an apolitical authority.

Defined as "the science of human settlements," Ekistics was initially formulated by Doxiadis during his work in Greece, and it promised to synthesize the input of economics, geography, sociology, anthropology, and other sciences. Emblematic of a modernist ambition to coordinate the entire system of knowledge about the physical environment, Ekistics' multidisciplinary approach had a twofold goal. The first goal was to reject the ethos of the individual signature-designer and to emphasize the necessity of addressing basic human needs, well beyond functionalist or technological concerns.[9] The second goal of Ekistics aimed to reinvent architects and planners as development experts by emphasizing the significance of the physical environment in promoting socioeconomic development in the post–World War II era.[10] Ekistics' commitment to international urbanization, industrialization, and socioeconomic modernization was in tune with the agenda of international development institutions to restructure the so-called underdeveloped countries of the world according to the paradigm of the industrialized West. However, Doxiadis's emphasis on a rational and scientific planning approach conveniently obscured such ideological leanings. His standard claim was that Ekistics' clients were simply the "common people" of any society, "communist and capitalist alike."[11] From the perspective of the Iraq Development Board, such a claim to scientific neutrality conveniently concealed the anti-Communist fears and pro-Western alliances that motivated the IDB's own modernizing agenda. Furthermore, Doxiadis's pledge that social, economic, racial, and ethnic inequalities could be managed away by benevolent technocrats promised to make his firm's interventions more acceptable to the highly diverse citizenry of Iraq.

Another equally important reason for Doxiadis's appeal was that, even as he claimed that Ekistics would apply scientific truths transnationally, he promised to make his interventions amenable to local cultural preferences. Doxiadis pledged not to act like a "magician planner" who "has all the solutions up his sleeve and he pulls them out like rabbits."[12] Often implying criticism of the new cities, like Brasilia in Brazil and Chandigarh in India, Doxiadis promised that his firm's proposals would emerge out of exhaustive surveys and research programs that would "diagnose" each locale's needs and potential (notice the scientific and medical authority assumed), and that he would overcome the functionalist, universalist, and ultimately Eurocentric and homogenizing preoccupations of other modernist approaches.[13] His dual claim both to scientific legitimacy and cultural sensitivity was the right combination for the Iraq Development Board, whose eagerness to provide architectural symbols of the modern state was accompanied by a desire to champion a shared ideal of national identity and pride.

RESTRUCTURING THE CITY

To understand the context of Doxiadis's proposal for Baghdad, it is important to remember that the city had been experiencing dramatic transformations since early in the twentieth century, when its administration changed hands from the Ottomans to the British. In 1921, when the British established the constitutional monarchy that brought the Hashimites to power in the newly formed Iraq, Baghdad became the capital of the new nation, and since then, it grew by leaps and bounds, both in size and population. In 1932, Iraq became independent, but after a series of tribal and ethnic revolts, military coups and counter-coups, it was reoccupied by the British, who installed a pro-Western government in 1941. From the 1920s to the 1940s, Baghdad's population tripled, reaching more than half a million, and the city burst out of its centuries-old confines—circumscribed by the settlement of Rusafah on the east bank of the Tigris, Al-Karkh on the west bank, and Kazimiyah and Azimiyah farther north. Especially after the 1920s, with the construction of a flood protection dyke that stretched from the Tigris north of Azimiya to the Diyala River east of Karradah, the urban reach of Baghdad expanded laterally in two directions: northwest toward Azimiyah, and southwest toward the Diyala (fig. 4.1).[14] Some large-scale government-sponsored developments (e.g., the 1920s Waziriyah) introduced systematic layouts, broad avenues, and suburban neighborhoods that stood in stark contrast to Rusafa's medieval feel—characterized by souks and narrow, tunnel-like residential streets running under the projecting wooden upper-stories of the densely built houses.[15]

In the 1950s, with the establishment of the Iraq Development Board, Baghdad experienced an even more rapid transformation, and by the time Doxiadis Associates began to implement its master plan, Baghdad had become a magnet for new businesses and also the site of ambitious experiments by

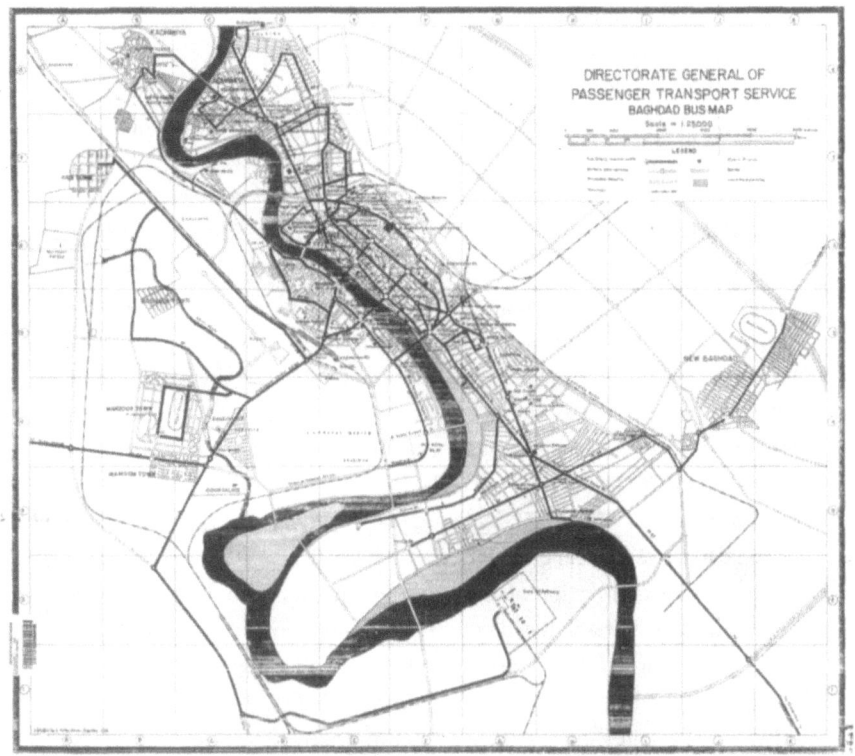

FIG. 4.1. *Map of Baghdad, 1957. University of Illinois Map Library.*

world-famous architects.[16] Le Corbusier was invited to build a mammoth sports stadium; Walter Gropius, of The Architects Collaborative, to design a university campus; Alvar Aalto to design a civic center; Frank Lloyd Wright to design an Opera House; and there were others.[17] Iraqi architects, most of whom had been educated in Europe, also became involved; these included Mohamed Makiya, Kahtan Awni, and Rifat Chadirji.

The Doxiadis Associates master plan was based on a planning model of urban expansion, control, and efficiency that Doxiadis would later call "Dynapolis."[18] Meaning "dynamic city," Dynapolis was one of the many neologisms that Doxiadis coined, which made a glossary a necessary feature of his later books. The core idea of Dynapolis was for the city to expand continually along one axis, to avert congestion, and for the business district to grow along this axis, controlled by zoning and the siting of public buildings, road systems, and green areas. Residential areas would also expand continually, along the core's flanks, echoing the open-ended logic of other "linear city" concepts, such as Arturo Soria y Mata's 1882 Ciudad Lineal, Tony Garnier's 1901 Cité Industrielle, and the Soviet Linear Cities of the 1930s.[19]

The concept of Dynapolis was to guide Baghdad's orderly expansion and become a symbol and instrument for creating an efficient modern capital. Doxiadis Associates identified the Tigris River as the reference for establishing the central axis of growth. Even though the concept theoretically allowed for indefinite urban expansion, Doxiadis set the ideal population limit of the future Iraqi capital at three million inhabitants—about three times larger than the 1958 population. This idealized population figure suggested certain maximum geographical limits for the city, defined by an elongated rectangle oriented along the main northwest-southeast axis of the river (see fig. 4.2).[20] This rectangular area was subdivided by a system of roads which incorporated some of the existing major roads, but which also suggested that the opening of new roads would be adapted to the rectilinear pattern of the new city. The new road system would provide "an easy connection of the city to the country," to tie the city into a larger regional schema.[21] Residential sectors and subsectors would also be arranged according to this rectangular grid, but modified in the center to accommodate the commercial district. The commercial district would include the existing old city center and also the new commercial centers that were expected to emerge along the main axis of the Dynapolis. The new commercial centers would have to abide by the rectilinear logic of the road system and residential grid. The same logic would also guide the placement of industrial districts, which would be pushed to the edges of the city, so as to preserve the uniformity of the residential and commercial districts. Any gaps left between the imposed grid and the winding river would be designated "green space," the firm's attempt at resolving competing rectilinear and organic geometries.

The master plan revealed a preoccupation with visual order, uniformity, and regularity, and a wholesale preference for low-density building and wide streets. Such aesthetic preferences were common among planning experts working in Baghdad at the time, and they were emphasized repeatedly, as much as the need for fresh water, electric power, and sewage systems.[22] The plan's blanket dismissal of the old city's urban density failed to recognize its social role and ignored the fact that the colorful souks of the old city, despite their narrowness and darkness (or because of it!), had an immense social value. The shortcomings of such a preoccupation with an aesthetic of order and regularity would become even more pronounced in the specific housing projects proposed by Doxiadis, described below.

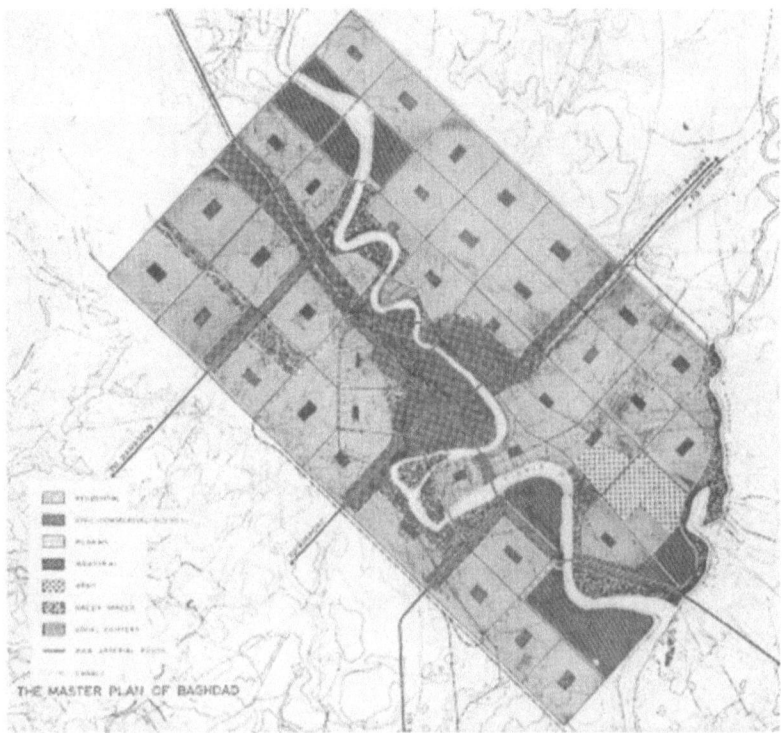

FIG. 4.2. *Master Plan for Baghdad, Iraq, 1958. Cover illustration for "Progress of the Housing Program," Doxiadis Associates Monthly Report no. 46, May 1959.*

A MODEL COMMUNITY IN WEST BAGHDAD

The Doxiadis Associates' restructuring of the city along functional lines became the basis for the design of a model community in the west part of the city. The Western Baghdad Development Scheme was planned to house a population of 100,000 inhabitants, either through government-funded housing or though self-help housing. The scheme proposed different "community sectors" of 7,000 to 10,000 people, with each sector providing administrative, social, educational, health, and other community buildings, shopping centers, green areas, coffee houses, and mosques (see figs. 4.3 and 4.4). Echoing the social and functionalist logic of the "neighborhood units" of the post–World War II British New Towns, the plan provided key social facilities within walking distance, favoring pedestrian movement. Even though the overall plan emphasized dynamic growth, the size of each sector was predetermined and the dimensions of each plot, roads, and public

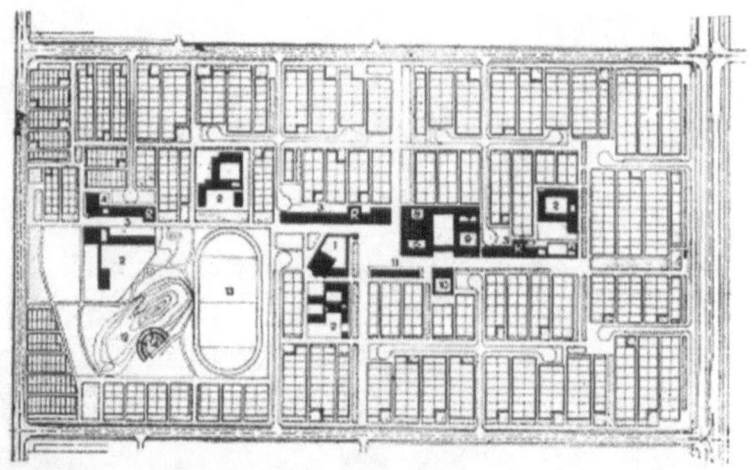

1 Mosque
2 School
3 Market
4 Public Baths
5 Coffee Houses
6 Administration
7 Red Crescent
8 Cultural Centre
9 Public Health Centre
10 Police Station
11 Shops
12 Public Park
13 Sports Ground
14 Open Air Theatre

FIG. 4.3. *Plan of community sector in West Baghdad. From Constantinos A. Doxiadis*, Architecture in Transition, *109*.

FIG. 4.4. *Model of community sector in West Baghdad. From Constantinos A. Doxiadis*, Architecture in Transition, *113*.

areas within it were also prescribed in an effort to preserve each sector's human scale.

Doxiadis Associates' logic of functional separation extended to the system of social ordering. Each community sector of Western Baghdad would be broken down into smaller socio-spatial units arranged hierarchically. The smallest, called "community class I," would comprise from ten to twenty families of similar income levels. A grouping of three to seven such communities would comprise a "class II" community, which would also have a homogenous economic status. House types would also correspond to this income-based hierarchy, but each promised to provide the basics of sanitation and safety. The hierarchical logic continued: An agglomeration of class II communities plus an elementary school would be designated as a "class III" community. Class III communities made up of different income groups, plus a market and shops, a teahouse and a mosque, could constitute a "class IV" community, also known as the "community sector" comprising seven thousand to ten thousand individuals. This "community sector" would constitute "the basic element" of Baghdad's urban plan, and it was actually a prototype for the basic element of many of the cities that were subsequently designed.[23] Doxiadis Associates' overall plan for West Baghdad was actually a plan for a class V community (combining a group of class IV sectors), which would join other parts of the city to create a class VI community (Baghdad) that would then join larger regional communities, and so on.

Doxiadis tried to contextualize his abstractions of "scales" and "hierarchies" by arguing that the smaller class I, II, and III communities corresponded to community sizes found in Iraqi towns and villages.[24] The larger-scale communities, then, were justified as new phenomena that were necessitated by the advanced transportation and communication technologies of the modern era. The vision of a multiplicity of communities aimed to provide a corrective to British versions of "self-contained" neighborhoods in New Towns, which prescribed an optimum size for neighborhoods, and which already were being criticized for failing to account for people's increasing dependence on the automobile and for the new industrial need for the mobility of populations.[25] Doxiadis Associates hoped to introduce some flexibility to the idea of optimum size by inscribing each community within larger ones. Ironically, however, the firm continued to be bound by a hierarchical logic that oversimplified the complexities of the urban environment by assuming that communities and sub-communities could neatly fit into each other, and by too precipitously accepting the notion of the social and economic harmony of parts and wholes.

A similar preoccupation with an efficient ordering of the city was reflected in the way social groups were organized. The small homogeneous residential communities that Doxiadis Associates defined (class I and II), that would then interact (on a class III level and beyond) with one another, were meant to promote the slow and controlled intermixing of social classes and the gradual "development of social balance amongst the several classes of the citizens."[26] This was Doxiadis Associates' attempt at social engineering, in tune with the Iraqi regime's campaign to eliminate sectarian and tribal divisions. Doxiadis Associates' proposals, however, remained oblivious to the specific demographic dynamic of the city (caused, e.g., by the emigration of most of the city's Jewish population to Israel after 1947, or the influx of rural populations, including many Christians and Kurds from the north and Shi'as from the south). For all of the firm's reports, Doxiadis Associates never acknowledged these transformations and avoided any specific reflection on the city's intricate tribal, nomadic, ethnic, and other social formations that created tight communities inside the city. The proposals were instead confined to vague references to the "proper" grouping from among different communities that would allegedly create "a healthy community spirit."[27] A look at the plan gives us a hint as to what the "proper" grouping of social groups actually meant: the plan usually called for middle-class housing to be inserted between upper-income and lower-income neighborhoods, as if to prevent the direct contact of people from opposite ends of the economic spectrum. Some residential sectors were even separated by "green spaces" that acted as soft barriers between classes. In short, the proposed design strategies had more to do with an administrative ordering of the society than with any vision of social equity. Such preoccupation with the rational ordering of both the urban fabric and the society, understood more in visual and aesthetic terms, was typical of twentieth-century high-modernist urbanism and its grand vision for the rational engineering of social life.[28] The irony, in Doxiadis's particular case, is that he had systematically framed Ekistics as an anti-stylistic approach that deemphasized aesthetics in favor of responding to basic human needs.

LOCAL PARTICULARITY IN THE FUNCTIONAL PLAN

Certain aspects of the master plan attempted to accommodate local social habits and formal vocabularies, as if to insert local character into the rational methodology of housing. One gesture was the introduction of a so-called gossip square for every grouping of ten to fifteen attached houses. These squares were to serve as "a modern substitute for the traditional gathering

FIG. 4.5. *Gossip square in Baghdad.* From Ekistics *(June 1958): 281.*

places of tribal life," and would facilitate the transformation of the village dweller into an urban dweller (see fig. 4.5).[29] The gossip square was an idea that originated with the Egyptian architect Hassan Fathy, who joined the Ekistics group in 1957, and its name was apparently inspired by the observation that similar loci existed in the traditional neighborhoods of Baghdad and that these were usually the places where neighborhood women would gather.[30] Overlooking the deep-rooted gender stereotyping (not to mention the orientalist bias) that the name "gossip square" implied, the firm embraced the concept as a planning element that demonstrated its cultural sensitivity. The strategy was effective in attracting favorable press. A *New York Times* report, for example, argued that the new housing in Baghdad compared favorably to other modernist interventions:

> Iraqi housing authorities, instead of razing the existing slums and erecting tenements on their site, are creating groups of new sub-hamlets in the adjoining countryside to provide the close family and tribal relationship the rural Arab knew in his ancestral home. . . . The sub-hamlets are built

in groups of ten or fifteen small attached houses beside a pedestrian way, at the end of which is a small gossip square.[31]

The article went on to praise Doxiadis Associates' interventions, giving them an anti-Communist spin! By nurturing a strong sense of community, the article claimed, the new housing was combating the void and loneliness felt in other, unsuccessful urban environments, which were threatening to make urban dwellers "overly susceptible to conversion by Communist agents."[32] In other words, the desire for harmony and community spirit was intimately tied to the anxieties of the Cold War.

In addition to the gossip square, the Doxiadis plan also called for the inclusion of hammams and mosques in each sector, and the occasional covered market with a roof shape reminiscent of the traditional souks. Such gestures, however, revealed more about the orientalist nostalgia of the plan's authors (Why were mosques and hamams the building types singled out?) than they reflected any profound understanding of Iraqi public life, of the intense heterogeneity of its society, or of the inhabitants' aspirations to modernity. Overpowered by the plan's modular functionality, these gossip squares, hamams, and mosques appeared as mere relics of a past, subsumed by the grand formal and social order of Dynapolis.

A similar criticism could be extended to Doxiadis Associates' studies of local climate and formal vocabularies. Climatic conditions were treated abstractly, in terms of solar exposure, wind patterns, and rainfall data, and were never really an integral part of the material choices, spatial conceptions, or larger design sensibilities of the plan. Doxiadis Associates may have recognized the open-air courtyard and colonnaded upper gallery as typical of the region's residential architecture, but the firm's own reinterpretation of these elements in its standardized "house types" pushed such courtyards to the side or back of each unit, where they lost their original climate benefits and secluded qualities (see figs. 4.6 and 4.7).[33] Similarly, Doxiadis Associates' attempts to reinterpret traditional wooden window screens with reinforced concrete produced larger patterns of openings that were not nearly as effective in promoting cooling breezes, softening harsh sunlight, or providing a sense of privacy. This is why, despite all the research and experimentation, in terms of microclimate, Doxiadis Associates' housing units compared unfavorably to the old city's mud huts with their movable roofs.[34] In the end, the courtyards and screens of the old city were compartmentalized in the plans for the new city into mass production elements. Moreover, the firm's insistence on attaching specific functional uses to each space—which, incidentally, echoed early modernist preoccupations with functional simplicity and single-use zoning—overlooked the multiplicity of purposes in domestic space, failing to recognize, for example, the inhabitant's tendency to migrate from room to room, depending on daily and seasonal comfort considerations.[35] What ultimately prevailed was an aesthetic imperative of standardization, which left little opportunity to contemplate a more cultured conception of the human subject, or to conceive of development itself as a cultural process tied to place.

CONCLUSION

Despite the Iraqi government's attempts to secure political stability through modernization and the nurturing of national pride, a military coup in July 1958, led by General Abd al-Karim al-Qasim, brought about the brutal deposition of the Hashimite monarchy and its replacement by a revolutionary republic with socialist leanings (until, eventually, a series of coups d'état would eventually establish the Baath Party as the only legitimate party). In this new climate, modernization plans changed direction and now emphasized a more anti-Western version of nationalism that left no room for the kind of universalism Doxiadis had advanced. By 1959, even local architects like Makiya and Chadirji, who had previously collaborated with Doxiadis Associates, shifted direction toward the valorization of local cultural roots. Under these circumstances, Doxiadis Associates' commission was cancelled in May 1959, leaving the Athens-based firm out of the new building boom in Baghdad in the subsequent decade.[36] By the time of their departure, however, Doxiadis Associates had constructed hundreds of dwelling units (some in western Baghdad, but also a few on the northeast side of the city and near the Army Canal)—housing that would set a precedent for many of the firm's future projects.[37] After Doxiadis Associates' left Iraq, their master plan for Baghdad was abandoned, although it occasionally became a reference point for later proposals. The handful of neighborhoods Doxiadis Associates developed on the northeast side of the city, for example, became the starting point for an enormous residential area that expanded along a rectilinear pattern and that became known as Al Thawra.[38]

Looking back at the master plan today, one can smile at the naive certainty of Doxiadis's predictions for the future, which, for all their comprehensive claims, failed to account for the impact of war, international trade sanctions, political and military relationships, and the other geopolitical power dynamics which, we now know, would shape Baghdad's future. (Even Doxiadis's

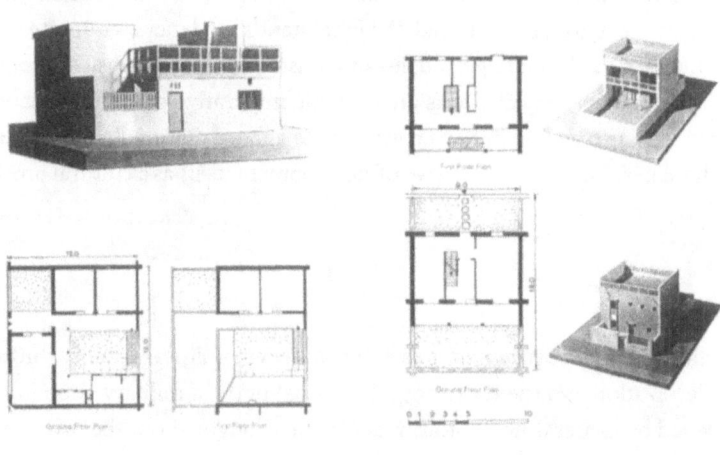

FIG. 4.6. *House types in West Baghdad. From Doxiadis Associates, "The Housing Program of Iraq," 11–12.*

FIG. 4.7. *Upper-income housing in West Baghdad. From Doxiadis Associates, "The National Housing Program of Iraq," 53.*

prediction of an ideal population of three million inhabitants grossly underestimated the growth of the city, whose population now stands at four and a half million). One must concede, nonetheless, that for all the pitfalls of Doxiadis's interventions, his firm's attempt to contemplate the dilemmas of Iraq's post-imperialist identity compares favorably when viewed against the rigid appropriations of the local heritage, as seen in the work of Frank Lloyd Wright and his orientalized references to the tales of *A Thousand and One Nights,* or in the later Baath regime's populist distortions of the country's cultural heritage that treated concepts of local tradition and heritage as entirely unambiguous.[39] Despite its flaws, Doxiadis Associates' plan was significant in contemplating the role of architecture and planning in the messy reality of postcolonial nationhood. And, in fact, because of the ironies of his intervention, Doxiadis's tactics of physical and social restructuring have gained an altogether new relevance today, when new strategies for reconstruction and nation-building in Iraq are being debated all over again.

NOTES

This material will appear in a revised version as "Back to the Future: Doxiadis's Plans for Baghdad, 1955–58," in a forthcoming issue (2007–8) of the *Journal of Planning History.*

1. For the Iraq Development Board's funding and its activities at the time, see Fahim Issa Qubain, *The Reconstruction of Iraq: 1950–1957* (New York: F. A. Praeger, 1958), vii, xi; Ishan Fethi, "Contemporary Architecture in Baghdad," *Process Architecture* (May 1985): 112–32; and Kathleen Langley, *The Industrialization of Iraq* (Cambridge, Mass.: Harvard University Press, 1961), 81. For a more recent, critical discussion of the IDB's social agenda, see Joseph Siry, "Wright's Baghdad Opera House and Gammage Auditorium: In Search of Regional Modernity," *Art Bulletin* (June 2005): 365–11.

2. Waldo Bowman, "A Modern Mesopotamia Is Molded," *Engineering News-Record,* December 12, 1957, 34–54.

3. "Development in Iraq: Special Survey," *The Economist* 183, no. 5939 (June 22, 1957): 14–page supplement after p. 1076 [Summary reprinted in *Ekistics* 5, no. 28 (January 1958): 45–48.].

4. P. W. Macfarlane, "The Plan for Baghdad, the Capital of Iraq," *Housing Review* 5 (November–December 1956): 193–95; and Minoprio & Spencely and P. W. Macfarlane, "Plan for Baghdad, Iraq," in *Architecture in the Middle East,* special issue of *Architectural Design* 27 (March 1957): 74–78.

5. Doxiadis Associates, "The Master Plan of Baghdad," *Monthly Bulletin* 9 (January 1960).

6. For the IBRD role in Iraq, see World Bank, *The Economic Development of Iraq: Report of a Mission Organized by the International Bank for Reconstruction and Development at the Request of the Government of Iraq* (Baltimore: Johns Hopkins University Press, 1952); and Kahdim al-'Eyd, *Oil Revenues and Accelerated Growth: Absorptive Capacity in Iraq* (New York: Praeger, 1979).

7. After receiving the commission in Iraq, Doxiadis Associates was solicited by many emerging nation-states, and by 1959 Doxiadis's Athens-based firm had established branches not only in Baghdad, but also in Karachi, Beirut, Addis Ababa, Khartoum, and Washington, D.C.

8. As Floyd Ratchford, the American development consultant who collaborated with Doxiadis in Iraq, would put it, Doxiadis "represents something new on the international 'technical assistance' scene." Later, a *New Yorker* article would explain Doxiadis's success as follows: "Doxiadis has the sort of European abilities that are needed—he is up on the latest planning techniques, and he runs his firm with northern (or, 'western') efficiency—but, being a Greek, he is free of the imperialist stigma" (Christopher Rand, "The Ekistic World," *The New Yorker*, May 11, 1963, 53).

9. Doxiadis had obviously assimilated some of the contemporary architectural debates in Europe and the United States that rejected mechanistic views and emphasized the multiplicity of human needs, non-functionalist concerns, sentiments, emotions, and values. For an overview of the key debates in the European post–World War II architectural scene, see Sarah Williams Goldhagen and Réjean Legault, eds., *Anxious Modernisms* (Montreal: Canadian Centre for Architecture; Cambridge, Mass.: MIT Press, 2000).

10. For Doxiadis's arguments on the alignments between Ekistics and international development, see, e.g., "Report by C. A. Doxiadis, Expert, Greece," in *Mass Housing in Rapidly Developing Tropical and Subtropical Areas* (Rotterdam: International Council for Building Research Studies and Documentation, 1959), 1–38 and esp. 6–7.

11. Constantinos A. Doxiadis, "The Science of Ekistics," *Architektoniki* 3, no. 13 (1959): 9–72 (quotation on p. 13).

12. Constantinos A. Doxiadis, "The Rising Tide and the Planner," *Ekistics* 7, no. 39 (January 1959): 4–10 (quotation on p. 6).

13. Ibid.

14. John Gulick, "Baghdad: Portrait of a City in Physical and Cultural Change," *Journal of the American Institute of Planners* 33, no. 4 (1967): 246–55.

15. For a description of Waziriyah and Rusafah, see Gulick, "Baghdad," 246,

250. See also John Searles, "City Problems Observed in Iraq, Greece, Germany," *Journal of Housing* (March 1959): 91–94.

16. "Architects Build Modern Baghdad," *Christian Science Monitor,* April 2, 1958, sec. 2. (Summary reprinted in *Ekistics* 5, no. 32 (May 1958): 244–46.)

17. Fethi, "Contemporary Architecture in Baghdad," 127. For a more recent overview of the modernization of Baghdad in this period, see Nicolai Ouroussoff, "In Search of Baghdad," *Los Angeles Times,* December 14–16, 2003.

18. Constantinos A. Doxiadis, "Dynapolis, The City of the Future," Articles—Papers/2529, Constantinos A. Doxiadis Archives, Athens, Greece.

19. Linear cities were often mentioned in commentaries about Dynapolis; see, e.g., Richard Llewelyn-Davis, "Town Design," *Town Planning Review* (October 1966), [157]-72.

20. In its later versions, Dynapolis would advance in only one direction, but in its first Baghdad version, its planned growth was towards two opposite directions.

21. Doxiadis Associates, "The Master Plan of Baghdad," *Monthly Bulletin* 9 (January 1960): 1–8. Doxiadis Associates inserted every city into a grand schema of a global network of cities that was supposed to establish an equilibrium with the earth's natural environment. For a discussion of Doxiadis's vision of a global urban network, see Panayiota Pyla, "Gray Areas in Green Politics," *Thresholds* 14 (Spring 1997): 48–53 and Panayiota Pyla, "Ecumenopolis, Ecumenokepos, and Doxiadis's Environment-Development Politics," in M. Christine Boyer, Anna Hardman, and Alexandros-Andreas Kyrtsis, eds., *Space and Progress: Constantinos Doxiadis's Ekistics and the Global Context of Post World War II Planning, Architecture, Urbanization and Reconstruction* (Springer, forthcoming).

22. See, for example, "The Master Plan of Baghdad" and "The Housing Program of Iraq" (1959) (Constantinos A. Doxiadis Archives, Athens, Greece), especially the section titled "The Program for Urban Amelioration." For similar views expressed by other planning experts, see Floyd Ratchford and Bleeker Marquette, "Tale of Two Countries: Spain, Iraq," *Journal of Housing* 16 (January 1959): 8–12, 18; and P. W. Macfarlane, "The Plan for Baghdad, the Capital of Iraq," *Housing Review* 5 (November–December 1956): 193–95.

23. "The National Housing Program of Iraq." *Architectoniki* 13 (January–February 1959): 42–46.

24. Constantinos A. Doxiadis, "Architecture, Planning, and Ekistics: Abstract of the Third Part of a Lecture Series Given at the Massachusetts Institute of Technology, Spring 1957," *Ekistics* 7, no. 42 (April 1959): 293–96.

25. Doxiadis's close colleague, Jaqueline Tyrwhitt, pointed to the pitfalls of the New Towns and to the advantages of Doxiadis's reinterpretation of neighborhood units; see Jaqueline Tyrwhitt, "Outline of Background Paper for Expert

Group Meeting on Planning and Development of Satellite and New Towns, 1964," Harvard Loeb Library Documents, Graduate School of Design, Harvard University. For the broader, U.N. debates on the New Towns, see United Nations, *Planning of Metropolitan Areas and New Towns* (New York: United Nations, 1967). For a summary of the criticism that surrounded the British New Towns in the 1950s, see Stanley Buder, *Visionaries and Planners* (New York: Oxford University Press, 1990), 187–89.

26. Doxiadis Associates, "Iraq Housing Program," Doxiadis Associates Pamphlet, no. 5, September 1959.

27. Ibid.

28. The pitfalls of High Modernist urbanism and its technocratic utopianism are insightfully exposed in James C. Scott, *Seeing Like a State* (New Haven, Conn.: Yale University Press, 1998).

29. "Tribal Housing in Iraq," Special to the *New York Times* from Baghdad, Iraq, May 14, 1958; abstracted in *Ekistics* 5, no. 33 (June 1958): 280–82.

30. For an analysis of Fathy's collaboration with Doxiadis in Iraq and elsewhere, see Panayiota Pyla, "Hassan Fathy Revisited: Postwar Discourses on Science Development, and Vernacular Architecture," *Journal of Architectural Education* 60:3 (February 2007): 23–29.

31. Ibid. For other examples of the positive reception to Doxiadis's Baghdad project, see B. S. Saini, "Housing in the Hot and Arid Tropics," *Design* 5 (August 1961): 18–24; and Ezra Ehrenhrantz and Ogden Tanner, "The Remarkable Dr. Doxiadis," *Architectural Forum* 114, no. 5 (May 1961): 112–16.

32. "Tribal Housing in Iraq," 280.

33. See, e.g., Hassan Fathy, Aris Deimezis, Nikos Kyriou, and A. Marinos, "Thermal Comfort," April 15, 1958, 1–2, document R-GA 108, Doxiadis Associates (Fathy Archives), Athens; and Doxiadis Associates, "A Regional Development Program for Greater Mussayib, Iraq, 1958," *Ekistics* 6, no. 36 (October 1958): 149–86.

34. Gulick, "Baghdad," 252.

35. Fethi, "Contemporary Architecture in Baghdad," 117.

36. In the 1960s, local firms took a huge volume of work, and after the creation of the first School of Architecture in Iraq, in 1959, the number of local professionals grew dramatically.

37. A summary of the buildings that were completed appears in Doxiadis Associates, "Progress of the Housing Program," *Monthly Report* 46, prepared for the Government of the Republic of Iraq (Athens, May 1959). Also see Gulick, "Baghdad," 253.

38. Under Saddam Hussein, this area became infamous for the poverty and misery of the mostly Shia inhabitants, but it would be unfair to blame that on

Doxiadis Associates' plans and not on the regime's own negligence toward its citizens.

39. For Wright's proposals for Baghdad, see Siry, "Wright's Baghdad Opera House and Gammage Auditorium"; and Neil Levine, *The Architecture of Frank Lloyd Wright* (Princeton, N.J.: Princeton University Press, 1996). For a reflection on Saddam Hussein's interventions in the 1980s, see William Brantley, "The Search for Baghdad," *Urban Land* 63 (2004): 49–55.

5 Democracy, Development, and the Americanization of Turkish Architectural Culture in the 1950s

SIBEL BOZDOĞAN

With the landslide election victory of the Democrat Party (DP) on May 14, 1950, Turkey's early republican period came to a decisive end. Abandoning the secular authoritarianism, statist economic policies, and nationalist isolationism of the Republican Peoples' Party during the previous two decades, the DP regime promoted populist democracy, private enterprise, and a more ambitious regional role for Turkey in the post–World War II international order. Sending 15,000 troops to the Korean War (and suffering a total of 3,514 casualties) was a price the new regime was willing to pay in order to join the American-led Western alliance in a sharply divided Cold War world. The foundational, Western-oriented cultural politics of the nation (as established by the national hero Kemal Ataturk in the 1930s) continued into this new period, but the meaning of "Western" shifted considerably, from "European" to "American." Two major American exports, namely, "modernization theory" in the social sciences and the "international style" in architecture, began to shape perceptions of democracy, modernity, and the "good life" in Turkey. At the same time, after two decades of relative insignificance in the shadow of the new capital of Ankara, the old imperial capital of Istanbul enjoyed a spectacular revival under the new DP regime and became the showcase for massive urban modernization projects.

These shifts in Turkish culture and politics were far from smooth, nor did they occur without resistance. The traditional republican elites (the military, the bureaucracy, and the Kemalist intelligentsia) resented the new economic policies of the DP government, which depended on agricultural exports and foreign aid and replaced the earlier ideals of national self-sufficiency and industrialization through the agency of the state. Nor were the ambitions of the DP entirely free of ambiguities. The DP slogan, of turning Turkey into "a little America," was accompanied by an equally strong ambition to turn Turkey into an important regional power in the Eastern Mediterranean, with strong ties to other Muslim countries of the Middle East. In fact, Turkey's textbook case of internationalization and modernization was accompanied, in the official discourse of the time, by a seemingly contradictory renewal of nationalist and religious themes. The homogenization of Turkish society (through the departure of ethnic minorities) accelerated under the DP regime, and many of the early republican restrictions on religious expression were lifted, in what amounted to a populist reclamation of the Islamic/Ottoman heritage of the nation. Such relaxation of the radical secularism of the early republic, although gaining conservative, popular support for the DP, antagonized the republican elites, who saw themselves as the guardians of Kemalist reforms against Islamic reactionaries—a conflict which, to this day, has proven to be endemic to Turkish society and politics.[1]

In this essay, I offer a broad overview of how Turkish architectural culture positioned itself, in the 1950s, between international architectural currents and the specific circumstances of national modernization in Turkey—of how the imported high-modernism of the post–World War II period acquired specific meanings within the political context of Turkey under the DP government. I suggest that rather than being the passive recipients of an imported aesthetic, Turkish architects became active participants in the localization and naturalization of an "international style," transforming both their professional culture and local building practices as a result.

NATIONAL MODERNIZATION AND INTERNATIONAL STYLE

To understand the internationalization (read Americanization) of Turkish architectural culture in the 1950s, it is important to begin with the concept of modernization as it was articulated by American social scientists and "area studies" experts. In Daniel Lerner's classic study titled *The Passing of Traditional Society: Modernizing the Middle East* (1962), and in other similar books (such as Bernard Lewis's *The Emergence of Modern Turkey* [1961]), Turkey was heralded as one of the most successful models of a universally defined process of modernization better known as "modernization theory." Central to modernization theory was a basic dichotomy between modernity and tradition, in which the former was presented as an unambiguous blessing and the latter as an obstacle to its realization. It was postulated that as societies became more "modern"—through increased literacy, increased mobility, a new spirit of enterprise, the use of communication technologies, urbanization, and other such indicators—their traditional traits and cultural practices such as fatalism, religion, and a lack of curiosity about the world would give way to new patterns of thought and behavior that would be largely derived from the institutions and values of American society. That these predictions proved to be mistaken—that, for example, increased mobility and urbanization resulted in a strengthening rather than slackening of religious practices in Turkey, did not change the fact that America was perceived as the ideal democratic society by the followers of DP, including religious and traditional Turks who admired the freedom of religious expression in America as an alternative to the much-resented radical secularism of the Kemalist revolution.[2]

The extensive fieldwork and empirical research methods employed by the proponents of "modernization theory" were particularly effective in lending a scientific aura to what Frederic Jameson sees as a euphemism for the penetration of capitalism.[3] In Daniel Lerner's book, for example, based on his studies in Balgat, a Turkish village near Ankara, and conducted between 1950 and 1954, the transition from traditional to modern society is equated with consumerism and entrepreneurship: it required individuals who were no longer content with older values of self-sufficiency. The ability to imagine oneself as someone else or as being somewhere else, especially in America, was a major criterion distinguishing the "moderns" from the "traditionals"—something that Daniel Lerner tabulated in the form of an "empathy index." Lerner wrote: "Empathy endows a person with the capacity to imagine himself as the proprietor of a bigger grocery store in the city, to wear nice clothes and live in a nice house, to be interested in what is going on in the world and to get out of his hole."[4] Furthermore, the more traditional societies changed along these lines, the happier and more in control of their destinies they were supposed to feel—a relationship that Lerner expressed in his so-called "dysphoria index."

Whatever our qualms about quantifying happiness, or about modernization theory in general, Turkey's future seemed bright in 1950. Owing to that country's strategic importance for the American policy of containing Communism and Soviet expansion during the Cold War, Turkey was included in the Marshall Plan of 1947 and admitted to NATO in 1952. American governmental and private agencies channeled generous packages of development aid and technical assistance to Turkey so as to modernize its agricultural and industrial production and its transportation network. This does not mean that Americanization and "modernization theory" were accepted wholesale across the political spectrum. The oppositional theories of "dependency," "American imperialism," and "arrested development" that would inform the ill-fated Turkish Left for the next two decades were all rooted in these socioeconomic shifts of the 1950s. For example, Niyazi Berkes, a prominent intellectual and a leading critic of the inequalities of the capitalist world system, argued that the real objective of American aid through the Marshall Plan was not to help Turkey develop its own economy in a planned fashion; rather, it was to help with the reconstruction of Europe, by subordinating the Turkish economy to Europe's, as a supplier of agricultural products and raw materials, and by eliminating all the Kemalist obstacles to foreign capital and private enterprise.[5]

Nevertheless, the fact that in the first few years of its rule the DP was able to deliver a brief "economic miracle" (largely due to the specific conditions of the Korean War, a boom in agricultural exports, and favorable foreign-exchange rates) offered ample grounds for optimism in the early 1950s. That Turkey was admitted to the "Western club" for geopolitical reasons, rather than as a result of any real acceptance of the need for cultural integration was not an issue for either side in the 1950s.[6] For a brief euphoric period, identity and difference were rendered irrelevant by geopolitics, and architects were ready to celebrate this. Although the centrality of the nation-state as the primary agent of modernization remained unchallenged, Turkish architects now abandoned the search for a "Turkish national style" and dropped their earlier misgivings about the term "international style." With a new sense of belonging to an international community of modern nations, they embraced the new supranational aesthetic of bureaucratic and technocratic efficiency (as best symbolized by the recently completed U.N. Building in New York), which eschewed any cultural references to any particular nation and sought to evoke a happier, democratic, and hopefully wealthier future for all.

The canonic Istanbul Hilton Hotel (1952–55), designed by Skidmore, Owings and Merrill (SOM) with Sedad Hakki Eldem as the local collaborating architect, is the indisputable marker of this major ideological and aesthetic shift in Turkish architectural culture, as well as the textbook case of modern architecture's role in Cold War politics (see fig. 5.1). A prime location overlooking the Bosporus was allocated to the Hilton project by the Turkish government, and the construction was publicly financed by the Turkish Pension Funds (Emekli Sandığı). Additional funds came from the Economic Cooperation Administration (ECA) of the U.S. government, which saw the project, whose location bordered the Soviet Union, as a political and strate-

FIG. 5.1. *Model of the Istanbul Hilton Hotel. Skidmore, Owings and Merrill, with Seddad Hakki Eldem, 1952–55. From* Arkitekt, *no. 3–4 (1952): 59.*

gic investment. As Annabel Wharton and others have observed, to enter the Istanbul Hilton was to gain admission to "a little America," the paradigm of benevolent and democratic capitalist society that the DP regime embraced as its model.[7] In terms of its political, economic, and social implications, the Hilton project generated significant national debate and even opposition at the time. Yet few would disagree with the fact that its design and construction opened up a new direction and a period of experimentation in modern Turkish architecture, releasing it from the ideological charge of national expression and from the earlier obsession with "Turkishness."

Using the Istanbul Hilton's catalytic role in the transformation of modern Turkish architecture as a starting point, the first general observation I want to make in this essay is that the feelings of "optimism" and "imagination" that are central to modernization theory deserve more attention than they typically receive in critical histories of modern architecture—especially as they provide a countervailing weight for the term "anxiety" that Sarah Goldhagen and Rejean Legault have employed to characterize post–World War II modernism.[8] It is only when one looks beyond the West and toward the decolonizing and modernizing nation-states of the Middle East, Asia, and Latin

America that one can clearly see this brief moment of optimism attached to the aesthetic and ideological precepts of international style, and precisely at the same time that these ideas were beginning to be questioned in Europe and the United States.

The optimism and democratic connotations of an imported modernization theory were not the only factors favorable to the internationalization of Turkish architectural culture in the 1950s. Equally important was the fact that the Turkish state had largely succeeded in homogenizing the society and creating a national bourgeoisie, thereby removing a major motivation for the search for a distinctly "Turkish" national style. With the departure of Greek, Armenian, Levantine, and other minorities,[9] the mass migration of Turkish peasants into major cities, and the resulting ethnic homogenization of the population, the Turkishness of the nation was no longer contested: it could now be taken for granted. Hence, expressing Turkishness through architecture was no longer an urgent need: it was superseded by the desire to adopt the supranational language of modernism and technological progress as visual testimonies to the success of Turkish national modernization in the international arena. Most Turkish architects were still committed nationalists, despite the aesthetic shifts in their work, but nationalism was no longer a matter of style to be derived from historical or vernacular precedents. Rather, it was a matter of national pride in the internationalization and increased competence of the profession—in the increasing domination in construction projects by Turkish, rather than foreign, architects.[10]

The most prominent of these architects was Sedad Hakki Eldem, the powerful leader of the "national architecture movement" of the 1930s and 40s, who surprised everyone by "going international" in the 1950s.[11] I would argue that the now-famous collaboration between SOM's Gordon Bunshaft and Sedad Eldem, during the design and construction of the Hilton Hotel, actually made a bigger impression on the latter than he would ever admit. Although in later, revisionist accounts of his own career, Eldem has denounced the international style of the 1950s, he produced some of his most interesting work during this brief period—work that has often been left out of the more canonical accounts of his career, which prefer to focus on his lifelong search for a national style along the lines of the traditional Turkish house.

In Eldem's partially built scheme for a motel and beach facilities in Florya, Istanbul (1956–59), for example, he unapologetically displays the international influences of the post-Hilton years. His use of a reinforced concrete structure with thin, pre-cast concrete slabs, wide cantilevers, and an overall feeling of lightness, especially in the perspective renderings of the beach facilities, has prompted historians to detect the influence of Richard Neutra, among others.[12] This is a plausible assumption, given the popularity of Neutra's work among Turkish architects and students in the 1950s.[13] A better-known and better-preserved testimony to the "internationalist" phase of Eldem's career is the villa for Rıza Derviş on Büyükada (largest of the Prince Islands) in Istanbul, built in 1956–57. The open plan of the villa that allows for a merging of interior and exterior on the garden level, the light, reinforced concrete structure with its wide cantilevering terrace projecting above the ground floor, and the absence of the traditional pitched roof collectively mark the most conspicuous departure in Eldem's residential work from his signature "Turkish house type." At the same time, the interior still suggests continuity with Eldem's earlier ideas on the compatibility of traditional Turkish *wohnkultur* with modernism: the fireplace as the modern hearth, built-in components, light furniture, and, most conspicuously, the stylized, abstract tile patterns that Eldem designed for the Hilton Hotel and used repeatedly thereafter.

The same post-Hilton tendencies can be observed in the 1950s work of Emin Onat, the other leading proponent of the "national architecture movement," along with Sedad Eldem and Paul Bonatz—the three of them having collaborated in a number of nationalist state monuments of the 1940s. Onat's shift from his Germanic architectural culture of the previous decade to an American/Internationalist one coincided with his brief, and ultimately disastrous, political career as a DP deputy after 1954. Eldem and Onat set the paradigm for the early republican architect whose professional identity was intimately tied to the ideology of the nation-state. Like them, almost all practicing architects of the 1930s and 1940s were either educators working within the architectural and engineering schools, or salaried government employees working within the planning and technical units of various government ministries: railway stations were designed by the Ministry of Transportation; schools by the Ministry of Education, and so on (which also accounts for a certain degree of aesthetic uniformity in these buildings). Given their strong ties to the state, it is not surprising that Eldem and Onat were quick to align themselves with the new regime after 1950, and to offer their services for its new architectural and urban initiatives.

It was, however, the advent of an entirely new, younger generation of architects whose careers coincided with the new commitment to international style that brought a significant organizational transformation of professional practice. Although the practice of providing major public architectural and planning services within the state bureaucracy continued during the DP government, the emergence of private clients, especially for residential and commercial buildings, coupled with the broader emphasis on the role of the private sector in Turkey's new development strategies, facilitated the emergence of what architectural historians consider to be the first truly "private" architectural firms and the first major "partnership" models.[14] Some of the most prominent architectural practices/partnerships of modern Turkish architecture emerged in this period, such as the partnership of Haluk Baysal and Melih Birsel, which has produced residential designs of very high quality reflecting the international trends of the 1950s. In 1954 the Turkish Chamber of Architects was established (with 720 members) as a licensing and regulating body, affirming the profession's autonomy and independence from the state. These structural changes in practice constitute an important backdrop to the aesthetic transformation of modernism in the 1950s.

CORPORATE AMERICAN STYLE MEETS "MEDITERRANEAN MODERN"

The primary role of America in the internationalization of the profession in Turkey in the 1950s is amply documented. In his recently published semi-autobiographical work, *Architectural Anthology of the 1950s Generation*, Enis Kortan remembers how his fascination with the "American modern" was triggered by a special 1953 issue of *L'Architecture d'aujour d'hui*, on "American Architecture," a copy of which he kept with him at all times.[15] This fascination, Kortan writes, especially his "mesmerizing encounter with Mies Van der Rohe's Fransworth House," was an important factor in luring him and a number of his friends to America, to see these modern marvels and seek work in the offices of SOM, Marcel Breuer, Saarinen and Yamasaki, among others. News items and announcements in the professional journal *Arkitekt* also reveal that in the 1950s summer training programs and various exchanges were offered to Turkish architects and engineers by the U.S. government through Fulbright grants. Furthermore, these exchanges were not one-sided: in 1956 the Americanization of Turkish architectural culture became even more official with the establishment of a new school of architecture in Ankara, as one of the first components of the Middle East Technical University. The University of Pennsylvania was among the founders of the school, and its committee, headed by G. Holmes Perkins, played a major role in mediating between the Turkish and U.S. governments.[16] The school's curriculum and orientation were conspicuously "American," breaking away from the earlier influence of Germans on architectural education in Turkey.

Yet to characterize the emerging aesthetic tendencies of the post-Hilton years as exclusively "American" would be to overlook the plurality of "international style" in the 1950s. Indeed, even the Istanbul Hilton did not represent the paradigmatic "American corporate modern" of SOM, as exemplified by their canonic Lever House in New York. Rather, the hotel was drawn from the work of Le Corbusier, with its use of a reinforced concrete frame, horizontally proportioned block, *pilotis,* and a roof terrace. The precedent for this signature "Hilton style," or the "tropicalization of modernism," was the Caribe Hilton, in San Juan, Puerto Rico. That hotel, completed in 1949, was designed by Torro, Ferrer and Torregrosa, and it appeared in *Arkitekt* two years before the Istanbul Hilton did. Overall, the architectural production of the 1950s in Turkey displays varying degrees of influence between the two basic architectural "types" prevailing in the architectural culture at large: the two-sided, egg-crate block displaying the grid of the reinforced concrete frame, after "the Hilton style"; or the glass-curtain wall "draped" in front of the structural frame, after the American office tower epitomized by the Lever House.

Given the limitations of technical expertise within the Turkish building industry, it is not surprising that high-rise towers clad in glass-curtain walls remained a formidable technological challenge in Turkey until much later—with the single proud exception, perhaps, of Ankara's so-called "Skyscraper" (Gökdelen), designed by Enver Tokay and built between 1959 and 1964. Indisputably, the more common paradigm was the Hilton's horizontally placed slab-block, raised on *pilotis* and expressing the logic of the reinforced concrete frame on its façade grid—a formula that was repeated in numerous hotels, apartments, and office buildings of the time. There were also a number of important in-between works, which used the glass-curtain wall in conjunction with the basic two-sided prismatic block lifted on *pilotis* and topped with the characteristic Corbusean roof. The Anadolu Club Building on Büyükada (Prince Island) in Istanbul, the winner of a major national competition in 1959, is the most notable and refined example of this hybrid idea. Designed by the uncompromising and very important Turkish modernist architect, Abdurrahman Hanci, in collaboration with Turgut Cansever (who would later abandon international-style modernism for regionalist expressions and Islamist philosophies), the Anadolu Club consists of a three-story main block raised upon a transparent ground level and topped at the roof level with a conspicuously Corbusean "parasol" (see fig. 5.2).

One particularly characteristic detail of the 1950s aesthetic was the use of perforated bricks or pre-cast concrete grills for the circulation shafts or exterior corridors, which worked both as sunscreens and decorative façade elements. In the post–World War II years, these characteristic devices for

FIG. 5.2. *Anadolu Club, Büyükada, Istanbul (1951–57)*, by Abdurrahman Hanci and Turgut Cansever. From Arkitekt, no. 295 (1959): 50.

"aestheticized light and climate control" were distinct features of a prolific, "tropicalized" or "Mediterraneanized" modernism, from the Caribbean to the Middle East and beyond. Examples of this style, in the work of Ed Stone and Joseph Stein in India, or Walter Gropius and Josep Lluis Sert in Baghdad, were particularly appealing to Turkish architects, especially in the context of Turkey's stated ambitions to be a regional power in the Eastern Mediterranean. Many Turkish architects acknowledge these international influences in their published writings and interviews, whereas references to the more "orientalist," or culturally tinted, styles of Islamic architecture, such as the traditional wooden grill, or *mashrabiyya*, are far less common. This is an important point in differentiating the "localization" efforts of the 1950s from the discourses of identity and cultural difference that emerged much later. In the 1950s, the terms "culture" and "locality" largely signified climate, terrain, and geography.

Even when orientalist evocations were to a certain extent inevitable, as in the case of hotels, the inspiration for the use of curves and non-orthogonal forms (such as shells, domes, vaults, and spirals, which in the 1950s were frequently used in conjunction with the geometric grid of the façades) was derived more from international references than oriental ones. Hilton Hotel is again the paradigmatic example. Orientalizing interpretations dominate most accounts of Hilton's auxiliary structures, designed by Sedad Hakki Eldem (see figs. 5.3, 5.4): the roof of the pool restaurant is associated with the domes of Ottoman mosques; the curving entrance canopy is nicknamed "the flying carpet," and many commentators make a point of highlighting their visual contrast with the geometry of the reinforced concrete frame. These allusions to the "sensuous curves" of the Orient (in both the popular media and the architects' own statements at the time) are undoubtedly useful for attracting tourism, but they also obscure the fact that architects

FIG. 5.3. *Istanbul Hilton Hotel pool restaurant. Sedad Hakki Eldem.*

FIG. 5.4. *Entrance canopy of Istanbul Hilton Hotel. From* Architectural Forum, *December 1953.*

looked at such shell structures and parabolic vaults primarily as the latest and most progressive technological innovations of international modernism. In most cases, their sources of inspiration were more Niemeyer and Nervi than mosques and flying carpets. For example, Eldem's pool restaurant for the Hilton is much less evocative of Istanbul's domes than it is of a very similar restaurant at the "La Concha" Hotel (literally, the "Seashell" Hotel) in San Juan, Puerto Rico, designed, once again, by Torro, Ferrer and Torregrosa. This form was simply a recurring element built into the vocabulary of international hotel design in the 1950s.

Other building types with comparable programmatic requirements (such as offices and apartment blocks) also adopted this distinctive aesthetic trope of the 1950s, juxtaposing the geometric grid of the main block (with identical cells for offices or apartment units) with a singular and more sculptural shell structure to cover restaurants, assembly halls, or other non-repetitive components of the program. In one of the most significant competitions of the post-Hilton years, Nevzat Erol's winning design for the Istanbul City Hall (1953) employed this same formula (see fig. 5.5). A parabolic cross-vault marked the roof of the assembly hall in front of the main block, and another, single parabolic shell and a thin, curving slab covered the roof restaurant. Another innovative use of a parabolic vault is Vedat Dalokay's unbuilt competition project for the Kocatepe Mosque in Ankara (1957), which reinterprets the classical Ottoman mosque with an innovative thin-shell concrete structure touching the ground on four supports. This important project testifies to the fact that, in the 1950s, rather than trying to orientalize new buildings by making allusions to mosques, Turkish architects sought to modernize them, even for the case of a traditional "oriental" building type like the mosque.

Whether it is the aesthetic of the reinforced concrete frame or the more sculptural form of the shell or vault accompanying it, the most significant buildings of the 1950s in Turkey were conceived as "modern monuments" to adorn Istanbul—singular objects that made a statement about the new DP regime's commitment to modernize and beautify the city. What is often overlooked in any discussion of Istanbul's "international-style" buildings is that their connotations of newness, optimism, and modernity were further accentuated by their particular location and its relationship to its surroundings. Under the personal direction of the Turkish prime minister, Adnan Menderes, the DP regime made the modernization of Istanbul one of its most publicized political priorities. In what many historians have called a "populist public relations campaign," large avenues were cut through the city fabric and entire areas were cleared around Ottoman monuments to highlight the historical and tourism potential of the city.[17] At the same time, the "modern monuments" of international style were placed as new and highly visible landmarks—for example, on a hilltop within a public park (the Hilton Hotel), at a busy intersection (City Hall), or along a new coastal road connecting the city to the airport (the Çınar Hotel). Their "international" architectural styles notwithstanding, most were strategically situated "Istanbul buildings," acquiring their meaning from the city itself—something that has been overlooked by later condemnations of "international style" as a generic, placeless architecture that disregards context.

DEMOCRATIZING MODERNISM: HOUSE AS SHELTER OR LUXURY?

It was, however, the translation of the multistory, slab-block type from such singular modern monuments to the realm of urban housing that gave the architecture of the 1950s its distinct visual character. Whereas in the early republic the paradigm of the modern house was the single-family villa within a garden, after 1950 Turkey's rapid urbanization and the concomitant housing shortage led to the emergence of designs for apartment blocks that adapted the same international aesthetic of the reinforced concrete frame. The paradigmatic Ataköy Cooperative Development, in Istanbul, built along the coastal road to the airport, was one of the first experiments undertaken utilizing long-term credits from the newly established Emlak Bank. Consisting of different types of medium- and high-rise apartment blocks spaciously arranged in a park according to a site plan by the Italian architect Luigi Piccinato, the Ataköy experiment symbolized the new standards of modern living. Designed by various Turkish architects, the Ataköy apartments are to this day quite successful architecturally as examples of reinforced concrete, high-rise blocks with aestheticized climate-control devices, roof terraces, and spacious units (see fig. 5.6). Nonetheless, as many commentators have observed, they have fallen short in responding to the housing needs of the urban poor, catering instead to the wealthier, upper-middle classes.

The Ataköy case illustrates what appears to be the defining paradox of Turkish architectural culture in the 1950s: namely, the conflict between a socially concerned interest in housing as the central question of modern democracies, and an aesthetic preoccupation with the idea of the dwelling as a designed product to house modern lifestyles. If we return to the Hilton Hotel for a moment, we can read the same paradox into its famous "honeycomb façade," as *Architectural Forum* called it in 1953. On one hand, the stacking of identical units (whether hotel rooms, offices, or apartments) was evocative of a democratic efficiency—that is to say, everyone gets the same

FIG. 5.5. *Istanbul City Hall. Nevzat Erol, 1953.*

cell. On the other, the interior of the hotel room signified American notions of modern comfort, consumption, and living the "good life" through technological amenities: air conditioning, private baths, hot water, wall-to-wall carpeting, and a radio cabinet in every room. This paradoxical and distinctly American ideal of democratizing comfort and luxury permeated the entire discourse on "the modern home" in the 1950s. In the pages of *Arkitekt*, "Existenzminimum" and the "Neue Sachlichkeit" were out; large kitchens with electric appliances, dishwashers, refrigerators, and a family-dining corner were in. Architectural and popular magazines of the time are full of articles on American homes, many of them translated from American journals through the agency of the U.S. Information Services in Istanbul.[18] The role of USIS in translating American foreign policy and strategic goals into cultural propaganda, and the complicity of *Arkitekt* in this process, is an important topic, but one beyond the scope of this essay.[19]

At the same time, in the discourse of modernization and development, also introduced to Turkey by American social scientists, experts, and planners, the house was seen not so much as a consumer object that could provide the good life, but rather as a basic need—as shelter. Charles Abrams, the prominent planner and housing expert who later published *Man's Struggle for Shelter in an Urbanizing World*,[20] came to Turkey on a research trip in 1951 and later prepared a report for the United Nations on the conditions and problems of housing and urbanization in Turkey. That same year, another report on housing, planning, and building construction was prepared for the Turkish government by an SOM team led by the same Gordon Bunshaft who would design the Hilton Hotel the following year.[21] Throughout the 1950s, the need for urban housing, especially in response to the massive migration to the cities from the countryside, remained a monumental social, economic, and political challenge for the DP government. Just to cite some figures: Turkey's urban population, which grew by 20.1 percent in the decade 1940–50, reached a growth rate of 80.2 percent between 1950 and 1960.[22]

Although ultimately ineffective against the magnitude of the housing problem, the care that at least some architects put into reconciling the conflicting demands of housing large numbers of people, while at the same time creating a sense of aesthetic refinement and conceptual experimentation, was unmatched for a long time afterward. Particularly noteworthy is the work of Haluk Baysal and Melih Birsel, which, as Ela Kacel analyzes in detail, was able to transform international modernism into a non-canonic, "ordinary" residential architecture that is today hardly discernable from the surrounding urban fabric.[23] In their most characteristic work, Baysal and Birsel have taken the basic multistory slab block and have experimented with its sections to create duplex units stacked within the main grid of the reinforced concrete frame—not unlike Le Corbusier's conception of the Unité d'Habitation. Furthermore, they have elaborated this idea into a flexible schema that can accommodate considerable typological variation in different projects. For example, in the apartment block for the Lawyers' Cooperative, in Mecidiyeköy, Istanbul (1960–61), instead of the usual two-sided, freestanding matchbox, they have stacked twelve stories of duplex units within an L-shaped arrangement (one wing perpendicular to the street and the other parallel to it), thereby giving expression to the corner condition on the exterior of the building (see fig. 5.7). In a later project, in Yeşilköy, a suburb of Istanbul, the same idea of manipulating the section to create duplex units was repeated, this time by transforming the corridor into an open-to-the-sky, two-level interior street, resulting in one of the most interesting, but understudied housing schemes of modern Turkish architecture (see figs. 5.8, 5.9).

Collectively, the more refined examples of 1950s apartment blocks illustrate that once the basic "type" was established (i.e., the prismatic, two-sided slab block, often raised on *pilotis*), the aesthetization of modernism was largely a matter of façade design. In contrast to the characteristically early republican preoccupation with volumetric compositions, architects in the 1950s engaged in a "surfacing of modernism"—a treating of the façade as a form of "modern decoration" expressing the programmatic and structural properties of the building.[24] On this topic, an article by Frederick Gibberd,

FIG. 5.6. *Ataköy Cooperative Housing development, Istanbul.*

FIG. 5.7. *Apartment block for Lawyers' Cooperative in Mecidiyeköy, Istanbul. Haluk Baysal and Melih Birsel, 1960–61.*

FIG. 5.8. *Low-rise, high-density housing in Yeşilköy. Haluk Baysal and Melih Birsel.*

FIG. 5.9. *Concrete grid with infill in the Yeşilköy apartment block. Haluk Baysal and Melih Birsel.*

titled "Expression in Modern Architecture" (Modern Mimaride Ifade) was reprinted in *Arkitekt* in 1953 (translated from *Architects' Journal*). As the Turkish historian Ali Cegizkan compellingly illustrates in his book, the article was received with great interest in the Turkish architectural scene.[25] Not only in hotels and office buildings, but also in the newly emerging typology of urban apartment buildings for the middle class, the reinforced concrete frame was used as a grid to be filled in with a geometric composition of glazed areas, brick or plastered infill walls, wooden or concrete grills, and/or cantilevering balconies (see fig. 5.10). Contrary to Sedad Hakki Eldem's subsequent dismissal of the period, as producing "buildings that looked like boxes, drawers or radios,"[26] this "surfacing of modernism," or the celebration of the reinforced concrete frame, has produced considerable aesthetic quality and variety.

CONCLUSION

As many critics have pointed out,[27] modernization theory was the work of American social scientists and "area studies" experts, who offered an academic foundation to the expansion of American political, military, and economic interests throughout the world in the aftermath of World War II. Yet the positive psychological effect of this theory on the emerging nations of the postcolonial world was enormous, giving them grounds to hope that although historical and cultural differences separated them from the experiences of the industrialized West, they too could "make it" one day, by following this linear, predictable, and "scientific" model of development. Whereas the older colonialist/orientalist constructs that were based on essentialist cultural categories suggested a built-in inferiority, modernization theory defined a universal process that applied to all societies. For architects, modernization theory played a progressive role in replacing nationalist obsessions with identity with a focus on the real and trans-national problems of modernization—like development, urbanism, housing, construction, and infrastructure.

Before the end of the decade of the 1950s, however, modernization theory was proving incapable of delivering on its promise—something even Daniel Lerner would admit.[28] Societies were indeed changing, but they were turning out to be "modern" in their own ways and not always in accordance with the predictions of modernization theory. The realization that Turkey would not be "a little America" was hard enough; harder still was the realization that the international modern aesthetic that architects were beginning to internalize and localize was rapidly turning into something else, as a

FIG. 5.10. *Facade detail of apartment block in Ankara. Nejat Ersin, 1956–60. Photograph courtesy of Ali Cengizkan.*

FIG. 5.11. *Example of the "modern vernacular."*

result of social, political, and economic (i.e., extra-architectural) reasons characteristic of peripheral modernities. The modern slab-block apartment, a symbol of modern comfort and the "good life" when accompanied by good design and landscaping, such as the consideration of appropriate angles of sun and ventilation, was breeding a faceless and congested urbanscape under the pressure of the speculative apartment boom. The Hilton's celebrated façade grid was being endlessly repeated in an anonymous "modern vernacular" of lesser examples constructed with inferior technical and financial means (fig. 5.11). Meanwhile, the DP's massive demolitions and attempts at urban renewal in Istanbul were already running into difficulties of financing and a lack of coordination, and the damage they wrought upon Istanbul's historical urban character was drawing an increasingly harsh and more vocal criticism. Above all, the new squatter belts around the major cities were growing at a rate beyond

FIG. 5.12. *Istanbul Hyatt Regency Hotel.*

all earlier estimates. The country was not able to attract as much foreign investment as expected; corruption and mismanagement of funds were rampant; and, most ominously, the populist policies of the DP regime and the relaxation of the militantly secular foundations of the republic were drawing increasing opposition from the military establishment.

The end of both the DP regime and the faith in international-style modernism came very abruptly, on May 27, 1960, when tanks rolled and the army took control of Turkey, in what would be the first of a series of military coups. This was the first sign that Turkey's transition to "democracy" was going be interrupted and difficult, just as its overall modernization project and the architectural modernism of the 1950s would be. Having risen to grace along with the DP regime, the "international style" now fell from grace with the collapse of that regime, giving way to a new experimentalism—with organic architecture, regionalism, new brutalism, and the other revisionist trends of the 1960s. The loss of faith in modernization theory prepared the ground for discourses of identity and cultural difference to reemerge with a vengeance, which reached its peak in the 1980s. Thereafter, as the role of the nation-state as the primary agent of modernization diminished, and as the transnational forces of globalization began to dramatically transform Turkish culture and society, along with its urban landscape, many architects began turning to historical and vernacular precedents in an iconographic search for identity.

One of the greatest ironies of the history of modern architecture is that "international-style modernism" has flourished during periods of strong identification with the nation-state, while the re-emergence of the discourse of identity and difference has coincided with the more recent era of transnational globalization. I want to conclude with a contemporary image that illustrates these shifts which took place after the 1980s. In figure 5.12, one can see the old Istanbul Hilton in the background, and in the foreground the more recent Hyatt Regency Hotel. In a compelling example of what Stuart Hall calls "the global production of localities,"[29] the Hyatt displays many stylistic references to the traditional "Turkish house." But it has utilized this well-established nationalist iconography to symbolize the slick luxury of a five-star hotel, part of an international chain, and has thus inverted its meaning. I will leave it to the reader to decide which of the two hotels in the photograph is more "international."

NOTES

1. See Reşat Kasaba, "Populism and Democracy in Turkey, 1946–1961," in *Rules and Rights in the Middle East,* ed. Ellis Goldberg, Reşat Kasaba, and Joel Migdal (Seattle: University of Washington Press, 1993), 43–68.

2. For example, the prominent author Peyami Safa in his editorials in the 1950s looked at America as a model of a religious society "where you cannot find one neighborhood without a church"—a critical reference to the absence of mosque construction in Turkey in the early republican period. Safa's essays are collected in a volume entitled *Din, irtica, inkilap* (Religion, reaction, revolution) (Istanbul, 1971).

3. Fredric Jameson, "Notes on Globalization as a Philosophical Issue," in *The Cultures of Globalization,* ed. Fredric Jameson and Masao Miyoshi (Durham, N.C.: Duke University Press, 1998), 54–77.

4. Daniel Lerner, *The Passing of Traditional Society* (New York: Free Press of Glencoe, 1964), 412.

5. For a critique of Americanization and the DP years from within and from the left, see N. Berkes, *Turk dusununde bati sorunu* (Ankara: Bilgi Yayınları, 1975), 146–61; and N. Berkes, *Turkiye'de cagdaslasma* (Ankara: Bilgi Yayınları, 1975).

6. This is in stark contrast with the predicament of Turkey's bid for EU membership today. As a "club" defined in terms of shared cultural and political val-

ues, rather than as a strategic military alliance like NATO, the EU is hesitant, at best, if not outright reluctant, to consider Turkey as part of the "Western club."

7. Annabel Jane Wharton, *Building the Cold War* (Chicago: University of Chicago Press, 2001), 22.

8. Sarah Williams Goldhagen and Réjean Legault, eds. *Anxious Modernisms* (Montreal: Canadian Centre for Architecture; Cambridge, Mass.: MIT Press, 2000). In her paper, "Americanization and Anxiety: Istanbul Hilton Hotel by SOM and Eldem," presented at the 2001 ACSA International Conference in Istanbul, Esra Akcan also discusses the ambiguities of the design of the Istanbul Hilton Hotel in terms of this "anxiety" about standardization, homogenization, and the disappearance of cultural difference.

9. E.g., Istanbul's population changed from 75.3 percent Muslim and 26 percent non-Muslim in 1935, to 90 percent Muslim and only 10 percent non-Muslim in 1960. Most of the non-Muslims left after the imposition of a heavy "wealth tax" exclusively on minorities in the 1940s.

10. See Z. Sayar's editorial in *Arkitekt*, no. 9–12 (1954), on the occasion of the establishment, with 720 members, of the Turkish Chamber of Architects.

11. See Sibel Bozdoğan, S. Ozkan, and E. Yenal, *Sedad Hakki Eldem: Architect in Turkey* (London: Butterworth, 1990).

12. See, e.g., U. Tanyeli, "1950lerden bu Yana Mimari Paradigmalarin Degisimi ve Reel Mimarlik," in *75 yilda değişen kent ve mimarlik*, ed. Y. Sey (Istanbul, 1998), 241.

13. This fact is noted by Enis Kortan in his semi-autobiographical account of 1950s architecture in Turkey, *1950'ler kuşağı mimarlik antolojisi* (Istanbul: Yem Yayinlari, 1997).

14. See U. Tanyeli, "Haluk Baysal, Melih Birsel," *Arredemento Mimarlik* (April 1998): 72–79.

15. Kortan, *1950'ler kuşağı mimarlik antolojisi*, 29.

16. Perkins even prepared the first proposal for the campus plan of METU in Ankara in 1959. This project was not implemented, and the campus was eventually built in the 1960s according to the design of the Turkish architects Altüg and Behruz Çinici; see Arif T. Payaslıoğlu's *Barakadan kampusa, 1954–1964* (Ankara: METU Publications, 1996), which is a history of METU's establishment.

17. For a detailed account of the urban interventions of the DP regime, see Ipek Akpinar, "The Rebuilding of Istanbul after the Plan of Henri Prost, 1937–1960," Ph.D. diss., Barttlet School, London, 2003.

18. See, e.g., "Bir Amerikan mutfaginin tertibati" (The organization of an American kitchen), in *Arkitekt*, no. 7–10 (1950): 158–61, 166.

19. On this topic, I would like to acknowledge Ela Kacel of Cornell Univer-

sity, whose doctoral research on "Intellectualism and Consumerism: Ideologies, Practices, and Criticisms of Postwar Modernism in Turkey and the United States" is ongoing.

20. Charles Abrams, *Men's Struggle for Shelter in an Urbanizing World* (Cambridge, Mass.: MIT Press, 1964).

21. See Skidmore, Owings and Merrill (SOM), "Town Planning and Housing in Turkey," report prepared for the Turkish Ministry of Public Works, December 1951.

22. Y. Sey, "Cumhuriyet döneminde konut," in *75 yilda değişen kent ve mimarlik*, ed. Y. Sey (Istanbul, 1998), 285.

23. Ela Kacel, "Rethinking Ordinary Architecture in Postwar Turkey," paper presented to the Docomomo Conference, New York, September 2004.

24. I have borrowed the phrase "surfacing of modernism" from the special issue of *Perspecta* (no. 32 [2001]), edited by Ann Marie Brennan, Nahum Goodenow, and Brendan D. Moran and entitled "Resurfacing Modernism." I use the term in the same double-sense, as both a preoccupation with façade and to denote the "emergence" of modernism on the cultural agenda.

25. Ali Cengizkan, *Modernin saati* (Ankara, 2002), 219–27. The Frederick Gilberd article was published in *Arkitekt*, nos. 1–4 (1953): 53–61.

26. Sedad Hakki Eldem, "50 yillik cumhuriyet mimarligi," *Akademi*, no. 8 (July 1974): 11.

27. See, e.g., D. C. Tipps, "Modernization Theory and the Comparative Study of Societies: A Critical Perspective," *Comparative Studies in Society and History* 15 (1973): 199–226.

28. Daniel Lerner, "Turkey: From the Past," in *The Turkish Administrator: A Cultural Survey*, ed. Jerry R. Hopper and Richard I. Levin (Ankara: Public Administration Division, US AID, 1968).

29. See Stuart Hall, "The Local and the Global," in *Culture, Globalization, and the World-System*, ed. Anthony D. King (Binghamton: Dept. of Art and Art History, State University of New York at Binghamton, 1991).

6 Temporal States of Architecture

Mass Immigration and Provisional Housing in Israel

ROY KOZLOVSKY

This essay examines the provisional architecture of the *ma'abaras* (transit towns) that were built to temporarily house immigrants who came to Israel during the period of "mass immigration" (1948–51), and were to be dismantled without a trace once the Israeli government settled these immigrants in permanent housing. Official Israeli historiography depicts the creation of the *ma'abaras* as an improvised response to the problems caused by mass immigration. This study problematizes that account, and with it the understanding of temporary architecture. It recovers the history of the *ma'abara* so as to delineate an inherent contradiction of Zionism as first and foremost a modernist project that attempted to create a nation-state by radically altering the course of history, while presuming that this could be done rationally and peacefully, according to a plan. This tension informs the construction of the *ma'abaras* as negative temporal and spatial voids into which the effects of accelerated historical transformation were to be channeled and contained without compromising Zionism's utopian self-image. But along with its material aspects, the *ma'abara* was also a social unit in which the political agency of its inhabitants and their status as autonomous citizens were temporarily suspended. My contention is that these two characteristics of the *ma'abara*—as an instrument of planning and as a mode of governance—are inseparable because the Zionist nation-building project, from its inception, necessitated the momentary disempowerment of its subjects.

ABSORBING MASS IMMIGRATION

Historically, the *ma'abara* was devised in response to the crisis of mass immigration that followed the establishment of Israel in 1948. In just three years, Israel's Jewish population had doubled, from 650,000 to 1.2 million (see fig. 6.1). Initially, the government assembled the immigrants into "immigration camps," where they were documented, medically examined, and then billeted to available housing, which included resettlement in evacuated Palestinian towns and villages. However, in less than a year, all housing options were exhausted, the camps ceased to function as relay centers, and the ever-increasing number of stranded immigrants remained for indefinite periods in the camps' tents and barracks, dependent on soup kitchens for daily subsistence. This failure to provide newcomers with the elementary necessities of shelter, food, employment, education, and health services soon threatened the very legitimacy of the new government. With disillusioned camp inhabitants storming the Knesset on several occasions, the minister of agriculture and development Pinhas Lavon warned that "one day a hundred thousand such people, cooped up in the camps without any other outlet could get together and rise up against us, and cause an explosion that would blow away both the government and the Knesset."[1]

Levi Eshkol, who was in charge of the Jewish Agency's Settlement Department, confronted Prime Minister David Ben Gurion with similar alarm: "In the past three months death stared us in the face. . . . How could we bring Jews and settle them in tents? . . . If only we could repress our inclinations and decide to conduct the immigration according to some plan . . . satisfying both the needs of the immigrants and the needs of the state."[2]

The mass immigration to Israel has been seen as a spontaneous and messianic event, one that reflected the collective aspirations of Jews of the Diaspora to return to their ancestral homeland. But Eshkol's plea demonstrates that mass immigration was in fact the outcome of an explicit and contested policy promoted by Ben Gurion. Two strategic imperatives were behind the promotion of an unrestricted inflow of people, despite the risks and hardships this policy entailed. First, the government was concerned that Eastern European and Arab states would halt the outflow of their Jewish subjects to Israel. Restricting immigration while it was still free (albeit expensive—the Czechoslovakian government extorted a fee for each emigration certificate) would have left some Jewish communities behind, and, in the case of Arab countries, vulnerable to acts of retribution. Second, rapid immigration was strategically used

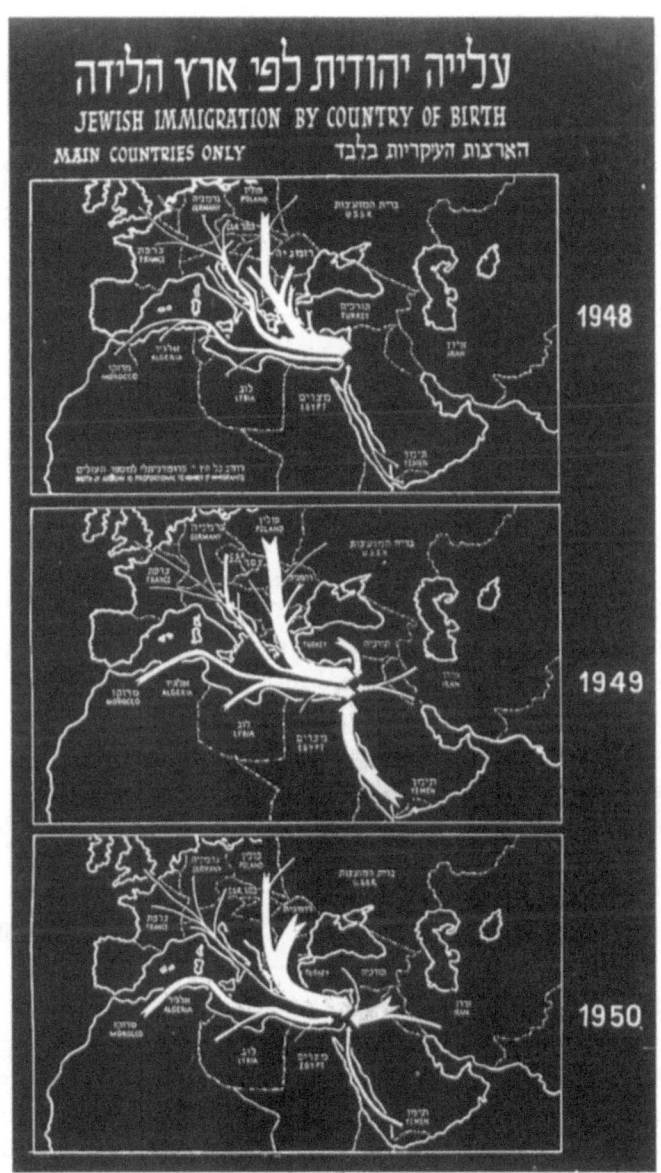

FIG. 6.1. *"Jewish immigration by country of birth,"* 1948, 1949, and 1950. From Statistical Abstract of Israel, no. 2 (Jerusalem: Central Bureau of Statistics, 1950/1951).

by the state to take possession of territories that, prior to the War of Independence (1947–49), were populated by Palestinians. As Ben Gurion stated, "We have conquered territories, but without settlements they have no decisive value.... Settlement—that is the real conquest! The future of the state depends on immigration."[3]

The result of this counter flow of two populations—Jews flowing in to the new state of Israel, and Palestinians being driven out to neighboring Arab states—was the simultaneous emergence of two complementary, but ideologically opposed, landscapes of roughly the same size: the Palestinian refugee camp and the Israeli *ma'abara*.[4] Both were designed to prevent their inhabitants from settling permanently, but they had completely different purposes. In this essay, however, I will analyze only the case of the Israeli *ma'abaras* and the politics of impermanency that applied to them.

The concept of the *ma'abara* was an invention of Levi Eshkol, as a way to replace the "immigrant camp" system. It was a way to maintain the pace of immigration while containing its explosive political impact. Between 1950 and 1951, 129 *ma'abaras* were built, housing one out of every three Israelis. While the emergence of the *ma'abara* appears to have been chaotic and improvisatory, the communities themselves had an orderly, rational appearance. This can be seen in an aerial photograph, captioned "A neighborhood unit in the town of Yokneam, being constructed by the immigrants living in provisional shacks along the road" (see fig. 6.2), which was used in official representations of the *ma'abara*. The photo provides the starting point for my critique of the concept of the *ma'abara*.

In the photo, the *ma'abara* of Yokneam can be seen in the valley below, and on the hilltop above is the New Town of Upper-Yokneam. The photograph implies an easy transition from the temporary to the permanent. The prospective settlers of Upper-Yokneam would be housed for the duration of construction in the temporary settlement below, which in turn would be dismantled once its inhabitants had moved up the hill. This rationale provided a justification for the *ma'abara* as a self-destructing, disposable architecture: the eventual displacement and uprooting it projects is represented as progress, as a necessary stage in the ascension uphill toward the ideal, modern design of the permanent settlement. However, the orderly situation projected by this image was in no way typical. More often than not, the *ma'abara* would be erected without the assuring proximity of the permanent settlement, and the efficient transition between the transitory and the permanent only rarely materialized, causing widespread conflict on the ground. This suppressed reality will be recovered by examining the design

FIG. 6.2. *"A neighborhood unit in the town of Yokneam, being constructed by the immigrants living in provisional shacks along the road."*

and organization of the *ma'abara* along its three distinct scales—the prefabricated shelter unit, the individual settlement, and the nationwide distribution of *ma'abaras*.

THE PREFABRICATED HUT

The Yokneam *ma'abara* was composed of hundreds of single-family tin huts. Other *ma'abara* dwelling units might consist of wooden shacks, aluminum cabins, canvas huts (a wood structure with canvas walls), or tents (see fig. 6.3). These motley structures were imported from Canada, the United States, Finland, Sweden, and even Japan. Because shelter suppliers were paid in foreign currency, these temporary structures were as expensive as permanent dwellings built with local materials and labor. Levi Eshkol's report to the government in October 1951 illuminates why such an economically wasteful policy was nevertheless pursued:

Temporal States of Architecture 143

FIG. 6.3. *Prefabricated huts being assembled at the Ra'anana Absorption Center for New Immigrants, March 15, 1949. Photograph by Eldan David.*

> In order to build 20,000 dwellings this season, we need time, money and materials, so nobody will live in tents. . . . 3,000 huts are nearly completed and in one or two weeks will be populated. An additional 6,000 huts and canvas-huts will be ready by next month, and we have to prepare the foundations and floors before they arrive at the port.[5]

The deployment of prefabricated technologies at such scale and speed was the result of a political dilemma: the government could either adjust the pace of immigration to the capacity of the building industry to construct permanent homes, or it could accelerate immigration beyond that ability and bridge the gap with the rapid deployment of temporary structures. Given these choices, the state employed the prefabricated shelter kit as a way to bypass the temporal limitations imposed by conventional construction methods.

THE PROVISIONAL SETTLEMENT UNIT

Viewed from the air, there are striking affinities between the provisional and the permanent settlements at Yokneam. Both are composed of one or two types of repeatable structures, differentiated only by their layout pattern. The permanent town is comprised of thinly spaced apartment blocks arranged as an ideal community following the neighborhood unit model,[6] whereas the *ma'abara* is composed of single-family huts densely placed in the grid layout of a military camp. These differences in density and geometry were the result of the contrasting concepts of temporality and economy that governed the planning of the two settlements. The plan of the transitory settlement was partly determined by economic efficiency: since water pipes were in short supply at the time, the placement of the units was determined by the most efficient layout for a water-supply system (see fig. 6.4). The excessive density of the settlement was also the result of an intentional strategy that sought to reinforce the transitory status of the *ma'abara* by suppressing the possibility that the inhabitants might settle there, transforming what was intended to be a transitional living arrangement into something more permanent. This strategy becomes apparent when one compares the arrangement of housing in the *ma'abara* with the unrealized plan for emergency housing that was developed by Louis Kahn in 1949.

Kahn had been commissioned by the Jewish Agency, the quasi-governmental organization responsible for immigrant resettlement, to develop plans both for the immediate production of 40,000 housing units and for the mechanization of the Israeli housing industry. He devised an inexpensive method for mass-producing semi-permanent concrete homes. Each prefabricated unit would be placed on an individual lot with enough room for its subsequent enlargement, which allowed the *ma'abara* to gradually develop into a permanent community (see fig. 6.5). This plan was never realized, perhaps because it was conceived only to attract American investors, yet its significance lies in the fact that it provided an alternative settlement model to the *ma'abara*. In contrast to Kahn's plan, the huts in the typical *ma'abara* were densely spaced, with little open space between them, precisely in order to prevent the inhabitants from expanding them into permanent homes. The design of the *ma'abara* was cunning in its resistance to any deviation from its temporary status, a strategy whose purpose can be appreciated by studying the nationwide distribution of the *ma'abaras*.

THE NATIONWIDE SYSTEM OF *MA'ABARAS*

Roughly half of the 129 *ma'abaras* that were built in Israel were sited in the center of the country, adjacent to already established towns and cities, where their residents could benefit from existing services and employment opportunities. The other half were scattered across the landscape according to a

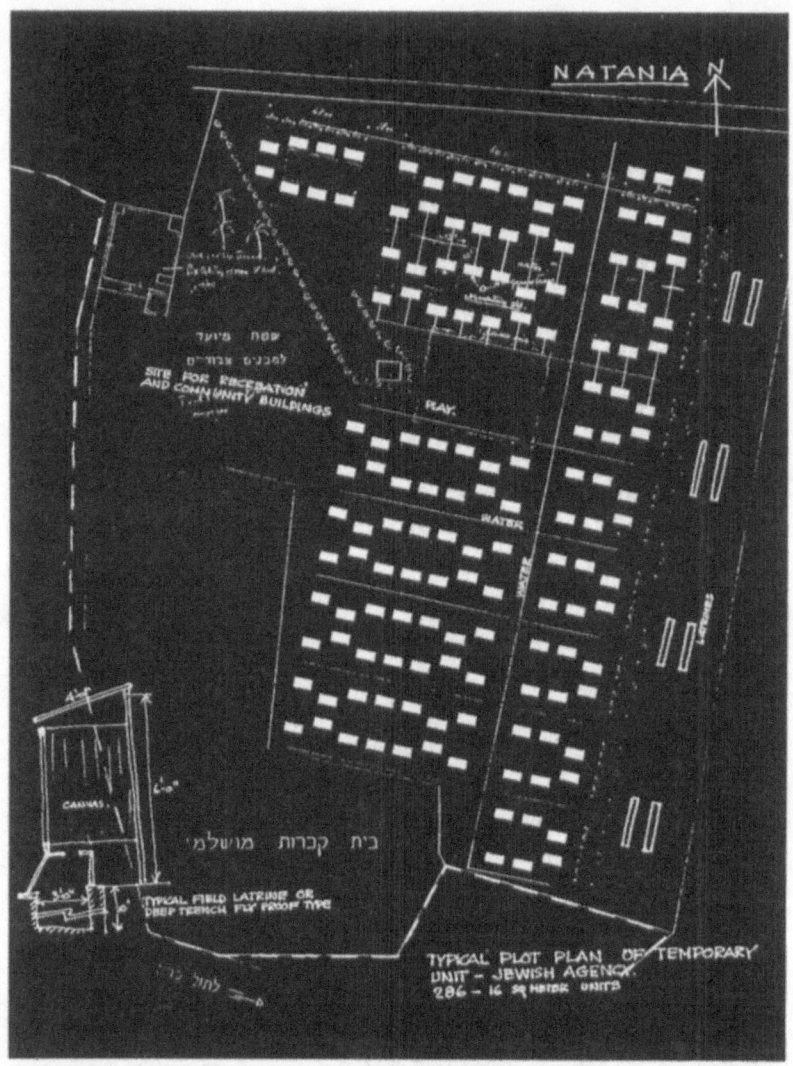

FIG. 6.4. *Typical plan of a* ma'abara, *with water-system layout.*

national plan. Yokneam, for example, was located in an undeveloped region, but its location in an isolated area was of strategic importance: it was built along a critical road that connected the center of the country with its northern provinces. Thus, the system of transit camps, devised to absorb the demographic shock of mass immigration until permanent settlements could be prepared, was at the same time instrumental for determining the future layout of the country according to a preconceived plan. This plan

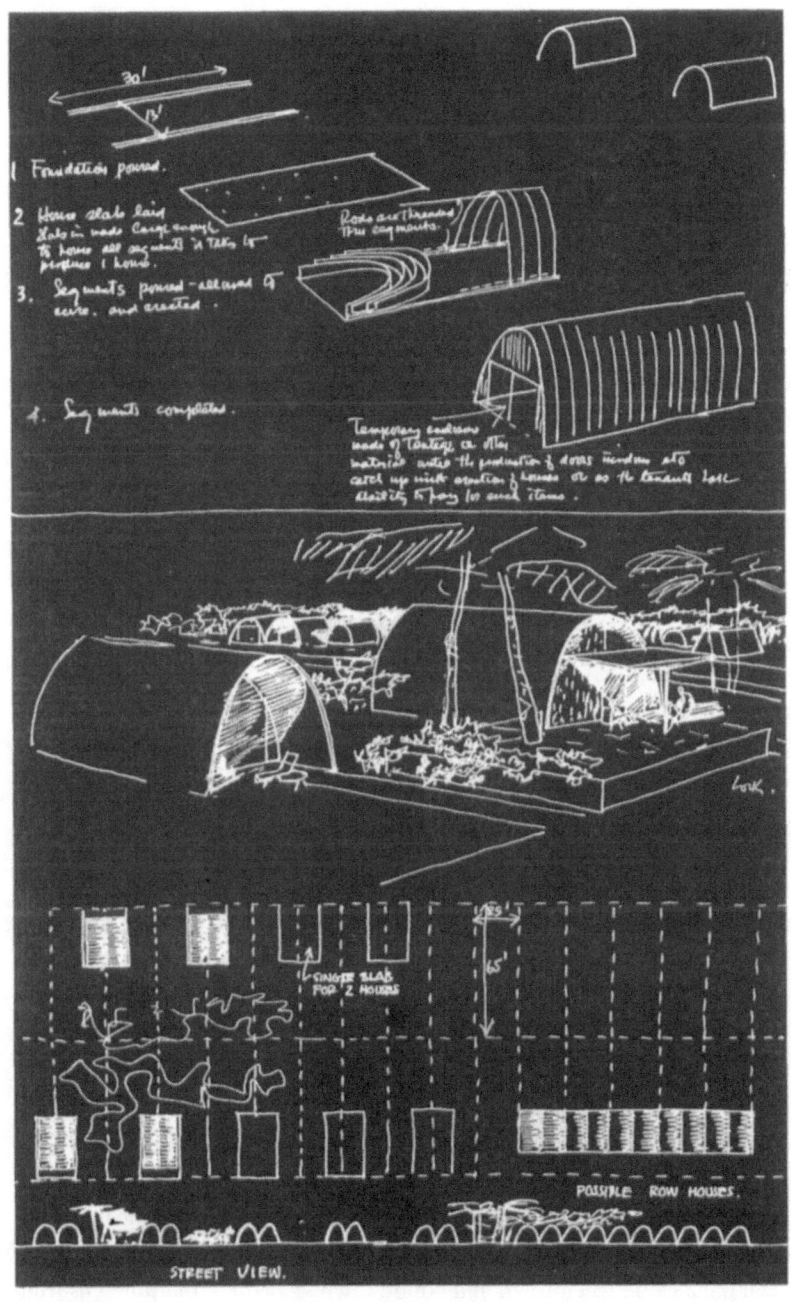

FIG. 6.5. *Louis Kahn's plan for semi-permanent shelter, 1948–49. Reproduced with permission of the Architectural Archives of the University of Pennsylvania.*

was prepared by the Planning Department under the direct patronage of the prime minister.

Staffed by architects and regional planners who were committed to the ethos of modernism, the department was in a unique position to pursue the radical ideals of modern planning: it had at its disposal a vast reserve of nationalized land, large numbers of immigrants to settle, and the crucial backing of the political establishment. The planners sought to avoid "any repetition of the mistakes made in vaster and richer countries."[7] They were especially obsessed with creating an ideal distribution of population between city and country, a statistical abstraction of some theoretical significance during the interwar period, yet one that was considered a critical issue in the Israeli context. The planners alarmed the public to the fact that in 1948 Israel's ratio of urban to rural population was the highest in the world, with 82 percent of the Jewish population living in the country's three major cities, and 43 percent living in Tel Aviv alone. The planners considered this ratio undesirable for a variety of theoretical and pragmatic reasons. Militarily, the concentration of population in urban areas was considered dangerous, given the technologies of modern warfare[8]; politically, the Jewish population was concentrated along the Israeli coastal strip, leaving the hinterland empty of Jewish settlement; economically, it was believed that many small cities were more efficient and more stable than a handful of large cities[9]; in terms of health policy, prewar planning theory maintained that infant mortality and the spread of tuberculosis and other health problems were caused by overcrowding and the lack of open space. There was yet another motive for the policy of decentralization: according to the official development plan of 1951, Israel's polarized pattern of urbanization "resembled that of colonial territories." The plan sought to replicate the historical pattern found in "small Central and West European countries which are economically, physically and sociologically similar to Israel."[10] The aim of the planners was to create, ex nihilo, a settlement pattern that would appear to have been shaped by centuries of evolution, in order to naturalize the artificiality of the Zionist nation-state.

The planning authorities feared that, left to themselves, immigrants would settle near existing cities and centers of employment, exacerbating the problem of urban density (see fig. 6.6). By forcing immigrants to settle in a more dispersed pattern, the planners could achieve what they regarded to be an ideal balance between town and country, while at the same time ensuring the colonization of the empty regions of the nation, including those areas that had previously been inhabited by the Palestinians. The main instrument of this resettlement policy was to be the New Town program—the establish-

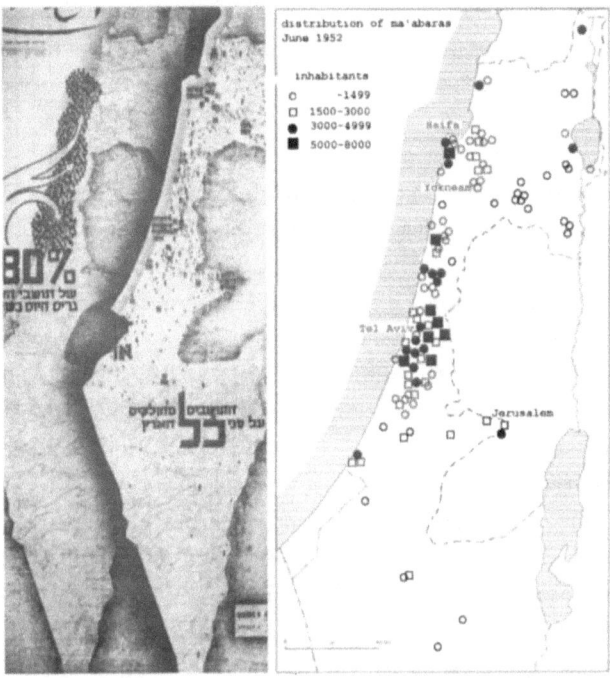

FIG. 6.6. *Poster promoting population dispersal, 1951 (left), and actual geographical location of* ma'abaras, *June 1952 (right).*

ment of twenty-eight cities modeled on the British New Town.[11] In this scheme, the *ma'abaras*, by suspending people in space and time until they could be permanently settled, would function as human reservoirs for populating the New Towns. When the *ma'abaras* were "liquidated" and their inhabitants resettled in the New Towns, those who refused to relocate according to plan were forced to remain in the *ma'abaras* well into the 1960s, even as immigrants who arrived after 1953 were immediately given permanent housing. The rudimentary conditions of the temporary settlements were used as leverage against the very people who inhabited them, forcing them to comply with the role assigned to them in the overall national plan.[12]

The rationale for maintaining residents in temporary housing was different in the case of the more favorably located *ma'abaras*. Housing Ministry administrators worried that these residents might end up owning land with potential real estate value:

> The *ma'abaras* at the center of the country occupy expensive land adjacent to main transportation routes, and the rapid development of their surroundings has informed the inhabitants of the possibility, which is not unfounded, of gaining possession of the land as a consequence of their long settlement on it.... Until now we have seen the erroneous location of specific *ma'abaras* on expensive sites as wasteful. This waste can develop, in specific lots, into wholesale theft of property.[13]

The insistence on the temporary status of the *ma'abara* was one way to resolve the contradiction between two forms of ownership: legal deed and possession through use. Denied the right of possession, its inhabitants could be displaced to other locations according to the national policy of population distribution, and the vacated land could be put to a more rational use. Yet the dismantled *ma'abaras*, once they became available for redevelopment, were often distributed to housing societies and construction companies affiliated with Israel's political parties. One of these societies that received favorable treatment was Shikun Ovdim (Workers' Housing), an organ of the Histadrut labor union led by Ben Gurion's Labour Party. What actually informed the politics of *ma'abara* clearance, then, was the self-interested notion that accidental gain by individuals was considered "theft," whereas political gain was seen as corresponding with the common good.

POPULATING THE IMAGE

The aerial image of Yokneam suggests that the transition from the temporary *ma'abara* to the permanent New Town was efficient and frictionless. The aerial point of view and the symmetrical, abstract composition of the image give no sense of a human presence, only feeble traces of which are discernable. The photo's ideological function is to suppress the point of view of the *ma'abara*'s inhabitants and their everyday living conditions. At ground level, the *ma'abara* provided only a rudimentary existence (see fig. 6.7). Large families had to fit into the standard living space of 160 square feet, and were offered deficient educational and health services. Due to these conditions, child mortality rates in the *ma'abaras* were so high that in the early 1950s, they contributed to the doubling of the national child mortality rate. As these temporary conditions were prolonged by the state's failure to liquidate the *ma'abaras*, Israel's established society became anxious that the *ma'abaras* would breed social degeneracy and political radicalism. Several investigative committees were commissioned to examine the living conditions in the *ma'abaras*.

FIG. 6.7. *An immigrant family from Iraq at Yokneam Ma'abara. In the foreground is Ma'abarah Yokneam, and in background a new housing project for the immigrants living in the* ma'abara. *Photograph by Cohen Fritz, dated April 26, 1952.*

According to a 1955 report: "In Tel Yeruham there is no phone and the nearest doctor is 53 kilometers away . . . garbage is collected once every two weeks . . . in Tira an average of 5.5 people live in one room, in Kurdani 336 people share one shower, in Karkur there is one toilet for 53 people."[14]

That such conditions could persist for so many years is indicative of the imbalance of power that was inscribed into the *ma'abaras*. Their systematically disempowered residents were dependent upon and marginalized by the veteran society and by the institutions under its control, a circumstance that allowed the state to act contrary to the will or the "self-interest" of the immigrants. When some inhabitants of geographically isolated *ma'abaras* refused to accept their assigned position in the national dispersal plan and migrated "independently" to *ma'abaras* in more prosperous regions, those responsible for immigration policy recommended radical measures, such as denying work and food to any settler who relocated without prior authorization.[15] Since in this period essential commodities were distributed by means of a rationing system and work permits were required in order to be legally employed, it was still possible to coerce the population into staying in a specific place. This example demonstrates that in order to function properly, beyond their physical design, the *ma'abaras* had to rely on a supplementary system of power.

Temporal States of Architecture 151

It also points to another role of the *ma'abaras*, articulated in official state documents:

> The term *"ma'abara"* has not been clearly defined. The *ma'abara* differs from the immigrant camp in that its inhabitants are self sufficient, while those in the camps received bed and board for free. . . . The inhabitants of the *ma'abara* live upon wage labor. In other words, *"ma'abara"* means a fixed group of settlers residing in temporary dwellings.[16]

This definition centers on the employment status of the *ma'abara*'s residents, since one of the state's original objectives was to relieve itself of the burden of feeding and supporting the idle residents of the immigrant camp. The first *ma'abaras* were defined as "labor villages," and their inhabitants were employed in relief projects such as construction, forestation, and land conservation.

Manual labor was seen as an ideological mechanism for changing the occupational structure of the new Jewish nation, from one of merchants thriving on the labor of others, to one of a people living off their own physical labor. The administrators of the Housing Ministry maintained that, "Construction acts as a kind of natural vocational school for new immigrants. The majority of new immigrants come from the middle classes and are not accustomed to physical labor. . . . Under such circumstances the construction industry acts as an important and desirable transitional stage."[17]

The faint foot trails that can be seen in the photograph connecting the Yokneam *ma'abara* with the New Town above it were carved into the hillside by a heterogeneous group of immigrants as they were transformed into a disciplined labor force. Once construction of the New Town was completed, other relief projects were organized. Among them, foresting the landscape became the main employment for those immigrants who had been placed in the geographically remote *ma'abaras* at the margins of the national economy.[18] The surplus of labor was channeled into a national program of soil reconstruction, as one component of "green" Zionism's project of nature conservation.[19] This progressive policy was linked to another kind of reconstruction discourse. In his opening address to the second Knesset in 1951, Ben Gurion identified labor and ecology as pedagogical and symbolic components of nation building: "We must plant many hundreds of thousands of trees on . . . a quarter of the area of the state. . . . We are a nation at the beginning of repairing the corruption of generations, corruption which was done to the people and corruption which was done to the land."[20]

The unequal relations of power that were built into the *ma'abara* made it possible to objectify their inhabitants as construction material for nation building. Indeed, the concept of "labor therapy" was an integral component of, not contingent to, to the *ma'abara* project. As such, it problematizes official accounts of the *ma'abaras* as having come into existence as a response to the challenges posed by mass immigration, since it appears that there was a preexisting theory of how the *ma'abaras* should function that preceded their praxis. The concept of the *ma'abara*, I would argue, was not the result of the event of mass immigration, but rather one of the elements that made that event conceptually possible in the first place, since from its inception, the Zionist movement had inscribed the concept of the transitory settlement as a necessary component of its modern nation-building project.

SCRIPTING THE TRANSITIONAL

A scenario that incorporated temporary architecture, mass immigration, and the will to design a nation was first scripted by Theodor Herzl (1860–1904) some fifty years prior to the establishment of the state of Israel. With his 1896 publication of *The Jewish State*, Herzl transformed Zionism from a messianic movement based on religious sentiments into a modern, organized movement. Written as a manual for nation building, the book outlined the organizational methods for relocating the Jewish population of Europe to another (as yet unspecified) continent, as well as the means for establishing a secular nation-state, for which Herzl also supplied an ideal constitutional and social framework. The book's instant success transformed Herzl from a journalist and failed playwright with little interest in Zionism into the movement's leader. By arming the Zionist movement with the instruments of planning as a method for mastering its future, Herzl also transformed Zionism into an effective political movement of international scope. Herzl's overriding desire was to appropriate modernity as the new faith of the Jewish people: "We are a modern people already, wanting to become the most modern among peoples."[21] This desire manifested itself in an uninhibited belief in progress and reason as the means for mastering historical change. Contrary to more evolutionary or organic visions of Zionism, which favored the slow, gradual acculturation of a Jewish cultural entity in Palestine, Herzl assumed that a nation could be instantly created, if it were only guided by the right plan.[22] As he stated, "From the start, everything will be determined according to plan . . . we will use all the sociological and technical achievements not only of the time in which we live, but also of the future times . . . with unprecedented chances of success."[23]

Herzl and his followers believed they could establish an ideal society, as they had the advantage of starting from scratch and could avoid both repeating the mistakes of other nations and the contingencies of unplanned historical change. In his follow-up novel, *Old New Land*, published in 1902, Herzl declared that it was possible to "establish our Society without inherited drawbacks. . . . Nations with unbroken histories have to carry burdens assumed by their ancestors. Not we."[24] His preference for a creationist, expert-driven mode of statecraft over an evolutionary process determined Herzl's concept of planning. He envisioned the colonization of Palestine as a rapid event, a feat he presented as unproblematic, since unlike the military planners of the Napoleonic wars, "we had only to settle half a million people by the autumn."[25] Herzl's blasé attitude to such a radical undertaking reflects an uncritical integration of military strategy to civic affairs. The mobilization of society along military principles was ingrained in the details of Herzl's plan. With his proposal that the new country's labor force, the first to immigrate, should be temporarily housed in prefabricated shelters that could be purchased wholesale to cut expenses, Herzl anticipated the deployment of the *ma'abaras* that would take place nearly fifty years in the future: "I ordered five hundred barracks from France—a new kind that could be taken apart like a tent and put together in an hour."[26] Not only did Herzl script transient architecture as a logistical necessity to the Zionist project, he also proposed using labor to transform immigrants into citizens. In *The Jewish State*, he envisioned that "Jews will enter the new land under the sign of labor," and he advocated labor therapy to discipline the masses into middle-class values: "By their labor [the unskilled] will gain the right to own their own houses . . . if they give evidence of good behavior for a period of three years. In this way we will develop a diligent people who can be readily employed. A man with the discipline of three years' work behind him is ready for life."[27]

The concept of the *ma'abara* as a spatio-temporal void was inscribed into Zionism as a necessary, even advantageous, stage for creating a modern nation-state. It secured the conception of both Palestine and the Jewish people as empty, abstract entities that could be shaped by disinterested experts and universal parameters of science and reason, without having to negotiate existing historical structures or the diversity of interests. Such a conception allowed the Zionist movement to envision a mode of action that circumvented political process, since it refused to acknowledge conflicting desires and interests, or to allow their political negotiation through compromise or struggle.

TESTS AND REHEARSALS

During the actual colonization of Palestine, Zionist planners submitted the concept of transitory architecture to a series of small-scale, concrete tests. An illuminating case is the "tower-and-stockade" settlement, a technique that was invented during the Arab Rebellion of 1936–39 for building cooperative village settlements in hostile territory against the resistance of Palestinian militias. A settlement was initially comprised of a prefabricated fortified nucleus that was transported and assembled on site in one day. At a later stage, the settlement would grow out of its protective cocoon and metamorphose into its final, utopian form (see fig. 6.8). The success of the experiment validated the hypothesis that the contingent and violent process of colonization could be contained in the scaffolding, allowing the finished architectural object to communicate a purified, ideal image of the Zionist project.

In addition to this local experiment, Herzl's scenario for the accelerated movement of people was rehearsed under emergency conditions in 1942, when Ben Gurion proposed to bring in a million Jewish refugees from Europe in *ten* days: the D-day of Zionism. A debate ensued, with critics claiming that "hundreds of thousands of unemployed masses will explode our country. . . . We must transfer immigrants in a planned, ordered method, and not in a catastrophic way."[28] To contain the risks of mass immigration, Ben Gurion commissioned a group of experts to prepare the "Million Plan," which included a complete design for a system of camps to house the influx of refugees until they could be settled and employed. The plan was elaborated with great detail, even calculating the caloric value of the meals that were to be prepared in the camps' kitchens.[29] The existence of the "Million Plan" requires us to reevaluate the way in which the story of the *ma'abaras* has been told, since it now appears that the concept of the *ma'abara* was in fact the precondition for, not the effect of, mass immigration. Revising the official history of the *ma'abara* by inverting the sequence of cause and effect points to a fundamental contradiction in Zionism's practice of modern planning. The discipline of planning was developed to rationalize and coordinate the process of modernization, rendering it more efficient and less disruptive to society. But in the case of the *ma'abaras*, planning became an altogether different instrument: it was used to radicalize and compress history, and to introduce new risks and

FIG. 6.8. Beit Yosef "tower-and-stockade" settlement. Top: The settlement in 1937, after having been built in a single day. Bottom: The settlement in its final form, 1939. Reproduced with permission of the Zionist Central Archive, Jerusalem.

upheavals. It allowed Zionism to calculate the risks of accelerated social and geographical change, and to promote extreme policies such as doubling the population in three years and managing hundreds of thousands of immigrants in military-like conditions, all the while maintaining that such upheavals could be contained in the transition phase without lasting negative consequences.

THE PERFORMANCE STAGE

The performance of the immigration script on a mass scale did not replicate the results of the small-scale rehearsals. While most of the *ma'abaras* were dismantled in the mid-1950s when their inhabitants were relocated into permanent settlements, the temporary stage produced unforeseen, long-term distortions in Israel's social structure. The residents of the *ma'abaras* received inferior medical and educational services and suffered from poverty and endemic unemployment, and the kind of work available to them was mostly manual labor. As the *ma'abaras* spatially separated longtime citizens from immigrants, they retarded the integration of the immigrants into the political and economic system. Since the population of the *ma'abaras* was made up predominantly of Sephardic Jews—72 percent versus 22 percent of Ashkenazi origin—whereas the veteran society was predominantly Ashkenazi, the *ma'abaras* initiated a process by which Israel's Jewish population became divided along ethnic lines.[30] The enduring correspondence between class and ethnicity in Israeli society, and its origin in the *ma'abara*, led to the emergence of a counter-narrative in which the memory of the *ma'abara* was made into a signifier of social and political inequality. Contemporary Sephardic identity is grounded upon the perception of the *ma'abaras* as representing an act of violence and humiliation inflicted upon them by the Ashkenazi "establishment." Shimon Ballas, in his 1964 novel, *The Ma'abara*, gave voice to the experience of Iraqi immigrants living in the *ma'abaras* with the following words:

> It appears to me that since the Babylonian exile, never such a horrible holocaust has been inflicted upon the Jews of Mesopotamia as the holocaust it presently suffers. This enlightened and ancient community was crushed to dust and dispersed upon desolate and foul places called *ma'abaras*. . . . Is this not exile?[31]

The above passage should be read, beyond the narrow discourse of identity politics, as furthering a more structural critique of Zionism and its un-homely conception of space. Ballas claims that the Zionist project reproduced the very conditions it attempted to negate—dispersion, exile, and disempowerment. Yet he also advances the critical possibility of maintaining a diasporic position from within a nationalistic culture. And as condemning as this passage is, it represents only one voice out of the multitude of experiences that are enacted in the novel, in which everyday life in its vitality and impurity is shown to undermine the official design of the *ma'abara*.

Such unforeseen and unintended outcomes of life in the *ma'abaras* leads to the conclusion that the concept of the transitory allowed Zionism to maintain its utopian vision of territorial and social harmony, while also enabling it to act and to exercise power, both in relation to the Jewish subjects who would inhabit those voids, and the Palestinians, whose prior presence and displacement would remain as a void in the nation's collective memory. And it is precisely here that the violence of this mechanism brings a local subjectivity into being. In a dialectical manner, the local is that which resisted its negation and silencing by a modernist discourse that assigned it a transitory, empty space.

NOTES

An earlier version of this essay appeared as "Necessity by Design," in *Perspecta* 34 (2003): 10–19.

1. Statement made April 22, 1949 (see Tom Segev, *1949: The First Israelis* [New York: Free Press, 1986], 136). The Knesset is the Israeli parliament.

2. Statement made January 2, 1950 (see Segev, *1949*, 140). Eshkol replaced Lavon as minister of agriculture and development in 1951.

3. Ben Gurion to Foreign Ministry staff, April 12, 1949, in Segev, *1949*, 97.

4. In the three years after May 1948, 685,000 immigrants entered Israel, while approximately 700,000 Palestinians became refugees.

5. "The Situation in the Ma'abaras" (in Hebrew), Government Meeting Memorandum, October 11, 1951, Session 2, Article 11, Israel State Archive.

6. The American sociologist Clarence Perry developed the concept of the neighborhood unit in the 1920s as a strategy for creating self-sufficient urban communities by organizing residential development around services catering to the family. It was popular with postwar English planners, and subsequently with Israeli planners as well.

7. Aryeh Sharon, *Physical Planning in Israel* (Jerusalem: Government Press, 1951); quote is from the English supplement, p. 3. Sharon, a graduate of the Bauhaus, was the head of the Planning Department.

8. Anatole Solow, an expert from MIT, advised the Israeli government in 1949 to implement the American postwar strategy of decentralization as a defense against a possible future atomic war. In a 1954 speech on settlement policy, Ben Gurion noted: "We are living in the era of total war. . . . The more settlements are smaller and better dispersed, the danger diminishes" (David Ben Gurion, *On Settlement: Collected Speeches, 1915–1956* [in Hebrew] [Tel Aviv: Hakibbutz Hameuchad, 1986], 116).

9. Israeli planners inferred from the Great Depression that the key to economic stability lay in geographical patterns of settlement: "It is of interest that during the great economic crisis which Germany and America experienced in the twenties, the large cities and purely agricultural areas were the main victims, whereas the small and medium towns with their well-balanced economy stood firm" (Sharon, *Physical Planning in Israel,* 4).

10. Ibid., 4. Israeli planners found pseudo-scientific justification for their "organic" dispersal ideology in Walter Christaller's "central place theory," which was based on a mathematical analysis of settlement patterns in South Germany.

11. Eighteen New Towns were established between 1948 and 1951, and ten more by 1957. In contrast, the British project consisted of "only" eleven New Towns between 1946 and 1955. Patrick Abercrombie, the author of the Greater London Plan (1944), which envisioned the relocation of a million Londoners into New Towns, was commissioned by the Israeli planners to persuade Ben Gurion to pursue this policy. In their meeting, Ben Gurion is reported to have remarked that "it was easier to do so in Israel, where we had only to direct the immigrants into the development areas and new towns" (Aryeh Sharon, *Kibbutz + Bauhaus* [Tel Aviv: Massada, 1982], 79).

12. Haim Darin-Drabkin, "Economic and Social Aspects of Israeli Housing," in *Public Housing in Israel: Surveys and Evaluations of Activities in Israel's First Decade, 1948–1958* (Tel Aviv: Gadish, 1959), 33. As late as 1963, there were still 15,300 people living in *ma'abaras*.

13. "Plan to Liquidate *Ma'abaras*—Permanent Housing for Immigrants" (in Hebrew), September 17, 1952, document G 5558/19, Israel State Archive.

14. "Committee for the Coordination of Social Services in the *Ma'abaras*" (in Hebrew), Ministry of Labor, July 1954, document G 5558/3903, Israel State Archive.

15. Yosef Weitz, the director of the Settlement Department, reported that he was "partaking in several measures to stop the migration of new settlers from place to place without our prior authorization. One of the measures recommended is preventing the relocation of food rationing cards without our approval" (Dvora Hacohen, *The Grain and the Millstone* [in Hebrew] [Tel Aviv: Am Oved, 1998], 194).

16. "Committee for the Coordination of Social Services in the Ma'abaras" (in Hebrew), July 1954, document G 5558/3903, Israel State Archive.

17. Darin-Drabkin, *Public Housing in Israel*, 78.

18. The pace of forestation correlates with the construction of the *ma'abaras*: in 1949, 2,910 dunams (1,000 square meters) were forested. In 1950, that figure had risen fourfold, to 12,650 dunams, and in 1951, fourfold again, to 56,400 dunams (see Shaul E. Cohen, *The Politics of Planting* [Chicago: University of Chicago Press, 1993], 64).

19. Zionist planners were associated with the first wave of modern environmentalism. Several Israeli planners graduated from the Berlin-Charlottenburg technical school, a prewar center of ecological and regional planning that promoted the ethics and aesthetics of sustainable development, especially soil and water conservation. Regretfully, a critical history of "green" Zionism is yet to be written.

20. Cohen, *The Politics of Planting*, 61.

21. Theodor Herzl, *The Jewish State* (Northvale, N.J.: Jason Aharonson, 1997), 195.

22. Such as Ahad Ha'am's brand of "cultural Zionism," which proposed to establish a cultural center in Palestine, rather than a nation-state, or Franz Oppenheimer's plan for an incremental settlement process.

23. Herzl, *The Jewish State*, 194.

24. Theodor Herzl, *Old New Land* (New York: Herzl Press, 1987), 78.

25. Ibid., 228.

26. Ibid., 205.

27. Herzl, *The Jewish State*, 156. Herzl was influenced by Edward Bellamy's 1888 utopian novel, *Looking Backward*, and especially Bellamy's idea of the industrial army, in which labor was performed as a contractual duty that gained citizens the right to society's collective goods. Hence Herzl's original design for the Jewish state's flag, which had seven stars representing the seven-hour workday as the foundation of his "third way" approach to resolving the conflict between capital and labor.

28. See Eliezer Kaplan (the future finance minister) to Ben Gurion, in Dvora Hacohen, *From Fantasy to Reality: Ben Gurion's Plan for Mass Immigration, 1942–1945* (in Hebrew) (Tel Aviv: Ministry of Defence Press, 1994), 114.

29. Hacohen, *From Fantasy to Reality*, 130.

30. Miriam Kachensky, "The Ma'abaras," in *Immigrants and Ma'abaras* (in Hebrew), ed. Mordechai Naor (Jerusalem: Yad Ben Zvi, 1986), 75. This unequal ratio was not the result of an intentional discriminatory policy, but rather the contingent product of the specific timing in which each Jewish Diaspora group arrived in Israel.

31. Shimon Ballas, *The Ma'abara* (in Hebrew) (Tel Aviv: Am Oved, 1964), 51.

7   Modernisms in Conflict

Architecture and Cultural Politics in Post-1967 Jerusalem

ALONA NITZAN-SHIFTAN

Shortly after the 1967 War, when Israel occupied East Jerusalem and the Old City formerly governed by Jordan, the feverish building of the unilaterally unified city began. Jerusalem mayor Teddy Kollek, who wanted a bounded and efficient city, fought against the government's plans to extend Jerusalem's boundaries into the occupied territories. Lodged between national and urban interests, he invited the elite of Western architecture—Buckminster Fuller, Louis Kahn, Lewis Mumford, and Bruno Zevi, among seventy other luminaries of the newly established Jerusalem Committee—to discuss and approve his multidisciplinary master plan. Rather than endorsing this modernist blueprint, however, these invited critics attacked the plan as transgressing Jerusalem's "natural charm and spiritual beauty."[1] Their criticisms provoked a series of confrontations between architectural, municipal, and national institutions. The result was a dramatic break with the modernist landscape that had predominated in pre-1967 Jerusalem (see figs. 7.1 and 7.2).

Having to do with one of the world's most emotionally charged cities, this criticism raised a set of poignant questions: How should Jerusalem be constructed under the new Israeli rule? Should it be a universal spiritual center or a metropolitan Israeli capital? And what conception of architectural modernism might best embody these alternatives? This essay examines these questions through the prism of post–World War II architectural culture and its criticism of the seemingly unified modernist movement in architecture. The latter was codified in seminal texts, exhibitions, and institutions that

FIG. 7.1. *David Anatol Brutzkos, Upper Lifta, 1960s. Reprinted from* Israel Builds *(Israel Ministry of Housing, 1965)*.

FIG. 7.2. *Salo Hershman, Gilo, Cluster 11, 1970s. Reprinted from* Israel Builds *(Israel Ministry of Housing, 1988), 112.*

identified it with the international style, functional planning, and urban renewal projects. Post-1967 Jerusalem provided an opportunity for postwar architects to revise and situate the resultant modernisms that were often entangled in modernization projects. Their intervention, via architectural criticism, in the politics of space in Jerusalem demonstrates how information extraneous to the Zionist ethos and the Palestinian-Israeli conflict nonetheless profoundly affects their course.

The essay analyzes this intervention by focusing on how the Jerusalem Committee directly inserted postwar architectural knowledge into the Israeli planning process. In the committee's plenary meetings, in 1969, 1973, and 1975, the debates pertaining to physical planning were particularly heated.[2] At the very first of these meetings there was already a demand for the creation of a subcommittee for town planning. That subcommittee met only once, in December 1970. During its deliberations, which this essay examines in detail, Jerusalem became a testing ground where two modernisms competed for supremacy. The first of these, the modernization of Jerusalem as carried out by Israeli planners, was predicated on the logic of "progress and development"—the bedrock of Zionist planning.[3] It demanded comfort and efficiency for every Israeli and Palestinian alike, within the bounded city, thus assuming a neutral definition of "residency" in what was (and remains) a deeply divided city. The second approach exemplified the post–World War II architectural culture of the diverse international membership of the Jerusalem Committee,[4] and grew out of a shared criticism of the modern movement in architecture and an anxiety toward its cooptation in modernization projects. This latter group's call for regional and monumental expression was geared toward the spatial realization of the idea of Jerusalem as a spiritual center. The competition between these two modernisms, which I call "developmental" modernism and "situated" modernism, respectively,[5] affected issues concerning democracy, religion, orientalism, and the ideology of nation-building, all of which related to the pressing question of whose history, religion, and nationality would be given form in the built landscape of modern Jerusalem.

Throughout the 1970 debate, the international committee criticized the Israeli planners in the name of universal values—that is, their objections reflected the then current discussions among architects regarding the crisis of the modernist city. Kollek's guests considered themselves victims of the urban renewal projects and inner-city highways that had destroyed the traditional patterns of American cities, and they came to Jerusalem to protect that historic city from a similar destiny.[6] It was the apparent rigor and neutrality of these professionals as they debated the role of architecture in modernization projects that enabled the committee to have such a far-reaching impact on the politics of space in Jerusalem. But the operation of the committee, with an overwhelmingly American presence and with no Muslim members, demonstrated the degree to which the debate had already been politicized. Both the Israelis and the international critics, mostly Jews and Christians, focused their discussions on Jerusalem as the hub of the three monotheistic faiths, whereas Muslims saw the city as a battleground between two competing nations. Since they could not join this advisory body without legitimizing Israeli rule over Jerusalem, Muslims of all nationalities declined to participate. Instead, they were represented by "experts"—orientalist proxies chosen by Kollek—and, as a result, Islamic claims for Jerusalem were confined to religious issues. The intervention of the international committee thus demonstrates the cultural politics of global practice in a local site—a site of contention between Muslims and Jews, Palestinians and Israelis, over the possession of territory and history.

TWO MODERNISMS CLASH

The 1970 meeting presented a rather unusual occasion. Mayor Kollek, acutely aware of the international attention that was focused on Jerusalem after 1967, invited about thirty renowned architects and town planners from nine countries to participate in the Subcommittee for Town Planning. He urged the five major Israeli planning agencies to voluntarily submit their coordinated 1968 Jerusalem Masterplan and its complements for the subcommittee's scrutiny.[7] The reviewers included such luminaries as Louis Kahn, Lewis Mumford, Bruno Zevi, Buckminster Fuller, Christopher Alexander, Philip Johnson, Nikolaus Pevsner, Moshe Safdie, Lawrence Halprin, and Isamu Noguchi, to mention a few.

These esteemed representatives of postwar architectural culture voluntarily arrived in Jerusalem on December 19, 1970, to participate in the three-day meeting of the subcommittee. The invitees had received comprehensive reports about the Israeli planning documents prior to their arrival. In Jerusalem, they attended an intense program of lectures and site visits before they began their formal deliberations, with forty Israeli architects, planners, and government officials in attendance. These formal discussions were organized around thematic sessions and were open to the press, but closed to the public. The public *was* invited to listen to the committee's concluding remarks, however, an event which many young Israeli architects remember as being professionally formative.

Earlier that year, in August 1970, public debate on the 1968 plan had already begun. The original plan called for a clearly bounded city, but the Israeli government had violated this urban dictate by confiscating more than 4,000 acres of East Jerusalem land, in order to build residential neighborhoods that would territorially fix Israeli rule over the recently occupied territory (see fig. 7.3). This act provoked a local and international uproar. Kollek sided with those critics who argued that the politicians had abused the professional integrity of the master plan in the name of settlements and had compromised aesthetics in favor of occupation. Given this overheated atmosphere, reported by the news media worldwide, expectations for the December 1970 meeting of the Jerusalem Committee architects ran high. The planners expected to receive the professionals' support, but instead they were surprised by the committee's criticism. Municipal architect Arthur Kutcher later reported:

> At a hastily called special session, closed to the public, the members of the Committee expressed their feelings about the plans to the Israeli authorities. Most of them were enraged by what they had seen. Some of them wept, others were nearly hysterical, and at least one was taken ill. The officials, who had expected the usual pat on the back given by such convocations of visiting firemen, were completely amazed. It had apparently never occurred to them that anyone would take a town plan so to heart.[8]

The unequivocal rejection of the plan devastated and confused the Israeli planners. "The foreign critics," wrote the *Jerusalem Post*, "were not wielding a scalpel on the Masterplan, but a guillotine."[9] Surprisingly, the committee's criticism addressed neither the internationally contested designation of Jerusalem as a unified Israeli capital, nor the public's frustration with the urban implications of the confiscation of land in East Jerusalem. Their critique, by focusing on the malaise of modernist urbanism, made the plan into a referendum against the imposition of the Zionist modernist blueprint on the city of Jerusalem.

THE JERUSALEM COMMITTEE

From the outset, the creation of the Jerusalem Committee with an international membership had been a political act. It was done on the initiative of Mayor Kollek, who had limited power in the arena of state politics. Kollek was a sharp politician and a masterful administrator. In 1969, in an effort to transcend the limitations of his own power, he invited the seventy luminaries of

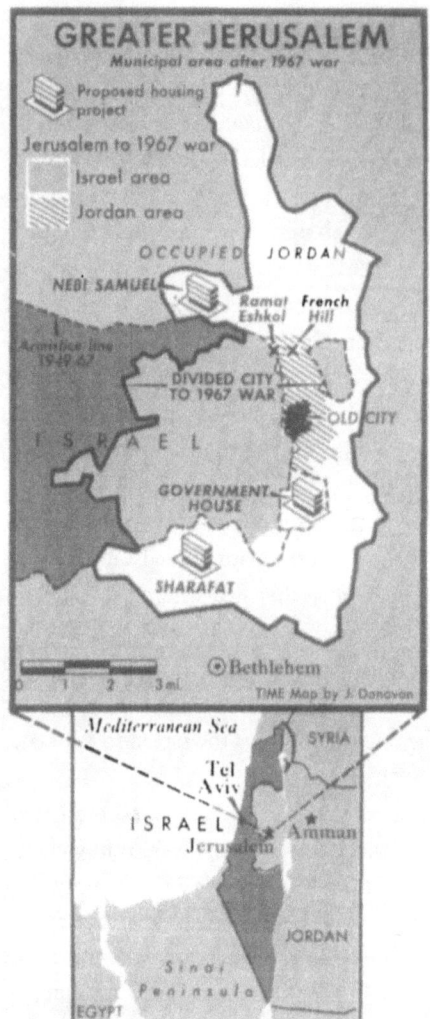

FIG. 7.3. Map of Greater Jerusalem after August 1970 confiscation. From Time, March 1, 1971.

the Jerusalem Committee to come to Jerusalem to oversee the Israelis' work there. On that occasion, he assured the committee members that, "The problem is not ours alone, as residents of the city; it belongs, in a sense, to the entire world, to all those people who are Jerusalemites in their hearts and minds."[10] By submitting the Israelization of Jerusalem to international surveillance, Kollek was endeavoring to legitimate his own mandate to govern Jerusalem, not just in an official, political sense, but according to moral and aesthetic precepts as well. Kollek reported with some satisfaction that only

FIG. 7.4. *Teddy Kollek (former mayor of Jerusalem), Louis Kahn, and R. Buckminster Fuller in Jerusalem. Photo by Isamu Noguchi, 1969. Courtesy of the Isamu Noguchi Foundation.*

one invitee had refused to join the committee, and that was because of the occupation of East Jerusalem.[11]

The beautification of Jerusalem represented the frontier of Kollek's cultural policy, and the architects became his indispensable agents (see fig. 7.4). When Buckminster Fuller suggested that Jerusalem should become "desovereignized," a "world-man-territory" of world citizens, because it "is at the still center of the revolving forces of history," Kollek remained aloof,[12] since the power of his agenda lay in the strict separation of politics and planning. "This city has to live regardless of politics," he insisted. "What we want are competent opinions on town planning."[13]

The committee's autonomy, international membership, and professionalism gave it critical weight—its members had received a mandate to speak in the name of universal values in the realms of aesthetics and humanism. They had been given a unique opportunity to reexamine the boundaries of architecture and its modernist legacy in an area saturated with history and symbolism—an area that had previously provoked much antagonism among modernists of the *Neue Sachlichkeit* persuasion.[14] In Jerusalem, as members of a late modernist club, criticizing themselves, they were free to experiment

Modernisms in Conflict 167

with the architectural trends that had flourished in the previous decade, such as regionalism, new brutalism, organicism, and the new tendencies toward preservation, so as to find the professional tools that would be the most adequate for Jerusalem.

As a leading forum for such debates, the periodical *Architectural Design* consequently observed about the committee: "All too conscious of the politically explosive background to their deliberations, the Committee had endeavored to keep to basic planning issues common to all cities and people irrespective of race or creed."[15] The seeming neutrality of this debate was arguably its greatest achievement. By advancing cultural rather than territorial politics, it allowed the imperial underpinnings of the debate about Jerusalem to be hidden beneath the discussion and debate about its beautification.

THE ZIONIST BLUEPRINT: 1968 JERUSALEM MASTERPLAN

The 1968 Jerusalem Masterplan had its roots in a plan originally commissioned in 1964 by Mayor Kollek's predecessor, Mordechai Ish Shalom, who established an interdisciplinary professional team to coordinate the various agencies involved in planning for the modernization of the city.[16] Shalom chose as his principal planners the brothers Zion and Avia Hashimshoni and Yoseph Schweid, who were members of the professional and academic establishment of Zionist modernist planning. Zion Hashimshoni had already had a leading role in Israel's first ultramodernist master plan.[17] Avia Hashimshoni, the team leader (and the author of Israel's first architectural history) was a professor of architecture at the Technion, where in the mid-1960s he represented the modernist-functionalist camp in Israel's sole architectural school.

The 1968 plan inherited from its Zionist predecessors the logic of an ordered environment, but stressed the benefits of urban forms.[18] Its goal was threefold: to create the blueprint for a national, civic-municipal, and universal town-planning. First, it sought to enhance the civic importance of the presumed national capital; second, it sought the well-being of the city's inhabitants; and third, it sought to reinforce the significance of Jerusalem's religious sites. These goals were translated into a set of objectives for which the plan provided detailed physical "solutions."[19] The plan's numerous diagrams depicted the desired relationship between the built and natural landscape, by specifying a plain architecture and by exhibiting a certain distrust of visual expressiveness (see fig. 7.5). The plan specified a contained city, geared to the everyday needs of its residents. To achieve this, it called for a modernist infrastructure, extensive road systems, and the convenient distribution of urban and civic activi-

FIG. 7.5. *The City and the Metropolitan Space. Reprinted from 1968 Jerusalem Masterplan (Jerusalem: Jerusalem Municipality, 1972), 63.*

ties.[20] The meticulous research and careful statistical analyses of the planners, packed into diagrams and colored maps, gave it a scientific aura.

DEVELOPMENTAL VS. SITUATED MODERNISM

That the master plan had "no vision, spirit, theme or character" was the most generally held assessment of it by the international committee. "We were not given a clue to an aspiration," Louis Kahn protested at the 1970 meeting. "We were given a problem analysis."[21] The plan's method of "solving" the problems of Jerusalem evoked the committee's worst fears of architecture's demise in the face of giving precedence to scientific and administrative operations. The committee's discussions were saturated with anxious talk over the prospect of turning Jerusalem "into a modern, International Style *ville radieuse*—skyscrapers, massive housing projects, freeway spaghetti, and all."[22] The journalist Amos Elon suggested that the proposed road system would turn ancient Jerusalem into a pictorial "gas station sacred to the three religions."[23]

The conflict seemed inevitable: the international committee, acting on behalf of "world cultures," had taken upon itself the mandate of protecting the city from the bite of modernization, which threatened Jerusalem, in particular, because of that city's political importance.[24] Israelis, for their part, were not thrilled to be expected to live like cultural relics.[25] Kollek put it more bluntly: "You would like to drive up in big cars but you want us in Jerusalem riding on donkeys. No matter how charming and picturesque that might be, the rest of the world forges ahead into the 21st century."[26]

Given these contradictory pressures, how was such a city to develop? The committee argued that, since it was impossible to deny the weight of the aesthetic and spiritual qualities of Jerusalem, the blueprint for its growth had to be sought *within* the discipline of architecture. The architectural critic Wolf von Eckardt stressed that Jerusalem required unique skills for translating "poetic-subjective experiences such as sacredness, charm and mystery into architectural design terminology of stone, concrete and asphalt."[27] Christopher Alexander insisted that the "answer to how one makes this a religious city should be present in the morphology of the existing plan."[28] And Louis Kahn concluded: "Jerusalem deserved the aura of the unmeasureable."[29]

Each of their comments echoed the debates over the tenets of post–World War II modernism. Modernism had started as an avant-garde movement with social underpinnings for rational planning, technological innovation, and bare aesthetics. Its stress on functionalism, mass production, and proper infrastructure, as well as its famous call for separating the city into secluded zones of work, habitation, recreation, and transportation, was intended to redeem the nineteenth-century industrial city from its severe urban predicament. During the interwar period, the abstract and internationalist discourse of modernists came under attack from many nationalist regimes.[30] After World War II, however, the already established Modern movement gained enormous power, which led not only to the architectural reconstruction of a devastated Europe, but to complementary modernization projects in many postcolonial nation-states, all of which furthered modernism's universalizing mission.

The 1968 plan exemplified a universal developmental logic that had already come under attack by a younger generation of architects during the 1950s and 1960s. Aldo van Eyck, for example, a prominent Dutch architect and member of Team X, complained that orthodox modernists had created "just mile upon mile of organized nowhere, and nobody feeling he is somebody living somewhere."[31] Van Eyck's generation lamented the loss of such notions as hierarchy, community, identity, and place in the well-administered, yet thoroughly alienating modernist urban environments. They asked how one might forge an identity between people and place through architectural means. They questioned why modern architecture had failed to perform this task of representing and identifying people with their physical environments, a task that fell within architecture's traditional province.

Post–World War II architects contended that in the race to improve the human condition, modern architecture had forgotten the man within—his (and it was always "his") sense of place and heritage. In order to redeem an impoverished and ugly modernist urbanness, and in an effort to restore the discipline's autonomous values, they looked back to an architecture before modernism. They were responsible for gradually lifting the modernist ban on revisiting past traditions, and they started looking at history, the vernacular, and nature to find authoritative architectural guidelines for situating modernism between people and their places.[32]

Modernist architecture, having disparaged the traditional tools of the trade, could now finally enjoy, as Denys Lasdun put it, a "physical awakening." Louis Kahn led the return to "architecture as it has always been" by eclipsing formal precedents in favor of timeless architectural principles: "our relations to earth, sky, fire and water; the myriad ways of defining space and controlling light, of relating materials and structure to all these elements, of establishing systems of order (including disorder)."[33] Architects now sought similarly timeless rules from within vernacular traditions, rules that were dictated primarily by instincts regarding habitation, rather than by rational planning.[34] Christopher Alexander suggested, for example, that instead of creating rational, artificial cities, architecture should emulate the stratification and inconsistently built patterns of older cities.[35]

This vibrant new architectural climate made the prospect of advising on the building of Jerusalem particularly attractive, and it brought architects to the city on a voluntary basis. In all probability, however, the only thing that this diverse body of critics fully shared was a common enemy: institutional modernist urban planning as it was represented in urban renewal schemes that could be found worldwide. The committee's architects found the enemy in the 1968 Jerusalem Masterplan and passionately criticized its ideology and methodology. But because their debate was itself ideological, with respect to Jerusalem, the encounter between the two modernisms had a great impact on issues pertaining to democratic practices, religion, and orientalist imagery, and finally, on the relationship between nation and state in a situation in which only one of the competing nations enjoyed complete sovereignty.

ONE CENTER VS. TWO CORES

The 1968 plan advocated an inner city that would be nestled within a larger bounded city. The inner loop would encircle two clearly distinguished centers—one religious, the other civic—that would be paired rather than fused. The former would contain historical and religious sites, and would be centered on the newly seized Old City; the latter would be comprised of state institutions and would be located within the government precinct of West Jeru-

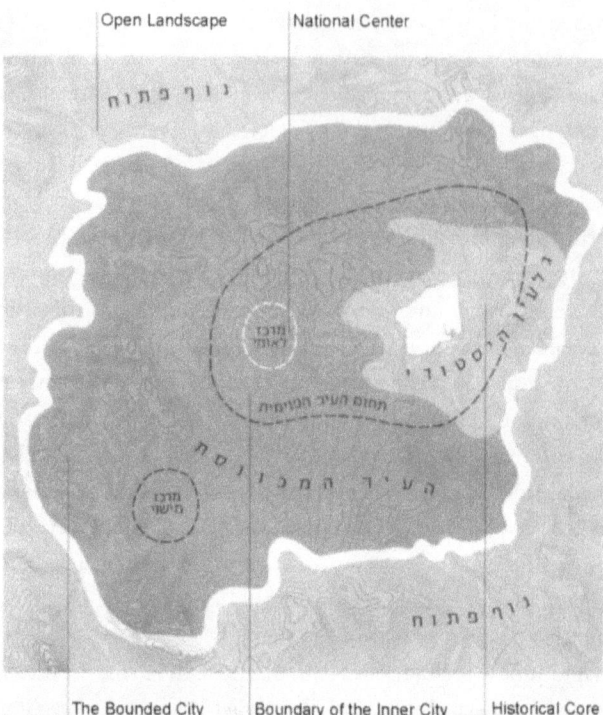

FIG. 7.6. *1968 Jerusalem Masterplan schema for the city structure.* Reprinted from 1968 Jerusalem Masterplan *(Jerusalem: Jerusalem Municipality, 1972)*, 62.

salem (see fig. 7.6). According to this plan, these clearly bounded cores were to be symbolically and aesthetically self-contained.

The international committee objected to the symbolic bifurcation of the city. A modernist capital could exist anywhere, the visiting architects thought, but for Bruno Zevi, for example, Jerusalem was more than just the people who lived there. According to his colleagues in the committee, a spiritual center of such magnitude and beauty had to emanate from the core of the Old City outward in order to achieve a unified image of civil and spiritual coherence. In so arguing, they ignored the political difficulties of such a proposition. Under this view, religious sites would have been overburdened with symbolic state power, thus imposing on an already contested site a problematic mesh of religious and state power.

One of the committee's favorite targets was the Central Boulevard that the Israeli planners had proposed. The boulevard would run from Mt. Scopus, the former Israeli enclave in East Jerusalem, to the national memorial at Mt. Herzl in the far end of West Jerusalem, threading along its way two academic campuses, the city center, and the government precinct. Connecting the most important civil institutions and national monuments of Israel, the Israeli planners saw the boulevard as making an urban statement expressing the role of Jerusalem as the capital of their state. To Lewis Mumford, the boulevard, which would be wide enough to accommodate military parades, showed that "the municipal authorities have been faithfully carrying out their assigned duties in the spirit of Baron Haussmann, without realizing that it is to Isaiah that they must look for guidance." Isaiah, the biblical prophet whose loving vision of Jerusalem Mumford contrasted to Haussmann's Paris, suddenly emerged as the great hero of Jerusalem in its post-1967 incarnation.[36] This was the kind of ethno-religious symbolism the plan's authors had shied away from. By proposing the Central Boulevard as a thread linking the civil centers of the state, they hoped to create a dialogue between the symbols of the Israeli state and those of the religious faiths represented in the Old City.

In their effort to privilege representation over politics, the international committee overlooked this important democratic distinction between religion and the state. In 1970 the other nation claiming Jerusalem was Jordan, whose capital at Amman was far away. When Jordan withdrew its claims to Jerusalem, in 1988, the consequences were great: after Jordan's withdrawal, the demand to make Jerusalem a capital for both the Palestinians and the Israelis could no longer be denied. A separate and confined religious core that contained all of Jerusalem's symbolic resources might have encouraged the Israeli and Palestinian states to develop their national institutions separately while sharing the same symbolic nucleus. But that did not happen. On the contrary, the institutional presence of the state at such sites—one could cite Israeli military ceremonies that have taken place at the Western Wall, for example—has created a predicament of long-lasting political impact.

ORIENTALISM AND SPIRITUALITY IN BRICK AND MORTAR

The team that authored the master plan considered the representational demands of the international committee untenable. The Israeli team was more geared toward convenience and efficiency, and therefore gave priority to the symbolic function of Jerusalem as the capital of Israel and to its operation as a contemporary city.[37] They interpreted the Jerusalem Committee's criticism regarding the form and image of the city as being of a kind with the attitudes of the former British colonials. They took this "British mandate imagery," the aestheticization of which is described in Annabel Wharton's essay in this volume, with a grain of salt. In particular, they dismissed what they considered to be an irrelevant enthusiasm for the exotic Orient, which, to their dismay, was fascinating to the post-1967 War Israeli public as well.[38] How, they wondered, could Israelis prefer insignificant Ottoman buildings over the civic symbols of the "Unified Capital"? Identifying edifices like the city walls as "Ottoman"—considered a decadent period in Zionist memory—robbed the powerful image of "the walled city" of its potency (see fig. 7.7).

Advocating a vibrant central business district, a massive transportation infrastructure, and a dense modernist city with identifiable urban boundaries, the drafters of the plan intended to privilege Jerusalem's civic values over its religious overtones. They saw the criticism of the plan and its values as originating with the cultural disposition of their international critics, who represented the Christian aspiration for Jerusalem: a heavenly Jerusalem on Earth.[39] The Israelis felt that such an untenable aspiration would require the planner to "provide a dramatic physical expression to the spiritual values of Jerusalem. He has to physically plan houses, palaces, streets, squares, gardens and boulevards that express 'heavenly Jerusalem,' embody her, and glorify and elevate her spirituality."[40] The Israeli planners dismissed such ideas as emotional naiveté that prevented foreign critics from recognizing Jerusalem's needs as contemporary city. Thus, they argued for a different option that would recognize "the spiritual value of everyday life, which has to exist by moral vow. This value overcomes the value of the naive urge to tie spiritual life with external material expressions."[41] Intriguingly, by linking "this view [to] the spirit of the Torah which emanated from Jerusalem," they married their choice of modernist planning to the Jewish mistrust of visual monumentality and its emphasis on the sacredness of the every day.

Israeli planners thus mobilized a powerful strategy: they divested the committee's criticism of its universality by locating its arguments within a Western cultural context, despite the Jewish origins of many of the committee's members. They presented the critics' demand that they design a townscape of Oriental beauty as an idolatry that would undermine the tenets of the Jewish religion. Taking just such a landscape as his object of inquiry, W. J. T. Mitchell warned that it "becomes a magical object, an idol that demands human sacrifices, a place where symbolic, imaginary, and real violence implode on an actual social space."[42] By locating his argument in the holy landscapes of Israel and Palestine in the 1990s, Mitchell pointed to the immense power of aesthetics to escalate the conflict, just as Daniel Monk had demonstrated for the Mandate period.[43] More importantly, Mitchell also pointed out the dan-

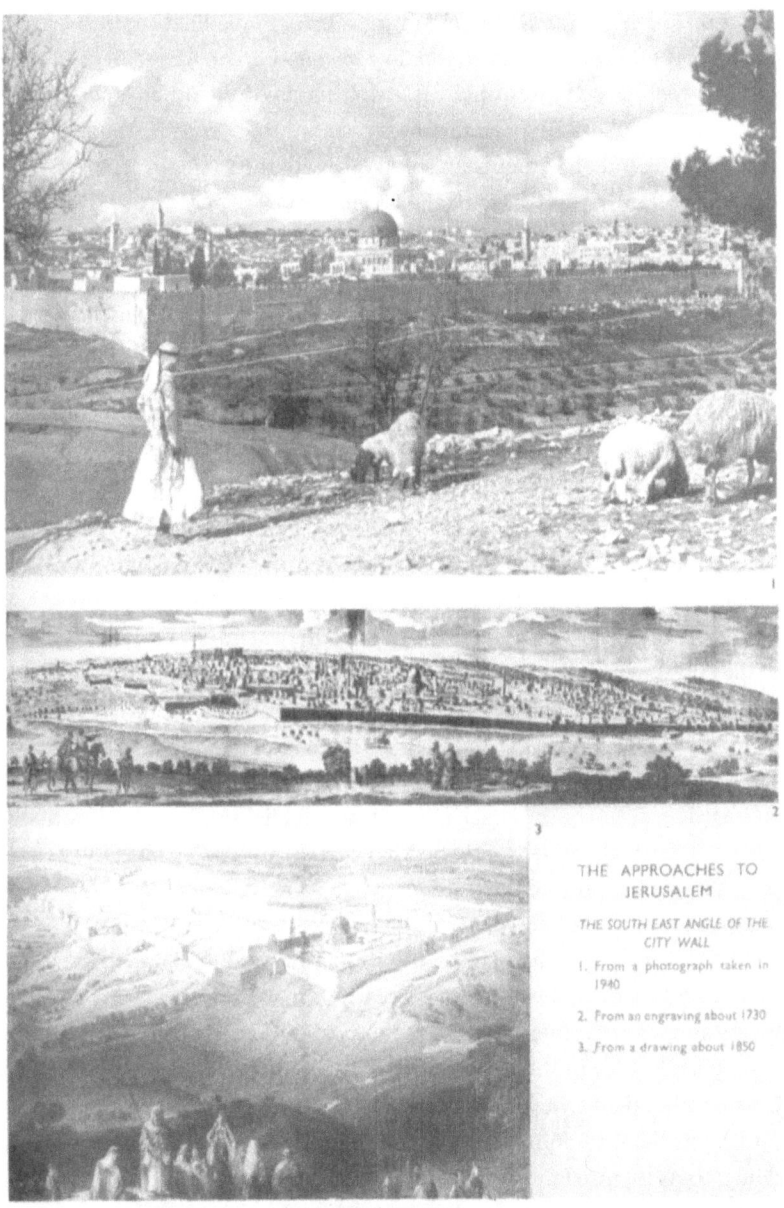

FIG. 7.7. *"The Approaches to Jerusalem." Reprinted from Henry Kendall,* Jerusalem: The City Plan; Preservation and Development during the British Mandate, 1918–1948 *(London: H. M. Stationery Office, 1948), 1.*

ger of solidifying nationalism and imperialism in sanctified landscapes and poetic geographies. The international committee's encouragement of this tendency would aid in just such a transformation of the urban landscape of post-1967 Jerusalem. By objecting to the committee's ideas, the authors of the master plan aligned themselves not only with the values of Judaism, but, more importantly, with those of the Israeli *state*.

RELIGION, NATION, AND STATE

At an early session of the gathering, Yossi Schweid, one of the principal authors of the original 1968 plan, indicated that he and his colleagues were operating according to the values upon which the Israeli state had been founded.[44] In contrast, the Italian politician Bruno Zevi, an influential proponent of organic architecture and a zealous Zionist, insisted that the "present plan [is] an instrument against Israel," and that "Jerusalem is something more than [the] people living there."[45] Deeply involved in the discussion, he next exclaimed: "This is collective hara-kiri. Everybody has abdicated. There has been no effort to have a new vision of life."[46] In the end, at the public session of the entire subcommittee chaired by Louis Kahn and attended by the Israeli planners and the press, it was agreed that the overall plan for the city should highlight its importance as a religious center, a learning center, a capital city, and a regional center, in that order.[47] In one sentence, Kahn had reversed the entire value system of the Israeli master plan: highlighting Jerusalem's importance as the Israeli capital would no longer be the overriding objective of the plan; that would only be the third objective on a list of four, with the city's importance as a religious center at the top.

Kahn's reversal of the plan's contested priorities highlights the tension that existed between the different parties who made claims on Jerusalem. In their statements, the international invitees, as well as their Israeli hosts, made constant reference to the city's religious groups—Christians, Muslims, and Jews—rather than to its political actors—the international community, the Jordanians (later to be replaced by the Palestinians), and the Israelis. In so doing, they disguised the national conflict over ruling Jerusalem by overemphasizing the pacifying spiritual realm of shared monotheism.

Rather then engaging with the great complexity of the city of Jerusalem, the place in which they wished to situate their revised modernism, the invitees limited their discussions to their own areas of expertise—architecture and urban planning—and, as a result, their criticism was focused exclusively on those aspects of the plan. They simply ignored the existing political tensions, and only critiqued the architectural and aesthetic implications of active beautification.

What the Jerusalem Committee called for was a timeless vision for the city. Such a vision should be based, the argument went, on Jerusalem's spiritual and educational qualities, that is, on religious and historical motifs. The demand to thematize Jerusalem was rife with complexities. Such a theme, or narrative, had to be grasped by means of spatial configurations and visual imagery. But whose narrative should Jerusalem's image represent? The "correct" answer was the universal narrative of the three monotheistic religions. This universal theme had to be internationally determined; this was exactly the reason for convening the Jerusalem Committee.

Muslims, as was mentioned, declined to participate, since they felt their participation would only serve to legitimize Israeli rule over Jerusalem. In their absence, Kollek solicited other experts on the subject of Islam. Their role was particularly crucial in the 1975 plenary session of the Jerusalem Committee. Bernard Lewis, for example, the renowned orientalist scholar, conducted the session on Jerusalem as a center for three religions. After the presentations of Judaism and Christianity, Lewis explained that circumstances had prevented the desirable presentation of Islam by a Muslim and then went on to elaborate on the great tradition of Jewish scholars of Islam, concluding: "It is therefore a great tradition of detached objective and sympathetic scholarship that the school of Islamic Studies in the university in this city builds, and it is from this university that we draw our pseudo or crypto-Mufti for this evening." To suggest that an academic orientalist can articulate an authorized Islamic position implies a view of Islam as mere religious essence, which ignores its inextricable links to the political force of Arabs claiming Jerusalem. This kind of "detached and objective" scholarship of "crypto-Muftis" was attacked by Edward Said in his seminal work, *Orientalism*, written in 1978. Lewis, Said's most eminent scholarly rival, was one of the consultants "protecting" the interest of Islam, which attests to the shortcomings of this endeavor.[48] The "monotheistic world," minus its Muslim contingent, consisted of Jews and Christians, whose respective international power was grossly disproportionate to each other and to that of Muslims and whose interests in an Israeli nation-state were also disproportionate.

Among Israeli Jews, those with growing nationalist tendencies happily yielded to the committee's aesthetic ideals for Jerusalem. Whereas post-1967 shifts in Israeli society are beyond the scope of this essay, it is sufficient to say that the pre-1967 modernist practices of the Israeli planning agencies fell short when it came to symbolizing the metaphoric 1967 historical moment of a

Jewish people returning to their biblical land. Moreover, many Israelis felt that Jerusalem was their business card to the world. Refusing to see Jerusalem as a highly modernist city seemed to be the only reasonable course, because modernism would not be able to address the unique spatial qualities of the Holy City, embedded as they are in an Oriental cityscape. According to Louis Kahn, this was the only approach that could grant Israel "the spiritual right to consider itself custodian of Jerusalem . . . from all others who consider it their sacred city."[49]

With such statements, we arrive at the crux of what Edward Said has called "essentialist universalism," a kind of historicism in which universalism as a value is the exclusive right of Westerners.[50] Israelis were allowed to join this Western club only on the condition of complying with its rules. Of course, this articulation of a universal ideal ignored the people who actually lived in the city of Jerusalem, or those in the state of Israel for whom the city was not only holy, but was also a civic center, an everyday city, and, more importantly, a city divided between two nations. The pressing demand to "thematize" Jerusalem meant that the civic symbolism of the state had to be subordinated to ethno-religious themes. The Israeli state, stripped of its modernist attire, had to symbolize its capital as a Jewish or, rather, monotheistic, center in order to legitimize its cause.

THE BEAUTIFIED CITY

When Israel turned to the West for legitimization, it had to accept an idea of Jerusalem as a spiritual site of pilgrimage, as it had already been envisioned by the British mandate that proceeded to translate nineteenth-century orientalist depictions of the city into the language of modern town planning. Attuned to his advisors, Kollek's post-1967 project of beautifying Jerusalem followed this course, which eventually led to a dramatic break with the developmental modernism that had hitherto predominated in the city. Visitors to Jerusalem can easily appreciate the result of these efforts: the greenbelt of parks surrounding the Old City clearly privileges an orientalist visual image as the overwhelming symbol of the city.

The visual control over the urban landscape image was enabled by the institutional changes the committee provoked. One of the reports, "following the Committee's Second Plenary Session" in 1973, specified, for example, that the city had "established a Municipal Ecology Section; rejected a number of proposed high-rise buildings; expanded and continued work on the Jerusalem Gardens; left the area outside the Damascus Gate undeveloped; listed 108 buildings and 14 areas to be preserved, in the first stage of a city-wide preservation program; reduced the highway system described in the master plan and instituted new traffic systems in the City's center, and established a comprehensive planning exhibition, open to the public, in the Citadel."[51]

This image advanced by these municipal measuresis echoed in many of city's preservation projects, such as the reconstruction of the Jewish Quarter, the landscape design of the Sherover and Hass promenades on the southern edge of the sacred basin, and the architectural design of projects like the Mammila complex and the Hebrew Union College campus. Even the design of the housing settlements in East Jerusalem, to which Kollek was opposed, bore the mark of this identifiable post-1967 Jerusalem style.

The force of this restored urban landscape lies in its "matter-of-fact" experience—or rather, in its obviousness, in the feeling that it was always already there. It is exactly the landscape that Mitchell describes as verb rather than noun—"a process by which social and subjective identities are formed."

> Landscape as a cultural medium has a double role with respect to something like ideology: it naturalizes a cultural and social construction, representing an artificial world as if it were simply given and inevitable, and it also makes that representation operational by interpellating its beholder in some more or less determinate relation to its givenness as sight and site. Thus landscape . . . always greets us as space, as environment, as that within which "we" (figured as "the figure" in the landscape) find—or lose—ourselves.[52]

The landscape the committee sought for Jerusalem was one that would enable Israelis not only to find themselves as a nation, but one that would allow Westerners to find in Jerusalem their imagined geography of the Holy Land. It was, thus, a landscape whose beauty was imbued with the colonial perception that brought to life, for Europeans, "the greatest collective landscape mirage the human imagination has ever projected for itself."[53]

Jerusalem's projected landscape exists by a process by which "universal" or "Israeli" Jerusalems are produced at the same time that the "Palestinian" one is concealed. In identifying this process in Kollek's beautification project, I argue that the "know-how" for bringing it to fruition is lodged in the disciplinary knowledge of architecture, which thus has become an active participant in the politics of space in Jerusalem. By way of conclusion, I will therefore contrast this beautification project, that is, the normalization of a politically charged aesthetic perception of the city, with the heated disciplinary discussion that occurred on modernism and modernization.

CONCLUSION

Mayor Kollek had limited power in the arena of state politics. Turning to cultural politics instead, he attempted to legitimize Israeli rule over Jerusalem on moral and aesthetic grounds. The architects and planners of the Jerusalem Committee, convened by him, were therefore entrusted with a strictly professional mandate. While other plenary sessions of the Jerusalem Committee raised issues of a political nature, the sessions conducted by the architects and planners enjoyed a professional aura, a practical edge, and an uncontested credo. Intimidated by Jerusalem's predicament, they preferred to remain secure within their disciplinary knowledge, which emanated from the contemporary crisis of the modernist city.

The ensuing debate became a confrontation between developmental and situated modernisms. At the time, development modernism was questioned, in the context of some modernization projects that had devastated historic urban patterns and had created efficient environments devoid of communal identity and poetic expression. When the Jerusalem Committee criticized the 1968 plan, it aimed to protect the city from such a destiny, not only in the name of moral and aesthetic values, but in the name of humanism and dignity. They argued that the systematic diagrams of the master plan failed to demonstrate that people are far greater than statistical data awaiting functional solutions.

The resultant focus of the international guests on the universal spiritual and aesthetic values of the city consistently avoided the intricate relations between the city's image and its representation of the conflict. This was apparent particularly in three domains of criticism. First, the denounced master plan suggested a dual core for the city, which separated its historic and civic centers. The committee favored instead a unified symbolic nucleus emanating its orientalist beauty onto the entire urban fabric, a proposal that undermined the democratic separation between state and religious faith, as well as the potential of having two civic centers for two states with a shared symbolic core. Second was the identification of the guests' seemingly neutral quest for urban beauty, with the British colonial conception of Jerusalem as a visual idea in Western cultures. The offended Israeli planners revealed the committee's quest to prioritize urban beautification as what Edward Said would later call an "essentialist universalism" that prepared Jerusalem's landscape for its Western audience.

Third was the issue of three faiths vs. two nations. The committee's self-imposed mandate of guarding the city by protecting its urban beauty meshed ethics and aesthetics. This was exactly the mind-set Mayor Kollek triggered in 1969, when he invited the Jerusalem Committee's world luminaries with the following appeal: "The physical beauty of Jerusalem embodies the universal spiritual truths basic to all faiths and people. To enhance the natural charm of Jerusalem is to make manifest a belief in the love of beauty and the desire for peace inherent in all mankind."[54] At the outset, granting aesthetics such moral weight was predicated on a conception of a city of three monotheistic faiths, each containing a mosaic of ethnicities, rather than a city that could potentially become a capital for two rival peoples. This seemingly neutral position, which granted all faiths a share in the city's sanctity, evoked colonial policies that spatially regulated the city according to religious affiliation.[55] For Kollek, the plurality of his "mosaic policy" was a way to undermine Palestinian claims in the name of a wishful cosmopolitanism under Israeli custody.[56] International critics succumbed to this view because what the three religions shared was the city's symbolic core, the image of which embodied their imagined Jerusalem. By insisting that this visual idea would affect the entire city, they believed they could combat what they perceived to be the anticipated ugliness of developmental modernism, and thus secure the Jerusalem they sought.

The resultant committee's demand to "thematize" Jerusalem, that is, to ethnicize its image, has left Arab claims unaccounted for while forcing and enforcing Jerusalem's "sanctity" on Jews. The historical moment of conflict between these two modernisms unraveled a remarkable reversal: foreign critics further entangled the Israeli state in its constitutive bind, the subordination of civic symbolism to ethno-religious themes, while the modernist Israeli planners moved away from such an overtly symbolic emphasis.

Failing to recognize the spatial politics embedded in administrative planning and everyday functioning for a contested city, the foreign critics threw out the baby—the 1968 master plan—with the bathwater. The result of the alternative focus on urban design was a sense of beauty that elevated the spirit of selected members. For others, beautified Jerusalem presented "landscape as a place of amnesia and erasure, a strategic site for burying the past and veiling history with 'natural beauty.'"[57]

NOTES

This essay is part of a manuscript in preparation, tentatively titled "Designing Politics: Architecture and the Making of 'United Jerusalem.'" It is based on my doctoral dissertation at MIT (2002). I would like to thank Mark Jarzombek, Stanford Anderson, and Sibel Bozdoğan for their critical role in developing this project.

1. Teddy Kollek to Lewis Mumford, March 26, 1969, Mumford Archive, University of Pennsylvania, Philadelphia.

2. The three meetings took place in the first decade following the war (1967–77). The archival research on the plenary meeting of 1978 and the activity of the Jerusalem Committee thereafter are beyond the scope of this essay.

3. For writings on Zionist/Israeli planning, see S. Han Troen and Noah Lucas, *Israel: The First Decade of Independence* (Albany: SUNY Press, 1995), and Haim Yacobi, *Constructing a Sense of Place* (in Hebrew) (Burlington, Vt.: Ashgate, 2004); see also Zvi Efrat, *The Israeli Project* (Tel Aviv: Tel-Aviv Museum of Art, 2004), and Yehuda Shenhav, *Merhav, Adamah, Bait* (Jerusalem: ekhon Van-Lir; Tel-Aviv: Ha-Kibutz Ha-Meuhad, 2003).

4. For post–World War II architectural culture, see Joan Ockman and Edward Eigen, *Architecture Culture* (New York: Rizzoli, 1993), and Sarah Williams Goldhagen and Réjean Legault, *Anxious Modernisms* (Montreal: Candian Centre for Achitecture; Cambridge, Mass.: MIT Press, 2000).

5. The term "developmental" refers to studies of high modernism (see, e.g., J. C. Scott, *Seeing Like a State* (New Haven, Conn.: Yale University Press, 1998), and Wolfgang Sachs, *The Development Dictionary* [London: Zed Books, 1992]). The term "situated" is borrowed from Goldhagen's account of Louis Kahn, who was the most influential architect of the Jerusalem Committee (S. W. Goldhagen, *Louis Kahn's Situated Modernism* [New Haven, Conn.: Yale University Press, 2001]).

6. Jane Jacobs, *The Death and Life of Great American Cities* (New York: Vintage Books, 1992).

7. The subcommittee analyzed four documents: the 1968 Master Plan for Jerusalem; the Outline Townplanning Scheme for the Old City and its Environs; A Plan for the Central Business District; and the Jerusalem Transportation Plan for 1985.

8. Arthur Kutcher, *The New Jerusalem* (London: Thames & Hudson, 1973), 88.

9. Abraham Rabinovich, "Planners under Fire," *Jerusalem Post*, December 25, 1970, 20.

10. *The Jerusalem Committee: Proceedings of the First Meeting*, 13.

11. A. Rabinovich, "Leading World Architects Meet in Jerusalem," *Jerusalem Post*, December 18, 1970, 5. The single holdout was a Jew from Berlin, who refused to visit Jerusalem as long as it remained occupied.

12. Fuller quoted in Avrahami, "Jerusalem's Not So Golden Plan," 210; see also A. Rabinovich, "Idealized Jerusalem at Engineers Congress," *Jerusalem Post*, December 17, 1970, 8. On Fuller's ideas, see Meier, "Planning for Jerusalem."

13. A. Rabinovich, "Leading World Architects Meet in Jerusalem," *Jerusalem Post*, December 18, 1970, 5.

14. The term *Neu Sachlichkeit* is usually translated as "the New Objectivity" (see Kenneth Frampton, *Modern Architecture* [New York: Oxford, 1980], 130–148). For the development of the debate on urbanism in the modern movement, see Lewis Mumford, *The Ciam Discourse on Urbanism* (Cambridge, Mass.: MIT Press, 2000).

15. Avrahami, "Jerusalem's Not So Golden Plan," 209.

16. The planners employed a large, multidisciplinary team of architects, planners, geographers, and economists, who entered into four years of intensive, full-time work. Among the workers and consultants were graduates of planning schools in the United States who had previously worked in Washington, D.C., on problems pertaining to social and ethnic conflict. They enlivened the local discourse of urban planning with talk about new methodologies. The planning team was unique, in that its composite institutional structure, made up of professionals from many disciplines, prevented the rule of any single interest. It regularly conducted two sets of meetings, corresponding to the two hierarchical tiers of ministerial officials from the various participating government agencies. The team produced numerous interim reports that testify to the consistency of their approach. Many of these reports can be found in the library of the Ministry of Housing. The final document, which contains much more visual material, perhaps as a result of the Jerusalem Committee's criticisms, was ultimately presented in 1968, and was published in Hebrew in two impressive volumes in 1972 and 1974. Those who worked on the plan still consider it one of Israel's most impressive planning documents ever. A list of the team members can be found in David Kroyanker, *Jerusalem* (Jerusalem: Zmora-Britan, 1988).

17. For that plan, see Aryeh Sharon, *Physical Planning in Israel*. For Sharon's English account of its making, see "Planning a New Land," in Sharon, *Kibbutz + Bauhaus* (Stuttgart: Kramer Verlag, 1976), 76–95.

18. During early statehood, a national campaign that privileged rural settlement was prevalent. The shift of focus toward urban forms was greatly influenced by the Israeli effort to unite East and West Jerusalem in 1967. For the role of the city in Zionist culture, see Erik Cohen, *The City in the Zionist Ideology*.

19. See Aviah Hashimshoni et al., *1968 Jerusalem Masterplan* (Jerusalem: Jerusalem Municipality, 1972), 1:9–15.

20. Ibid., the entire plan.

21. Louis Kahn quoted in Abraham Rabinovich, "Planners Under Fire," *Jerusalem Post*, December 25, 1970, 20.

22. W. von Eckardt, "Jerusalem the Golden."

23. Amos Elon, "Jerusalem as a Gas Station Sacred to the Three Religions,"

Haaretz, December 14, 1970, 8. Elon's remark was made in response to the release of the transportation master plan, prepared by the Ministry of Transportation in collaboration with the Jerusalem master plan office.

24. Ari Avrahami, "Planning for Change," a sidebar in Avrahami, "Jerusalem's Not So Golden Plan," 215.

25. Yoseph Schweid, one of the master plan's authors, had already voiced this concern, at the 1968 Symposium on the Image of Jerusalem: "With all due respect to the noble sentiments of the large part of the civilized world who sees in this country a possession that needs to be treated as a preserve—we do not see ourselves as living on a preserve. There are landscapes in this country which require museam guard. But our first consideration must be the actual needs of life in this country" (see Avi-Yona et al., "A Symposium on the Image of Jerusalem").

26. Teddy Kollek quoted in Meier, "Planning for Jerusalem," 57.

27. Wolf von Eckardt, "Summing Up a Period," a postscript to Kroyanker, *Jerusalem*, 452.

28. Tamar Eshel Archive in Jerusalem's Municipal Archive, City Hall, Jerusalem.

29. Louis Khan quoted in Abraham Rabinovich, "Planners Under Fire," *Jerusalem Post*, December 25, 1970, 20.

30. Fascist Italy and Kemalist Turkey are famous exceptions.

31. Aldo van Eyck quoted in Smithson and Team X, *Team 10 Primer*, 15.

32. Some examples of writings of great influence in this debate are: Rudolf Wittkower, *Architectural Principles in the Age of Humanism* (London: Warburg Institute, University of London, 1949);Bernard Rudofsky, *Architecture without Architects*; (New York: Museum of Modern Art, 1964); Sibyl Moholy-Nagy, *Native Genius in Anonymous Architecture* (New York: Horizon, 1957); D.W. Thompson, *On Growth and Form* (Cambridge, U.K.: Cambridge University Press, 1961).

33. See Stanford Anderson's account of disciplinary memory in connection with the work of Louis Kahn: "Memory in Architecture (Erinnerung in Der Architektur)" (*Daidalos* 58 [1995]: 35).

34. See Moholy-Nagy, *Native Genius;* Rudofsky, *Architecture without Architects;* Smithson and Team X, *Team 10 Primer*.

35. Alexander, "A City Is Not a Tree."

36. Another example of this kind of thinking occurred during the first plenary session of the Jerusalem Committee, when Judge Hayim Cohen confessed his admiration for the prophet who celebrated the city as one would celebrate a lover (see H. Cohen, "Eternal Jerusalem," in *The Jerusalem Committee: Proceedings of the First Meeting*, 9–12).

37. Hashimshoni et al., *1968 Jerusalem Masterplan*, 49.

38. For the British fascination with the Orient, see Fuchs, "Representing

Mandatory Palestine." For the return to the British colonial paradigm, see Nitzan-Shiftan, "Israelizing Jerusalem."

39. The team made no mention of Christianity in particular. However, the notion of "heavenly Jerusalem" is a clear and erroneous reference to Christian tradition, in which "heavenly Jerusalem" is an abstract notion devoid of corporeal expression. For the notion of "heavenly Jerusalem" in Christian culture, see Prawer, "Christianity between Heavenly and Earthly Jerusalem."

40. Hashimshoni et al., *1968 Jerusalem Masterplan*, 11.

41. Ibid.

42. W. J. T. Mitchell, "Holy Landscape," 5 (electronic version).

43. Daniel B. Monk, *An Aesthetic Occupation* (Durham, N.C.: Duke University Press, 2002).

44. Yehuda Ha'ezrahi quoted in Avi-Yona et al., "A Symposium on the Image of Jerusalem," 38.

45. Tamar Eshel Archive.

46. A. Rabinovich, "Jerusalem Committee Repudiates Master Plan," *Jerusalem Post*, December 22, 1970, 8.

47. Ibid.

48. Bernard Lewis introduced "Dr. Wilson, who teaches Arabic literature at the Hebrew University and who is the author of a number of writings on the subject" (see *The Jerusalem Committee: Proceedings of Third Plenary Meeting*, 13). For the debate between Lewis and Said, see Edward Said, *Orientalism* (New York: Pantheon, 1978). For a response, see "The Question of Orientalism" in Lewis, *Islam and the West* (New York: Oxford University Press, 1993), 99–118.

49. "U.S. Architect Says: Faulty Presentation." *Jerusalem Post*, December 25, 1970, p. 5.

50. Said, "Orientalism Reconsidered."

51. See The Jerusalem Committee, "Background Information," 1978, in the Jerusalem Municipal Archive.

52. W. J. T. Mitchell, *Landscape and Power* (Chicago: University of Chicago Press, 1994), 1–2.

53. Mitchell, "Holy Landscape," 2.

54. First letter of invitation from Teddy Kollek to Lewis Mumford, March 26, 1969, Mumford Archive, University of Pennsylvania, Philadelphia. Similar letters were sent to all the members of the Jerusalem Committee.

55. For the transition from Ottoman to British rule, see Salim Tamari.

56. For further discussion of Kollek's "mosaic policy," see Roger Friedland and Richard D. Hecht, *To Rule Jerusalem* (New York: Cambridge University Press, 1996).

57. Ibid.

8 Palestinian Remembrance Days and Plans
Kafr Qasim, Fact and Echo

WALEED KHLEIF AND SUSAN SLYOMOVICS

In memory of Waleed Khleif, who died of cancer on July 31, 2006

Even when facts are not in dispute, some people want to remember, others want to forget. When facts are in dispute, the divide between those who want to remember and those who want to efface widens. How are memories and commemorative practices metonyms for the larger Palestinian predicament, in particular for Palestinians' rights as citizens of Israel and for Israel's responsibility to its Palestinian Arab population? Azmi Bishara, the Palestinian Israeli philosopher, asserts in a much-quoted statement: "There could not begin to be an equality until stones mark the graves of what were once villages, nor an historic compromise until Palestinians obtain their tombstones; the victim must be recognized in order for him to forgive."[1] In Bishara's succinct aspiration for a solution are subsumed a series of necessary steps: an accommodation to alternate historical truths,[2] a recognition of Palestinians as victims, the restoration of their former sites of habitation (if only as memorials, according to Bishara's radical proposal), and, finally, the victim's right of choice to accept or refuse these processes. Indeed, the first memorial to the contested history of the Palestinians and Israelis was erected, in the form of a monument near Sakhnin in the Galilee, to mark "Land Day" and to commemorate six Palestinian Israelis killed in 1976 during protests of Israeli seizures of Palestinian land.[3] The monument has been described as "a watershed of identity and memory, when the Palestinian identity of the Arabs in Israel started to gain presence in the public space."[4] The right to place memorials dedicated to the eradicated Palestinian past within

Israeli public space is an example of the notion of "historical justice," defined in recent historiography as an alternate, sometimes parallel path. Unlike solutions to problems between nations that are resolved in conventional, courtroom-centered, criminal justice venues, historical justice assumes that the act of recognizing and acknowledging an historical truth is itself a form of justice.

In this essay, using the lengthy, contested historical struggle of Palestinians in Israel as background, we focus on how architecture (local and international design competitions), ritual (annual commemorations), and public performance (especially poetry and the erection of monuments) have been enlisted as ways to revise entrenched historical accounts about the Palestinian past within Israel.[5] Following James Young's definitions as applied to Holocaust memorials, we find it useful to "distinguish a memorial from a monument only in a broader, more generic sense."

> There are memorial books, memorial activities, memorial days, memorial festivals, and memorial sculptures. Some of these are mournful, some celebratory: but all are memorials in a larger sense. Monuments, on the other hand, will refer here to a subset of memorials; they are the material objects, the sculptures and installations used to memorialize a person or a thing.... A memorial may be a day, a conference, or a space but it need not be a monument. A monument, on the other hand, is always a kind of memorial.[6]

While some commemorative monuments have appeared in Palestinian Arab villages within Israel, many projects remain plans; they represent the will to build with scant hope of realization. This is spectacularly so for the proposed memorial to the 1948 Israeli massacre of Palestinians at Deir Yassin, on a site opposite to and within view of Jerusalem's Yad Vashem Museum to Holocaust Victims.[7]

As a case study, our essay focuses on the 1956 massacre at Kafr Qasim and on the ways in which the memory of the massacre and of the victims is kept alive. The massacre occurred on Thursday, October 29, 1956. On the eve of the 1956 Sinai campaign, shortly after 5:00 P.M., Palestinian citizens of Israel from the village of Kafr Qasim—men, women, and children—were returning home at the end of the workday, unaware that a curfew had been declared during their absence, when they were shot by units of the Israel Defense Force charged with protecting Israel's border. The majority of the workers were killed at the western entrance to Kafr Qasim, a few in the center of the town, and some to the north of the town center. This last group, known as the "women's group," consisted of fourteen women, a boy, and four men. Over time, at each of the locations where the Kafr Qasim villagers were murdered, a variety of ephemeral gestures and site-specific installations have appeared. We analyze these efforts at commemoration constructed by the inhabitants of Kafr Qasim, including the creation of Palestinian art, monuments, and performances that have been shaped by the massacre. Thus, in the aftermath of Kafr Qasim, we have chosen to study Palestinian Israelis' and Jewish Israelis' symbolic and ritual gestures. These performative manifestations reveal past and present issues of culpability, the power of memory and memorializing, the civic motivation of the Palestinian minority population to erect monuments, the public acceptance of moral responsibility, the acknowledgment of wrongdoing that is communicated between opposing parties, and the nature of the historical truth that governs relations between Jewish Israelis and Palestinian Israelis.[8]

KAFR QASIM: POST-1948 HISTORY AND THE 1956 MASSACRE

During the Israeli-Jordanian armistice talks that began on March 4, 1949, Jordan ceded a strip of territory designated by Israeli historiographers as the "Little Triangle." As a result of the cession, approximately 20,000 Palestinian Arabs living in fifteen villages, among them Kafr Qasim, were added to the Jewish Israeli population (see fig. 8.1).[9] The historian Benny Morris had provided an account of the political and military conditions that existed in the Triangle and of how Israeli plans to expel those Arabs on the Israeli side of the cease-fire line were disrupted:

> There was apparently no "clean" way to pressure the Arabs into leaving. The inhabitants of Baqa al Gharbiya, At Taiyiba, Qaqun, Qalansuwa, Kafr Qasim, At Tira and the Wadi 'Ara villages stayed put. As [Moshe] Sharett [Israel's Foreign Minister from 1948 to 1954] put it on 28 July: "This time . . . the Arabs learned the lesson; they are not running away. It is not possible in every place to arrange what some of our boys engineered in Faluja [where] they chased away the Arabs after we signed an . . . international commitment. . . . There were warnings from the UN and the U.S. in this matter. . . . There were at least 25–30,000 . . . whom we could not uproot.[10]

Until 1967, the village of Kafr Qasim was situated at a distance of only one kilometer from Israel's eastern border with Jordan, at the easternmost point of what was once thought of as Israel's *beten rakhah* (soft underbelly)—the

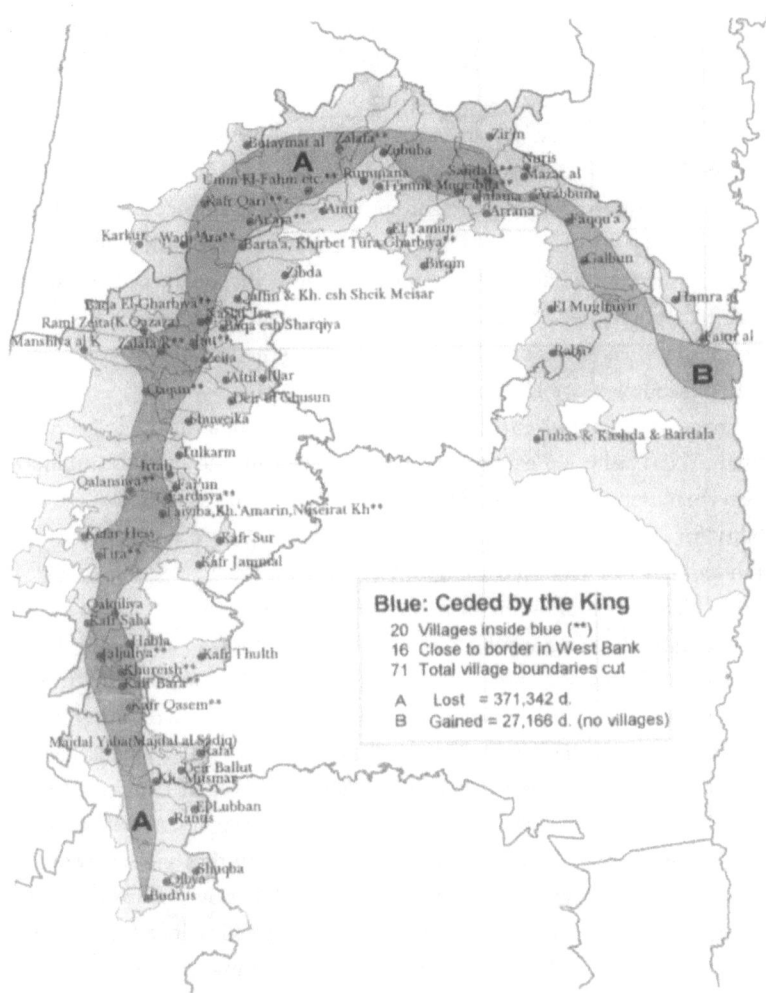

FIG. 8.1. *1949 Map of the Little Triangle: Kafr Qasim (in shaded area) ceded to Israel. Adapted from the* Survey of Palestine, *by the Palestine Land Society, London, 2002, and Salman Abu Sitta. Reproduced by permission of Salman Abu Sitta.*

densely populated, narrow coastal strip of Israel that extended only fifteen kilometers, from the Mediterranean Sea to the Jordanian border. The Palestinian villages on both sides of the border share specific legal and sociocultural features. On the Israeli side, however, inhabitants of the Little Triangle are neither refugees nor "present absentees" (defined as Palestinians who are internal refugees, displaced from their original homes and lands but still resid-

Palestinian Remembrance Days and Plans 189

ing within the borders of Israel). On the Jordanian side, the United Nations Relief and Work Agency (UNRWA) does not classify border villagers as refugees.[11] Nonetheless, Palestinians on both sides of the 1949 Israel-Jordan armistice boundary lost considerable agricultural land to Israel, depending upon which side of the border they found themselves. Palestinians living in Jordan were dispossessed of their lands by the new lines of partition, and Palestinian Israelis were dispossessed as a result of land expropriation by the state of Israel under succeeding emergency regulations that promoted Jewish settlements along Israel's borders with Jordan as strategic defense units.[12] The Kafr Qasim villagers, as dispossessed farmers on the Israeli side, were transformed into low-wage laborers.[13]

Since 1948, according to the ethnographic account of anthropologist Abner Cohen, Kafr Qasim has exemplified what Cohen calls the "border situation." The term is useful for understanding subsequent Israeli discourses about responsibility for crimes and indemnities, as these govern future relations between Arab and Jew in Israel. According to Cohen: "A distinct category ... are villages, which (a) lie literally on the most strategically sensitive part of the [Israeli-Jordanian] border, (b) are cut off by that border from close associate villages, only a few miles away within Jordan, (c) are in intense interaction with the Jews in Israel with whom they have great economic interests, and (d) are seriously caught up in the strife between Israel and the Arab world."[14] The larger pattern of "intense interaction" between Arab and Jew that Cohen identifies inevitably owes much to the Palestinians' intertwined experience of massacre, trials, reconciliation, pardon, memory, and monuments that is the story of Kafr Qasim, even though most Arab villages in Israel, Cohen avers, can be regarded as border villages.[15] Certainly, Kafr Qasim's geographical location close to a contested, militarized border contributed to the ensuing tragedy. Benny Morris notes that between 1949 and 1956, Israel's "free-fire policy" prevailed along the border and resulted in a series of "atrocities,"[16] as well as contributing to the massacre that led Palestinian Israelis to conclude that their expulsion, or worse, was imminent.[17] A hint of their worst fears (which requires an as yet unwritten, thickly descriptive ethnography of the culture of fear among Palestinian Israelis during the 1950s) is offered by Abd at-Tamam, a Palestinian Israeli artist from Kafr Qasim, who recalls having lived through the 1956 events, when he was twelve years old, that continue to inform the content of his paintings. When asked by an interviewer, "Who buried the dead?" at-Tamam replied:

> People from the neighboring village of Jaljulya. We were in our houses. They brought people from Jaljulya to dig the graves. They were frightened.

> They were told that each one should dig a grave. They thought [the graves] were for themselves. We learned this afterward. On that same day imprisoned [in our homes] we didn't know. They took the notables to identify the bodies. It was a shocking thing, a man whose two sons went to work and did not return and he threw aside the cover, looked and saw that it was his son. The people of Jaljulya buried them twenty centimeters in the ground. After this, people dug and brought out the bodies from the graves and buried them again.[18]

Abd at-Tamam's testimony highlights a significant aspect of the earliest post-massacre moments. Palestinians feared that they were literally being forced to dig their own graves, a situation that resonates uncomfortably with genocidal techniques elsewhere. The closure ritually and traditionally enacted between legitimate mourners and a dead body was disrupted by Israeli dismissal of burial practices, to the degree that any Palestinian, not a family member, might act as a gravedigger and mourner. The Kafr Qasim villagers' immediate response, after an enforced hiatus of two days before they were even permitted to approach the cemetery, was to reclaim their dead from shallow graves dug in haste and fear and to re-inter the bodies on their own terms. This was described to us by interviewees as a collective act of resistance, meant to assuage wounds and reclaim normal funerary rites. As with burial sites in distant lands, for the Palestinian diasporic dead, the Kafr Qasim cemetery became the first site permitted to display commemorative monuments, in the form of graves and headstones etched with the word "Martyr" (see figs. 8.2 and 8.3). Since that first year, the space of the cemetery, the headstones, and the annual ceremonies anchor, sustain, and inspire subsequent projects that build upon and spread outside of the spatial confines of both Muslim sacred and Israeli state-approved burial grounds in order to scatter physical markers of the massacre throughout the town.

But in the beginning there was fear, confusion, and ignorance, compounded by the villagers' forced confinement in their homes in the aftermath of the massacre:

> There was imprisonment [in our houses]. People could not go out. I heard neighbors shouting: "Has yours returned?" "Did your father return?" Those who stayed outdoors died. After two, three days, I don't remember exactly, the notables arrived and went from house to house and asked for hoes and axes. The more older adults knew immediately that this was to dig graves. People knew that whoever did not return home, had died. After

FIG. 8.2. *Entrance to Kafr Qasim Martyrs' Cemetery. Photo by Susan Slyomovics.*

FIG. 8.3. *Kafr Qasim Cemetery, 2006 project to paint the martyrs' graves green. Photo by Susan Slyomovics.*

two days, they permitted people to go to the cemetery to know the victims. There were some who thought that all the people in the village had died so they ran away. There were wounded people in the hospital. I saw no woman screaming or shouting, none weeping or shedding tears. A kind of dryness. An interior pain. No words. No words whatsoever. People sat and looked at each other.[19]

In general, when we speak of gestures of apology, accountability, and truth telling, roles are assigned designating certain persons or governments as perpetrators who need to acknowledge wrongdoing, while at the same time describing the situation of those who were set upon as victims. Kafr Qasim is not only an extreme case, but an exemplary one: it is anomalous because these Palestinian villagers remained in their ancestral homes and homelands, but it is characteristic because their agricultural lands were taken away. Residents of Kafr Qasim were neither Palestinian refugees nor "present absentees" within Israel, yet after the massacre they were officially, symbolically, and legally recognized as victims of the state of Israel. The people of Kafr Qasim remained in their home territory after 1948 (despite subsequent land expropriations to establish a neighboring Jewish settlement), exhibiting what Palestinians in Israel term *thabat* (generally defined as an immoveable, quiet, physical force of nature, when a peasant unreflectively stays put, grips the land, and refuses to leave). In contrast, when Kafr Qasim became nationally and internationally known as an example of the state's violence against its own citizens, after the 1956 massacre, articulated as fundamental to the new vocabularies and strategies for Palestinian Israelis in the 1960s was the notion of *ṣumūd*: a purposeful, nationalistic struggle with the same end of staying put physically on the land that evolved into marking this struggle publicly. Thus, Ibrahim Sarsur, head of Kafr Qasim's municipal council during our 1998 fieldwork, insists from hindsight that the massacre in his village had the unintended consequence of dispelling the culture of fear that pervaded the lives of Arabs in Israel, certainly for himself, born after the massacre, and that it had thereby contributed an emotional and moral force to the *samidin* who stayed put:

> The massacre of Kafr Qasim completely liberated the inhabitants of Kafr Qasim, especially the young, from the tight manacles of military rule in the 1950s and 60s. The young stopped being afraid and decided to transform the first memorial day to the massacre, organized in 1957, as a sign

of the beginning of the struggle against fear and suspicion from military rule, from its representatives and from all of its activities in Kafr Qasim and outside.[20]

The conceptual shift from *thabat* to *ṣumūd* does not reveal itself easily through overt actions, such as a mass reburial, but it does signal, if not help lay the foundations for innovative collective history-making processes and architectural planning. While the notion of *ṣumūd* has received much attention in literary and historical analyses of Palestinian-Israeli confrontations, and although *ṣumūd* is a consequence of violence, to be emphasized are its nonviolent and creative realizations in Kafr Qasim, embodied in conceiving and erecting memorializing projects. Certainly, in the early years after the massacre, the ways in which both sides understood the pursuit of peaceful relations differed, as military trials interspersed with a ceremony of reconciliation unfolded. Questions arise concerning the ways in which the Israeli pursuit of justice through the military courts is compatible in any way with Israel's declared pursuit of reconciliation. In turn, what are the ways in which the immediate village reburial transforms traditional Muslim gravesites at the Kafr Qasim cemetery into national Palestinian monuments? What public and political events have emerged dynamically in the lives of Palestinians and in relation to Israeli gestures based on the pivotal moment of the massacred, twice-buried, annually commemorated Palestinian body?

ISRAELI STATE RESPONSES: MILITARY COURT TRIAL, COMPENSATION AND ṢULḤA (CEREMONY OF RECONCILIATION)

After a year-and-a-half-long, highly publicized military trial (lasting from January 15, 1957 to October 16, 1958), and two years after the shootings in Kafr Qasim, eleven members of the Border Police, including the battalion commander, Major Shmuel Malinki, were sentenced to lengthy prison terms. In contrast, in a second, swift military trial, the responsible brigade commander, Issachar Shadmi, was convicted of a minor administrative offence and sentenced to pay a fine equivalent to a penny.[21] All the convicted border policemen were freed after three years, having received presidential pardons or administrative reductions of their sentences, which were served in a Jerusalem sanitorium and not in prison. Lieutenant Gabriel Dahan, found guilty of killing forty-three citizens, was sentenced to seventeen years. He too was freed after three years, to be rehabilitated and appointed in 1960 as an officer for Arab affairs in the nearby municipality of Ramleh. When Dahan retired, Kafr Qasim villagers reported to us that his newest assignment was as a security guard in the shopping mall at Rosh ha-Ayin, a nearby Jewish settlement that had been built on expropriated Kafr Qasim agricultural lands. The initial Israeli response to the massacre relied on criminal law, although the criminal process was limited and suborned by amnesties for all the perpetrators. Nonetheless, the Kafr Qasim trials establish a clear legal precedent in Israeli civil and military law that following orders or transmitting the order to shoot is sufficient grounds for determining guilt if murder is the consequence, even if the transmitter of those orders to shoot does not have murderous intentions. Following such legal terminology, a black flag had been raised, and thus a "partnership in crime" is invoked.[22]

On November 10, 1957, a year after the massacre, but in the midst of the first trial, a Public Committee, hastily formed to consider compensation for the wounded and slain of Kafr Qasim, indemnified inheritors of the slain. An exception was the one pregnant victim, Fatimah Salih Sarsur, whose family was allotted an additional 1,000 pounds, "in consideration of the fact that she was in the last days of her pregnancy at her death."[23] Fatimah and her unborn child represent both a real and a symbolic instance of contestation between Arab and Jew. During the trial, testimony was presented by sixteen-year old Hana Sulayman Amir, a survivor of the massacre, who described the killings of seventeen people in the third group of women. Hana's testimony, after she repeated the words of the two Israeli officers as they confronted and then shot the pregnant Fatimah, continue to resound in text and image: Officer Shmuel Malinky said to Sergeant Shalom Ofer, "Kadur ehad maspik" (A single bullet is sufficient).[24] Fatimah's fecund female life, cheaply and easily dispatched, was cut short as she was about to produce a child, part of a future generation that fuels Jewish fears about high Arab fertility and low Jewish birth rates, in the ultimate demographic war between Arab and Jew.[25] One bullet, two lives expended, and a penny fine for fifty lives relegated Palestinians to abuse by the dominant culture and left them unable to defend their own land and homes. Another consequence of Fatimah's death is that the number of Palestinians killed by the Israeli Border Police continues to be a figure in dispute: Israelis acknowledge thirteen injured and forty-nine dead, whereas Palestinians count fifty dead because they include as a fiftieth victim the unborn child carried by the pregnant Fatimah. At the base of the monument and fountain constructed inside the municipality complex in 1973, the people of Kafr Qasim memorialized the fifty dead with forty-nine white headstones inscribed with the names of the dead; the fiftieth remains starkly blank (see fig. 8.4). Adel Badir, our tour guide and a member of the commemoration committee, explained the choice of a fountain with water: life continues like a stream and because all the water in the monument flows upward to one source, symbolizing that the fate (*masirah*) of all the victims, even the unborn, was the same.[26]

In the rush to supply tidy endings, the Public Committee's report ended with a recommendation to both sides to set up a ṣulḥa ceremony in Kafr Qasim, at government expense, as soon as possible and "in accord with customary Arab tradition" (be-hetem la-masoret ha-'aravit ha-mekubelet).[27] The reconciliation ceremony and the financial compensation report were intimately related in time and content. On November 20, 1957, more than a year after the Kafr Qasim massacre, a mere seventeen days after the Public Committee's recommendation and in the midst of the first trial, a ceremony staged by Israeli authorities in the village of Kafr Qasim was designated by Israeli authorities with an Arabic word, ṣulḥa, which in the Arabic-speaking world denotes a ceremony of reconciliation. The ṣulḥa is a much-studied sociocultural event in Western and Israeli anthropology. Israeli anthropologist Abner Cohen undertook fieldwork in 1958, not long after the massacre in Kafr Qasim.[28] Cohen's village descriptions are especially important to appreciate the contrasting Arab and Jewish viewpoints of the subsequent trial, reconciliation efforts, and indemnities that resulted from the massacre; Cohen illustrates the differences between Jewish Israeli justice and "Arab justice," the latter being a term applied by Cohen to complex Palestinian and Arab juridical institutions such as *sulh* (reconciliation) and *ṣulḥa* (reconciliation ceremony), as they were conducted among Kafr Qasim's *hamulahs* (village clans). Cohen concludes that "Perhaps the most serious divergence between Arab concepts of justice and those implicit in Israeli legislation is the abolition, in Israel, of the death penalty. This abolition runs counter to the Arab notion of justice based on retribution, although allowance is made in Arab justice for the payment of blood money."[29] Eliminating the death penalty, however, is no guarantee that the state will not find other means to execute its citizens: witness the killings at Kafr Qasim. It seems possible that Israel's Arabists, many of whom are and were responsible for ruling over as well as studying the Arab population, share Cohen's fieldwork conclusions that "Disputes are not regarded by [Arab] villagers as settled until indigenous procedures of arbitration and reconciliation took place. Often the [Israeli] police themselves helped in setting these procedures in operation. In some of the cases the police were requested by the villagers not to take the disputants to courts, when the matter was settled according to 'Arab Justice.'"[30] Given that Cohen's fieldwork took place a year after the Kafr Qasim massacre, his ahistorical research findings are strikingly oblivious to the reasons why Palestinian villagers in Israel, under military rule from 1948 to 1964, preferred local legal controls to the Jewish Israeli courts. Nonetheless, how to account for the spectacle of an Israeli government appropriating and financing traditions of Arab justice? Moreover, Ibrahim Sarsur informed us during our 1998 visit that he and other inhabitants had come to see this ṣulḥa as a response to a wrongful murder, powered by the need to cover up by denial and betrayal. Sarsur, repeating the experiences of his parents' generation, corroborated Abd at-Tamam's story of the terrified Jaljulya gravediggers brought to bury the Kafr Qasim victims while their families remained under house detention, but Sarsur also maintains that the planning for the ṣulḥa ceremony, forced upon the villagers, was long intended, perhaps from the horrific moment when the village *mukhtar* was brought to identify the dead bodies of his villagers, and then discovered among the dead the corpse of his own son, and turned to the officer in charge: "Why was my son killed? What did he do?" The military governor replied: "Tomorrow you will eat *savīh* [an eggplant and chickpea dish] and everything will work out."[31]

Sarsur's description of the ṣulḥa is a powerful testimony of the event:

> The food was prepared, the food was not eaten. Village inhabitants and a small part of the victims' families were brought to a tent erected in the only village school. During the forced ṣulḥa, notables participated from neighboring Arab villages that were an integral part of the regime's rule in the State of Israel. The media reported that the ṣulḥa was conducted according to the best of Arab tradition. The massacre, according to this definition, was kind of a quarrel of village clans that ended in a ṣulḥa, food, drinks, peace. Ben-Gurion needed a ṣulḥa before the end of the trial of the murderers, a ṣulḥa that supposedly enabled him to make a deal with Malinki and the rest of the soldiers: after the inhabitants of Kafr Qasim forgive, there is no reason for the murderers to remain in jail. "It is a moral obligation to free them," Ben-Gurion claimed. The second reason for Ben-Gurion wanting a ṣulḥa is that it would "release" the Israeli government from any further responsibilities towards the victims. . . .
>
> From many conversations I have had with victims' families it emerges that pressure was applied to them and strong threats including threats of deportation and being fired in order that they should participate in the ṣulḥa process. Until today, in Kafr Qasim, there is no one who agrees with the manner of treatment of the government of Israel concerning the massacre and its consequences.[32]

The ṣulḥa, that is, the true Arab reconciliation ceremony, publicly mediates disputes among and between individuals, families, and clans; the ṣulḥa is not intended to resolve conflicts between persons and governments. Yet the conundrum remains: since Arab justice in Israel is devalued by Israeli Jewish views of the Arab population, for whom did the Israeli government organize the Kafr Qasim ṣulḥa, and why? Not for the mourning families who were forced to attend and participate in their degradation, Sarsur insists.[33] A contemporary newspaper account ends with the words of Hamdelelullah Sarsur, a son of one of the victims: "Not one member of the bereaved families would come to the proposed ṣulḥa with the man standing trial for killing 43 [sic] villagers. He charged that the villagers were 'forced' to sign in favour of the Rashish Committee finding."[34] Is this an instance of the state of Israel, while encountering the Arab native as the embodiment of an effaced past, romanticizing useful fragments of Arab culture to be embraced for the moment (e.g., during a ṣulḥa)? Is there a culinary parallel in the journalist's report that "an Arab-style meal was served by Shekem, the Israeli army catering organization"?[35] Can the state of Israel simulate, or does the state mock, Arab justice for the Arabs? Israel's leaders reproduced early anthropological "culturalist" views of the Arab world, in which Israel's own culturally constructed stereotypes keep non-Western groups as frozen representatives within unvarying societies that are resistant to historical time and contexts. So, too, the Western and Israeli scholarly interest in the Arab *hamulah* (the clan system) is similarly theorized as a static, internally coherent social system, unaffected by the external impact of colonialism.[36] Linked to *hamulah* studies are detailed descriptions of the ṣulḥa, viewed by anthropologists as a parallel mode of social control achieved by means of a set of relationships among the patrilineal Arab clan system. A potent mix of orientalism, the weight of Israeli military rule and administrative control over Arabs in Israel, and crude pressure on the Kafr Qasim families to participate underlies the discourse of a ṣulḥa as a process toward healing and reconciliation.

Although the Israeli government appropriated Arab juridical terms and traditions, the villagers of Kafr Qasim explained to us that at least they were able to endure the ceremony and gain ironic relief from Ashkenazi Jewish Israeli mispronunciations of ṣulḥa that mistakenly transformed the middle consonant "h" (the voiceless pharyngeal fricative) to "kh" (the voiceless uvular fricative). Thus, ṣulḥa (reconciliation), whenever articulated by Jewish Israeli voices during the ceremony, was heard and understood by Kafr Qasim villagers to mean *sulkhah*, which means "a butchery" and "a flaying."[37] Shared notions of political and historical truths or, minimally, a shared consensus between the two opposing groups were strikingly absent. For the villagers of Kafr Qasim, there was no dearth of evidence that customary social and cultural institutions and relations (kinship network, clan system, legal modes of maintaining social peace) were not stable, unadulterated systems operating in a peaceful context, but systems profoundly altered by conflict, terror, and high-intensity threats. There was no reconciliation and no peace during the ṣulḥa, but instead Sarsur describes a slow, painful butchery, as if the participants were being skinned alive again.

A FIRST MEMORIAL: PALESTINIAN POETRY

Open your gates, O our village
Open them to the four winds
And let fifty wounds glow with fire.
Kafr Qasim,
A village dreaming of grain, violet flowers,
And flocks of pigeons:
"Mow them all down in one full sweep,
Mow them down."[38]
They mowed them down.
. . . .
If only I buried all the dying words,
If only I had the strength of the cemetery's silence,
O you the hand that plays music, O shame for fifty strings,
If only I could write my history with a scythe,
My life with an axe,
And the song of a lark.[39]

In the felt absence of meaningful justice and restitution for Kafr Qasim's dead, and as a counter-performance to the trial and the ṣulḥa, Palestinian poets and Arabic poetry perform the roles of judge, historian, teacher, and memoirist of the massacre. Tawfiq Tubi, then a member of Israel's Knesset as a representative of the Communist Party, recounted during our interview that on November 7, 1956, a week after the massacre, he decided to break the silence.[40] The first newspaper article about the events appeared on November 23, in *al-Ittihad*, the Arabic-language newspaper of the Israeli Communist Party. Authored by Tubi in the form of a *mudhakkarah* (a term denoting both a memorial and report), the article was widely distributed, appearing eventually as a separate pamphlet in Arabic, Hebrew, and English.[41] The Palestinian poet Tawfiq Zayyad spoke with Tubi, who provided details and fresh accounts, indeed the closest thing to an eyewitness, his being a parliamentarian who arrived a few days after the massacre. Zayyad, in turn, met with a close circle of poets and friends. The poem, as the first memorial, emerged immediately after the 1956 massacre, whereas monuments were not erected until 1973; thirteen years after the massacre, villagers still fearful of building their first architectural statement on the actual site of the massacre, instead placed the sculpture in the town core, adjacent to the main municipality building, instead of at the stated preference for a monument, on the specific sites of the massacre (see fig. 8.4).[42]

While physical memorials beyond the cemetery walls had to wait, poetry emerged to articulate the archive of written and oral testimony. Annually, poetry is declaimed and accompanied by a procession through the village that stops at the massacre sites and ends at the cemetery, for prayers and the placing of wreaths. According to Waleed Khleif, his generation of Palestinian Arab writers (in their teens and twenties the year of the massacre) derived poetic inspiration from the *Ittihad* article authored by Tawfiq Tubi, and from Zayyad's account to Khleif and his fellow poets about what Tubi saw. The mantle of the poet as the conscience of the community was first taken up by Tawfiq Zayyad. Zayyad produced a *malhamāh,* a heroic cycle consisting of four poems,[43] dated November 1956, a few weeks after the event, although the poems were to be later performed only at the first anniversary of the massacre, a year after their composition, in November 1957, in the courtyard at Mary's Well, the central plaza of Nazareth. Khleif, who was present to read his poetry, recalls an audience of more than five thousand people. The occasion, the content, and the style of Zayyad's cycle heralded the beginnings of "the literature of resistance" (*adab al-muqāwamāh*).[44] Traditional romantic poetry—as practiced in Palestine, for example, by Jamal Qawar, Michael Haddad, and Yusuf Nakhleh—is complemented by another vision from a new generation of writers, those living *fi-al-dākhīl* (inside)—the Palestinian Arab inhabitants of the state of Israel after 1948 who became renowned throughout the Arabic-speaking world for voices committed to politically engaged poetry. Zayyad's poem, "On the Trunk of an Olive Tree," presents the olive tree as a symbol of communal rootedness, identity, and resistance. The poet values the tree for a different kind of materiality. Denied a voice and paper and pen to publish, the poet proclaims novel uses for the olive tree, appropriate to the Palestinian struggle, which permits him to "carve all that has

FIG. 8.4. *1973 monument and fountain in Municipality Square, with a blank headstone for the fiftieth victim of the massacre. Photo by Susan Slyomovics.*

happened / all my secrets / on an olive tree in the courtyard of the house / I shall carve my story and all the seasons of my tragedy, my sighs." Poetically, the poet's personal attachment to the tree and its deep and long-living roots in the soil, as the steadfast bond, *sumūd*, between Palestinians and the land have been invested with heightened symbolic meanings. For poets, the commonplace in the material environment permits both the writing of the message and the sending of a message to the world, mediated by the tree. As have other Palestinian poets, Zayyad has kept his promise: "I shall carve Kafr Qasim I will not forget / I shall carve Dayr Yasin, rooted in memory."

Although a first-anniversary commemoration was held in Kafr Qasim,[45] it is the second-anniversary event commemorating the massacre, on October 27, 1958, which produced poems speedily memorized throughout the Arabic-speaking world. Only during the second year were details of the trials and descriptions of perpetrators and victims made available to the public. Published court proceedings allowed poets of the resistance generation to imagine that the massacre had actually taken place before their eyes. No one from the village of Kafr Qasim, which lies approximately sixty kilometers from Nazareth, attended the early commemorations, since the Israeli Military Laws in effect from 1948 to 1964 prohibited Arabs within Israel from traveling from their officially designated residences without permits. Likewise, every year memorial ceremonies for the dead were held in the Kafr Qasim village cemetery, although in the early years, as villagers recount in interviews, each third week of October, Israeli authorities declared the village a closed area, an action that prevented outsiders from entering.

Because the villagers of Kafr Qasim could not attend the memorial service held on their behalf in Nazareth without violatiing Israeli military law, a group of poets—namely, Mahmud Darwish, Tawfiq Zayyad, Waleed Khleif, Salim Jubran, Samih al-Qasim, Issam Abassy, and Hanna Abu Hanna—drove by car to participate in the local Kafr Qasim village ceremonies in 1958. On the spot where many of the villagers were killed—where a large memorial tombstone would eventually be erected for the twenty-third anniversary of the event, on October 20, 1979, and renovated for the fiftieth anniversary in 2006 (see fig. 8.5)—the delegation of poets joined other villagers in the *fātihah*. Khleif recounts that they all walked to the village cemetery where the victims were buried. Ali Ibrahim al-Ali, the shaykh and imam of Kafr Qasim led prayers for the souls of the dead. The procession of men and women stopped at the three additional spots where their kin had been killed, then gathered at the main square. The Israeli authorities permitted a religious ceremony and silent procession, but forbade any speechmaking. Standing on a raised platform, the first and only poet able to speak was Waleed Khleif. He began, "Will Kafr Qasim be forgotten and the blood of the victims in vain be sh[ed]?" (Kafr qasima nansa wa-dammu al-dahaya sudan yuh—[rahku]?). Khleif recalls that in mid-syllable of the first line of his poem, while pronouncing the word "shed," multiple club blows rained down upon him from more than 250 Israeli security police who were monitoring the procession.[46] The delegation of poets was hustled into a border police command car, beaten with swagger sticks, jailed together for less than a week, and fined. Charges of illegal entry into a closed military area and inciting a riot by inflammatory speech—all without a military permit—were eventually dropped. While in Bet Lid prison, the poets continued their poetic speechmaking and declaimed and created more poetry. Poems, never uttered in Kafr Qasim before their intended audience, were subsequently published in *al-Ittihad*.

The poetry of those poets who were briefly imprisoned together—Mahmud Darwish, Samih al-Qasim, and Hanna Abu Hanna—is politically focused, anchored in the reality of oppression and the experience of persecution, and this poetry illumines facets of Arab life in Israel in the 1950s. Mahmud Darwish's poem, "al-Qatil raqm 48" ("Victim Number 48") was set to music by Marcel Khalifeh in 1972 and became a popular hit song throughout the Arabic-speaking world.[47] Darwish's poem is about Fathi Uthman Isa, who was twelve years old when he was shot and killed along with other members of his family. His body was found on a rock farthest from the entrance to the village and at some distance from where the others were killed. Thus, Fathi was one of the first to die, and he was garlanded with roses and the moon, romantic items borrowed from Palestinian folklore to describe the magical world of childhood:

> They found in his chest a garland of roses and the moon
> while he lay discarded, dead on a rock.
> They found in his pocket some pennies,
> they found a matchbox, and a travel permit,
> on his arm freshly-drawn tattoos.
> When his brother grew up and went searching for work
>   in the city markets,
> they imprisoned him.
> He was not carrying a travel permit,
> He was carrying a tattered satchel
> and some other boxes.
> O children of my country,
> this is how the moon dies.

In Mahmud Darwish's poem, "Uyun al-mawtā alā al-abwāb" ("The Eyes of the Dead on the Doors"),[48] the victims' eyes, wandering restlessly and unburied through the village and through our consciousness, are represented metaphorically as the "ten candles" of the ten dead boys and girls. Darwish pointedly asks, How is it possible to speak about massacred children?

> What do you bring to the ten candles that lit up Kafr Qasim,
> Only more hymns about doves
> and skulls?
> They don't want and we don't repeat
> our laments, they don't bargain

    the commandment of shed blood seeks our help to resist.
    At night, they knock on every door,
    each door, every door,
    they beg not to heap earth on their precious blood.
    Their eyes, extinguished, address us to castigate:
    "Do not bury us with dirges, but keep our memory steadfast,
    so that we may prepare your night for the glitter of new light."
    O Kafr Qasim,
    from the victims' coffins, a banner raised shall proclaim:
    Stop, stop,
    stop and think.
    No, no, do not yield to shame.
    You have been billed to repay debts exacted by the storm
    as shadows fall.
    O Kafr Qasim.
    we will not sleep as long as you have your cemetery and nightfall
    and the commandment of shed blood is not to be forgotten
    and the commandment of blood calls for our help
    so that we may resist.

Darwish's poem has been directly incorporated into the annual commemorative performances in Kafr Qasim. On the evening of October 29 each year, a gathering is held outdoors and attended by dignitaries. Forty-nine children, each of them dressed in black and bearing torches, march on to the stage. Behind them, the master of ceremonies reads the names of the dead; as each name is read, the child carries the torch, douses it, and leaves the stage. At the end of the reading of the names, the stage is in utter darkness and silence is preserved.[49]

PALESTINIAN POETRY, PERFORMANCE, AND MEMORIALS

Samih al-Qasim, in the poem "Li-yādin dhallāt tuqāwim" ("To a Hand that Still Resists"), includes quiet funeral obsequies and private laments to mourn what happened at Kafr Qasim. Here, the poet conveys his reaction when he first arrived at the village:

    Then I came.
    Your trusting children welcomed me
    We recited the *fatihah*.

> In your children's eyes,
> O you women with wounded eyes,
> the river is dried out, and the doves' song is dead
> while I, O Kafr Qasim,
> I grant no dirges to the dead, but praise
> the hand that still resists.

Al-Qasim's poem concludes with words to his fellow Palestinians, playing with the echo of a well-known folk proverb: "Khellīh fī-al-qalb yijrāh walā bayn an-nas yifdāh" (Let it continue wounding the heart, never let it be exposed to people). He proposes an alternative: Were this wound to remain in the heart for generations, waiting the day to emerge, al-Qasim the poet, in contrast, will not be silenced. His rhythmic proclamation, the village name chanted three times, is linked to the blood of its victims, who will one day bring about a future resistance movement:

> All that we said is insignificant,
> what is inside the heart remains in the heart
> from one generation to the next.
> Until the river resurrected
> and the doves burst into songs
> Then I fill the universe with relentless screams:
> Kafr Qasim
> Kafr Qasim
> Kafr Qasim
> Your blood is still unavenged
> But we shall resist.

The Palestinian Israeli poet Hanna Abu Hanna tells how an individual, even among the fifty dead, not only counts to those who love and grieve, but also evokes anguish that endures for days, weeks, years, and decades. Each victim's death possesses a unique history and form, yet of what import were the fifty massacred? Abu Hanna asks and answers these questions:

> How can we forget the bitterness of our past
> and in the present narrate our tragedies
> and still we have chains choking us
> as betrayal moves quickly to banish what remains of us?
> . . . .

> How can we forget the bitterness of our past
> and how our present still proclaims our tragedy?

How our present still proclaims our tragedy, Abu Hanna insists. Kafr Qasim stands metonymically, the physical attached to its referent, a part standing for the whole, for the many fates of Palestinians since 1948. For Palestinian poets within Israel, Kafr Qasim is within the culture of resistance, the refusal to go into exile, the injunction to stay and build with the quality of steadfastness required of those remaining on the land. Poets employ a poetic conceit in which they make poetry about their silencing, while the martyr's voice, muted by death, is never stilled and still cries out to us. For the dead of Kafr Qasim, and for those who continue to mourn, martyrdom has forged yet one more strong and chilling connection with the home village: Al-sha'b yuthbut (The people stay put). This connection means, however, that only the dead are certain to remain, as corpses buried where they belong in their ancestral village. Is it only then, Abu Hanna muses, that we can speak of Palestinians safely of the soil and in the homeland?

Poetry and memorializing have taken divergent paths. Poems preceded monuments and memorials historically in time. An early Samih al-Qasim poem about the Kafr Qasim massacre depicts only words as memorials, without any material monument or commemorative marker:

> No monument, no flower, no remembrance
> Not one poetic verse, no curtain,
> No blood-soaked rag from a shirt
> Worn once by our innocent brothers
> No stone with names inscribed on it
> Nothing, O the shame!
> Their ghost still circling
> Dig up their graves in Kafr Qasim's ruins.[50]

Al-Qasim's poem, composed in the 1950s, documents the early facts but not the subsequent memorializations: the memorials built in the 1970s within the city hall complex; the memorial at the old village entrance constructed in 1976, on the occasion of the twentieth anniversary; the memorials at the cemetery; the well-attended annual services; the 1973 memorial, renovated and enlarged in 2006; the addition of a large monument created by Ibrahim Hijazi, a sculptor from Haifa, in the shape of a torch, gesturing to Darwish's poem of the martyr as candle (with the flame under construction as of this writing, in 2006); and the youth project to paint all the martyrs' coffins green, so their numbers and location are visually prominent to mourners (see fig. 8.5). At the different sites of the massacre throughout Kafr Qasim there are memorials, plaques, and monuments in constant states of conception, construction, and renovation, while, until recently, visitors who approached the main village entrance from the highway were greeted by these words on a billboard: "Kafr Qasim, Balād al-shūhadā" (Kafr Qasim, Village of Martyrs).

WHY THE KAFR QASIM MASSACRE DOES NOT FADE AWAY

> After it was evident to you little by little the details of that horrific deed,
> After it was revealed to you the darkness, its size, stripped bare like a monument,
> You viewed in contrast the government communiqués, the announcement of the "wounded," the vague pallid announcement,
> You didn't know even if it was intended for them . . . because of the abyss between the horrific facts and the echo.[51]

At the forty-first anniversary, in 1997, the then minister of tourism Moshe Katsav was present to voice an apology as a representative of the Israeli government. Kafr Qasim's then mayor Ibrahim Sarsur told us that he countered by calling on the government to return 6,000 dunams (1,500 acres) of confiscated village lands, a request that was never implemented. Justice minister Yossi Beilin reiterated the government position, "that Israel could not take responsibility for the massacre, saying that the government at the time did not order the shootings."[52] Even as attempts to force government recognition persisted, as early as the 1980s the people of Kafr Qasim voted to set aside precious land for a memorial park with sculptures. Architectural plans depicted a multipurpose building, to include a cultural center, archives, museum, and facilities for visitors (see fig. 8.6).

Twenty years after the ceremony, in 1986, to lay the cornerstone for the planned museum and archive site, and as part of the fiftieth commemoration ceremony on October 29, 2006, a permanent space for exhibiting the story of the 1956 massacre was finally dedicated and inaugurated. It did not conform to the municipality's original architectural vision; nevertheless, historical displays, maps, photography, books, and artwork found a home in the new Community Center (Merkaz Kehīlāti) for the municipality of Kafr Qasim, subsidized by the Israeli state (see figs. 8.7 and 8.8).[53]

Notable among the many artifacts at the museum is Abd at-Tammam's

FIG. 8.5. *Memorial tombstone erected for the twenty-third anniversary of the massacre, October 20, 1979, and then renovated for the fiftieth anniversary in 2006. In front of the memorial tombstone, on the traffic roundabout, a statue of a torch with flame was under construction during the fiftieth anniversary year. Photo by Susan Slyomovics.*

iconic painting of the single penny, the derisory fine levied against one of the perpetrators. The painted penny formerly hung behind the mayor's desk; as of the October 26, 2006, opening ceremonies, it is housed in the section of the museum designed by Shlomo Khayat, the architect of the building, intended for the gymnasium and workout rooms. In December 2006, when Susan Slyomovics interviewed Khayat, who was born in Egypt and is also a planner and a landscape designer (he was educated at Cairo's School of Architecture and also the École des Beaux-Arts in Paris), he listed the design challenges he faced once he had been hired to build the center. Before Khayat undertook the Community Center assignment, in 2001, this project of an edifice consecrated to the 1956 massacre had begun when the municipality arranged for a 2,000–square-meter, poured concrete platform for the proposed site. Further construction, after the building foundations were laid, was halted due to lack of money. Instead, by 2003, funding amassed from various Israeli ministries and government agencies helped pay to complete the building, but according to strict, state-mandated guidelines that regulate all community centers within Israel and include complex templates for

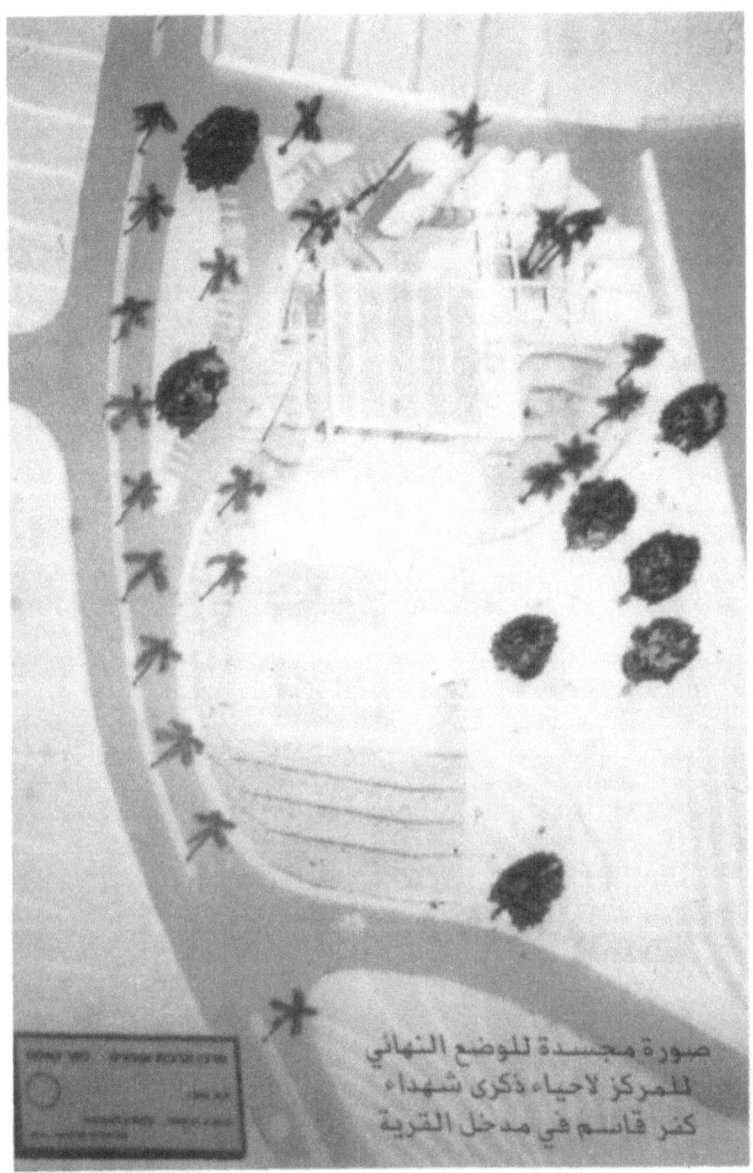

FIG. 8.6. *Architectural plans for a multipurpose building to commemorate the massacre, with a cultural center, archives, museum, and facilities for visitors. Courtesy of the Kafr Qasim Municipal Archives.*

FIG. 8.7. *Memorialization of the forty-nine martyrs, at the entrance to Kafr Qasim Community Center, 2006. Photo by Susan Slyomovics.*

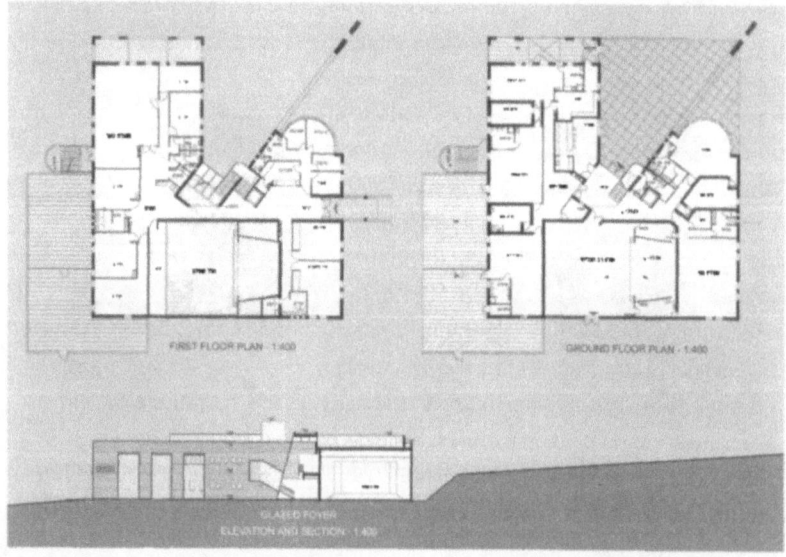

FIG. 8.8. *Architectural plans for the Kafr Qasim Community Center, courtesy of Shlomo Khayat, Khayat Architects, Jerusalem. Instead of sports room (studio guf), the ground floor houses the museum.*

FIG. 8.9. *Aerial view of Kafr Qasim Community Center, 2003. Courtesy of Shlomo Khayat.*

budget, architectural plans, landscaping, as well as the function, allocation, and use of interior and exterior spaces (e.g., daycare facilities, parking, terraces, classrooms, auditoriums, gymnasium, etc.). Since Kafr Qasim already had a sports center nearby, as well as a senior citizen center, the municipality re-purposed a section of the ground floor of the Community Center. Khayat informed Slyomovics that he was unaware of the first floor transformation from athletic rooms into a small museum devoted to the "living memory" of the 1956 massacre, a reuse of space completed in time for the fiftieth-anniversary ceremonies in 2006 (see fig. 8.7). Nor had he seen, at the time of our interview, the addition of forty-nine ceramic dishes shaped like sunflowers and bearing the names of each martyr, as if they were headstones lining the entrance (see fig. 8.9).

Perhaps Kafr Qasim's persistent museum-making (to the extent of transforming interior spaces within Israel's state-mandated architectural structures) bears some relationship to the political activism of Ibrahim Sarsur, a former mayor of Kafr Qasim and leader of a branch of the Islamic Movement of Israel headquartered in Kafr Qasim. He ran for a parliamentary seat during Israel's March 2006 elections, advocating one united party representation for the 20 percent of Israel's population that is Palestinian. His platform, to protect Arab villages from land seizures and improve school and job opportunities, employed the slogan: "Rights are not given. They are taken."[54] For Sarsur and for the people of Kafr Qasim, the stories of Arabs and Jews in Kafr Qasim from 1948 until today, especially the books, sculpture, commemoration days and anniversaries, architectural plans, even poetry—all understood in this essay as various memorializing operations—are not detachable from the daily lives of Palestinian since the establishment of the state of Israel. The ways in which the Palestinian Arab minority of Israel chooses to enshrine national and group memory have evolved dynamically, but also in relation to Israel's institutional forms of architecture, construction, and remembrance. Palestinian Israelis in Kafr Qasim have created memorials, a small museum, and commemorative holidays to drive home certain national lessons: first and foremost, to stay put, as the *samidīn* of Kafr Qasim have done; second, to create a shared national experience embodied in material ways to bind successive generations as the generation of the massacre dies out; third, to articulate a Palestinian historical perspective that differs from prevailing Jewish Israeli ones; and fourth, to reconstruct memory in performance-based enactments and architectural forms as one task for Palestinian Israelis in their journey for the recognition of their rights as citizens.

NOTES

This essay belongs to our larger project on the Kafr Qasim massacre (see the review by Hossam Abou-Ela, in *Al-Ahram Weekly*, April 15–21, 1999, available at weekly.ahram.org.eg/1999/425/cu1.htm. Unless indicated, translations from the Hebrew and Arabic are by Waleed Khleif and Susan Slyomovics. We are grateful to Ibrahim Sarsur, Adel Bedir, and Adnan Taha of Kafr Qasim, as well as various members of the municipality. We thank Shlomo Khayat for his generosity with information, architectural plans, and photographs. For readings and comments, we are grateful to Kamal Boullata, Tamar Katriel, Salman Abu Sitta, and Ruth Iskin.

1. Azmi Bishara, "Representations of the 'Other' in Israeli Culture," presented at the conference on "The 'Other' as Threat: Demonization and Anti-Semitism," June 12–15, 1995, Hebrew University, Jerusalem.

2. Here, the term "alternative historical truths" evokes the work of revisionist historians; see, e.g., Benny Morris, "The New Historiography: Israel Confronts its Past," *Tikkun* 3, no. 6 (1988): 19–23, 99–102.

3. Kamal Boullata, "Facing the Forest: Israeli and Palestinian Artists," *Third Text* 7 (1989): 77–95.

4. Tamer Sorek, "Memory and Identity: The Land Day Monument," *ISIM Newsletter* 10 (2002): 17.

5. For excellent studies of the broader historical and political background, which is not our focus here, but upon which we have relied, see Hillel Cohen, '*Arvim tovim* (Jerusalem: Keter, 2006); Rubik Rozental, ed., *Kefar kasem: Eru'im ve-mitos* (Tel Aviv: ha-Kibuts ha-Me'uhad, 2000); Shira Robinson, "Local Struggle, National Struggle: Palestinian Responses to the Kafr Qasim Massacre and Its Aftermath, 1956–66," *International Journal of Middle East Studies* 35 (2003): 393–416; and Shira Robinson, "Commemoration Under Fire: Palestinian Responses to the 1956 Kafr Qasim Massacre," in *Memory and Violence in the Middle East and North Africa*, ed. Ussama Makdisi and Paul A. Silverstein (Bloomington: Indiana University Press, 2006). Robinson's observation, made in both of the essays cited here, that "it is difficult to find a Palestinian poet who has *not* written about the massacre," serves as our own point of departure.

6. James E. Young, *The Texture of Memory: Holocaust Memorials and Meaning* (New Haven, Conn.: Yale University Press, 1993), 4.

7. Daniel A. McGowan and Marc H. Ellis, eds., *Deir Yassin Remembered: The Future of Israel and Palestine* (New York: Interlink, 1998).

8. The scholarship on memory in relation to both Jewish and Arab gestures and acts concerned with the massacre is vast. In this essay, Waleed Khleif looks at Palestinian Israeli experiences through works of poetry, and Susan Slyomovics examines place and material culture. See also Susan Slyomovics, *The Object of Memory* (Philadelphia: University of Pennsylvania Press, 1998).

9. Benny Morris, *Righteous Victims* (New York: Knopf, 1999), 249–52.

10. Benny Morris, *The Birth of the Palestinian Refugee Problem, 1947–1949* (Cambridge: Cambridge University Press, 1987), 249.

11. According to Shadia Matar, "A Palestinian refugee is a person whose normal residence was Palestine for a minimum of two years preceding the conflict in 1948, and who, as a result of the conflict, lost both his home and his means of livelihood and took refuge in one of the countries where UNRWA provides relief (Jordan, Lebanon, Syria, West Bank, Gaza)" (Shadia Matar, "Palestinian Refugees, a Material and Spiritual Homeland" [in Italian], *Mediterranean: Un Mare di Donne*, no. 3 [http://www.medmedia.org/review/numero3/en/art7.htm]).

12. On the Israeli government's confiscation of land from its Arab citizens, see Menachem Hofnung, *Democracy, Law, and National Security in Israel* (Aldershot, U.K.: Dartmouth, 1996).

13. See Henry Rosenfeld, "Processes of Structural Change within the Arab Family," *American Anthropologist* 60 (1958): 1127–39; Henry Rosenfeld, "From Peas-

antry to Wage Labor and Residual Peasantry: The Transformation of an Arab village," in *Process and Pattern in Culture*, ed. Robert A. Manners (Chicago: Aldine, 1964).

14. Abner Cohen, *Arab Border-Villages in Israel* (Manchester, U.K.: Manchester University Press, 1965), 17–18.

15. Ibid., 17.

16. Morris, *Israel's Border Wars, 1949–56: Arab Infiltration, Israeli Retaliation, and the Countdown to the Suez War* (New York: Oxford University Press, 1993), 432–34.

17. On "Plan Mole" (Miftsa' Hafarforet), an army program for Israel's Border Patrol to execute the "transfer" (expressed in English) of Arabs from the Triangle in case of war with Jordan, see Tawfiq Tubi, *Kafr Qasim al-majzarah wa-al-'ibrah* (Tel Aviv: Israeli Communist Party Publications, 1996), 77.

18. Ariella Azoulay, *Ekh zeh nireh lekha?* (Tel Aviv: Babel, 2000), 140.

19. Ibid., 139–40.

20. Ibrahim Sarsur, "Beyn ha-ṣulḥa veha-andarta," in *Kefar kasem: Eru'im vemitos*, ed. Rubik Rozental (Tel Aviv: ha-Kibuts ha-Me'uhad, 2000), 199.

21. Transcripts in Hebrew of the trial are published in Moshe Kordov, *Ahat esreh kumtot yerukot ba-din: Parashat Kefar-Kasm* (Tel Aviv: A. Narkis, 1959).

22. Nor would the military trial of soldiers serve as a deterrent to future hostilities, despite a famous verdict by Israeli judges (who were borrowed for the army trial from the civil court system) that condemned "manslaughter by army personnel" (in Hebrew, "harigah 'al yidey ish tsava'"), asserting that soldiers must refuse "a patently illegal order that carries a black flag of criminality." The "black flag criterion" of Kafr Qasim was evoked five years later, in 1961, during a more internationally famous trial, when Israeli judges condemned Adolf Eichmann to death for his role in exterminating European Jews. On the concept of "the black flag," see also Rozental, *Kefar kasem*, 117–77; and Leora Bilsky, "Kufr Qassem: Between Ordinary Politics and Transformative Politics," *Adalah's Review* 3 (2002): 69–80.

23. The full report of the Public Committee (known as the Rashish report, after Pinchas Rashish, mayor of Petah Tikvah) appears in Rozental, *Kefar kasem*, 237–39; see also "Four Hundred Attend Sulha at Kafr Qasim," *Jerusalem Post*, November 21, 1957, 1, 3.

24. Hana Sulayman Amir's testimony was recounted by Ibrahim Sarsur (interview, Kafr Qasim, January 13, 1998).

25. See Rhoda Ann Kanaaneh, *Birthing the Nation: Strategies of Palestinian Women in Israel* (Berkeley: University of California Press, 2002).

26. Interview with Adel Badir, Kafr Qasim, January 13, 1998.

27. "Report of the Public Committee for Indemnities to the Dead and

Wounded of Kafr Qasim, Petah Tikvah, 10 November 1957," in Rozental, *Kefar kasem*, 239; see also Robinson, "Commemoration Under Fire"; and Robinson, "Local Struggle, National Struggle."

28. See Cohen, *Arab Border-Villages in Israel*; Abner Cohen, "Hamula," *Encyclopaedia of Islam*, 3:149–50. Although Cohen renamed the pseudonymous Triangle village Bint el-Hudud (Arabic for "Daughter of the Borders"), he noted that "the whole village had been in mourning for the many villagers who had been killed in an incident two years earlier" (87). Cohen's ethnography is a transparent document, his disguise purportedly confected to protect his informants and their locations, and it should be reread in terms of the legal fallout from a suppressed legacy of civilian dead. On the identity of the village where Cohen did his fieldwork, see Dan Rabinowitz, *Antropologyah veha-Palestinim* (Raananah, Israel: Institute for Israeli-Arab Studies, 1998), 93–117.

29. Cohen, *Arab-Border Villages in Israel*, 135.

30. Ibid., 139–40, note 3.

31. Sarsur, "Beyn ha-ṣulḥa veha-andarta," 198.

32. Ibid., 199. For a different description, see Lea Ben-Dor, "Marginal Column," *Jerusalem Post*, November 22, 1957, 1.

33. Interview with Ibrahim Sarsur, Kafr Qasim, January 13, 1998.

34. "Kafr Kasim Counsel Reject Terms of Payment," *Jerusalem Post*, November 18, 1957, 3.

35. "Four Hundred Attend Sulha at Kafr Qasim," *Jerusalem Post*, November 21, 1957, 3.

36. For critiques and overviews of Western and Israeli anthropology on the *hamula*, see Talal Asad, "Anthropological and Sociological Studies on the Arabs in Israel: A Critique," *Journal of Palestine Studies* 6 (1977): 41–70; Talal Assad, "Anthropological Texts and Ideological Problems: An Analysis of Cohen on Arab Villages in Israel," *Economy and Society* 4 (1975): 274; Elia Zureik, *The Palestinians in Israel: A Study in Internal Colonialism* (London: Routledge Kegan Paul, 1979); and Aziz Haidar, *The Palestinians in Israel: Social Science Writings* (Kingston, Ontario: NECEF Publications, 1987). See also Gil Eyal, "Beyn mizrah le-ma'arav: Ha-si'ah 'al ha-kfar ha-'aravi bi-yisra'el," *Teoriya u-Bikoret* 3 (1993): 39–55. Eyal contrasts the current discursive objectification of the Arab village (which produced harsh military-rule policies) by Jewish Israelis with the pre-1948 state period, which romanticized the Arab village as a locus for an authentic Jewish identity rooted in biblical ways. See also Susan Slyomovics, *The Object of Memory* (Philadelphia: University of Pennsylvania Press, 1998), chap. 3.

37. Interviews with Ibrahim Sarsur and Adel Bedir, January 1988, Kafr Qasim.

38. Darwish quotes a soldier's orders, "Mow them down," taken from pub-

lished trial transcripts, to describe the killing of a group of thirteen village men, who were lined up and then shot.

39. In 1958, Mahmud Darwish composed a *shi'ir malhami* (heroic poem), in six parts, about the massacre at Kafr Qasim. The excerpts reproduced here are from the first poem in the cycle, entitled "Mughanni al-damm" (Acre: Dar Hijazi li-al-nashr, 1967); the translation appears by written permission of the author.

40. Interview with Tawfiq Tubi, December 1998, Haifa. For an English-language account of the event and for trial transcripts, see Sabri Jiryis, *The Arabs in Israel* (New York: Monthly Review Press, 1976), 140–53.

41. Tubi, *Kafr Qasim al-majzarah wa-al-'ibrah*, 31 (for *mudhakkarah*, see 34–44).

42. Group interview with municipal counselors, Kafr Qasim, January 13, 1998.

43. See Tawfiqu Zayyad, "Kafr Qasim," in *Kalimat muqatilah* (Acre: Matba'at al-Jalil, 1970), 86–101. In the same collection there is another poem about Kafr Qasim and Dayr Yasin, entitled "On the Trunk of an Olive Tree"; partial English translations for the poem are in *The Palestinian Wedding*, collected and translated by A. M. Elmessiri; line drawings by Kamal Boullata (Washington, D.C.: Three Continents Press, 1982), 55–57; and in Barbara McKean Parmenter, *Giving Voice to Stones: Place and Identity in Palestinian Literature* (Austin: University of Texas Press, 1994), 75–76.

44. The literary critic Hussein Kadhim traces the first use of the term "literature of resistance" to the Jordanian writer Isa al-Na'uri, who, he says, used the term at an October 16–20, 1961, conference in Rome (see Hussain Kadhim, *The Poetics of Anti-Colonialism in the Arabic Qasidah* [Leiden: Brill, 2004], viii). Others credit the Palestinian writer Ghassan Kanafani; see his *Adab al-muqāwamah fī Filastīn al-muhtallah, 1948–1966* (Beirut: Dār al-Ādāb, 1966).

45. The English-language speeches of Pinhas Rashish, mayor of nearby Petah Tikva, Eliahu Agasi of the Histadrut, and Abdel Aziz Zubi of the Jewish-Arab Association are summarized in "Memorial Meeting in Kfar Kassim," *New Outlook*, November–December 1957, 52.

46. Waleed Khleif, "Kafr Qasim," *Al-Ittihad*, November 5, 1957 (reprinted in *Majallat al-Adib* [Lebanon], October 1959).

47. Mahmud Darwish in Tawfiq Tubi, *Kafr Qasim al-majzarah wa-al-'ibrah* (Tel Aviv: Israeli Communist Party Publications, 1996, 164–65 (the fifth poem in the epic cycle).

48. See Mahmud Darwish, "The Eyes of the Dead at the Door," in Tubi, *Kafr Qasim al-majzarah wa-al-'ibrah*, 165–66 (poem 6 of the *malhamah*).

49. See also videos of the annual commemorations produced in Kafr Qasim, available through the municipality of Kafr Qasim.

50. Samih al-Qasim, "Kafr Qasim," *al-Ittihad*, November 1, 1957; another English translation appears in El-Messiri, *The Palestinian Wedding*.

51. Natan Alterman, "Tehom ha-meshulash," *Davar*, November 7, 1956.

52. Joel Greenberg, "School Official Wants to Mark Israeli Atrocity," *New York Times*, October 7, 1999.

53. On the Israeli community-center movement and the history of its predecessor government organization, the MATNAS (the Hebrew acronym for Center for Culture, Youth, and Sport), see Haim Hazan, *A Paradoxical Community* (Greenwich, Conn.: JAI Press, 1990).

54. Thanassis Cambanis, "Candidate Striving to Give Arab-Israelis a Voice," *Boston Globe*, March 23, 2006, A16.

PART III *Overviews and Openings*

9   Global Ambition and Local Knowledge

GWENDOLYN WRIGHT

When Walter Gropius began a decade-long master plan for Baghdad University in 1953, the sensuous curves, courtyards, and *mashribiya* screens of his buildings projected orientalist fantasies in high-tech concrete (see fig. 9.1).[1] During these same years, Josep Lluis Sert infused the American Embassy in Baghdad (1955–61) with his personal ideas about tropical conditions and the larger Mediterranean realm.[2] A half-century later, confronting new American efforts to reconstruct the Middle East, it seems incumbent to ask why stalwart modern architects would have chosen to engage this local context in such conspicuous ways. Premonitions of postmodernism? Surely this label is too narrowly construed in terms of Western cultural fashions, including the notion of an autonomous architecture culture. These designs, and others like them, instead show the inherent volatility of modernism—perhaps especially in the tumultuous Middle East. Ever-present local meanings and practices shift continuously, in part by negotiating the global flow of capital and politics, images, and ideas.[3]

The geopolitical arena of "Western architecture" has engaged the Middle East and North Africa since the idea first coalesced under the Romans. Early-twentieth-century modernism drew from the white cubic forms of these vernaculars, even as colonialism's *mission civilisatrice* claimed to embody shared principles of social equality and scientific rationality. Connections intensified after World War II, prompted by a fuller understanding of indigenous architecture, especially its environmental adaptations, but even more so by

FIG. 9.1. *Proposed entry to University of Baghdad Auditorium. Walter Gropius and TAC, 1953–58.*

new universals, notably a free-market economy, advanced technologies, and nuclear families at the micro-level. The Middle East became a prime site to implement W. W. Rostow's "takeoff" stage of modernization—in principle, a process through which all societies had to proceed, although, as with earlier concepts of civilization, the highest level closely resembled the West's own dominant values.[4] Critics of the late-1960s and the decade of the 1970s rebelled against these claims, condemning the disruptive inequities of international development and urban renewal, attacking modern architecture as an inhumane abstraction that looked just the same all over the world.

In fact, as with Gropius and Sert in Baghdad, modern architects in the Middle East during the 1950s and 1960s often made reference to local cultures—if only by simplistic assumptions about the past and the future. These allusions show the ongoing role of history and locale as inspiration, integration, and resistance. "Staging the modern has always required the non-modern," contends Timothy Mitchell. "The production of modernity involves the staging of differences."[5] Only in modern times can people worry about the fate of traditions: whether certain practices or places should be abolished, transformed, or preserved. Of course, the very word "tradition" shifts attention from complex historical legacies to vague or mythic ideals. Anthropologists insist that traditions have always been in flux as well as embedded, but architects prefer their own bifurcated analysis, excoriating "outdated" attitudes and settings, as if these impediments to progress could be surgically removed, while extolling "authentic vernaculars" as organic, indeed, timeless. Such imaginary realms, supposedly uncontaminated by the pastiche and commercialism of modern life, can only exist in the long-ago or far-away. This is a tourist's perspective, what Mitchell has called the world-as-exhibition, and Aziz al-Azmeh, a celebration of primal innocence.[6] Yet architects, then and now, must confront the paradoxical relationship between tradition and modernity wherever they design. "Rather than doing away with tradition," asserts the geographer Jane Jacobs, "globalization has delivered new conditions for its emergence; installed new mechanisms for its transference; and brought into being new political imperatives for its performance."[7]

Post–World War II architecture in the Middle East reveals distinct patterns, but no simple formulas. The ambiguity makes it easy to fall back on such dichotomies as modern vs. traditional, West vs. non-West, or foreign vs. indigenous. This essay proposes instead a series of triads—admittedly, another artifice, but one that is considerably more flexible. I will explore modern architecture and urbanism in three nations over three decades, roughly the period from 1945 to 1975—a time span that marks the start of Lebanon's civil war; an upsurge of new construction in Saudi Arabia, funded by profits from OPEC's oil embargo; and Anwar Sadat's neoliberal Infitah policy in Egypt. Three overlapping tendencies in architecture culture were all, to some extent, modern responses as well. Even as the heroic international style reached its apogee, some Westerners sought to revitalize formal dogmas by tapping into the "authenticity" of local cultures; their universal vernacular emerged from the dense, irregular settlement patterns of Moroccan *ksours*, Dogon huts, and Mediterranean villages, prompting architects to cite similar "precedents," or "justifications," for their modern designs.[8] Meanwhile, several indigenous architects espoused a more circumscribed design approach, supposedly able to sustain cohesive community life, based on traditional Arab-Islamic construction principles (see fig. 9.2), while historic preservation emerged as a profession with its own universal principles, although strategies varied from one nation to another. Intellectual frameworks outside the design professions also played a role. First was the notion of the "colonial situation," suggesting how hegemony was exercised—and contested—after independence.[9] Second came the modernization theories of Pax Americana. Third, the rise of interdisciplinary area studies in American universities focusing on critical regions like the Middle East with its vast oil resources and political antagonisms in the wake of Israel's formation out of Palestine in 1948.[10]

The goals of architectural patronage in the region were clear in principle,

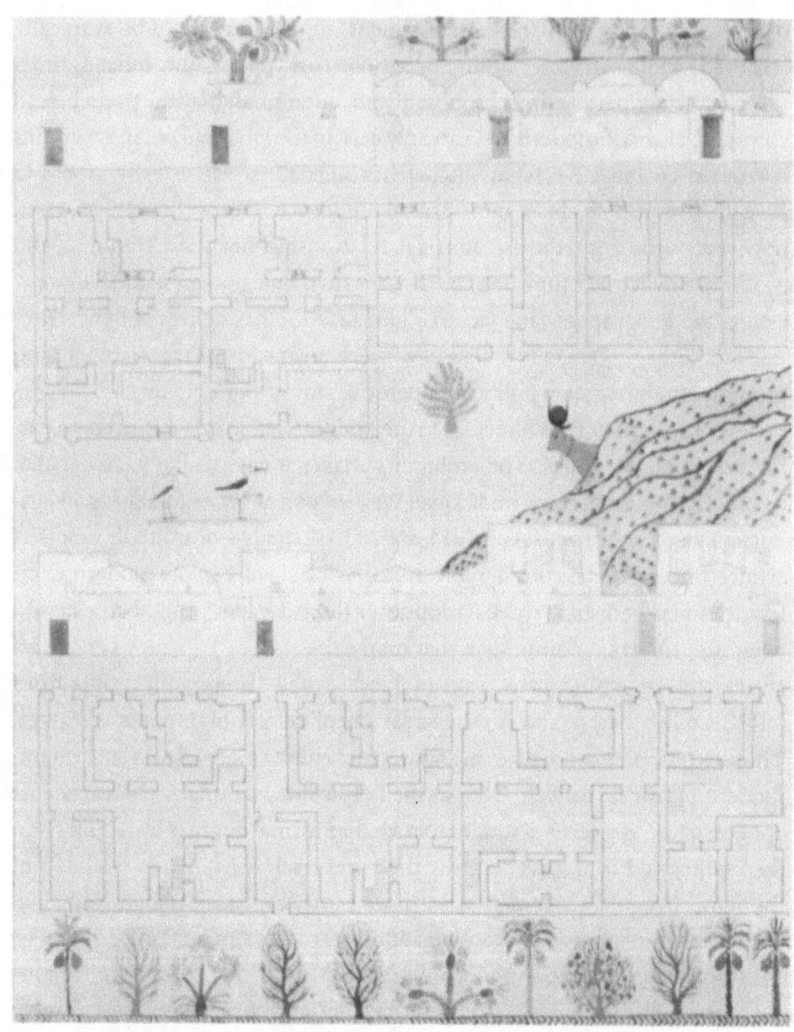

FIG. 9.2. *Sketch of the village of New Gourna, Egypt. Hassan Fathy, 1945–48. Courtesy of the Aga Khan Trust for Culture. Photo by Gary Otte.*

if less so in practice: the import and training of professional experts; installation of modern infrastructure; state provision of social services like education and health care; national housing programs; a historic preservation agenda; and the rise of a profit-driven private sector, both local and transnational. Most architects were ardent modernists, as were their clients, who employed terms like *hadith* (new or modern), *'asri* (contemporary or modern), and *madani* (civilized or refined).[11] The majority of designers hailed from the United States, Europe, and occasionally Japan, though many were local, at least to the region, and often affiliated with the Arab Bureau of Architects, Planners, and Technical Consultants in Cairo, a product of Nasser's pan-Arab vision. The region's historical richness and cultural vitality, especially in the ancient cities, prompted modernists to incorporate references to local history—or at least historical fantasies—while preservationists and neo-traditionalists sought, usually in vain, to protect monuments, building practices, and social life from the force Joseph Schumpter has labeled capitalism's "creative destruction." Most designers had good intentions, whatever their stylistic preferences. They sincerely hoped to situate modern architecture, making it less intrusive and more inspiring. Yet the effects of modern architecture extend far beyond individual buildings. A much larger, less distinct picture is critical to evaluating even relative successes and failures.

Modernism and neo-traditionalism coexisted in the Middle East. The cities of the region did not experience a cultural battle between opposing architectural camps, in part because they were confronting other, more pressing, soon overwhelming urban problems. There, as elsewhere, urban problems responded to local, national, and international events. But conditions were magnified in the chaotic, contentious, and often impoverished nations that now called themselves the Third World. According to some observers, modern architectural buildings in the Middle East might look like frightful distortions, whimsical anomalies, chaotic disasters, or exhilarating opportunities. As with any modern city, all these perspectives were accurate.

The post–World War II era was simultaneously prosperous and incendiary in Lebanon. Lebanon had gained formal independence with the end of the French Mandate in 1943, but American interests quickly assumed a dominant role there. In 1951, the United States underwrote a pipeline across Lebanon to transport Saudi and Iraqi crude oil. When insurrection broke out in 1958, the Marines invaded, ostensibly to prevent a Communist threat, installing former general Fuad Shihab as president. Multiple strata of history underlay the bright modern surface of Beirut, the capital city called the "Pearl of the Middle East"; some provided stable foundations reaching back millennia, but others proved to be dangerous fault lines. Long-standing antagonisms between Maronite Christians, Muslims, and Druze produced a highly ineffective, byzantine government apparatus for sharing power. More recent conflicts also festered, especially those surrounding Israel's expulsion of Palestinians, hundreds of thousands of whom ended up in refugee camps on the outskirts of the city. Pressures mounted as massive amounts of capital investments and rural in-migration transformed the economics of real estate. Beirut's residential population tripled between 1952 and 1964, reaching almost 900,000 people.

The influence of France continued to dominate architectural education and practice. The major figure in architecture was Michel Ecochard, who had first worked as an archaeologist in Syria and Lebanon under the Mandate, then sought to assuage Lebanon's root-bound cultural tensions using the orthodox modern formulas of CIAM (the Congrès International d'Architecture Moderne).[13] Ecochard's initial, 1943 master plan for Beirut, modified and expanded over the next twenty years, adhered to CIAM rules: extensive clearance and selective preservation in the center (see fig. 9.3); a modern, "healthy city" (later two) alongside the "ailing city"; and a rational street-grid linked to high-speed expressways along the coast. Despite repeated efforts and formal approval of his 1964 plan, these rational urban analyses had little effect on the city's development.[14] Ecochard's architecture proved to be more lasting, if isolated, with sensitive adaptations of historical buildings for civic purposes, together with several handsome, well-sited modern schools and hospitals from the 1950s.

Others, too, seemed confident that Euro-American "technical know-how" could unite and modernize Lebanon. Information and design ambition were available in abundance. Under the auspices of the U.S. Operations Mission, Constantinos Doxiadis began gathering extensive data and photographs for a nationwide housing initiative in the mid-1950s, a project that was abruptly derailed by the "Crisis of 1958."[15] In consolation, Doxiadis would design a new Government Center just outside Beirut in 1963, of which only the Ministry of Telecommunication was built. Like most architects, whether foreign or Lebanese, Doxiadis rejected any reference to the "pastiche" of Mandate-era colonial styles, convinced that functional modernism would guarantee progress and unity. Some advocated Bauhaus exercises in "type forms" and "a pure language of lines, shapes, colors, and materials."[16] Bold geometries characterized government buildings. The chaste cubic volumes of the Union Nationale (1952) and the Ministry of Justice (1959), by the Lebanese architect Antoine Tabet, conveyed order and permanence. André Wogenscky, a Frenchman who had worked with Le Corbusier in Paris and with ATBAT-Afrique in Casablanca, designed several public buildings in collaboration with Maurice Hindieh, a young, French-trained Lebanese. Their most important commission, the 1965 Defense Ministry, combines a dramatic sculptural façade with a rational plan (see fig. 9.4).[17] International stars were imported, including Alvar Aalto and Alfred Roth, who designed a major office building and commercial center in 1963.

FIG. 9.3. *Photomontage of a proposed urban renewal and preservation project in central Beirut, Lebanon. Michel Ecochard, 1963. Courtesy of the Aga Khan Trust for Culture.*

Unfortunately, these visions focused on talent and convictions about the future, rather than engaging the real dilemmas of the time, including clear evidence of overpopulation, hyperspeculation, sectarian strife, and ensuing environmental disasters. Development in the city center, headquarters for all major businesses and the nucleus of exchange between diverse neighborhoods, was more chaotic than dynamic, since profit seemed the only common value. This critique is not simply a matter of hindsight. Soon after leaving

FIG. 9.4. *Lebanese Defense Ministry, Beirut. André Wogenscky and Maurice Hindieh, 1965. Courtesy of André Wogenscky and Maurice Hindieh.*

Beirut's Technical Bureau (the city's planning department), which he directed from 1956 to 1959, the Palestinian Saba George Shiber condemned the central business district as the embodiment of "our utter state of laissez faire, anti-civicism, cupidity, disorder, caprice, and extreme materialism"; he also lambasted the majority of that area's architecture as "loud and jarring, pirated or plagiarized."[18]

Domestic architecture showed a similar tension, seemingly innovative, but in fact dangerously neglectful of social conditions. The best houses combined modern Euro-American villas with regional traditions in massing and environmental controls. Samir Khairallah and Pierre el-Khoury deftly interpreted new typologies in light of the region's topography, climate, and social mores. Market-rate housing was another story altogether. Small walk-up apartment buildings were demolished, to be replaced by large high-rises with elevators; demure balconies inflated into terraces supported by concrete columns, orientated to distant views rather than the street below. Expensive luxury residences dominated the urban market, creating a precipitous shortage for other classes. Even with commerce on the ground floor, this new housing helped speed a shift from collective life in extended-family clans to privacy in nuclear families—though clans would assert considerable power during the civil war. More egregiously, nothing was done to alleviate problems in the fast-growing squatter settlements outside the city.[19]

The great international hotels helped fuel an image of Beirut as a cosmopolitan Mediterranean paradise appealing to tourists from the Gulf to Europe and the United States. An early and lavish example was Edward Durrell Stone's Phoenicia Inter-Continental of 1954.[20] Other kinds of businesses soon followed, hoping to lure investment in a similar manner. Irving & Jones designed the Middle East headquarters of the American Life Insurance Company with colonnades and a rooftop aluminum grill, which they supposedly derived from Islamic *mashribaya* screens, ignoring the fact that this "typical" Islamic decoration was rare in the Levant.[21] In contrast, Samir Khairallah skillfully incorporated traditional references in his commercial and educational buildings. The American University in Beirut created a course in Regional Architecture in 1964, the first in the Middle East.[22] President Shehab, recognizing the nascent desire for national self-expression, emphasized a personal preference for pointed arches in a 1963 state commission for a building to promote Lebanese handicrafts. Taking the cue, Jacques Aractingi and Pierre Neema designed a building that features structural columns that rise up to an allusion of arches under the roof slab (see fig. 9.5).[23] Even the U.S. *Area Handbook* of 1968 noted the tendency to infuse modernism with traditional Arabic architectural motifs.[24] Other non-Western cultures shared these sentiments. Many Lebanese architects admired Brazil and Morocco for their vivid expressions of cultural pride and climactic adaptations. In 1962 Oscar Niemeyer was invited to build the International and Permanent Fair in Tripoli.[25]

Despite these sentiments, the pace of construction and the lack of regula-

FIG. 9.5. *Center for Lebanese Handicrafts / Maison de l'Artisan, Beirut. Jacques Aractingi and Pierre Neema, 1963.*

Global Ambition and Local Knowledge 229

tions encouraged widespread demolition.[26] A private citizens' group tried to raise public awareness, with little success. The Department of Antiquities was transferred to the Ministry of Tourism, which concentrated on excursions to the Hellenistic ruins at Baalbek. Only one urban site seemed sacred, Beirut's central markets, or souks, as if continuity there could assure harmony and resolve antagonisms that ranged from glaring social inequalities to angry collective memories. These attitudes resound today with Solidere, the private development association that oversees reconstruction in Beirut's central core. In an effort to erase the disturbing reminders of violent destruction during fifteen years of civil war, all new architecture in the area must evoke the regional modernism of the Mandate era—including Rafael Moneo's 1996 design for the new souks.[27] Solidere is confident in the unifying power of its design solution, just as Shihab's post-1958 government had been in its commitment

Petroleum was key to Saudia Arabia's modernism—and to the power of its traditional rulers. When Abdul Aziz al Saud (known as "Ibn Saud" in the West) declared himself king of a unified nation in 1932, he marked the occasion by bringing the new nation's first automobile to his palace in Riyadh. Six years later, an American company discovered the first major oil supply and created a joint venture with the king. The U.S. Department of State and the U.S. Navy, having decided that access to Saudi oil was a national priority during World War II, backed further explorations and renamed the venture Aramco (the Arabian American Oil Company).[28] Aramco engineers constructed up-to-date housing, educational, medical, and shopping facilities for some 150,000 employees and their families—gridiron desert enclaves with an eerie resemblance to American suburbs.[29] Saudi officials took these settlements as a model for development in the early 1950s. Aramco generously agreed to help, bringing in the Bechtel Corporation to equip the entire country with electricity, sewage systems, paved roads, bridges, rail links, an airport, and prefabricated dwellings in new "town-sites" (see fig. 9.6).[30] If architecture remained functional and plain, the base had been transformed.

Saudi rulers did mix tradition, luxury, and new technologies in their own royal complexes. The Emir Saud commissioned two extravagant palaces in the early 1950s, both entirely in concrete: the Qasr el-Hokm in Riyadh and another just outside at Nasiriyyah. These qualities continued to define later, even larger royal complexes when Saud became ruler following his father's death in 1953. One, an entirely new palace at Nasiriyyah in 1956, is probably the world's first completely air-conditioned city, with more than nineteen miles of chilled-water pipes serving over 120 buildings.[31]

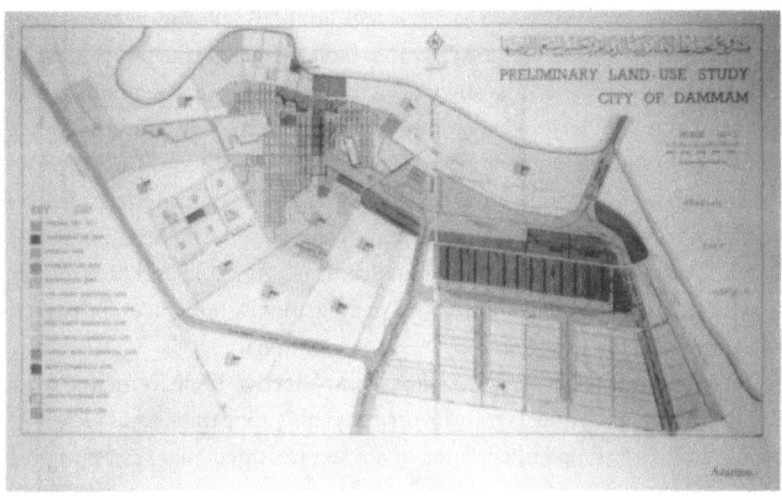

FIG. 9.6. *Plan for the "town-site" of Dammon, Saudi Arabia, by Aramco engineers, ca. 1950. From Shiber,* Recent Arab City Growth.

Meanwhile, two small Saudi towns catapulted to global status. In 1947 King Abdul Aziz commissioned Egyptian architect Sayed Karim to transform Jeddah into the kingdom's main business and commercial center. Demolition of the historic coral walls facilitated expansion, and the population grew almost tenfold, from some 30,000 people in 1947 to over 200,000 by 1960.[32] Development in Riyadh was equally spectacular. Abdul Aziz again tore down the city walls and commissioned a plan from Karim. Preferences for simplicity exerted a pronounced effect here, since adherence to the region's strict Wahabi fundamentalism had buttressed the Saudi clan's authority since 1803.[33] Traditional massing continued, albeit with slightly larger fenestration—though reinforced concrete, first used in the 1940s, soon became the material of choice. When Saud chose Riyadh to replace Mecca as the nation's political capital in 1953, Doxiadis was asked to prepare a master plan. After several years of study, he proposed vigorous interventions in "action areas," with cantilevers and covered passages to connect isolated buildings, but made scant provision for semi-private space, so essential to Islamic urban life, in new residential areas.[34] The UNDP initiated development programs, as yet unaware of the wealth that Saudi Arabia would accrue with the creation of OPEC in 1960.[35]

Minoru Yamasaki's flamboyant 1961 airport in Dhahran (see fig. 9.7), near Aramco's headquarters, anticipated a pivotal shift in taste and power. Crown Prince Faisal deposed Saud in 1964, and the new monarch emphatically

Global Ambition and Local Knowledge 231

embraced modernization—within certain limits. Education became paramount, albeit suffused with traditions as well as the latest technologies. To inaugurate his reign, Faisal commissioned the St. Louis-based Hellmuth, Obata & Kassabaum (HOK) to create a vast new campus for King Saud University (see fig. 9.8); and the Houston-based Caudill, Rowlett & Scott (CRS), one for the University for Petroleum and Minerals in Dhahran, close to Aramco's headquarters. Both campuses featured "Islamic" ornament, colonnaded arcades, and pointed arches. In marked contrast, Ahmed Farid Moustapha, an MIT-trained Egyptian, allowed no such historicist references for Riyadh University and the King Faisal University in Damman.

Faisal's modernization worked best in collective improvements. Massive infrastructure projects transformed Riyadh's appearance and its way of life.[36] WAISIA, a complex consisting of a water treatment plant and pumping stations designed by McDonald and Yakeley, encompassed an entire experimental village; water towers by the Swedish engineer Sune Lindstroem raised necessity to the status of art. Paolo Ghera's Central Market used a prefabricated system of vaulted concrete forms, while the simplicity of Trevor Dannat's conference center and the boldness of Kenzo Tange's King Faisal Foundation building assert confidence in international research and philanthropy.

Even sacred sites underwent radical alterations. The Saudi royal family proudly oversees Mecca and Medina, pilgrimage destinations for Muslims from around the world. Abdul Aziz had commissioned a new plan for Mecca from Sayed Karim in 1952, but almost a million pilgrims were arriving for the hajj by the mid-1960s, creating an urgent need for updating. Faisal, invested as King and Imam, ordered Mecca's Great Mosque and Medina's Mosque of the Prophet to be rebuilt and expanded; they now featured minarets, arcades, and elaborate ornamentation, none of which were familiar idioms in the peninsula. He then hired a British firm, Robert Matthew Johnson Marshall and Partners (RMJM) to prepare a new plan. RMJM insisted on gearing everything to the automobile, prompting the government to spend enormous sums on highways, tunnels through the mountains, and multistory parking facilities. While these interventions ran counter to the historic simplicity of the hajj, the tensile structure of pilgrim accommodations (Kenzo Tange, Frei Otto, and Rolf Gutbrod, 1964–67) and the later Hajj Terminal (Fazlur R. Khan for SOM, 1978–82) did embrace the historical forms and impermanent nature of this religious experience.[37]

Saudi resources expanded exponentially with OPEC's oil embargo in 1973. Gaudy architecture flourished outside the Old Towns in Jeddah and Riyadh,

FIG. 9.7. *Airport for Dharan. Minoru Yamasaki, 1961. Courtesy of Minoru Yamasaki, New York.*

FIG. 9.8. *King Saud University near Riyadh, corridor. HOK, 1964–82. Courtesy of Hellmuth, Obata & Kassabaum, St. Louis.*

as courtyard houses gave way to detached suburban villas and opulent multistory residential buildings. (A few enthusiasts justified the shift by claiming that apartment towers harked back to Saudi precedents.[38]) If traditional sentiments remained strong, the results were now highly self-conscious and often quite expensive. Fathy designed a few elegantly simple houses, but, for the most part, façades as well as interiors were bedecked with imitations of handcrafted Islamic detailing—now ridiculed as "cut-and-paste" or "Gulf clip-on" décor, as if similar phenomena did not appear elsewhere.[39] Architects, clients, and policymakers must always consider many factors, including cost; façades and ornament are rarely a simple matter of choosing either modernism or neo-traditionalism. Sometimes Western models were tried and discarded with good reason, as when Jeddah demolished the mammoth public-housing towers (likened to Pruitt-Igoe) built under the 1973 Rush Housing Program. Yet no one abided by the Muslim obligation for charity by improving the grim, isolated camps for foreign workers—who soon comprised almost one of every three people making Saudi Arabia home.[40]

When Sheik Mohammed Said Farsi, trained as an architect, became mayor of Jeddah in 1975, he commissioned a new plan from RMJM. Rejecting the aggressive modernization of Mecca as a model for Jeddah, both the client and the architect now adopted a policy of maximum conservation for the historic core and reoriented the city toward the Corniche, a magnificent curving road along the seashore, which soon became a prime setting for new architecture, both modern and neo-traditional.[41] The most notable examples are Abdelwahed El-Wakil's exquisite mosques, elegant houses, and a headquarters for Datsun. El-Wakil embraced historic building technologies and typologies, but he did so with a deep understanding of historical processes, seeking to "reinterpret [the constants] within the new context."[42] Official and corporate support certainly helped. Some residents complained that El-Wakil's Datsun complex drew upon the distinctive simple façades of Riyadh, rather than the more ornamented surfaces of Jeddah, but new regulations under Mayor Farsi adopted this "creolized" typology as a new vernacular.

Riyadh, the capital, became the largest building site in the world in the mid-1970s, issuing an average of seventy permits each day.[43] The results varied greatly, to be sure, in quality as in the range of formal idioms. The Saudi royal family now adopted a stylistic prescription consistent with its commitment to "Islamic solidarity," conservative social mores, and authoritarian government, even as it promoted advances in technology and economic development. Architectural preferences thus went far deeper than emulating the fashion for postmodernism in Western countries. These various, seemingly

FIG. 9.9. *Government offices, Qasr el-Hokm District, Riyadh. Franco Albini / Studio de Architettura, 1974–78.*

contradictory tendencies came together most clearly when Franco Albini and his Studio de Architettura won the 1974 competition for new government offices in Riyadh's Qasr el-Hokm (see fig. 9.9).[44] History itself could be sacrificed, so long as certain traditions were protected. Although the site had been the nucleus of Saudi regional government for over a century, most of the older structures were now demolished—except for Masmak Castle, a fortress of sun-dried mud where Abdul Aziz had staged his coup against the Ottomans in 1902, which was restored and preserved as a national monument.[45] Genuinely committed to local typologies, Albini incorporated the massive crenellated walls of the Najdi vernacular into the design. But Albini and his staff also presumed to draw from referents throughout the Arab-Islamic world, as if these coalesced into a fixed set of criteria and forms—or, in the caustic words of one Italian critic, "a statistical mean."[46]

American designers were equally complicit, using architecture to entrench the authority of multinational businesses and Saudi rulers. A deep respect for history as well as modern technology permeates the work of SOM's Bagladeshi-born engineer Fazlur R. Khan (1929–1982), who designed the Hajj Terminal and other innovative engagements with Saudi Arabian culture and climate.[47] In contrast, SOM's in-house research on urban precedents reveals an orientalist attitude knowledgeable about the past, at least superficially, yet disdainful of the present. The firm's 1978 pamphlet, *Urban Design Middle East: A Primer for Development*, echoes colonial-era prejudices, declaring without qualification that no significant advances in Arab design had occurred for over two-and-a-half centuries.[48] Like Albini, the authors drew freely from the entire Islamic world, including Istfahan, Seville, and Mughal India, all far from the Persian Gulf. Such references to "the Islamic city" hark back to French and British historians of the 1920s, who had used this artificial typology to legitimate colonial control over a vast region.[49] That unfortunate "tradition" reverberates in the claim that this rather cursory analysis of "logical precursors" would generate "a significant new Islamic urban tradition"—comprised of "organic forms," geometric ornament, a "desert vernacular," and the continuity of a conservative, hierarchical society—under the benevolent auspices of the firm and its powerful clients.[50]

Egypt had incorporated modern reforms ever since the Ottoman pasha Mehmet Ali transformed much of Cairo in the early nineteenth century, installing civic institutions and residential districts that laid the foundations for an indigenous middle class.[51] Yet if modernity was not alien, neither was it benign. After Britain formalized its imperial claim in 1882, the city's population grew precariously larger, more segregated, and more unequal. Wealthy Egyptians and Europeans lived in elegant luxury, often alongside one another in fashionable *raaqi* (upper-class) neighborhoods like Garden City, Heliopolis, and Zamalek, while the vast majority of Cairenes made do in the crowded dwellings and vivacious street life of *sha'bi* districts, which saw virtually no urban improvements.[52]

Conditions in Cairo certainly looked dire after World War II, while daily life in villages along the Nile remained relatively static. One might assume that neo-vernacular architecture would have flourished, given the international fame of Hassan Fathy's new village of Gourna (1945–48), near Luxor (see fig. 9.2). Yet Fathy's *Architecture for the Poor*, published in 1973, was written in English; an Arabic translation did not appear until the 1980s.[53] New Gourna itself was considered a failure in Egypt, at least as an official effort to remove the villagers from Old Gourna, so as to destroy their lucrative but illegal trade in tomb-robbing and demolish what Fathy considered their "uncivilized" self-built dwellings.[54] Nationalist sentiments were strong, and Egyptians were justly proud of their history. Sayyid Karim's magazine *Al-'Imara* (*Architecture*) initiated a call for "national identity in built form" in 1945, continuing these efforts until 1959. But few Egyptians of the Nasser era showed much interest in neo-Pharaonic, neo-Islamic, or other purportedly indigenous themes. This was considered *baladi*, a key word that means "traditional, local, and homely," in contrast with modern, international and cosmopolitan.[55]

More urgent national concerns took precedence over architectural idioms. Egypt had become independent in 1945, and the populace chafed at ongoing British ownership of the Suez Canal Zone. Tensions erupted in 1952 when crowds stormed the invisible barrier between Cairo's "two cities," setting fire to foreign hotels, clubs, shops, and movie palaces. Britain was forced to relinquish the Canal (but continued to operate it). King Farouk abdicated and the Revolution Command Council declared a Republic. Egypt's new leader, Colonel Gamal Abdel Nasser, espoused a broad vision: socialism at home, pan-Arab nationalism in the region, anti-colonialism throughout the Third World. This made him a hero for the multitudes, a Soviet ally, and a perceived threat to Western leaders.

Unfortunately, Cairo's situation worsened drastically after the 1952 revolution. Even the basic infrastructure of water and sewerage systems began to fail—that is, in the words of one commentator, "to fail even more seriously than had been the case hitherto."[56] The population exploded, from 2.4 million in 1950, to 5.7 million in 1980, by which time Cairo had become one of the world's most dense cities, in terms of population.[57] Assuming the role

FIG. 9.10. *Hall of the Arab League Headquarters, Cairo, Egypt. Mahmoud Riad, 1958–60. From* Cairo: A Life Story of 1000 Years.

FIG. 9.11. *Nile Hilton, Cairo. Welton Becket, 1953–59.*

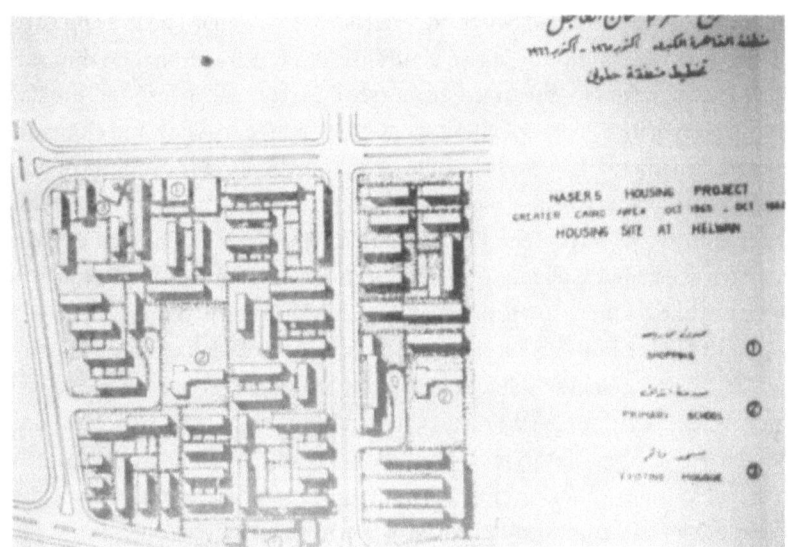

FIG. 9.12. *Abdul Nasser's Urgent Housing Project at Helwan, Greater Cairo, 1965–55*. From Shiber, Recent Arab City Growth.

of president in 1956, Nasser nationalized the Canal and ordered a municipal master plan to convert Cairo's recent development into a modern city.[58] Thoroughfares were cut through the maze of narrow alleys, but the wide streets soon became congested, dirty, and unbearably hot. Industrial subcenters were built on the periphery, anticipating the nationalization of the entire industrial sector in 1957. The government sponsored an international seminar on "The New Metropolis in the Arab World" in 1960. Funds were scarce, however, and Nasser favored rural land reform, industrialization, and military spending—especially after the debacle of the 1967 war with Israel.

Egyptian architecture of the 1950s and 1960s represents a truly international modernism, that is, it is a contentious amalgam of Communist, capitalist, and Third World technologies and aesthetics. Launched in 1952, the Mugamma, "a huge building in Stalin-Allée concrete," built to house the vast state bureaucracy, was the most significant new structure of the era, at least in its political and visual impact.[59] As Nasser played the major Cold War powers against each other for funds, Egyptian architects garnered most of the commissions. The lavish lotus-flower filigree of Naoum Shebib's Cairo Tower (Al Borg, 1956–61) flaunted the extravagant use of a CIA bribe. Several new skyscrapers faced the renamed Midan Tahrir (Liberation Square), most notably Galal Moemem's Radio and Television Center. Eager to show their love of culture, the Soviets underwrote the National Theatre and City of the Arts. The most elegant structure is the most traditional. Mahmoud Riad's headquarters for the Arab League (see fig. 9.10), built in 1958–60, evoked the city's remarkable Islamic heritage with its simple massing and eloquent mosaic ornament. The Arab League stood on the former grounds of the British barracks, across the river from Welton Becket's opulent Nile Hilton (1953–59) (see fig. 9.11). The Hilton revealed Pharaonic luxury rather than regional sensibilities; all guests enjoyed a panoramic view of the Great Pyramids, while the hotel turned a blank wall on the crowded medieval city.[60]

Cairo's acute housing shortage led to government interventions as early as 1946, when the English-trained engineer Ali al-Maligi Masa'ud designed 6,000 standardized units for a "Workers' City" in Imbābah.[61] The first 1,100 units, completed just before the 1952 revolution, became the model for Nasser's Urgent Housing (Masaakin el-Qadima) program of public housing during the 1960s. Soviet influence meant that the blocks were intentionally large in scale, standardized, and austere (see fig. 9.12). The *massaquin*, as they are called (the best translation would be "the projects," implying spartan structures and policies), proved to be prohibitively expensive, poorly located in terms of employment, and completely inadequate to the need, given the scale of in-migration from the countryside.[62] A different word, *ahali*, meaning "people," refers to privately built apartment buildings. Nasser also advocated de-concentration, with the first and largest of Cairo's new towns, Nasr City (Madinet Nasr, or "Victory City") providing uniform high-rises for state technocrats.[63]

Following Nasser's death in 1970, his protégé, Anwar Sadat, served as president until his assassination in 1980. Sadat threw out the Soviets and launched a disastrous attack on Israel in 1973. Then, seeking to salvage the nation's economy and reputation, he embarked on the Infitah ("Open-Door" policy) in 1974, vowing to modernize the city by promoting foreign investment. Once committed to modernism, Egypt now turned to Islamicist and neo-Pharaonic architectural motifs, especially in the center of Cairo and at resort towns, not for their vernacular familiarity and environmental benefits, but for populist allure and tourist appeal. Beholden to the West, especially the United States, Sadat's regime accentuated the most wasteful, unequal, and ostentatious aspects of 1970s modernity, including an infatuation with postmodern design. (Saad Ibrahim contends that Sadat's urban models were surely Houston and Los Angeles.[64]) Housing programs conspicuously favored the upper-middle class, even though almost half the population lived below the poverty level. New towns were often organized by profession, as in Madinat al-Awqaf ("The Engineers' City"), designed by Mahmoud Riad. Sadat's *masaakin*, or public-

This view, looking north from Bab al-Wazir consists of an entire cluster of monuments, from the Blue Mosque to the Palace of Alin Aq, covering a period of some four hundred years.

FIG. 9.13. *Sketch of Mosque-Madrasa of Amir Khayrbak, Cairo, ca. 1977, by Jim Antoniou, Director of the Medieval Cairo project.*

housing, policies espoused "a scientific solution": relocating the poor from central areas like Bulaq to distant sites, invisible to tourists, so that property values would soar in the "new heart of Cairo" with luxury housing, hotels, offices, and "centers of culture."[65] In fact, however, residential construction consisted principally of informal self-built shanties—an estimated 87 percent of the annual total by 1985.[66]

The historic core of Medieval Cairo (also called Old Cairo) remained relatively untouched until the end of Sadat's regime. Originally the town of Fustat, founded in 641 A.D., this area has one of the finest and largest concentrations of Islamic architectural history in the world. Nearly 4 square kilometers in size, its present occupants were mostly rural migrants to the city, at least half of them impoverished. Nasser's commitment to centralized authority had led him to nationalize all preservation efforts, even though the state Antiquities Department had neither the budget nor the expertise to maintain, much less restore, the more than six hundred listed monuments.[67] Recognizing the toll of neglect, Sadat's Antiquities Department asked European and American archaeological institutes to adopt individual buildings or neighborhoods.[68] UNESCO then sponsored a master plan for Medieval Cairo in 1980, the year of Sadat's assassination. Research drew on scientific data, maps, and photographic documentation; the staff identified six clusters of monuments, each viewed as a "heritage corridor" that would draw foreign visitors.[69] Publicity featured charming sketches of street life around the monuments (see fig. 9.13), prepared by the project's director, the American architect Jim Antoniou.

Antoniou's 1981 report suggests a concluding point for my essay. Historical continuity, he wrote, provides late-twentieth-century Cairo with "a means of avoiding cultural disruptions, preserving cultural identity, and establishing an organic link between the past, the present and the future."[70] These words reveal a change in architectural parameters. The altered framework split architecture into two separate, relatively autonomous camps, erasing much of the earlier cross-fertilization. Historically-minded design now looked myopically to the past, less concerned with creative play, environmentalism, or social life than with exacting archaeological criteria leavened by high-minded rhetoric. Modern architecture looked to the present and the developer's bottom line, which allowed for the latest fashions, but for little depth or vision. This generation of Egyptian architects, whatever their bent and their origins, whether indigenous or foreign, was no longer challenged by the complexities of history—including modernism's own founding beliefs in social progress.

A brief overview of post–World War II modern architecture in the Middle East raises some intriguing questions. How best to characterize the patterns as three seemingly consistent terms—modernism, history, and locale—were played out on different stages? What are the implications today, wherever one might be? Contemporary scholars, architects, and social activists around the world are raising similar issues.[71] They agree that local knowledge remains critical in an age of global economics and cultural fashions. There is no essence or truth here, as some would claim, but there are myriad particularities, distinctive places, and narratives. Each locale may be circumscribed, perhaps insular, but even parochial viewpoints suggest alternative ways to view the world—and ourselves.[72] Indeed, we modernists have our own types of provincialism.[73] Not only do we believe that the rest of the world should abide by our values, whether in political philosophy, popular culture, medicine, or architecture; we tend to explain the inevitable dissonance as other people's ignorance or as minor deviations from a norm.

These three nations show that modern architecture assumed many forms and generated diverse effects in a single region, indeed, in each country or city. Talent was only one of many variables. Good intentions confronted tenuous circumstances. Modernism's benefits and burdens co-existed in an unstable calculus: multinational investment, foreign interventions, cosmopolitan pleasures, and dangerous disparities in Lebanon; rapid wealth, technological development, and ultraconservative authoritarian leadership in Saudi Arabia; state socialism, ambitious social programs, and slow-moving bureaucracies in Egypt. New buildings responded to these circumstances—but always with exceptions to the rule. They could be visually disturbing, tedious, or inspiring; socially oppressive as well as enlightened; culturally exhilarating or debilitating—and often several conflicting qualities simultaneously.

References to regional vernaculars or historical traditions in architecture likewise showed common tonalities and unique effects. Seen in a positive light, these influences modulated modernist orthodoxy, generating distinctive appearances and richer meanings, even if these qualities were not always legible outside the context. Viewed from another perspective, however, they could be reactionary and divisive. Injurious traditions had repercussions that affected architecture, at least indirectly: an unregulated laissez-faire economy, hedonistic pleasures, and sectarian rivalries in Lebanon; autocratic leadership, conspicuous displays of wealth, and deeply conservative social mores in Saudi Arabia; bureaucratic inaction, deep cultural pride, and entrenched poverty in Egypt. Seeking to preserve a supposed purity or superiority in race, religion, nationhood, or cultural preferences, people often turn against other groups and alternative points of view. The critique can be extended to the traditions or habits of peripatetic architects and other modern citizens of the world who never question their ability to capture the nature of a place, even a large city, and what it needs, often in a fleeting visit.

Rather than relying on comparisons to explain this situation, I suggest a more flexible model of ongoing exchange. This shifts the focus from individuals or groups to more open-ended processes. The flow of ideas and images is multidirectional, not linear, with unpredictable results, as exchanges follow official and informal routes. This was certainly the case as modern architecture evolved in the Middle East. Historians usually trace the paths of elite professionals who emanated from Europe and the United States. We might consider the role of local or regional traditions, especially those with indisputable provenance; but we tend to neglect more popular currents, as well as the modern architectural trends of Morocco, Greece, Brazil, and other Third World nations, especially if they were modified or "corrupted" en route. These other processes are difficult to track, and even more so to classify: the impetus could be commercial or spiritual, creative or coercive; the results, awkward or inspired, mimetic or original. Yet this perspective helps reframe how we might think about modern architecture. Inherently global in formal and economic terms, it must have some flexibility, yet always remain particular to local contexts of history, geography, culture, and power.

NOTES

1. The original project for University City in Baghdad included 273 buildings designed by Gropius with The Architects Collaborative (TAC) and the Iraqi architect Hisham Munir. Political unrest limited the project to only a few dozen buildings, constructed mostly in the late 1960s. For commentary, see Hasan-Uddin Khan, ed., *The Middle East*, vol. 5 of *World Architecture, 1900–200*, ed. Kenneth Frampton (Vienna and New York: Springer, 2000), 5: 92–95; "Planning the University of Baghdad," *Architectural Record* 129 (February 1961): 107–22.

2. Samuel Isenstadt, "'Faith in a Better Future,'" *Journal of Architectural Education* 50 (February 1997): 172–78; Bastlund, *Josep Luis Sert, Architecture, City Planning, Urban Design* (Barcelona: Gustave Gili, 1968), 98–109.

3. I have drawn principally on Alfred E. Eckes and Thomas W. Zeiler, *Globalization and the American Century* (Cambridge, U.K.: Cambridge University Press, 2003); John R. Short, *Global Dimensions* (London: Reaktion, 2002); Kris Olds, *Globalization and Urban Change* (New York and Oxford: Oxford University Press, 2001); Michael Peter Smith, *Transnational Urbanism* (Malden, Mass.: Blackwell, 2001); Akira Iriye, *Cultural Internationalism and World Order* (Baltimore, Md.: Johns Hopkins University Press, 1997); and Anthony Giddens, *The Consequences of Modernity* (Stanford: Stanford University Press, 1990).

4. See Daniel Lerner, *The Passing of Traditional Society* (Glencoe, Ill.: The Free Press, 1958); Walt Whitman Rostow, *The Stages of Economic Growth* (Cambridge, U.K.: Cambridge University Press, 1960); as well as more recent indictments, such

as Timothy Mitchell, "The Object of Development," in *Power of Development*, ed. Jonathan Crush (London and New York: Routledge, 1995), 127–57. For background on the United States and the Middle East, see Mahmoud Mandami, *Good Muslim, Bad Muslim* (New York: Pantheon, 2004); Melani McAlister, *Epic Encounters* (Berkeley: University of California Press, 2001); Roger Owen, *State, Power and Politics in the Making of the Modern Middle East* (New York and London: Routledge, 2000); Irene L. Gendzier, *Notes from the Minefield* (New York: Columbia University Press, 1997); and David W. Lesch, ed., *The Middle East and the United States* (Boulder, Col.: Westview, 1999).

5. Timothy Mitchell, "The Stage of Modernity," in his *Questions of Modernity* (Minneapolis: University of Minnesota Press, 2000), 24, 26. Jean-Paul Bourdier, a scholar of "traditional" architecture in sub-Saharan Africa, acknowledges that "tradition identified as the past is a modernist idea" (see Bourdier, "Reading Tradition," in *Dwellings, Settlements and Tradition*, ed. Jean-Paul Bourdier and Nezar AlSayyad [Lanham, Md.: University of America Press, 1989], 38; and Nicholas K. Dirks, "History as a Sign of the Modern," *Public Culture* 2 [Spring 1990]): 25–32.

6. Timothy Mitchell, *Colonizing Egypt* (Cambridge, U.K.: Cambridge University Press, 1988); and Aziz al-Azmeh, *Islams and Modernities* (London: Verso, 1993). I am, of course, also indebted to the work of Edward Said, especially *Orientalism*, and his ideas about Orientalists' "unshakable abstract maxims [about] a general object, the whole Orient," and the "myth of arrested development."

7. Jane Jacobs, "Tradition Is (Not) Modern," in *The End of Tradition?* ed. Nezar AlSayyad (London and New York: Routledge, 2004), 32.

8. See Alison Smithson, ed., *Team 10 Meeting, 1953–1984* (New York, 1991); Sarah Williams Goldhagen and Réjean Legault, eds., *Anxious Modernisms* (Cambridge, Mass.: MIT Press for the Canadian Centre for Architecture, 2000), especially the essay in that volume by Felicity Scott, "Bernard Rudofsky: Allegories of Nomadism and Dwelling," 215–38; and Gwendolyn Wright, ed., *The History of History in American Schools of Architecture* (New York: Princeton Architectural Press, 1999), 39–46. Three books on "non-pedigreed" vernacular design became highly successful in the United States: Bernard Rudofsky, *Architecture without Architects* (New York: Museum of Modern Art/Doubleday, 1964); Amos Rapoport, *House Form and Culture* (Englewood Cliffs, N.J.: Prentice-Hall, 1969); and Paul Oliver, *Shelter and Society* (New York: Frederick A. Praeger, 1969). Anthony D. King juxtaposes the lyrical descriptions of dwellings in books like Rudofsky's with the denigrating appraisals of colonial and post-colonial officials who routinely demolished indigenous housing, rural as well as urban, in the name of modern standards (see King, *Urbanism, Colonialism, and the World Economy* [New York and London: Routledge, 1990], 53).

9. See Georges Balandier, "La situation colonial" (1955), reprinted as "The Colonial Situation: A Theoretical Approach," in *Social Change: the Colonial Situation*, ed. Immanuel Wallerstein (New York: Wiley, 1966), 34–61.

10. See Wendell C. Bennett, *Area Studies in American Universities* (New York: Social Science Research Council, 1951); Carl Leiden, ed., *The Conflict of Traditionalism and Modernism in the Muslim Middle East* (Austin: University of Texas Press, 1966); and Manfred Halpern, *The Politics of Social Change in the Middle East and North Africa* (Princeton: Princeton University Press, 1963). For later critiques, see Neil Waters, ed., *Beyond the Area Studies War* (Hanover, N.H.: University Press of New England, 2000); and Timothy Mitchell, "The Middle East in the Past and Future of Social Science," in *The Politics of Knowledge*, ed. David Szanton (Berkeley: University of California Press, 2004), 74–118.

11. Farha Ghannam, *Remaking the Modern* (Berkeley: University of California Press, 2002), 2.

12. Samir Khalaf and Per Kongstad, "Urbanization and Urbanism in Beirut," in *From Medina to Metropolis*, ed. L. Carl Brown (Princeton: Darwin Press, 1973), 117, 130. These figures do not include the equally stunning growth in Beirut's suburbs.

13. Marlène Ghorayeb, "The Work and Influence of Michel Ecochard in Lebanon," in *Projecting Beirut*, ed. Peter C. Rowe and Hasim Sarkis (Munich and New York: Prestel, 1998), 106–21; Ghorayeb, "Au croisement des cultures urbaines," *Maghreb Machrek*, no. 143 (Jan.-March, 1994): 162–89; and Ghorayeb, "Homage à Michel Ecochard," special issue of *Revue des Études Islamiques* 53 (1985).

14. Friedrich Ragette, "Reconstruction," in *The Middle East City*, ed. Abdulaziz Y. Saqqaf (New York: Paragon House, 1987), 267. Assem Salam speaks of the "coefficient of exploitation" driving development in "The Role of Government in Shaping the Built Environment,"(in Rowe and Sarkis, *Projecting Beirut*, 126). See also Jade Tabet, *Beyrouth* (Paris: Institut Français d'Architecture, 2001); May Davie, *Beyrouth* (Beirut: CERMOC [Centre d'Études et de Recherches sur le Moyen-Orient Contemporain], 2001); Jean-Luc Arnaud, ed., *Beyrouth, Grand-Beyrouth* (Beirut: CERMOC, 1997); Aida Boudjikanian, "Beyrouth 1920–1991," in *Le Liban aujourd'hui*, ed. Fadia Kiwan (Paris: CNRS Éditions, 1993); Pierre el-Koury, *Pierre el-Khory, Architecture, 1959–1999* (Paris, 2000); Jean-Pierre Gaudin, "L'Urbanisme au Levant et le mandat français," in *Architectures françaises outre-mer*, ed. Maurice Culot and Jean-Marie Thiveaud (Liège: Mardiga, 1992), 177–205; Udo Kultermann, *Contemporary Architecture in the Arab States* (New York: McGraw-Hill, 1999), 107–14; Samir Khalef and Philip S. Khoury, eds., *Recovering Beirut* (New York and Leiden: Brill, 1993); Gebran M. Yacoub, *Architectures au Liban*, 2 vols. (Beirut: Samir Abdo, 1993); Friedrich Ragette, ed., *Beirut of Tomorrow* (Beirut: American University of Beirut, 1983); Assem Salaam, "City Planning in Beirut and Its Out-

skirts"; Raymond S. Ghosen, "Beirut Architecture" in *Beirut: Crossroads of Cultures* (Beirut: Librairie du Liban, 1970), 167–202; and Soraya Antonius, *Architecture in Lebanon* (Beirut: Khayats, 1965).

15. See Hashim Sarkis, *Circa 1950* (Beirut: Editions Dar en-Nahar, 2003).

16. The Polish architect Karl Chayer and the Palestinian architect Georges Rayes were among those who made this argument (see Tabet, "From Colonial Style to Regional Revivalism," in Rowe and Sarkis, *Projecting Beirut*, 90–91).

17. John Hadidian, "A French Architect in Lebanon," *Architecture Plus* 1 (May 1973): 24–31.

18. Saba George Shiber, "Remarks about Urban Aesthetics and Architecture in the Arab World," in *Recent Arab City Growth* (Kuwait: Kuwait Government Printing Press, 1969), 213.

19. Eric N. Peterson, "Housing and Reconstruction," in Ragette, *Beirut of Tomorrow*, 46; Helmut Ruppert, *Beyrouth* (Beirut: Les Cahiers du Cermoc, no. 21, 1999), 30; Friedrich Ragette, *Architecture in Lebanon* (Beirut: American University of Beirut, 1974), 190; Harry H. Smith et al., *Area Handbook for Lebanon* (Washington, D.C.: Government Printing Office, 1968), 77–83; and Shiber, *Recent Arab City Growth*, 179, 737. Robert Saliba's *Beirut, 1920–1940* (Beirut: Order of Engineers and Architects, 1998) provides essential background.

20. Antoine Tabet built the St. Georges Hotel in 1932; Karol Schayer, the Carlton, in 1957; André Wogenscky and Maurice Hindieh, the Holiday Inn, in 1971 (see Joseph Fitchett, "From Khans to Khiltons," *Aramco World Magazine* 24 [Nov.–Dec. 1973]: 16–29).

21. Antonious, *Architecture in Lebanon*, 8.

22. Friedrich Ragette, "A Post-modern Approach to Reconstruction," in Ragette, *Beirut of Tomorrow*, 82.

23. Ragette, "Building on Tradition, 2," *Aramco World Magazine* 22 (July–August 1971): 7–8; and Ragette, "Maison de l'Artisan," in Khan and Frampton, *World Architecture*, vol. 5, *The Middle East* 5: 114–15.

24. Smith et al., *Area Handbook for Lebanon*, 119.

25. The fairgrounds remain only partially completed, another victim of civil war (see Oscar Niemeyer, "Feira Internacional e Permanente do Líbano en Trípoli," *Modulo* [1962], cited in Farès el-Dahdah, "On Solidère's Motto," in Rowe and Sarkis, *Projecting Beirut*, 73–77).

26. See Hana Abu Khadra, "A Pictorial Essay of the Reconstruction Process," in Saqqaf, *The Middle East City*, 279–80; and Lerner, *The Passing of Traditional Society*, 169.

27. See Rafael Moneo, "The Souks of Beirut," in Rowe and Sarkis, *Projecting Beirut*, 263–73; Robert Salilba, *Beirut City Center Recovery* (Beirut, 2004); Angus

Garvin and Ramez Maluf, *Beirut Reborn* (London: Academy Editions, 1996); and Saree Makdisi, "Laying Claim to Beirut," *Critical Inquiry* 23 (Spring 1997): 661–705.

28. The British controlled oil exploration throughout the Arabian peninsula in the 1920s, but had no success. Standard Oil was granted a concession in 1933 and discovered oil near Dammon in 1938. The renamed Aramco established a 50/50 distribution system with the Saudis in 1948; the corporation was also allowed to subtract its profit-share to the Saudis from its U.S. corporate income taxes (see Eckes and Zeiler, *Globalization and the American Century*, 140–43, 186–93; Gendzier, *Notes from the Minefield*, 38–41; Roy Lebkicher, George Rentz, and Max Steineke, *Aramco Handbook* [Dammen: Aramco, 1960]; Fouad Al-Farsy, *Saudi Arabia* [London: Stacey International, 1978]; Al-Farsy, *Modernity and Tradition* [London and New York: Kegan Paul International, 1990]; and Norman C. Walpole et al., *Area Handbook for Saudi Arabia* [Washington, D.C.: GPO, 1971]).

29. See Anthony Guise, *Riyadh* (London and New York: Stacey International, 1988), 16; *Riyadh Album* (London: Stacey International, 1983), 12–13; and Jon Parssinen and Kaizer Talib, "The Development of Dhahran (Saudi Camp) as a Community," in *The Arab City*, ed. Ismaïl Serageldin and Samir El-Sadek (Medina, Saudi Arabia: Arab Urban Development Institute, 1982), 177–83.

30. Eckes and Zeiler, *Globalization and the American Century*, 142; George A. Lipsky, *Saudi Arabia* (New Haven: Human Relations Area Files Press, 1959), 290–91; Shiber, *Recent Arab City Growth*, 191, 100; Saleh A. Al-Hathloul, "Tradition, Continuity, and Change in the Physical Environment," Ph.D. diss., MIT, 1981, 144–54; and Michael E. Bonine, "Cities of Oil and Migrants," *Proceedings of the International Conference on Urbanism in Islam* (ICUIT) 2: 340–55 (Tokyo: Middle Eastern Culture Center, 1989).

31. "Cooling for 13,000 Stores, the Alamo, and a Harem," *Architectural Forum* 114 (April 1961): 134. Frei Otto and Rolf Gutbrod built a royal residence and offices in Riyadh (1978) and then the magnificent limestone-based and tensile-roofed Towaiq Palace outside the city (1983). Abdelwahed El-Wakil espoused traditional forms in Jeddah's Al-Sulaiman Palace (1981), while Kenzo Tange designed a striking modern palace on the outskirts (1982).

32. Al-Farsy, *Saudi Arabia*, 129–31.

33. See Sherban Cantacuzino, "Conference Centre and Hotel, Riyadh, Saudi Arabia," *Architectural Review* 157 (March 1975): 213–14; Guise, *Riyadh*, 9–14; and Facey, *Dir'iyya and the First Saudi State*, 33–47. Abdul Aziz instituted a revival in 1912, the Ikhwan, or "Brotherhood" movement, which was even more spartan than Wahabism.

34. See Constantinos Doxiadis, *Riyadh Existing Conditions* (1968), *Riyadh Mas-*

ter Plan (1971), and *Riyadh Action Master Plan Technical Reports* (1979), all cited in Al-Hathloul, "Tradition, Continuity, and Change in the Physical Environment," 154–89; see also Francesco Tentori, "From Architecture of Petrodollars to Architecture for New Man," *Lotus* 18 (1978): 109, 114. The master plan was submitted in 1971 and approved two years later.

35. Al-Farsy, *Saudi Arabia*, 129–31.

36. See William A. Beling, ed., *King Faisal and the Modernisation of Saudi Arabia* (Boulder, Col.: Westview, 1980).

37. See Stefano Bianca, *Urban Form in the Arab World, Past and Present* (London: Thames & Hudson, 2000), 219–47; Bianca, "Designing Compatibility between New Projects and the Local Urban Tradition," in *Continuity and Change*, ed. Margaret Bentley Ševčenko (Cambridge, Mass.: Aga Khan Program for Islamic Architecture at Harvard and MIT, 1984), 21–28; and Walpole et al., *Area Handbook for Saudi Arabia*.

38. See Geza Feherari, "Towers in Islamic Architecture," *Arts and the Islamic World* 4 (Autumn-Winter 1986): 29–32.

39. For commentary, see Khaled Asfour, "Cultural Crisis," *Architectural Review*, no. 203 (special issue on the Middle East, March 1998): 52–60; Suha Özkan, "Regionalism within Modernism," in *Regionalism in Architecture*, vol. 1, ed. Robert Powel (Singapore: Aga Khan Award for Architecture and Concept Media, 1985), 8–16; and Larry Paul Fuller, "Building the Kingdom," *Texas Architect* 35 (January-February 1985): 60–61. Strangely enough, in Arabic the word *façade* means "corruption" (Shiber, *Recent Arab City Growth*, 214).

40. See John Close, "The Towers of Silence," *Saudi Business*, November 16, 1979, cited in Kaizer Talib, *Shelter in Saudi Arabia* (London and New York: Academy/St. Martin's Press, 1984), 128; Abdelmohsen M. Farahat and M. Numan Cebeci, "A Housing Project," in Serageldin and El-Sadek, *The Arab City*, 303–11; and Shiber, "Public Housing Policy Needed in Arab World," *Recent Arab City Growth*, 197–201. On the camps, see Hasan-Uddin Khan, "Introductionary [sic] Essay—Expressing Identities through Architecture," in Kahn and Frampton, *World Architecture*, vol. 5, xxix, xl.

41. RMJM's conservation of Jeddah's Old Town won an Aga Khan Award. On the evolution of the city, see James Buchanan, *Jeddah Old and New* (London: Stacey International, 1980); Saleh A. Al-Hathloul, "City Profile—Jeddah," *Cities* 8 (November 1991): 267–71; Kamel A. Komsani, "Jeddah," in *Arab Architecture: Past and Present*, ed. Antony Hutt (Durham, N.C.: Centre for Middle Eastern & Islamic Studies, 1983), 39–41; Mohammed Scharabi, "The New Town of Jubail and the Civic Center at Jedda," in *Islamic Cairo*, ed. Michael Meinecke (London: Deutsches Archäologisches Institut Art and Archaeology Research Papers, 1980), 100–104;

N. S. Farsi and H. I. Amer, "Islamic Architectural Features in the Arabian Peninsula and Their Reflection in Planning Old and New Jeddah," in Serageldin and El-Sadek, *The Arab City*, 184–90; and Angelo Pesce, *Jiddah: Portrait of an Arabian City* (Tucson, Ariz.: Falcon Press, 1974).

42. "Profile of El-Wakil," *Mimar* 1 (July-September 1981): 5, 47; Chris Abel, "Work of El-Wakil," *Architectural Review* 180 (November 1986): 52–60; Saleem Shahed, "Abedl Wahed El-Wakil," *Arts and the Islamic World* 1 (Winter 1983–84): 56–64; and Peter Rawstone, "A Bridge between Two Cultures [Interview]," *RIBA Journal* 97 (October 1990): 36–90.

43. *Riyadh Album*, 13. In addition to works already cited, other relevant publications on Riyadh include William Facey, *Riyadh, The Old City* (London: IMMEL Publishing, 1992); Facey, *Dir'iyyah and the First Saudi State* (London: Stacey International, 1997); Udo Kultermann, "Riyadh—The Arab City of the Twentieth Century," *Arcus* (January-February 1985): 84–90; Kultermann, "Contemporary Arab Architecture," *Mimar* 16 (April-June 1985): 42–53; Kultermann, *Contemporary Architecture in the Arab States*, 127–66; and M. A. Al-Hammad, "Riyadh: City of the Future," *Cities* 10 (February 1993): 16–23.

44. See Franco Albini et al., *Kasr-el-Hokm Area Revelopment Project Report* (Riyadh, 1974); Tentori, "From Architecture of Petrodollars to Architecture for New Man," including Marco Albini, "Urban Design," 114; Ali Shuaibi and Saleh Al-Hathloul, "The Justice Palace District, Riyadh," in Ŝevčenko, *Continuity and Change*, 37–84; and Al-Hammad, "Riyadh: City of the Future," 16–23. As bureaucracy expanded in the 1980s, so too did the Qasr el-Hokm district. The Jordanian Rasem Badran added a huge new mosque, courthouse, and museum complex (1979–92), and Ali Shuaibi of the Saudi Beeah Group built another courthouse at the Al-Kindi Plaza (1981–86). Each emphasized continuity with the past and continuity between architecture and the surrounding urban fabric; both received Aga Khan awards, as did Henning Larson's adjacent Ministry of Foreign Affairs.

45. Facey, *Dir'iyyah and the First Saudi State*, 48–61. Badran's additions of the 1990s suggest a growing tension about culture, memory, and modern space (see Badran, "On the Poetics of Place," in *Understanding Islamic Architecture*, ed. Attilio Petruccioli and Khalil K. Pirani [London: Routledge Curzon, 2002], 105–10; and Badran, "Historical References and Contemporary Design," in *Theories and Principles of Design in the Architecture of Islamic Societies*, ed. Margaret Bentley Ŝevčenko [Cambridge, Mass.: Aga Khan Program for Islamic Architecture at MIT and Harvard, 1988], 149–59).

46. Tentori, "From Architecture of Petrodollars to Architecture for New Man," 111.

47. See, in particular, Fazlur R. Khan, "The Islamic Environment," in *Toward an*

Architecture in the Spirit of Islam, ed. Renata Holod (Singapore: Aga Khan Awards, 1980), 32–43; Khan, "The Future of High Rise Structures," *Progressive Architecture* 53 (October 1972): 78–85; Khan, "The Bearing Wall Comes of Age," *Architectural and Engineering News* 10 (October 1968): 64–67; and Hasan-Uddin Khan, "Profile: Fazlur R. Khan," *Mimar,* no. 4 (April-June 1982): 35.

48. Skidmore, Owings and Merrill, *Urban Design Middle East* (Chicago: Skidmore, Owings & Merrill, 1978), 8. The pamphlet cites Rudofsky's *Architecture without Architects* and Rapoport's *House, Form, and Culture* as key sources.

49. See Janet Abu-Lughod, "The Islamic City"; Albert Hourani and Samuel M. Stern, eds., *The Islamic City* (Oxford: Cassirer; Philadelphia: University of Pennsylvania Press, 1970).

50. Skidmore, Owings and Merrill, *Urban Design Middle East,* 8.

51. See Khaled Fahmy, *All the Pasha's Men* (Cambridge and New York: Cambridge University Press, 1997); Mitchell, *Colonizing Egypt.*

52. The best book on the city's history remains Janet L. Abu-Lughod's *Cairo: 1001 Years of the City Victorious* (Princeton: Princeton University Press, 1971), although books by André Raymond (Cairo, 1993; Cambridge: Harvard University Press, 2000); Max Rodenbeck, *Cairo: The City Victorious* (New York: Alfred A. Knopf, 1999); and Samir Raafat, *Cairo, the Glory Years* (Alexandria: Harpocrates Publishing, 2003) provide captivating recent interpretations.

53. *Architecture for the Poor* (Chicago: University of Chicago Press, 1973), Fathy's lyrical account of his work in New Gourna, was based on his earlier, state-sponsored version, *Gourna: A Tale of Two Villages* (Cairo: Ministry of Culture, 1969), also written in English. See also T. Mitchell, "Making the Nation," in *Consuming Tradition, Manufacturing Heritage,* ed. Nezar AlSayyad (London and New York: Routledge, 2001), 235; and N. Al Sayyad, "From Vernacularism to Globalism," *Traditional Dwellings and Settlements Review* 7 (1995): 13–24.

54. Fathy quoted in the World Bank's "Staff Appraisal Report: Arab Republic of Egypt Tourism Project" (1979), cited in Mitchell, "Making the Nation," 218. By the 1980s, the government had banned the use of alluvial mud for traditional brick-making, hoping to limit the further loss of fertile soil for agriculture. Mitchell notes that the new efforts to relocate villagers into "minuscule and nondescript concrete-and-red-brick boxes" now include an ethnographic film about the village that is to be destroyed.

55. *Al-'Imara* (no. 5/6 [1945]) called "for a National Style of Architecture in Egypt" (cited in Mercedes Volait, *L'Architecture moderne en Egypt* (Cairo: American University of Cairo Press, 1993), 73. A special issue published in 1952 covered "Modern Architecture in Brazil." Karim had trained as an architect in Zurich in the mid-1930s. See also Terek Mohamed Rafast Sukr, *Early Twentieth-Century*

Islamic Architecture in Cairo (Cairo: American University of Cairo Press, 1993); and Udo Kultermann, "Contemporary Arab Architecture." The Social Building and the Engineers Syndicate were exceptions. I have not been able to consult Ms. Volait's Ph.D. dissertation, "Architects et architectures de l'Égypte moderne (1820–1969)."

56. Ronald Lewcock, "Conservation in Islamic Cairo," in *The Expanding Metropolis,* ed. Ahmet Evin (Singapore: Concept Media for the Aga Khan Award for Architecture, 1984), 50.

57. Jim Antoniou, "The Exploding City," *Arts and the Islamic World* 2 (Winter 1984–85): 35. Michael Sorkin points out that, with 20 million people, at 29 people per acre, the density today is six times that of Mexico City. Cairo's population continues to grow by some 350,000 per year (Sorkin, "Deciphering Greater Cairo," *Architectural Record* 189 [April 2001]: 83).

58. Many elements of the plan, including the focus on and sites for public housing on the West Bank of the Nile, had first been explored in Mahmoud Riad's 1932 thesis in Civic Design at the University of Liverpool's School of Architecture (see Volait, "Town Planning Schemes for Cairo," in *Mass Mediations,* ed. Walter Armbrust [Berkeley: University of California Press, 2000], 44–70; and Volait, *L'Architecture moderne,* 97–98).

59. Abu-Lughod, *Cairo,* 182–220.

60. Miles Copeland, *The Game of Nations* (New York: Simon and Schuster, 1969), 148–50; Raafat, *Cairo,* 213–15; Desmond Stewart, *Cairo* ["Cities of the World" series] (London: Phoenix House, 1965), 73; and Annabel Wharton, *Building the Cold War* (Chicago: University of Chicago Press, 2001), 41–54.

61. Volait, "Town Planning Schemes for Cairo," 63.

62. See Abu-Lughod, *Cairo,* 166; Farha Ghannam, "The Visual Remaking of Urban Space," *Visual Anthropology* 10 (1998): 265–80; Ghannan, *Remaking the Modern,* 6, 27–28; Frederic Shorter, *Cairo's Leap Forward* (Cairo: American University of Cairo Press, 1989); Nawal Mahmoud Hassan, "Social Aspects of Urban Housing in Cairo," *Mimar* 17 (July-September 1985): 59–61; Abou-Zeid Rageh, "The Changing Pattern of Housing in Cairo," in *The Expanding Metropolis,* 133–48.

63. Saad Eddin Ibrahim, "Cairo: A Sociological Profile," in Saqqaf, *The Middle East City,* 213; Mona Serageldin, "Cairo—1800–2000," 91–119, and Mohammed Salah-Eddin Hegab, "New Towns Policy," both in *The Expanding Metropolis,* 91–119, 171–91. Today, Nasr City has a population of more than 3 million living in modern high-rises.

64. Ibrahim, "Cairo: A Sociological Profile," 214. See also Raymond Hinnebusch Jr., *Egyptian Politics under Sadat* (Cambridge and New York: Cambridge University Press, 1985); John Waterbury, *The Egypt of Nasser and Sadat* (Princeton:

Princeton University Press, 1983); and Sadat's aptly named autobiography, *In Search of Identity* (Glasgow: Collins, 1978).

65. The economically strategic cities of the Suez Canal Zone, virtually abandoned after extensive Israeli bombing during the 1967 war, epitomize the dual approach to housing that now prevailed. In 1973, the UNDP and a consortium of British consultants, led by the ubiquitous RMJM, undertook "realistic" master plans for Suez and Port Saïd. Culpin Planning used a radical alternative at nearby Ismailia, upgrading the existing informal settlements and securing title rights for some 90,000 residents. While Culpin's project received an Aga Khan Award in 1986, a waterside tourist facility soon shifted development priorities back to the more familiar pattern (see "Housing in the Suez Canal Towns, *Third World Planning Review* 3 (May 1981): 8–200, especially Forbes Davidson, "Ismailia," 161–78; and Ismaïl Serageldin, "Ismailia Development Project, Ismailia, Egypt," in *The Architecture of Empowerment*, ed. Ismail Serageldin (London: Academy, 1997), 102–3.

66. Ashraf Salama, "Contemporary Cairo Demystified," *Archis* no. 1 (2002): 29–32; Rageh, "The Changing Pattern of Housing in Cairo," 133, 138; Mildred F. Schmertz, "Coping with Cairo," *Architectural Record* 173 (May 1985): 91; *Al-Ahram* (December 29, 1979, p. 3, and December 27, 1979, p. 3), cited in Ghannan, *Remaking the Modern*, 30, 32. Ghannan notes that the separate rooms with functional labels (e.g., "kitchen" or "bedroom") of Sadat-era *masaakin* emphasized greater privacy and more rational use of space than did Nasser-era projects. As with other "modern" public housing of the 1970s, female residents complained about smaller rooms and more isolated home life (Ghannan, *Remaking the Modern*, 43–66). Even cemeteries became squatters' housing, including the City of the Dead, with its remarkable Islamic monuments.

67. See Jim Antoniou, "Historic Cairo," *Architectural Review* 203 (March 1998): 73; George T. Scanlon, "Municipal Planning and Archaeology," in Serageldin and El-Sadek, *The Arab City*, 230–34. The current population of Medieval Cairo is estimated to be over 1.5 million.

68. Under Nasser, the annual maintenance budget for all registered medieval monuments in the city was only £600 (Rodenbeck, *Cairo*, 170).

69. The most spectacular result was the German intervention in the Darb Qirmiz, beginning in 1977, which became the nucleus for Cairo's first conservation area (see Antoniou, "Historic Cairo," 75–77; Michael Meinecke, "The Darb Qirmiz Project," in *Islamic Cairo*, 42–46). The site received an Aga Khan Award for preservation in 1983.

70. See N. AlSayyad, I. A. Bierman, and N. Rabbat, eds., *Making Cairo Medieval* (Lanham, Md.: Lexington Books, 2005); Caroline Williams, "Transforming the

Old," *Middle East Journal* 59 (2002): 458–75; Florian Steinberg, "Architecture and Townscape in Today's Cairo," *Ekistics* 38 (1991): 75–86; Evin, *The Expanding Metropolis,* 49–90 (on conservation programs). Cairo was chosen as the site of the 1989 Aga Khan Award for Architecture, to focus attention on the collective nature of this historical legacy (see James Steele, ed., *Architecture for Islamic Societies Today* [London: Academy, 1994]). A mark of the ongoing appeal is Neil Mac-Farquhar, "The Beating Heart of Medieval Cairo," *New York Times Magazine* (September 12, 2004): 27–35.

71. Preface to Jim Antoniou, *Islamic Cities and Conservation* (Paris: Unesco Press, 1981), 5.

72. E.g., see Frederick Cooper and Ann Laura Stoler, eds., *Tensions of Empire* (Berkeley: University of California Press, 1997); Mitchell, ed., *Questions of Modernity*; Walter D. Mignolo, *Local Histories/Global Designs* (Princeton: Princeton University Press, 2000); Beatriz Sarlo, *Scenes from Postmodern Life* (Minneapolis: University of Minnesota Press, 2001); Kwame Anthony Appiah, *Cosmopolitanism* (New York: Norton, 2006); Alexander Tzonis, Liane Lefaivre, and Bruno Stagno, eds., *Tropical Architecture* (West Sussex: John Wiley, 2001); and Jyoti Hosagrahar, *Indigenous Modernities* (London and New York: Routledge, 2005).

73. Clifford Geertz put it eloquently: "To see ourselves as others see us can be eye-opening," he wrote in the introduction to a collection of his essays. "But it is from the far more difficult achievement of seeing ourselves amongst others, as a local example of the forms of human life locally taken, a case among cases, a world among worlds, that the largeness of mind, without which objectivity is self-congratulation and tolerance a sham, comes" (Geertz, *Local Knowledge* [New York: Basic Books, 1983], 16).

74. See Dipesh Chakrabarty, *Provincializing Europe* (Princeton: Princeton University Press, 2000).

10 From Modernism to Globalization

The Middle East in Context

NEZAR ALSAYYAD

Looking at the problems of cities today, one cannot ignore the revolutionary developments that have occurred in the world since the 1960s. Trends such as the transnationalization of capital, the internationalization of labor, the steady increase in global trading and communication, and the ensuing competition between cities have led individuals, businesses, industries, and governments to attempt to position themselves globally.[1] It follows that in a globally compressed world, constituted of national societies that are becoming increasingly aware of their ethnic and racial roots, the conditions for the identification of individual and collective selves become very complex.[2] It is important to take into account that any theory of globalization must recognize the distinctive cultural and unequal conditions under which the notion of the "global" was constructed.[3] It also becomes difficult to comprehend globalization without recognizing the historical specificity of traditional cultures, their colonization, and their later emergence as nation-states.

At the heart of all of these issues is the question of identity. We see this very clearly in no place more than we do in the Middle East, where the very problematic traditional/modern dialectic is often invoked. Of course, all societies are constructed in relation to one another and produced, represented, and perceived through the ideologies and narratives of situated discourse.[4] For example, the definition of the "Middle East" as a category is very much dependent on the existence of a "West." Both terms are mainly defined in difference, constructed in opposition to the other, produced in a variety of postcolonial and anticolonial discourses, although neither of them constitutes a monolithic preexisting real subject itself.[5]

PERIODIZING MODERNITY IN THE MIDDLE EAST

In studying the relationship between the West and the Middle East and its effect on the corresponding identity of people and architecture, three historic phases may be discerned: the colonial period, the era of independence and nation-state building, and, the most recent phase, globalization. These phases appear to have been accompanied by three respective urban forms: the hybrid, the modern or pseudo-modern, and the postmodern. In this essay, I hope to demonstrate how constructed the notion of the Middle East has been and to show the fluidity of identity under both colonial and global conditions, often invoking examples from Egypt and other Arab counties in the Middle East. But I also want to make explicit that this historical periodization and the attempt to theorize modernity in the entire Middle East will always be an abstract exercise. Generalization about the diverse countries of the Middle East, a fragile geopolitical entity whose existence as a single cultural unit, can and should be always called into question, and may only be justified in the pursuit of general cultural knowledge of the region.

Before the era of colonialism in most of the Middle East, settlements largely took the form of traditional communities under pre-industrial and often insular conditions. Although some forms of economic exchange occurred between this world and that of the developed world, curiosity about the "other" was limited. The vernacular forms of dwellings and settlements were shaped primarily by sociocultural concerns and the surrounding natural environments. They also reflected, possibly at the subconscious level, the identity of their inhabitants.

Around the middle of the nineteenth century, the world witnessed the rise of modern industrial capitalism and the emergence of organized political dominance, represented by colonialism. The paradigm shift from the traditional to the colonial created a relationship of unequal cultural and socioeconomic exchange. And, if one analyzes the issues of identity in the Middle East, one must take this fact into account and understand the processes by which identity was violated, ignored, distorted, or stereotyped throughout history. For once the "backwardness" of this traditional Middle East population was established (at least in the minds of the great mass of citizens in the colonial motherland), reform was legitimized. This series of events did not necessarily have an effect on the physical fabric of cities; everywhere the colonists went, they introduced their own brand of settlements.

The colonization process affected the overall planning model that determined the patterns of urban development. This was the era when modernist ideas flowed from the countries of the West to the Middle East. Ironically, in the 1950s and 1960s, when many Middle East countries launched their wars of liberation and independence, the colonists resorted to an age-old urban strategy. Hundreds of traditional villages were destroyed in order to regroup the population in checkerboard resettlement towns under the banner of modernization. This uprooting operation, as in the case of the Algerian war, was meant to break the subversive influence of the rebels, rather than to improve conditions for the local population. The colonial era thus resulted in a hybrid urban condition and, subsequently, a certain architectural and urban language began to emerge, at least at the visual level, that unified the countries of the Middle East ruled by certain colonial empires—British, French, Italian, etc.

When the people of the Middle East started to rebel against this colonial world order, they had little conceptual language to employ in their drive to establish sovereignty. Often they were forced to use the terms of the existing order, with all its baggage of physical realities and ideological constructs, like the nation-state. Groups of people living in one region under a colonial power (but of different religions, languages, ethnicities, and traditions, as in the case of Iraq and Sudan), sharing little more than a colonial history, had to band together to achieve this new, "more advanced" stage of independence. The new political and governing bodies highlighted what few commonalities existed, and suppressed differences, in pursuit of the larger goal of freedom and independence. A national identity based on shorter-term political interest and the ideology of struggle emerged as the driving force behind many nationalist movements in the Middle East. Once independence was achieved, the glue that bound together the various groups no longer held. Indeed, the long ethnic civil wars in Sudan and the recent American occupation of Iraq have exposed these weaknesses in those states. The continuing conflicts between the different ethnic groups that formed these countries are testament to the true associations of their native populations, where ethnic origin or religious affiliation have been, or have reemerged as the prime definer of their collective identity.[6]

Again, the second phase of independence struggles and nationalism did not necessarily improve the quality of the built environment in the Middle East, nor did it resolve the conflicts that plagued the traditional settlements of those countries. During the era of colonialism, important and irreversible decisions were made that affected the production of the built environment. In the Arab Middle East, for example, new building codes requiring setbacks (based on Western norms) forced the traditional courtyard house out of existence in Egypt and much of the Arabian Peninsula. New construction often took the form of banal single-family dwellings that were unsuited for the climate of the Middle East. Also, in such societies, where privacy was cherished, major adaptations of these new forms were required. In some countries, entire efficient systems of construction were abandoned because they did not suit the modern era. The urban system fell grossly out of balance, and the urban environment of many Middle Eastern countries' societies became pseudo-modernized.[7]

An obsession with modernity accompanied the early years of nationalism and independence and preoccupied most governments in the Middle East, including the most conservative ones. As a result, the Western, particularly European, pattern of urban development continued to serve as the main frame of reference, especially for the urban middle classes who stepped in after independence to run the various bureaucracies of these new nation-states. During this period, after World War II, the construction of public housing was pursued in many parts of the world both, as an instrument of rebuilding and as a mechanism to achieve social justice. Despite the failures of many public housing projects in the West, the international influence of modernism was strong enough to assure that this public-housing model would be often copied in the Middle East without questioning its stability. Here, as with other developing nations, Middle East governments in rich and poor states alike often used public-housing projects as an instrument of nation-building in an attempt to gain the allegiance of the new citizenry. In Egypt, for example, under the nationalist-socialist regime of Gamal Abdel Nasser, thousands of public-housing blocks were built across the country. Suffering under the usual problems of such development—lack of maintenance, empty and unused spaces, the need to accommodate expanding families—many residents took matters into their own hands and took over these projects by reappropriating them in novel ways. Some built additions into public spaces, others took over ground floors to use as private vegetable gardens, and, in some cases, the project's community collaborated in erecting small neighborhood mosques to camouflage their interventions, which revealed a new tendency to resort to the power of religion to achieve their goals. Both ethnicity (e.g., Kurdish, Berber, Nubian) and religion (in this case, Islam) were becoming the preeminent forms of community identification in the Middle East.

We may consider globalization as the third phase in the relationship between the Middle East and the West, particularly at a time when the search for and the reconstruction of identity has become paramount. Once independence was achieved and the dust from the struggle had settled, the problems of national and community harmony began to surface. Where these issues were resolved, religious and political fundamentalisms began to flourish. To understand the impact of these forces on urbanism, closer attention must be paid to the difficulties associated with defining national identity. The primary elements of nation identity—race, language, religion, history, territory, and tradition—have always been essential but unequal components in its formation. The political units that formed most nations in the Middle East after the two World Wars were expected to be homogenous entities with a common culture. But the reality was otherwise, as these nation-states were mainly put together by international deals that displayed little interest in the will of the people who inhabited these lands. Again, Iraq is a case in point.

National identity as perceived by a government is inherently tied to the image it wishes to project in the international arena. Many Middle Eastern governments resorted to using local and foreign architects to help them create such a new national style. While many of these post-independence projects continued the modernist schema, some others totally retreated to older traditional forms, and sometimes to newly invented ones that claimed to be based on specific historical periods. The work of Ramzy Omar and Ali Nassar in Egypt was an extension of the modernist schema, but with a lot of attention to issues of climate and abstract symbolism. These two architects helped build a large number of structures for the newly constituted public sector in Egypt, which included hotels, schools, clubs, and even structures for Egypt's single party at the time, the Arab Socialist Union, representing the attempt to devise a modern architecture for Egypt that was based on universal principles but adapted for the Egyptian context. Anyone who lived in Egypt in the 1960s easily recognizes these buildings today, which are often referred to as the Socialist Architecture of Egypt. I am not only talking about these public buildings, but also about the vast numbers of five-story public-housing walk-ups discussed earlier.

There were a few who had earlier rejected the Western styles altogether, and here architect Hassan Fathy stands out as the lone ranger. His village of New Gourna, near Luxor, Egypt, provides an interesting story of grudging critical acclaim. New Gourna was planned in the 1950s as the new home for residents of an old settlement that existed among the archaeological sites of the ancient Theban necropolis, whom the Egyptian government wanted to evict from their houses. Fathy designed the village using elaborate mud-brick structures that he imagined represented indigenous traditions. However, in his search for the ideal vernacular form, he turned to the geometries and proportions of Islamic styles, particularly Mamluk, which had flourished in medieval Cairo several centuries earlier. Among other things, this resulted in the use of unfamiliar forms (domes and vaults) for the project, which the local people associated with the tombs and shrines of the dead. New Gourna was an elegant depiction of an idea, but when the villagers who were meant to live there refused to move in, the attempt to create a new community with no real economic or social justification was revealed as a costly mistake. And in the end it became all too clear that Fathy's true concern was with his standing among his Western architectural peers, not his struggling Egyptian colleagues. Nevertheless, on account of the publicity of his effort to adapt indigenous architectural forms to create a national style, and after winning the distinguished Aga Khan Award for Architecture, Fathy became something of a guru among Middle Eastern architects.[8]

Today, examples of Fathy-like architecture are widespread in the Egyptian landscape, often giving the mistaken impression that this is what vernacular architecture in Egypt has always looked like. What Fathy had inadvertently done was to resuscitate an old tradition, or to simply invent a new one based on an imagined continuous history and an assumed homogenous community, when neither existed. His project is, in fact, an excellent example of how architecture can provide some of the best illustrations to Benedict Anderson's brilliant and important thesis about imagined communities.[9] Only time will tell whether the imagery that Fathy created in Gourna will become a lasting national Egyptian style, unlike the short-lived modern style that emerged in Egypt's socialist period.

Of course, identity cannot be based on some myth from precolonial times. Many Middle Eastern nations have resorted to a past in which identity may coalesce as a solace against the perceived dominator, often forgetting that respect for the past must also include accepting and coming to terms with the architectural and urban legacy of colonization itself. In the 1920s and 1930s, when it was a monarchy, Egypt often resorted to its Pharaonic past to establish the symbols of its new nationhood. But its architects and planners, like Fathy, often borrowed more from its Islamic heritage as well. Other architects simply invoked both traditions without resolving any possible contradictions, and that resulted in interesting hybrid forms that some may consider uniquely Egyptian but still modernist. The work of Ali Labib Gabr is a good example of this creative but small group of practitioners from the 1940s.

GLOBALIZATION, IDENTITY, AND THE "OTHER" IN THE MIDDLE EAST

The problem of national identity is of course complicated by the extensive economic exchanges that characterize the world today. Not only do Middle Eastern nations have to mediate between precolonial and colonial legacies, between the traditional and the modern, but they must also deal with the effects of globalization and the New World Order. "Globalization" here refers to the process by which the world is becoming a single economic entity, characterized by information exchange, interconnected modes of production, and flows of labor and capital within a predominately capitalist world system. Indeed, the considerable migration from the former colonies in the Middle East and North Africa to the lands of their former colonizers in Europe and the infiltration of these ethnic subcultures into mainstream European societies cannot be dismissed. In fact, this demographic change has often been the cause of social conflict as these local subcultures, often Muslims, have resorted to ethnic, racial, or religious allegiances to keep from being swallowed up by the majority culture.[10] The current attempts at multiculturalism in Europe, and the struggles, often failed, of many European governments to cope with their minority Muslim populations, usually from Middle Eastern countries, may be a good example of a strategy to embrace difference as a fundamental constituent of national identity. It is ironic that as the national identity of the former European colonizers is being discussed and reassessed, often in an attempt to become more inclusive, the national identity of the formerly colonized nations of the Middle East and North Africa, like much of Eastern Europe and South Asia, is moving in the opposite direction, and is often becoming more exclusive and more directly linked to national origin or religious association. Indeed, the twentieth century has witnessed the return of states where belonging to a particular religious or ethnic group is a prerequisite for the enjoyment of full citizenship rights or status.[11] Here, Israel and Iran may be cases in point.

We must remember, however, that national identity is always undergoing a process of transformation and flux. While the contradictory forces of globalization may be playing havoc with traditional loyalties and values and challenging older ideologies and practices, a single "world culture" inclusive of Middle Eastern traditions remains a distant prospect. Thus, as Benjamin Barber points out in his appropriately titled book, *Jihad vs. McWorld*, Middle Eastern and Islamic nations want the veil, but they also want the World Wide Web and Coca Cola.[12] Timothy Mitchell, on the other hand, argued that Jihad is not antithetical to the development of McWorld, and that McWorld is really McJihad, a necessary combination of a variety of social logics and economic forces, often driven by and benefiting from the advances in communication technology that led to the emergence, particularly in the Middle East, of the current Jihadist movements, like Al-Qaida in the Muslim World.[13] Here, some Middle Eastern countries evolve their own local appropriations of many Western practices without ever embracing their logic. Similarly, for its part, the West continues to be interested in consuming the cultures and environments of Middle Eastern societies because of the exotic differences they offer, but without accepting their underlying premise. A good example here may be the fascination or the fixation that some Western countries have with Middle Eastern monuments and their emergence as financial patrons for monument preservation as part of what they define as "universal" heritage, even when the natives of those Middle Eastern and Central Asian countries, who are mainly Muslim, do not recognize or accept the historic value of such structures. The dynamiting of the Buddha Statues in Bamian, Afghanistan, under the Taliban regime is a case in point.

I have argued elsewhere that most people usually exhibit two conflicting sentiments toward tradition, culture, and the past. The first is to resort to culture and tradition out of fear of change—change that in and of itself may be inevitable. But protectionism against the unknown or the unfamiliar can, and often does, turn into fundamentalism. Some may simplistically argue that this position offers an explanation for the attitudes of some Middle Eastern nations and their people toward the West, but I believe that the matter is more complex than that and requires a more global perspective. The second sentiment, characterized by interest in the culture of the mysterious "other," an idea that generated the initial interest of European orientalists in the Middle East, emerges from a totally different feeling, that is, the desire to have the choice to merge with the "other" and share in a wider or a different collective consciousness. Indeed, we see this sentiment clearly represented among groups of Middle Easterners living in the West who have become thoroughly Westernized and are no longer interested in or comfortable with their Middle Eastern heritage, as well as among groups of Europeans and Americans who are residents and lovers of particular Middle Eastern countries. The tremendous movement of citizens across borders and the rise of protected ethnic minorities demonstrate that the two sentiments, both legitimate, are not necessarily contradictory. In fact, they may indeed occur simultaneously, or, alternatively, based on time and place.[14] I would argue that the interplay between these two sentiments shapes much of the attitudes of many First and Third World peoples, particularly those in the Middle East. It is here that much work and analysis need to be done to unpack the complexities of the relationships between the "Middle East" and the "West."

For those interested in the study of culture and urbanism in the Middle East in the era of globalization, there are some lessons to be learned.[15] First, one may argue that even as the many different nations converge into a "world culture," it is a culture marked by the management of diversity, rather than by the replication of uniformity. This so-called world culture, an idea made possible during the heyday of modernization, remains essentially a culture of dominant groups, in which the persistent diversity of the constituent local culture—as is the case with many Middle Eastern societies—is often a product of globalization itself. The second lesson involves the connection between this world culture and the nature and form of space and place as this culture is increasingly placeless. Indeed, it is a culture created through the rapid interconnectedness of local, national, and foreign communities, through flows of information whose logic is largely uncontrolled by any specific local society but whose impacts shape the lives of all these local societies.[16] Nowhere can this be better observed than in the Middle East. Here, the impact on urbanism is that cultural experience, even in the supposedly traditional Middle East, which is notorious for its resistance to change, will likely become less place-rooted and more information-based.

The case of the Middle East may in fact convince us that the so called "universal modernism," if one can talk about such a thing, is only or mainly a European phenomenon. The permanently hybrid nature of architecture and urbanism in the Middle East make it impossible to accept this "universal" notion. Hence, the rising tide of placelessness will not likely generate a uniform global response, since the underlying cultural diversity will find new and yet to be known means to manifest itself. Placelessness will not eventually undermine cultural diversity, but it will require different practices for the construction of the multiple and increasingly complex identities of the people of the Middle East.

Finally, and despite the world's preoccupation with globalization, the history of the world demonstrates a movement toward cultural differentiation and not homogenization, in which each individual belongs to many cultures and people have multiple cultural identities. In this sense, identity is always under construction and in constant evolution. For if hybridity is accepted as an inherent constituent of national identity, then the ensuing urbanism must be accepted as only a reflection of a specific transitional stage in the life of any society.[17] Indeed, globalization has made the issues of identity and representation in urbanism very cumbersome and has cast doubt on urbanism's ability to fully represent the peoples, nations, and cultures within which it exists. But since culture has become increasingly placeless, urbanism will likely become one of the few remaining arenas where one may observe how local cultures mediate global domination. Again, here the countries of the Middle East will be prime sites for such observations. But as the nations of this globalizing Middle East become more conscious of their religious convictions and ethnic roots, they are likely to seek forms and norms that represent these sub-identities, even if these send confused messages to a global audience that will ultimately deal with them through the spaces of flows.

In the end, while some may argue that there is a world of difference between the "true" modernity of a First World city like London or Paris and the "apparent" modernity of a Cairo or Beirut, much new research has demonstrated that citizens of Middle Eastern countries are articulating a project of active citizenship outside of the traditional institutional and state arenas. It is a unique modernity cognizant of the surrounding global and transnational current.[18] Whether the different nations that constitute the Middle East will be able to develop a new political culture and a spatial articulation beyond the slogans of traditionalism, religious revival, and anti-modernity is yet to be seen. The new claims to citizenship that have emerged recently may simply be a response to the perceived threat of the rising American Empire with its alternative democratizing models, as hegemonic as these may be. This raises for me the most important issue in studying modernity and modernism in the Middle East.

In *All That Is Solid Melts into Air,* Marshall Berman brilliantly illustrated how the modernity of Paris and St. Petersburg in the mid-nineteenth century was a modernity based on urban encounters in the newly-opened boulevards, which, in Paris, were often cut from the traditional fabric of the medieval city.[19] These new public spaces allowed the rich and the poor to come together in physical contact in new and unprecedented ways. Berman showed how this apparently similar modernity in both of these cities captured very different meanings. In Paris, it was a modernity of class encounter grounded in a particular liberal traditions, whereas in St. Petersburg, Berman argues, it was a "modernity of underdevelopment," bearing the apparent forms of the modern but lacking its processes, and marked more by a mix of mimicry and envy.

The globalizing changes that the Middle East has undergone in the last couple of decades, particularly in its confrontation with the West following the repercussions of 9/11, have opened up new experiences of modernity à la Berman. Are today's exclusive malls of Cairo, Beirut, Dubai, and Doha, where the totally veiled mix comfortably with the skimpily dressed, the new boulevards of a unique Middle Eastern modernity?[20] Will the attempt to reconcile "MacWorld" and Jihad lead to a new and different modernity? Or will we see a retreat to traditionalism without an abandonment of the fundamental premises of modernity, a sort of "Medieval Modernity" that deals with the new parameters of survival in an ever changing and globalizing world?[21] These are only a few of the important challenges that will face the theorists and historians of modernity in the twenty-first century.

NOTES

1. See Anthony D. King, ed., *Culture, Globalization, and the World-System* (Basingstoke, U.K.: Macmillan, in association with the Department of Art and Art History, SUNY at Binghamton, 1991).

2. Roland Robertson, "Social Theory, Cultural Relativity, and the Problems of Globality," in King, *Culture, Globalization, and the World-System*.

3. Many conceptions of globalization have been developed in the social sciences or are rooted in economic theories. This essay mainly draws from the field of cultural studies.

4. Janet Wolff, "The Global and the Specific: Reconsidering Conflicting Theories of Culture," in King, *Culture, Globalization, and the World-System*.

5. See Stuart Hall, "Old and New Identities, Old and New Ethnicities," in King, *Culture, Globalization, and the World-System*.

6. Nezar AlSayyad, "Urbanism and the Dominance Equation," in *Forms of Dominance*, ed. Nezar AlSayyad (London: Avebury, 1992).

7. Nezar AlSayyad, "From Vernacularism to Globalism: The Temporal Reality of Traditional Settlements," *Traditional Dwellings and Settlements Review* 7, no. 1 (1995): 13–24.

8. Ibid.

9. Benedict R. O'G. Anderson, *Imagined Communities* (London: Verso, 1983).

10. Nezar AlSayyad and Manuel Castells, eds., *Muslim Europe or Euro-Islam* (Lanham, Md.: Lexington Books, 2002).

11. Nezar AlSayyad, "Urbanism and the Dominance Equation," in *Forms of Dominance*, ed. Nezar AlSayyad (London: Avebury, 1992).

12. See Benjamin Barber, *Jihad vs. McWorld* (New York: Ballantine Books, 1995).

13. Timothy Mitchell, "McJihad: Islam in the U.S. Global Order," *Social Text* 20, no. 4 (Winter 2002): 1–18.

14. Nezar AlSayyad, "Culture, Identity, and Urbanism in a Changing World," in *Preparing for the Urban Future*, ed. Michael A. Cohen et al. (Washington, D.C.:

Woodrow Wilson Center Press; Baltimore: Distributed by the Johns Hopkins University Press, 1996).

15. Many of these lessons are collected in a series of essays, by Anthony King, Stuart Hall, Roland Robertson, Immanuel Wallenstein, Ulf Hannerz, and Janet Wolff, among others. The essays are from a symposium held at the State University of New York, Binghamton, in 1989 (see King, *Culture, Globalization, and the World-System*).

16. Manuel Castells, "The World Has Changed: Can Planning Change?" *Landscape and Urban Planning* 22, no. 1 (1992): 73–78.

17. Nezar AlSayyad, ed., *Hybrid Urbanism* (New York: Prager, 2001).

18. Paul Amar and Diane Singerman, eds., *Cairo Cosmopolitan* (Cairo: American University in Cairo Press, 2006).

19. Marshall Berman, *All That Is Solid Melts into Air* (New York: Penguin, 1988).

20. Nezar AlSayyad, "Whose Cairo?," in Amar and Singerman, *Cairo Cosmopolitan*, (Cairo: American University in Cairo Press, 2006), 539ff.

21. Ananya Roy and Nezar AlSayyad, "Medieval Modernity: Citizenship in Contemporary Urbanism," *Applied Anthropologist* 25, no. 2 (2005): 147–65.

Bibliography

HISTORY AND THEORY: MIDDLE EAST AND BEYOND

Ahmad, Aijaz. "Orientalism and After: Ambivalence and Metropolitan Location in the Work of Edward Said." In *In Theory: Classes, Nations, Literatures.* London: Verso, 1992.

Al-Azmeh, Aziz. *Islams and Modernities.* London: Verso, 1993.

AlSayyad, Nezar. "Culture, Identity, and Urbanism in a Changing World." In *Preparing for the Urban Future: Global Pressures and Local Forces,* edited by Michael A. Cohen et al. Washington, D.C.: Woodrow Wilson Center Press; Baltimore: Distributed by the Johns Hopkins University Press, 1996.

AlSayyad, Nezar, and Manuel Castells, eds. *Muslim Europe or Euro-Islam.* Lanham, Md.: Lexington Books, 2002.

Anderson, Benedict R. *Imagined Communities: Reflections on the Origin and Spread of Nationalism.* London: Verso, 1983.

Appadurai, Arjun. *Modernity at Large: Cultural Dimensions of Globalization.* Minneapolis: University of Minnesota Press, 1996.

Appiah, Kwame Anthony. *Cosmopolitanism: Ethics in a World of Strangers.* New York: Norton, 2006.

Baydar, Gulsum. "Toward Postcolonial Openings: Rereading Sir Banister Fletcher's History of Architecture." *Assemblage* 35 (1998): 6–17.

Berman, Marshall. *All That Is Solid Melts into Air.* New York: Penguin, 1988.

Bhabha, Homi K. *The Location of Culture.* London: Routledge, 1994.

Bourdier, Jean-Paul. "Reading Tradition." In *Dwellings, Settlements, and Tradition: Cross-Cultural Perspectives,* edited by Jean-Paul Bourdier and Nezar AlSayyad. Lanham, Md.: University of America Press, 1989.

Castells, Manuel. "The World Has Changed: Can Planning Change?" *Landscape and Urban Planning* 22, no. 1 (1992): 73–78.

Çelik, Zeynep. "Commemorating the Empire: From Algiers to Damascus." In *Edges of Empire: Orientalism and Visual Culture,* edited by Jocelyn Hackforth-Jones and Mary Roberts. Malden, Mass.: Blackwell, 2005.

Chakrabarty, Dipesh. "Postcoloniality and the Artifice of History." In *Unpacking Europe: Towards a Critical Reading,* edited by Salah Hassan and Iftikhar Dadi. Rotterdam: NAi Publishers, 2001.

———. *Provincializing Europe: Postcolonial Thought and Historical Difference.* Princeton, N.J.: Princeton University Press, 2000.

Cooper, Frederick, and Ann Laura Stoler, eds. *Tensions of Empire: Colonial Cultures in a Bourgeois World.* Berkeley: University of California Press, 1997.

Crinson, Mark. *Empire Building: Orientalism and Victorian Architecture.* London and New York: Routledge, 1996.

———. *Modern Architecture and the End of Empire.* Aldershot, U. K. and Burlington, Vt.: Ashgate Publishing Company, 2003.

Dirks, Nicholas K. "History as a Sign of the Modern." *Public Culture* 2 (Spring 1990): 25–32.

Eckes, Alfred E., and Thomas W. Zeiler. *Globalization and the American Century.* Cambridge: Cambridge University Press, 2003.

Geertz, Clifford. *Local Knowledge.* New York: Basic Books, 1983.

Gendzier, Irene L. *Notes from the Minefield: United States Intervention in Lebanon and the Middle East.* New York: Columbia University Press, 1997.

Giddens, Anthony. *The Consequences of Modernity.* Stanford, Calif.: Stanford University Press, 1990.

Goldhagen, Sarah Williams, and Réjean Legault, eds. *Anxious Modernisms: Experimentation in Postwar Architectural Culture.* Montreal: Canadian Centre for Architecture; Cambridge, Mass.: MIT Press, 2000.

Gunter, Ann C., and Stefan R. Hauser, eds. *Ernst Herzfeld and the Development of Near Eastern Studies, 1900–1950.* Leiden: Brill, 2005.

Hackforth-Jones, Jocelyn, and Mary Roberts, eds. *Edges of Empire: Orientalism and Visual Culture.* Malden, Mass.: Blackwell, 2005.

Hall, Stuart. "The Local and the Global." In *Culture, Globalization, and the World-System: Contemporary Conditions for the Representation of Identity,* edited by Anthony D. King. Binghamton: Dept. of Art and Art History, SUNY at Binghamton, 1991.

———. "Old and New Identities, Old and New Ethnicities." In *Culture, Globalization, and the World-System: Contemporary Conditions for the Representation of Identity*, edited by Anthony King. Binghamton: Dept. of Art and Art History, SUNY at Binghamton, 1991.

Halpern, Manfred. *The Politics of Social Change in the Middle East and North Africa*. Princeton, N.J.: Princeton University Press, 1963.

Hillenbrand, Robert. "Creswell and Contemporary Central European Scholarship." *Muqarnas* 8 (1991): 23–35.

Hobsbawm, Eric, and Terrence Ranger, eds. *The Invention of Tradition*. New York: Cambridge University Press, 1992.

Hourani, Albert, Philip S. Khoury, and Mary C. Wilson, eds. *The Modern Middle East: A Reader*. Berkeley: University of California Press, 1993.

Iriye, Akira. *Cultural Internationalism and World Order*. Baltimore, Md.: Johns Hopkins University Press, 1997.

Jameson, Fredric. "Notes on Globalization as a Philosophical Issue." In *The Cultures of Globalization*, edited by Fredric Jameson and Masao Miyoshi. Durham, N.C.: Duke University Press, 1998.

King, Anthony D., ed. *Culture, Globalization, and the World-System: Contemporary Conditions for the Representation of Identity*. Binghamton, N.Y.: Dept. of Art and Art History, SUNY at Binghamton, 1991.

———. *Urbanism, Colonialism, and the World Economy: Cultural and Social Foundations of the World Urban System*. New York: Routledge, 1990.

Lesch, David W., ed. *The Middle East and the United States: A Historical and Political Reassessment*. Boulder, Col.: Westview Press, 1999.

Lockman, Zachary. *Contending Visions of the Middle East: The History and Politics of Orientalism*. Cambridge, U.K.: Cambridge University Press, 2004.

McAlister, Melani. *Epic Encounters: Culture, Media, and U.S. Interests in the Middle East, 1945–2000*. Berkeley: University of California Press, 2001.

Mignolo, Walter D. *Local Histories/Global Designs: Coloniality, Subaltern Knowledges, and Border Thinking*. Princeton, N.J.: Princeton University Press, 2000.

Mitchell, Timothy, ed. *Questions of Modernity*. Minneapolis: University of Minnesota Press, 2000.

Nasr, Seyyed Hossein. *Traditional Islam in the Modern World*. New York: Kegan Paul International, 1990.

Nasr, Seyyed Vali Reza. "Religious Modernism in the Arab World, India, and Iran: The Perils and Prospects of a Discourse." *The Muslim World* 83, no. 1 (1993): 20–47.

Nochlin, Linda. "The Imaginary Orient." *Art in America* (May 1983): 118–31.

Northedge, Alaister. "Creswell, Herzfeld, and Samarra." *Muqarnas* 8 (1991): 74–93.

Olds, Kris. *Globalization and Urban Change*. New York: Oxford University Press, 2001.

Owen, Roger. *State, Power, and Politics in the Making of the Modern Middle East*. New York: Routledge, 2000.

Pyla, Panayiota. "Ecumenopolis, Ecumenokepos, and Doxiadis's Environment-Development Politics." In *Space and Progress: Constantinos Doxiadis's Ekistics and the Global Context of Post World War II Planning, Architecture, Urbanization and Reconstruction*, edited by M. Christine Boyer, Anna Hardman, and Alexandros-Andreas Kyrtsis. New York: Springer, forthcoming.

Reid, Donald Malcolm. "Cultural Imperialism and Nationalism: The Struggle to Define and Control the Heritage of Arab Art in Egypt." *IJMES* 29 (1992): 57–76.

Roy, Olivier. *Globalised Islam: The Search for a New Ummah*. London: C. Hurst, 2004.

Sachs, Wolfgang. *The Development Dictionary: A Guide to Knowledge as Power*. London: Atlantic Highlands: Zed Books, 1992.

Said, Edward. *Orientalism*. New York: Vintage, 1978.

———. "Orientalism Reconsidered." *Cultural Critique* (Fall 1985): 89–107.

Scott, James C. *Seeing Like a State: How Certain Schemes to Improve the Human Condition Have Failed*. New Haven, Conn.: Yale University Press, 1998.

Short, John R. *Global Dimensions: Space, Place, and the Contemporary World*. London: Reaktion, 2002.

Silberman, Neil Asher. *Between Past and Present: Archaeology, Ideology, and Nationalism in the Modern Middle East*. New York: Henry Holt, 1989.

Vale, Lawrence. *Architecture, Power, and National Identity*. New Haven, Conn.: Yale University Press, 1992.

Vernoit, Stephen, ed. *Discovering Islamic Art: Scholars, Collectors, and Collections, 1850–1950*. New York: I. B. Tauris, 2000.

———. "The Rise of Islamic Archeology." *Muqarnas* 14 (1997): 1–10.

Wharton, Annabel Jane. *Building the Cold War: Hilton International Hotels and Modern Architecture*. Chicago: University of Chicago Press, 2001.

ARCHITECTURE AND URBANISM: MIDDLE EAST

Abed, Jamal, ed. *Architecture Re-Introduced: New Projects in Societies in Change*. Geneva: Aga Khan Award for Architecture, 2004.

Abu-Lughod, Janet L. "The Islamic City: Historic Myth, Islamic Essence, and

Contemporary Relevance." *International Journal of Middle East Studies* 19 (1987): 155–76.

AlSayyad, Nezar, ed. *Forms of Dominance: On the Architecture and Urbanism of the Colonial Enterprise.* Aldershot, U.K.: Avebury, 1992.

———, ed. *Hybrid Urbanism: On the Identity Discourse and the Built Environment.* New York: Prager, 2001.

Antoniou, Jim. *Islamic Cities and Conservation.* Paris: UNESCO Press, 1981.

Asfour, Khaled. "Cultural Crisis." Special issue, *Architectural Review* 203 (March 1998): 52–60.

Badran, Rasem. "Historical References and Contemporary Design." In *Theories and Principles of Design in the Architecture of Islamic Societies,* edited by Margaret Bentley Ševčenko. Cambridge, Mass.: Aga Khan Program for Islamic Architecture at MIT and Harvard, 1988.

———. "On the Poetics of Place: The Communicabililty of an Architectural Image." In *Understanding Islamic Architecture,* edited by Attilio Petruccioli and Khalil K. Pirani. London: Routledge Curzon, 2002.

Baker, Philippa. *Architecture and Polyphony: Building in the Islamic World Today.* London: Thames and Hudson, 2004.

Barber, Benjamin. *Jihad vs. McWorld.* New York: Ballantine Books, 1995.

Bianca, Stefano. "Designing Compatibility between New Projects and the Local Urban Tradition." In *Continuity and Change: Design Strategies for Large-Scale Urban Development,* edited by Margaret Bentley Ševčenko. Cambridge, Mass.: Aga Khan Program for Islamic Architecture at Harvard and MIT, 1984.

———. *Urban Form in the Arab World, Past and Present.* London: Thames and Hudson, 2000.

Bozdoğan, Sibel. "The Aga Khan Award for Architecture: A Philosophy of Reconciliation." *Journal of Architectural Education* 45, no. 3 (May 1992): 182–88.

———. "Architectural History in Professional Education: Reflections on Postcolonial Challenges to the Modern Survey." *Journal of Architectural Education* 54, no. 4 (May 1999): 207–15.

———. "Journey to the East: Ways of Looking at the Orient and the Question of Representation." *Journal of Architectural Education* 41, no. 4 (Summer 1988): 38–45.

Bregel, Yuri. "Barthold and Modern Oriental Studies." *IJMES* 12 (1980): 385–403.

Burke, Edmund, III. "Orientalism and World History: Representing Middle Eastern Nationalism and Islamism in the Twentieth Century." *Theory and Society* 27, no. 4 (August 1998): 489–507.

Çelik, Zeynep. "Colonialism, Orientalism, and the Canon." *The Art Bulletin* 78, no. 2 (June 1996): 202–5.

———. *Displaying the Orient: Architecture of Islam at Nineteenth-Century World's Fairs.* Berkeley: University of California Press, 1992.

———. "New Approaches to the Non-West City." *Journal of the Society of Architectural Historians* 58, no. 3 (September 1999): 374–81.

Conner, Patrick. *Oriental Architecture in the West.* London: Thames and Hudson, 1979.

Davidson, Cynthia, ed. *Legacies for the Future: Contemporary Architecture in Islamic Societies.* New York: Thames and Hudson, 1999.

Davidson, Cynthia C., with Ismaïl Serageldin, eds. *Architecture Beyond Architecture: Creativity and Social Transformations in Islamic Cultures: The 1995 Aga Khan Award for Architecture.* London: Academy Editions, 1995.

Dufaux, Frédéric, and Annie Fourcaut, eds. *Le monde des grands ensembles.* Grâne: Creaphis, 2004.

Elsheshtawy, Yasser. *Planning Middle Eastern Cities: An Urban Kaleidoscope in a Globalizing World.* New York: Routledge, 2004.

Ergut, Elvan, and Belgin Ozkaya, eds. "Modern Architecture in the Middle East." *Docomomo Journal*, no. 35 (September 2006).

Frampton, Kenneth. "Prospects for a Critical Regionalism." In *The Anti-Aesthetic: Essays on Postmodern Culture,* edited by Hal Foster. Port Townsend: Wash.: Bay Press, 1983.

Frampton, Kenneth, Charles Correa, and David Robson, eds. *Modernity and Community: Architecture in the Islamic World.* London: Thames and Hudson, 2001.

Frishman, Martin, and Hasan-Uddin Khan, eds. *The Mosque: History, Architectural Development, and Regional Diversity.* New York: Thames and Hudson, 1994.

Holod, Renata, and Hasan-Uddin Khan. *Mosque and the Modern World: Architects, Patrons, and Designs since the 1950s.* New York: Thames and Hudson, 1997.

Hourani, Albert, and Samuel M. Stern, eds. *The Islamic City.* Philadelphia: University of Pennsylvania Press, 1970.

Kadhim, Hussein. *The Poetics of Anti-Colonialism in the Arabic Qasidah.* Leiden: Brill, 2004.

Khan, Hasan-Uddin. *The Middle East,* vol. 5 of *World Architecture, 1900–2000: A Critical Mosaic,* edited by Kenneth Frampton. New York: Springer, 2001.

Kultermann, Udo. *Contemporary Architecture in the Arab States: Renaissance of a Region.* New York: McGraw-Hill, 1999.

Mitchell, Timothy. "McJihad: Islam in the U.S. Global Order." *Social Text* 20, no. 4 (Winter 2002): 1–18.

Nalbantoglu, Gülsüm Baydar. "Beyond Lack and Excess: Other Architectures, Other Landscapes." *Journal of Architectural Education* 54, no. 1 (September 2000): 20–27.

———. "Toward Postcolonial Openings: Rereading Sir Banister Fletcher's 'History of Architecture.'" *Assemblage*, no. 35 (April 1998): 6–17.

Nalbantoglu, Gülsüm Baydar, and Wong Chong Thai, eds. *Postcolonial Space(s)*. New York: Princeton Architectural Press, 1997.

Nanji, Azim A. *Aga Khan Award for Architecture: Building for Tomorrow*. London: Academy Editions, 1994.

Nasr, Joe, and Mercedes Volait, eds. *Urbanism: Imported or Exported? Native Aspirations and Foreign Plans*. West Sussex, U.K.: Wiley-Academy, 2003.

Özkan, Suha, ed. *Faith and the Built Environment: Architecture and Behavior in Islamic Cultures*. Lausanne: Comportements, 1996.

Petruccioli, Attilio, and Khalil K. Pirani, eds. *Understanding Islamic Architecture*. London: Routledge Curzon, 2002.

Powell, Robert, ed. *Regionalism in Architecture*. Singapore: Aga Khan Award for Architecture and Concept Media, 1985.

Pyla, Panayiota. "Gray Areas in Green Politics." *Thresholds* 14 (Spring 1997): 48–53.

Roxburgh, D. "Au Bonheur des Amateurs: Collecting and Exhibiting Islamic Art, ca. 1880–1910." *Ars Orientalis* 30 (2000): 9–38.

Saqqaf, Abdulaziz, ed. *The Middle East City: Ancient Traditions Confront a Modern World*. New York: Paragon, 1987.

Serageldin, Ismaïl, ed. *The Architecture of Empowerment: People, Shelter, and Livable Cities*. London: Academy, 1997.

Serageldin, Ismaïl, and James Steele, eds. *Architecture of the Contemporary Mosque*. London: Academy Editions, 1996.

Serageldin, Ismaïl, and Samir El-Sadek, eds. *The Arab City, Its Character and Islamic Cultural Heritage: Proceedings of a Symposium Held in Medina, Kingdom of Saudi Arabia*. Medina: Arab Towns Organization, 1981.

Ševčenko, Margaret Bentley, ed. *Theories and Principles of Design in the Architecture of Islamic Societies*. Cambridge, Mass.: Aga Khan Program for Islamic Architecture at MIT and Harvard, 1988.

Slyomovics, Susan, ed. *The Walled Arab City in Literature, Architecture, and History: The Living Medina in the Maghrib*. London: Frank Cass, 2001.

Smith, Michael Peter. *Transnational Urbanism: Locating Globalization*. Malden, Mass.: Blackwell, 2001.

Steele, James, ed. *Architecture for Islamic Societies Today.* London: Academy, 1994.

ARCHITECTURE AND URBANISM: EGYPT

Abu-Lughod, Janet L. *Cairo: 1001 Years of the City Victorious.* Princeton, N.J.: Princeton University Press, 1971.

AlSayyad, Nezar. "From Vernacularism to Globalism: The Temporal Reality of Traditional Settlements." *Traditional Dwellings and Settlements Review* 7, no. 1 (1995): 13–24.

———. "Whose Cairo?" In *Cairo Cosmopolitan: Politics, Culture, and Urban Space in the New Middle East,* edited by Paul Amar and Diane Singerman. Cairo: American University in Cairo Press, 2006.

AlSayyad, Nezar, Irene A. Bierman, and Nasser Rabbat, eds. *Making Cairo Medieval.* Lanham, Md.: Lexington Books, 2005.

Amar, Paul, and Diane Singerman, eds. *Cairo Cosmopolitan: Politics, Culture, and Urban Space in the New Middle East.* Cairo: American University in Cairo Press, 2006.

Behrens-Abouseif, Doris. *Azbakiyya and Its Environs: From Azbak to Isma'il, 1476–1879.* Le Caire: Institut Français d'Archeólogie Orientale, 1985.

Davidson, Forbes. "Ismailia: From Master Plan to Implementation." In *The Architecture of Empowerment: People, Shelter, and Livable Cities,* edited by Ismail Serageldin. London: Academy, 1997.

Evin, Ahmet, ed. *The Expanding Metropolis: Coping with the Urban Growth of Cairo.* Singapore: Concept Media for the Aga Khan Award for Architecture, 1984.

Fahmy, Khaled. *All the Pasha's Men: Mehmet Ali, His Army, and the Making of Modern Egypt.* New York: Cambridge University Press, 1997.

Fathy, Hassan. *Architecture for the Poor: An Experiment in Rural Egypt.* Chicago: University of Chicago Press, 1973.

———. *Gourna: A Tale of Two Villages.* Cairo: Ministry of Culture, 1969.

Ghannam, Farha. *Remaking the Modern: Space, Relocation, and the Politics of Identity in Global Cairo.* Berkeley: University of California Press, 2002.

———. "The Visual Remaking of Urban Space: Relocation and the Use of Public Housing in 'Modern' Cairo." *Visual Anthropology* 10 (1998): 265–80.

Hinnebusch, Raymond, Jr. *Egyptian Politics under Sadat: The Post-Populist, Authoritarian-Modernizing State.* Cambridge, U.K.: Cambridge University Press, 1985.

Meinecke, Michael. "The Darb Qirmiz Project." In *Islamic Cairo: Architectural*

Conservation and Urban Development of the Historic Center, edited by Michael Meinecke. London: Deutsches Archäologisches Institut Art and Archaeology Research Papers, 1980.

Mitchell, Timothy. *Colonizing Egypt.* Cambridge: Cambridge University Press, 1988.

———. "Making the Nation: The Politics of Heritage in Egypt." In *Consuming Tradition, Manufacturing Heritage: Global Norms and Urban Forms in the Age of Tourism,* edited by Nezar AlSayyad. New York: Routledge, 2001.

———. *Rule of Experts: Egypt, Techno-Politics, Modernity.* Berkeley: University of California Press, 2002.

Pyla, Panayiota, "Hassan Fathy Revisited: Postwar Discourses on Science, Development, and Vernacular Architecture." *Journal of Architectural Education* 60:3 (February 2007): 28–39.

Raafat, Samir. *Cairo, the Glory Years: Who Built What, When, Why, and for Whom.* Alexandria, Egypt: Harpocrates Publishing, 2003.

Rabbat, Nasser. "The Formation of the Neo-Mamluk Style in Modern Egypt." In *The Education of the Architect: Historiography, Urbanism, and the Growth of Architectural Knowledge,* edited by Martha Pollak. Cambridge, Mass.: MIT Press, 1997.

Rageh, Abou-Zeid. "The Changing Pattern of Housing in Cairo." In *The Expanding Metropolis: Coping with the Urban Growth of Cairo,* edited by Ahmet Evin. Singapore: Concept Media, for the Aga Khan Award for Architecture, 1984.

Raymond, André. *Cairo.* Cambridge, Mass.: Harvard University Press, 2000.

Rodenbeck, Max. *Cairo: The City Victorious.* New York: Alfred A. Knopf, 1999.

Roy, Ananya, and Nezar AlSayyad. "Medieval Modernity: Citizenship in Contemporary Urbanism." *Applied Anthropologist* 25, no. 2 (2005): 147–65.

Sakr, Tarek Mohammed Refaat. *Early Twentieth-Century Islamic Architecture in Cairo.* Cairo: American University in Cairo Press, 1993.

Sanders, Paula. "The Victorian Invention of Medieval Cairo: A Case Study of Medievalism and the Construction of the East." *MESA Bulletin* 37, no. 2 (2003): 179–98.

Shorter, Frederic. *Cairo's Leap Forward: People, Households, and Dwelling Space.* Cairo: American University of Cairo Press, 1989.

Sorkin, Michael. "Deciphering Greater Cairo." *Architectural Record* 189 (April 2001): 83.

Steele, James. *An Architecture for People: The Complete Works of Hassan Fathy.* New York: Whitney Library of Design, 1997.

Sukr, Terek Mohamed Rafast. *Early Twentieth-Century Islamic Architecture in Cairo.* Cairo: American University of Cairo Press, 1993.

Volait, Mercedes. "Appropriating Orientalism? Saer Sabri's Mamluk Revivals in Late-Nineteenth-Century Cairo." In *Islamic Art in the Nineteenth Century: Tradition, Innovation, and Eclecticism,* edited by Doris Behrens-Abouseif and Stephen Vernoit. Leiden: Brill, 2006.

———. *Architectes et architectures de l'Egypte moderne (1830–1950): Genèse et essor d'une expertise locale.* Paris: Maisonneuve et Larose, 2005.

———, ed. *Caire-Alexandrie architectures Européennes, 1850–1950.* Cairo: Centre d'Études et de Documentation Économique, Juridique et Sociale, 2004.

———. *L'architecture moderne en Egypte et la Revue Al-'imara, 1939–1959.* Cairo: Centre d'Études et de Documentation Économique, Juridique et Sociale, 1988.

———. "Town Planning Schemes for Cairo Conceived by Egyptian Planners in the 'Liberal Experiment' Period." In *Mass Mediations: New Approaches to Popular Culture in the Middle East and Beyond,* edited by Walter Armbrust. Berkeley: University of California Press, 2000.

———. "Une Oeuvre Méconnue: Le Palais de Justice du Caire." *Monuments Historiques,* no. 200 (January–February 1996): 52–55.

Williams, Caroline. "Transforming the Old: Cairo's New Medieval City." *Middle East Journal* 59 (2002): 458–75.

ARCHITECTURE AND URBANISM: IRAN

Behdad, Ali. "The Powerful Art of Qajar Photography: Orientalism and (Self)-Orientalizing in Nineteenth-Century Iran." *Journal of Iranian Studies* (2001).

Diba, Kamran. *Buildings and Projects.* Stuttgart-Ban Cannstatt, W. Germany: Hatje, 1981.

Elm, Mostafa. *Oil, Power, and Principle: Iran's Oil Nationalization and Its Aftermath.* Syracuse, N.Y.: Syracuse University Press, 1992.

Foucault, Michel. "Iran: The Spirit of a World without Spirit." In *Michel Foucault: Politics, Philosophy, Culture,* edited by Lawrence D. Kritzman. London: Routledge, 1988.

Fromonot, Françoise, ed. *Nasrine Seraji: L'Architettura Come Territorio.* Melfi: Libria, 2002.

Gluck, Jay, and Noel Siver, eds. *Surveyors of Persian Art: A Documentary Biography of Arthur Upham Pope and Phyllis Ackerman.* Costa Mesa, Calif.: Mazda Publishers, 1996.

Grigor, Talin. "Recultivating 'Good Taste': The Early Pahlavi Modernists and

Their Society for National Heritage." *Iranian Studies* 37, no. 1 (March 2004): 17–45.

———. "(Re)Framing Rapid Modernities: American Historians of Iranian Architecture, Phyllis Ackerman and Arthur Pope." *Arris* 15 (2004): 39–55.

Jodidio, Philip, ed. *Iran, Architecture for Changing Societies: An International Seminar.* Turin, Italy: U. Allemandi for Aga Khan Award for Architecture, 2004.

Marefat, Mina. "Modern and Islamic: On Tehran." *Harvard Design Magazine* (Winter–Spring 1997): 42–45.

———. "The Protagonists Who Shaped Modern Tehran." In *Téhéran, capitale bicentenaire,* edited by C. Adle and B. Hourcade. Paris and Tehran: Bibliothèque Iranienne, 1992.

Rizvi, Kishwar. "Art History and the Nation: Arthur Upham Pope and the Discourse on 'Persian Art' in the Early Twentieth Century." *Muqarnas* 24 (2007).

———. "Religious Icon and National Symbol: The Tomb of Ayatollah Khomeini in Iran." *Muqarnas* 20 (2003).

Scarce, Jennifer. "Ancestral Themes in the Art of Qajar Iran, 1785–1925." In *Islamic Art in the Nineteenth Century: Tradition, Innovation, and Eclecticism,* edited by Doris Behrens-Abouseif and Stephen Vernoit. Leiden: Brill, 2006.

ARCHITECTURE AND URBANISM: IRAQ

Al-Khalil, Samir [Kanan Makiya]. *The Monument: Art, Vulgarity, and Responsibility in Iraq.* Berkeley: University of California Press, 1991.

al-Said, Shakir Hasan. *Fusul min tarikh al-haraka al-tashkiliyah fi al-Iraq.* 2 vols. Baghdad: Wizarat al-thaqafah wa al-ilam, 1983.

Batatu, Hanna. *The Old Social Classes and the Revolutionary Movements of Iraq: A Study of Iraq's Old Landed and Commercial Classes and of its Communists, Ba'thists, and Free Officers.* Princeton, N.J.: Princeton University Press, 1978.

Bernhardsson, Magnus T. *Reclaiming a Plundered Past: Archaeology and Nationalism in Modern Iraq.* Austin: University of Texas Press, 2005.

Brantley, William. "The Search for Baghdad." *Urban Land* 63 (2004): 49–55.

Chadirji, Rifat. *Concepts and Influences: Towards a Regionalized International Architecture.* New York: Routledge and Paul Kegan, 1986.

Davis, Eric. *Memories of State: Politics, History, and Collective Identity in Modern Iraq.* Berkeley: University of California Press, 2004.

Deyoung, Terri. *Placing the Poet: Badr Shakir Al-Sayyab and Postcolonial Iraq.* Albany: State University of New York Press, 1998.

Dodge, Toby. *Inventing Iraq: The Failure of Nation Building and a History Denied.* New York: Columbia University Press, 2004.

Elliot, Matthew. *Independent Iraq: The Monarchy and British Influence, 1941–1958.* London: I. B. Tauris, 1996.

Fethi, Ishan. "Contemporary Architecture in Baghdad." *Process Architecture* (May 1985): 112–32.

Gulick, John. "Baghdad: Portrait of a City in Physical and Cultural Change." *Journal of the American Institute of Planners* 33, no. 4 (1967): 246–55.

Haj, Samaira. *The Making of Iraq, 1900–1963: Capital, Power, and Ideology.* Albany: State University of New York Press, 1997.

Isenstadt, Samuel. "'Faith in a Better Future': Josep Lluis Sert's American Embassy in Baghdad." *Journal of Architectural Education* 50 (February 1997): 172–88.

Jalal, Ferhang. *The Role of Government in the Industrialization of Iraq, 1950–1965.* London: Frank Cass, 1972.

Levine, Neil. "Signs of Identity in an Increasingly One-Dimensional World," in *The Architecture of Frank Lloyd Wright.* Princeton, N.J.: Princeton University Press, 1996.

Makiya, Kanan. *Post-Islamic Classicism: A Visual Essay on the Architecture of Mohamed Makiya.* London: Saqi, 1990.

Makiya, Muhammad. "The Arab House: A Historical Overview." In *Proceedings of the 1984 Colloquium on the Arab House,* edited by A. D. C. Hyland and Ahmad al-Shahi. Newcastle, U.K.: University of Newcastle upon Tyne, 1986.

Marefat, Mina. "Wright's Baghdad." In *Frank Lloyd Wright: Europe and Beyond,* edited by Anthony Alofsin. Berkeley: University of California Press, 1999.

McMillen, Louis. "The University of Baghdad, Baghdad, Iraq." In vol. 4 of *The Walter Gropius Archive: The Work of the Architects Collaborative,* edited by Alexander Tzonis. New York: Garland Publishing, 1991.

Simon, Reeva Spector. *Iraq between the Two World Wars: The Creation and Implementation of a Nationalist Ideology.* New York: Columbia University Press, 1986.

Simon, Reeva Spector, and Elanor H. Tejirian. *The Creation of Iraq, 1914–1921.* New York: Columbia University Press, 2004.

Siry, Joseph. "Wright's Baghdad Opera House and Gammage Auditorium: In Search of Regional Modernity." *The Art Bulletin* 87, no. 2 (June 2005): 205–311.

Tripp, Charles. *A History of Iraq.* Cambridge, U.K.: Cambridge University Press, 2000.

Uthman, Fuad A. "Exporting Architectural Education to the Arab World." *Journal of Architectural Education* 31, no. 3 (1978): 26–30.

Zubaida, Sami. "The Fragments Imagine the Nation: The Case of Iraq." *International Journal of Middle East Studies* 34, no. 2 (2002).

ARCHITECTURE AND URBANISM:
MANDATE PALESTINE AND ISRAEL

Ahimeir, Ora, and Michael Levin, eds. *Modern Architecture in Jerusalem*. Jerusalem: Institute for Jerusalem Studies, 1980.
Asad, Talal. "Anthropological and Sociological Studies on the Arabs in Israel: A Critique." *Journal of Palestine Studies* 6 (1977): 41–70.
———. "Anthropological Texts and Ideological Problems: An Analysis of Cohen on Arab Villages in Israel." *Economy and Society* 4 (1975).
Azoulay, Ariella. *Ekh zeh nireh lekha?* Tel Aviv: Babel, 2000.
Ben Gurion, David. *On Settlement: Collected Speeches, 1915–1956* [in Hebrew]. Tel Aviv: Hakibbutz Hameuchad, 1986.
Benvenisti, Meron. *City of Stone: The Hidden History of Jerusalem*. Berkeley: University of California Press, 1966.
Biger, Gideon. *An Empire in the Holy Land: Historical Geography of the British Administration in Palestine, 1917–1929*. New York: St. Martin's Press, 1994.
Bilsky, Leora. "Kufr Qassem: Between Ordinary Politics and Transformative Politics." *Adalah's Review* 3 (2002): 69–80.
Cohen, Abner. *Arab Border-Villages in Israel: A Study of Continuity and Change*. Manchester, U.K.: Manchester University Press, 1965.
Cohen, Erik. *The City in the Zionist Ideology*. Jerusalem Urban Studies, no. 1. Jerusalem: Hebrew University Institute of Urban and Regional Studies, 1970.
Efrat, Zvi. *The Israeli Project: Building and Architecture, 1948–1973* [in Hebrew]. Tel Aviv: Tel Aviv Museum of Art, 2004.
Fiedler, Jeannine, ed. *Social Utopias of the Twenties: Bauhaus, Kibbutz, and the Dream of the New Man*. Translated by Miriam Neumann and William H. Boyle. Wuppertal: Muller and Busman Press, 1995.
Friedland, Roger, and Richard D. Hecht. *To Rule Jerusalem*. New York: Cambridge University Press, 1996.
Fuchs, Ron, and Gilbert Herbert. "Representing Mandatory Palestine: Austen St. Barbe Harrison and the Representational Buildings of the British Mandate in Palestine, 1922–37." *Architectural History* 43 (2000): 281–333.
Fuchs, Ron, and Gilbert Herbert. "A Colonial Portrait of Jerusalem: The Manipulation of Tradition in the Architecture of the British Mandate in Palestine." In *Invocations of Ethnicity, Nationalism, and Religion in Heritage Strategies*, edited by Rosemary Latter et al. Berkeley: Center for Environ-

mental Design Research, International Association for the Study of Traditional Environments, University of California at Berkeley, 1998.

Gitler, Inbal Ben-Asher. "C. R. Ashbee's Jerusalem Years: Arts and Crafts, Orientalism, and British Regionalism." *Assaph: Studies in Art History* 5 (2000).

Hacohen, Dvora. *From Fantasy to Reality: Ben Gurion's Plan for Mass Immigration, 1942–1945* [in Hebrew]. Tel Aviv: Ministry of Defence Press, 1994.

Haidar, Aziz. *The Palestinians in Israel: Social Science Writings.* Kingston, Ont.: NECEF Publications, 1987.

Harlap, Amiram, ed. *Israel Builds.* Tel Aviv: Ministry of Housing, 1977.

Hashimshoni, Aviah, et al. *1968 Jerusalem Masterplan.* Vol. 1. Jerusalem: Jerusalem Municipality, 1972.

Helphand, Kenneth. *Dreaming Gardens: Landscape Architecture and the Making of Modern Israel.* Charlottesville: University of Virginia Press, 2002.

Kachensky, Miriam. "The Ma'abaras." In *Immigrants and Ma'abaras* [in Hebrew], edited by Mordechai Naor. Jerusalem: Yad Ben Zvi, 1986.

Kanaaneh, Rhoda Ann. *Birthing the Nation: Strategies of Palestinian Women in Israel.* Berkeley: University of California Press, 2002.

Khleif, Waleed. "Kafr Qasim." *Al-Ittihad,* November 5, 1957. (Reprinted in *Majallat al-Adib* [Lebanon], October 1959.)

Kozlovsky, Roy. "Necessity by Design." *Perspecta* 34 (2003): 10–19.

Kroyanker, David. *Jerusalem: Conflicts Over the City's Physical and Visual Form.* Jerusalem: Zmora-Bitan, 1988.

Levin, Michael. *Modern Architecture in Israel.* London: Thames and Hudson, 2000.

Lieber, Alfred E. "An Economic History of Jerusalem." In *Jerusalem: City of the Ages,* edited by Alice L. Eckhardt. New York: University Press of America, 1987.

Matar, Shadia. "Palestinian Refugees, a Material and Spiritual Homeland" [in Italian]. *Mediterranean: Un Mare di Donne,* no. 3. http://www.medmedia.org/review/numero3/en/art7.htm.

McGowan, Daniel A., and Marc H. Ellis, eds. *Deir Yassin Remembered: The Future of Israel and Palestine.* New York: Interlink, 1998.

Mitchell, W. J. Thomas. "Holy Landscape: Israel, Palestine, and the American Wilderness." *Critical Inquiry* 26, no. 2 (2000): 199–223.

Monk, Daniel Bertrand. *An Aesthetic Occupation: The Immediacy of Architecture and the Palestine Conflict.* Durham, N.C.: Duke University Press, 2002.

Morris, Benny. *The Birth of the Palestinian Refugee Problem, 1947–1949.* Cambridge: Cambridge University Press, 1987.

———. *Israel's Border Wars, 1949–1956: Arab Infiltration, Israeli Retaliation, and the Countdown to the Suez War.* New York: Oxford University Press, 1993.

Nitzan-Shiftan, Alona. "Alternative Modernism: Erich Mendelsohn and the Tel Aviv Chug in Mandate Palestine." *Architectural History* 39 (1996): 147–80.

———. "Israelizing Jerusalem: The Encounter between Architectural and National Ideologies, 1967–1977." Ph.D. diss., MIT, 2002.

Parmenter, Barbara McKean. *Giving Voice to Stones: Place and Identity in Palestinian Literature.* Austin: University of Texas Press, 1994.

Rabinowitz, Dan. *Antropologyah veha-Palestinim.* Raananah, Israel: Institute for Israeli–Arab Studies, 1998.

Robinson, Shira. "Commemoration Under Fire: Palestinian Responses to the 1956 Kafr Qasim Massacre." In *Memory and Violence in the Middle East and North Africa,* edited by Ussama Makdisi and Paul A. Silverstein. Bloomington: Indiana University Press, 2006.

———. "Local Struggle, National Struggle: Palestinian Responses to the Kafr Qasim Massacre and Its Aftermath, 1956–66." *International Journal of Middle East Studies* 35 (2003): 393–416.

Rozental, Rubik, ed. *Kefar kasem: Eru'im ve-mitos.* Tel Aviv: Ha-Kibuts Ha-Me'uhad, 2000.

Segal, Rafi, and Eyal Weizman. *Civilian Occupation: The Politics of Israeli Architecture.* New York: Verso, 2003.

Sharon, Aryeh. *Kibbutz + Bauhaus.* Tel Aviv: Massada, 1982.

Shenhav, Yehuda ed. *Merhav, adamah, bait* [in Hebrew]. Jerusalem: Mekhon Van-Lir; Tel Aviv: Ha-Kibutz Ha-Meuhad, 2003.

Slyomovics, Susan, ed. *The Object of Memory: Arab and Jew Narrate the Palestinian Village.* Philadelphia: University of Pennsylvania Press, 1998.

Troen, S. Han, and Noah Lucas. *Israel: The First Decade of Independence.* Albany: State University of New York Press, 1995.

Tubi, Tawfiq. *Kafr Qasim al-majzarah wa-al-'ibrah.* Tel Aviv: Israeli Communist Party Publications, 1996.

Wasserstein, Bernard. *The British in Palestine: The Mandatory Government and the Arab-Jewish Conflict, 1917–1929.* 2d ed. Oxford: Basil Blackwell, 1991.

Wharton, Annabel Jane. *Selling Jerusalem: Relics, Replicas, Theme Parks.* Chicago: University of Chicago Press, 2006.

Yacobi, Haim, ed. *Constructing a Sense of Place: Architecture and the Zionist Discourse.* Aldershot, U.K.: Hants; Burlington, Vt.: Ashgate, 2004.

Zakim, Eric. *To Build and Be Built: Landscape, Literature, and the Construction of Zionist Identity.* Philadelphia: University of Pennsylvania Press, 2006.

ARCHITECTURE AND URBANISM: LEBANON

Antonius, Soraya. *Architecture in Lebanon*. Beirut: Khayats, 1965.

Arnaud, Jean-Luc, ed. *Beyrouth, Grand-Beyrouth*. Beirut: CERMOC, 1997.

Boudjikanian, Aida. "Beyrouth, 1920–1991." In *Le Liban Aujourd'hui*, edited by Fadia Kiwan. Paris: CNRS, 1993.

Davie, May. *Beyrouth, 1825–1975*. Beirut: CERMOC, 2001.

el-Dahdah, Farès. "On Solidère's Motto, 'Beirut: Ancient City of the Future.'" In *Projecting Beirut: Episodes in the Construction and Reconstruction of a Modern City*, edited by Peter G. Rowe and Hashim Sarkis. Munich: Prestel, 1998.

El-Khoury, Pierre. *Pierre el-Khory, Architecture, 1959–1999*. Beirut: Dar an-Nahar, 2000.

Garvin, Angus, and Ramez Maluf. *Beirut Reborn: The Restoration and Development of the Central District*. London: Academy Editions, 1996.

Ghorayeb, Marlène. "The Work and Influence of Michel Ecochard in Lebanon." In *Projecting Beirut: Episodes in the Construction and Reconstruction of a Modern City*, edited by Peter G. Rowe and Hashim Sarkis. Munich: Prestel, 1998.

Hamadeh, Shirine. "Creating the Traditional City: A French Project." In *Forms of Dominance: On the Architecture and Urbanism of the Colonial Enterprise*, edited by Nezar AlSayyad. Aldershot, U.K.: Avebury, 1992.

Khalaf, Samir, and Philip S. Khoury, eds. *Recovering Beirut: Urban Design and Postwar Reconstruction*. New York: Brill, 1993.

Khalaf, Samir, and Per Kongstad. "Urbanization and Urbanism in Beirut: Some Preliminary Results." In *From Medina to Metropolis: Heritage and Change in the Near Eastern City*, edited by L. Carl Brown. Princeton, N.J.: Darwin Press, 1973.

Makdisi, Saree. "Laying Claim to Beirut: Urban Narrative and Spatial Identity in the Age of Solidere." *Critical Inquiry* 23 (Spring 1997): 661–705.

Peterson, Eric N. "Housing and Reconstruction." In *Beirut of Tomorrow*, edited by Friedrich Ragette. Beirut: American University of Beirut, 1983.

Ragette, Friedrich. *Architecture in Lebanon: The Lebanese House during the 18th and 19th Centuries*. Beirut: American University of Beirut, 1974.

———, ed. *Beirut of Tomorrow*. Beirut: American University of Beirut, 1983.

Rowe, Peter, and Hashim Sarkis, eds. *Projecting Beirut: Episodes in the Construction and Reconstruction of a Modern City*. New York: Prestel, 1998.

Ruppert, Helmut. *Beyrouth, une ville d'orient marquée par l'occident*. Cahiers du CERMOC, no. 21. Beirut: Centre d'Etudes et des Recherches sur le Moyen-Orient Contemporain, 1999.

Saliba, Robert. *Beirut, 1920–1940: Domestic Architecture between Tradition and Modernity.* Beirut: Order of Engineers and Architects, 1998.

———. *Beirut City Center Recovery: The Foch-Allenby and Etoile Conservation Area.* London: Steidl, 2004.

Sarkis, Hashim. *Circa 1950: Lebanon in the Pictures and Plans of Constantinos Doxiadis.* Beirut: Dar en-Nahar, 2003.

Tabet, Jade. *Beyrouth: Portrait de ville.* Paris: Institut Français d'Architecture, 2001.

Yacoub, Gebran M. *Architectures au Liban.* 2 vols. Beirut: Samir Abdo, 1993.

ARCHITECTURE AND URBANISM: NORTH AFRICA

Abu-Lughod, Janet L. *Rabat: Urban Apartheid in Morocco.* Princeton: Princeton University Press, 1980.

Béguin, François. *Arabisances: décor architectural et tracé urbain en Afrique du Nord, 1830–1950.* Paris: Dunod, 1983.

Ben-Ghiat, Ruth, and Mia Fuller. *Italian Colonialism.* New York: Palgrave Macmillan, 2005.

Boussora, Kenza. "Regionalism: Lessons from Algeria and the Middle East." *Mimar* 36 (September 1990): 64–71.

Çelik, Zeynep. *Urban Forms and Colonial Confrontations: Algiers under French Rule.* Berkeley: University of California Press, 1997.

Cohen, Jean-Louis. "The Moroccan Group and the Theme of Habitat." *Rassegna* 14, no. 52 (December 1992): 58–67.

Cohen, Jean-Louis, and Monique Eleb. *Casablanca: Colonial Myths and Architectural Ventures.* New York: Monacelli Press, 2002.

Consoli, Gian Paolo. "The Protagonists." *Rassegna* 51 (September 1992): 58–59.

Culot, Maurice, and Jean-Marie Thiveaud, eds. *Architectures Françaises Outre-Mer.* Liège: Mardiga, 1992.

Fuller, Mia. "Building Power: Italy's Colonial Architecture and Urbanism, 1923–1940." *Cultural Anthropology* 3, no. 4 (November 1988): 455–87.

———. *Moderns Abroad: Architecture, Cities and Italian Imperialism.* London and New York: Routledge, 2007.

Gresleri, Giuliano, et al., eds. *Architettura italiana d'Oltremare, 1870–1940.* Venice: Marsilio Editori, 1993.

Husnéin, Adnan Ali. "Tracing Libyan Modernities: A Century of Urban Renovation in Tripoli, 1850–1950." Ph.D. diss., University of Washington, 2006.

McLaren, Brian L. *Architecture and Tourism in Italian Colonial Libya: An Ambivalent Modernism.* Seattle: University of Washington Press, 2006.

———. "The Architecture of Tourism in Italian Libya: The Creation of a Mediterranean Identity." In *Italian Colonialism: A Reader*, edited by Mia Fuller and Ruth Ben-Ghiat. New York: Palgrave, 2005.

———. "From Tripoli to Ghadames: Architecture and the Tourist Experience of Local Culture in Italian Colonial Libya." In *Architecture and Tourism: Perception, Performance and Place*, edited by D. Medina Lasansky and Brian McLaren. Oxford: Berg Press, 2004.

———. "The Italian Colonial Appropriation of Indigenous North African Vernacular Architecture in the 1930s." *Muqarnas* 19 (2002): 164–92.

———. "The Tripoli Trade Fair and the Representation of Italy's African Colonies." *The Journal of Decorative and Propaganda Arts* 24 (2002): 170–97.

Rabinow, Paul. "France in Morocco: Technocosmopolitanism and Middling Modernism." *Assemblage* 17 (April 1992): 52–57.

———. *French Modern: Norms and Forms of the Social Environment*. Chicago: University of Chicago Press, 1995.

von Henneberg, Krystyna. "Imperial Uncertainties: Architectural Syncretism and Improvisation in Fascist Colonial Libya." *Journal of Contemporary History* 31 (2) (April 1996): 373–95.

———. "Piazza Castello and the Making of a Fascist Colonial Capital." In *Streets: Critical Perspectives on Public Space*, edited by Zeynep Çelik, Diane Favro, and Richard Ingersoll. Berkeley: University of California Press, 1994.

Wright, Gwendolyn. *Politics of Design in French Colonial Urbanism*. Chicago: University of Chicago Press, 1991.

ARCHITECTURE AND URBANISM: SAUDI ARABIA

Al-Farsy, Fouad. *Modernity and Tradition: The Saudi Equation*. London: Kegan Paul International, 1990.

Al-Hathloul, Saleh A. "Tradition, Continuity, and Change in the Physical Environment: The Arab-Muslim City." Ph.D. diss., MIT, 1981.

Anderson, Irvine. *Aramco, the United States, and Saudi Arabia: A Study in the Dynamics of Foreign Oil Policy, 1933–1950*. Princeton, N.J.: Princeton University Press, 1981.

Beling, William A., ed. *King Faisal and the Modernisation of Saudi Arabia*. Boulder, Col.: Westview, 1980.

Bonine, Michael E. "Cities of Oil and Migrants: Urbanization and Economic Change in the Arabian Peninsula." In vol. 2 of *The Proceedings of the International Conference on Urbanism in Islam (ICUIT): October 22–28, 1989, the Middle Eastern Culture Center, Tokyo, Japan*. Tokyo: Research Project "Urbanism in

Islam" and the Middle Eastern Culture Center in Japan; distributed by Daisan-Shokan, 1989.

Buchan, James. *Jeddah Old and New.* London: Stacey International, 1980.

Facey, William. *Dir'iyyah and the First Saudi State.* London: Stacey International, 1997.

———. *Riyadh, The Old City: From Its Origins until the 1950s.* London: IMMEL Publishing, 1992.

Farsi, Mohamed Said. Foreword in *Jeddah Old and New.* London: Stacey International, 1980.

Farsi, N. S., and H. I. Amer. "Islamic Architectural Features in the Arabian Peninsula and Their Reflection in Planning Old and New Jeddah." In *The Arab City: Its Character and Islamic Cultural Heritage,* edited by Ismaïl Serageldin and Samir El-Sadek. Medina, Saudi Arabia: Arab Urban Development Institute, 1982.

Komsani, Kamel A. "Jeddah: Red Sea City of the Past, Present, and Future." In *Arab Architecture: Past and Present,* edited by Antony Hutt. Durham, England: Centre for Middle Eastern and Islamic Studies, University of Durham, 1983.

Pesce, Angelo. *Jiddah: Portrait of an Arabian City.* Tucson: Falcon Press, 1974.

Shuaibi, Ali, and Saleh Al-Hathloul. "The Justice Palace District, Riyadh." In *Continuity and Change: Design Strategies for Large-Scale Urban Development,* edited by Margaret Bentley Ševčenko. Cambridge, Mass.: Aga Khan Program for Islamic Architecture at Harvard and MIT, 1984.

ARCHITECTURE AND URBANISM: TURKEY

Akcan, Esra. "Modernity in Translation: Early Twentieth-Century German-Turkish Exchanges in Land Settlement and Residential Culture." Ph.D. diss., Columbia University, 2005.

Akpinar, Ipek. "The Rebuilding of Istanbul After the Plan of Henri Prost, 1937–1960." Ph.D. diss., Bartlett School, London, 2003.

Barillari, Diana, and Ezio Godoli, eds. *Istanbul 1900.* New York: Rizzoli, 1996.

Berkes, N. *Turk dusununde bati sorunu.* Ankara: Bilgi Yayinlari, 1975.

———. *Turkiye'de cagdaslasma.* Ankara: Bilgi Yayinlari, 1975.

Bernd, Nicolai. *Moderne und Exil: Deutschsprachige Architekten in der Türkei, 1925–1955.* Berlin: Verlag für Bauwesen, 1998.

Bilsel, Can. "Architecture in the Museum: Displacement, Reconstruction, and Reproduction of the Monuments of Antiquity in Berlin's Pergamon Museum." Ph.D. diss., Princeton University, 2003.

Bozdoğan, Sibel. "Against Style: Bruno Taut's Pedagogical Program in Turkey, 1936–1938." In *The Education of the Architect: Historiography, Urbanism, and the Growth of Architectural Knowledge*, edited by Martha Pollak. Cambridge, Mass.: MIT Press, 1997.

———. "Between Civilization and Culture: Appropriation of Traditional Dwelling Forms in Early Republican Turkey." *Journal of Architectural Education* 47, no. 2 (November 1993): 66–74.

———. *Modernism and Nation Building: Turkish Architectural Culture in the Early Republic*. Seattle: University of Washington Press, 2001.

Bozdoğan, Sibel, and Reşat Kasaba. *Rethinking Modernity and National Identity in Turkey*. Seattle: University of Washington Press, 1997.

Bozdoğan, Sibel, S. Ozkan, and E. Yenal. *Sedad Hakki Eldem: Architect in Turkey*. London: Butterworth, 1990.

Cengizkan, Ali. *Modernin saati*. Ankara, 2002.

Eldem, Sedad Hakki. "Toward a Local Idiom: A Brief History of Contemporary Architecture in Turkey." *Zodiac* 10 (1993–94): 38–53.

Ersoy, Ahmet. "On the Sources of the 'Ottoman Renaissance': Architectural Revival and Its Discourse during the Abdülaziz Era, 1861–76." Ph.D. diss., Harvard University, 2000.

Evin, Ahmet, and Renata Holod. *Modern Turkish Architecture*. Philadelphia: University of Pennsylvania Press, 1983.

Eydel, Katja. *The Invention of Turkey*. New York: Sternberg Press, 2006.

Hamadeh, Shirine. "Ottoman Expressions of Early Modernity and the 'Inevitable' Question of Westernization." *Journal of the Society of Architectural Historians* 63 (March 2004): 32–51.

Holod, Renata, and Ahmet Evin. *Modern Turkish Architecture*. Philadelphia: University of Pennsylvania Press, 1984.

Kandiyoti, Deniz, and Ayse Saktanber. *Fragments of Culture: The Everyday of Modern Turkey*. New York: I. B. Tauris, 2002.

Kasaba, Reşat. "Populism and Democracy in Turkey, 1946–1961." In *Rules and Rights in the Middle East: Democracy, Law, and Society*, edited by Ellis Goldberg, Reşat Kasaba, and Joel Migdal. Seattle: University of Washington Press, 1993.

Keyder, Çaglar, ed. *Istanbul: Between the Global and the Local*. Lanham, Md.: Rowman and Littlefield, 1999.

Kezer, Zeynep. "The Making of a Nationalist Capital: Ideology and Socio-Spatial Practices in Early Republican Ankara." Ph.D. diss., University of California, Berkeley, 1998.

Kortan, Enis. *1950'ler kusagi mimarlik antolojisi*. Istanbul: Yem Yayinlari, 1997.

Kuban, Dogan. *Istanbul: An Urban History.* Istanbul: Turkish Economic and Social History Foundation, 1996.

Meeker, Michael E. "Once There Was, Once There Wasn't: National Monuments and Interpersonal Exchange." In *Rethinking Modernity and National Identity in Turkey,* edited by Sibel Bozdoğan and Reşat Kasaba. Seattle: University of Washington Press, 1997.

Nalbantoglu, Gülsüm Baydar. "Tenuous Boundaries: Women, Domesticity, and Nationhood in 1930s Turkey." *Journal of Architecture* 7 (Autumn 2002): 229–44.

Ozyurek, Esra. *Nostalgia for the Modern: State Secularism and Everyday Politics in Turkey.* Durham, N.C.: Duke University Press, 2006.

Sey, Y. "Cumhuriyet doneminde konut." In *75 yilda degisen kent ve mimarlik,* edited by Y. Sey. Istanbul, 1998.

Wright, Alaister. "The Work of Translation: Turkish Modernism and the 'Generation of 1914.'" In *Edges of Empire: Orientalism and Visual Culture,* edited by Jocelyn Hackforth-Jones and Mary Roberts. Malden, Mass.: Blackwell, 2005.

Contributors

NEZAR ALSAYYAD is Professor of Architecture, Planning and Urban History, and Chair of the Center for Middle Eastern Studies at the University of California at Berkeley, as well as President of the International Association for the Study of Traditional Environments (IASTE). He is the author and editor of many books, including *Cities & Caliphs* (1991); *Forms of Dominance* (1993); *Consuming Tradition* (2000); *Hybrid Urbanism* (2001); *Muslim Europe/Euro Islam* (2002); *Urban Informality* (2004); *The End of Tradition* (2004); *Making Cairo Medieval* (2005); and *Cinematic Urbanism* (2006).

MAGNUS T. BERNHARDSSON teaches Middle Eastern History at Williams College. He is the author of *Reclaiming a Plundered Past: Archaeology and Nation-Building in Modern Iraq* (2005). He is now working on a book that will explore U.S.-Iraqi relations between 1920 and 1990.

SIBEL BOZDOĞAN teaches architectural history and theory courses at the Graduate School of Design, Harvard University, and at Bilgi University, Istanbul. She has published articles on the culture and politics of modern architecture, co-authored a monograph on the Turkish architect Sedad Hakki Eldem (1987), and co-edited an interdisciplinary volume, *Rethinking Modernity and National Identity in Turkey* (1997). Her book, *Modernism and Nation Building: Turkish Architectural Culture in the Early Republic* (2001), won the 2002 Alice Davis Hitchcock Award of the Society of Architectural Historians, and the Koprulu Book Prize of the Turkish Studies Association.

SANDY ISENSTADT teaches the history of modern architecture for Yale University's Department of the History of Art. He has written on post-World War II reformulations of modernism by the well-known émigré architects Richard Neutra and Josep Lluis Sert; on visual polemics in the urban proposals of Leon Krier and Rem Koolhaas; and on the history of American refrigerators, picture windows, landscape views, and real estate appraisals. His book, *The Modern American House: Spaciousness and Middle-Class Identity* (2006), describes the visual enhancement of spaciousness in the architectural, interior, and landscape design of American domestic design. His work has been supported with fellowships from the National Endowment for the Humanities, the Graham Foundation for Advanced Studies in the Fine Arts, and the Center for Advanced Study in the Visual Arts.

WALEED KHLEIF, a poet, is former director of the Nazareth Documentation Center and a member of the editorial committee of *al-Mawaqib*, a monthly literary journal. He is the author of several books of poetry and historical studies of Nazareth and pre–1948 Palestine.

ROY KOZLOVSKY is a doctoral candidate at the School of Architecture, Princeton University, and teaches at Parsons, The New School for Design, in New York. He has published articles on various aspects of postwar architecture, including essays on the spatial practices of the Beat writers, Team Ten urbanism, and playground design. His dissertation research on "Reconstruction through the Child: English Modernism and the Welfare State" has been supported by a Whiting Fellowship in the Humanities and a Woodrow Wilson Scholars Fellowship.

BRIAN L. MCLAREN is an Associate Professor in the Department of Architecture at the University of Washington, where he teaches architectural history and theory courses and design. He has published essays on architecture and culture during the period of the Italian colonization of Libya in the *Journal of Decorative and Propaganda Arts* (2002) and in *Muqarnas* (2002), and had co-edited a volume (with D. Medina Lasansky), *Architecture and Tourism: Perception, Performance, and Place* (2004). His writings on architecture and tourism in Libya have also appeared in *Italian Colonialism* (2005), and in his recently published *Architecture and Tourism in Italian Colonial Libya: An Ambivalent Modernism* (2006). His current book project is titled "Modern Architecture, Colonialism, and Race in Fascist Italy."

ALONA NITZAN-SHIFTAN is an architect, historian, and critic of the politics of architecture in cross-cultural and interdisciplinary contexts with a focus on post–World War II architectural culture. She holds a Ph.D. and an S.M.Arch.S. from MIT and is a Senior Lecturer at the Technion's Faculty of Architecture and Town Planning in Israel. Her research was sponsored by the Center for Advanced Study in the Visual Arts, the Getty/UCLA program, the Israel Science Foundation, and currently by the Frankel Center at the University of Michigan. She lectures and publishes widely on post–1967 Jerusalem, as well as on historiography, preservation, national identity and globalization in Israel and the United States. Her forthcoming book is titled *Designing Politics: Architecture and the Making of "United Jerusalem."*

PANAYIOTA I. PYLA is Assistant Professor of Architecture at the University of Illinois at Urbana-Champaign. She holds a Ph.D. in the History and Theory of Architecture from MIT, a Masters of Science in Architectural Studies, also from MIT, and a Professional Degree in Architecture from Rensselaer Polytechnic Institute. Her essays on modern architecture, development, and environmental politics in the Middle East have appeared in the *Journal of Architectural Education, Docomomo, and Thresholds.*

KISHWAR RIZVI teaches the history of Islamic art and architecture as well as seminars on modern architecture in the Middle East and South Asia. Her primary research is on representations of religious and imperial authority in the art and architecture of Safavid Iran, for which she has received an Alexander von Humboldt Foundation award (2007–8). She is finishing her book, *The Safavid Dynastic Shrine: Architecture, Piety and Power in Sixteenth- and Seventeenth-Century Iran.* She has also written on issues of nationalism and religious identity in the modern art and architecture of Iran, with articles appearing in *Muqarnas* (2003, 2007).

SUSAN SLYOMOVICS is Professor of Anthropology and Near Eastern Languages and Cultures at the University of California at Los Angeles. Her books include *The Object of Memory: Arab and Jew Narrate the Palestinian Village* (1998); *Women and Power in the Middle East* (co-edited with Suad Joseph, 2001); *The Walled Arab City in Literature, Architecture, and History: The Living Medina in the Maghrib* (2001); and *The Performance of Human Rights in Morocco* (2005).

ANNABEL WHARTON is the William B. Hamilton Professor of Art, Art History, and Visual Studies at Duke University. She received her Ph.D. at the Courtauld Institute of the University of London. Initially, her work focused on Byzantine and Late

Antique art, architecture, and urbanism; more recently, she has considered the relationship of modernity to pre-modernity, which she has written about in *Building the Cold War: Hilton International Hotels and Modern Architecture* (2001), and *Selling Jerusalem: Relics, Replicas, Theme Parks* (2006). She is currently working on a new project on *Architectural Agency, or How Abused Buildings Take Their Revenge*.

GWENDOLYN WRIGHT is Professor of Architecture in Columbia University's Graduate School of Architecture, Planning and Preservation. She has received numerous fellowships, including a Guggenheim. She is the author of *The Politics of Design in French Colonial Urbanism* (1991); scholarly essays about French architecture and urban design in Africa, North Africa, Southeast Asia, and the Middle East; editor of *The Formation of National Collections of Art and Archaeology* (1995), and the author of several books on American architecture and urbanism. She received both her Masters degree in Architecture and her Ph.D. from the University of California at Berkeley.

Index

Page numbers in italics indicate illustrations.

Aalborg museum (Denmark), 87
Aalto, Alvar, 87, 226
Abassy, Issam, 202
Abbasid period, 7, 83, 86, 88, 91
Aberdeen Free Press, 54
Abrams, Charles, 129
Achaemenid period, 10, 13
Afghanistan, 14, 262
Aga Khan Award for Architecture, 260
Al-Ali, Shaykh Ali Ibrahim, 202
Al-Ayubbi, Ali Jawdat, 87
Al-Azmeh, Aziz, 223
Al-Bahá, Sir Abbas Effendi Abd, 48
Albini, Franco, 236
Alexander, Christopher, 164, 170, 171
Algeria, 24, 62, 63
Algerian War, 257
Algiers, 7
Ali, Mehmet (pasha of Egypt), 236
Ali, Muhammad (viceroy and pasha of Egypt), 41
Al-'Imara (journal), 237
Al-Ittihad (journal), 199, 200, 202
Al-Mansur, and circular plan of Baghdad (8th century), 89
Al-Qaida, 262
Al-Qasim, General Abd al-Karim, 109
Al-Qasim, Samih, 202–6
Al-Rashid, Harun, 88
Al-Ruwad, 85
Allenby, General Edmund, 41
American Embassy Building Program, 23
Anderson, Benedict R. O'G., 31, 260
Anıt Kabir mausoleum (1953), 34n.33
Anglo-Palestine Bank, 48
Ankara, Turkey, 116; Academy of Fine Arts, 15; Kocatepe Mosque, 25, 26, 26; Middle East Technical University, School of Architecture, 123; Skyscraper (Gökdelen, 1959–64), 124
anthropology, 61, 99, 198, 222
anti-modern, 74, 264
Antoniou, Jim, 241, 242
Amir, Hana Sulayman, 195
apocalypse, 42, 56

293

Apollonj, Fabrizio Maria, 74
Arabian American Oil Company (Aramco), 230, 231
Aractingi, Jacques, 229
Architectural Design (journal), 168
Architectural Forum (journal), 128
Architettura e Arti Decorative (journal), 64, 69
Arda, Orhan, 34n.33
Arizona State University, 93
Arkitekt (journal), 123, 124, 129, 133
Armenians, 121
Arts and Crafts Movement, 46
Ashbee, C. R. (Charles Robert), 46, 48, 52, *52*, 53
Assyrian motifs, 86
Atatürk, Mustafa Kemal, 5, 15, 116
Athens, Greece, 39, 44, 109
At Taiyiba, Israel, 188
At-Tamam, Abd, 190, 191, 197, 207
automobiles, 21, 85, 88, 89, 105, 163, 169, 179, 202, 230, 232
Avesta, Sweden, 87
Awni, Kahtan, 101
Azerbaijan, 30n.3

Baalbek (Lebanon) Hellenistic ruins, 230
Baath Party, 109, 111
Babylon, 8, 86, 157
Baghdad, Iraq, 7, 28, 29, 81–96, 97–100, 101, 101–15, 125; American Embassy in, 21, 221; bridges, 84, 85, 98; gossip squares, 106, 107, *107*, 108; housing projects, 98, 103, *110*; Master Plan (1958), *103*; and Ministry of Foreign Affairs (1967), 91; and Monument for the Unknown Soldier, 91–92; New Towns, 103, 105, 149; 1960s building boom, 109; Ottoman Palace (1861), Serai, 81; slums, 85, 107; souk, 102, 108; and Western Baghdad Development Scheme, 103, *104*, 105
Baghdad Modern Art Group, 85

Baghdad University, 88–90, 101, 221–22, *222*
Balbo, Italo, 71
Balgat, Turkey, 118
Ballas, Shimon, 157, 158
Baltimore, Maryland, 48
Baqa al Gharbiya, Israel, 188
Barber, Benjamin, 261
Bauhaus, 226
Baysal, Haluk, 123, 130
Bechtel Corporation, 230
Becket, Welton, 240
Bedouins, 39
Behrenson, Bernard, 43
Behrenson, Mary, 43
Beilin, Yossi, 207
Beirut, Lebanon, 30, 225, 227, 264; American University in, 229; Center for Lebanese Handicrafts, *229*; Defense Ministry (1965), 226, *228*; Ministry of Telecommunication, 226; 1943 master plan, 226; Phoenicia Inter-Continental (1954), 229; Solidere, 230; souks, 230; Technical Bureau, 228
Ben Gurion (or Ben-Gurion), David, 140, 142, 152, 155, 197; and Labour Party, 150
Berbers, 63, 71, 258
Berkes, Niyazi, 119
Berlin, Germany, 8, 32n.12; Charlottenburg Technische Hochschule in, 13
Berman, Marshall, 264
Bethlehem, Israel, 45
Bey, Kemallettin, 13
Bey, Osman Hamdi, 13
Bey, Vedat, 13
Bhabha, Homi, 62
Bigger, Gideon, 47
Birsel, Melih, 123, 130
Bishara, Azmi, 186
Bonatz, Paul, 122
Bozdoğan, Sibel, 18, 20, 29, 116–38, 182, 289–90

294 *Index*

Brasilia, Brazil, 99
Brazil, 229, 244
Breuer, Marcel, 123
Buddha statues in Bamian, 262
Bunshaft, Gordon, 121, 130
Bury St. Edmunds, 42

Cairo, Egypt, 7, 9, 13, 30, 43, 236, 260, 264; and Arab Bureau of Architects, Planners, and Technical Consultants, 225; and Arab League headquarters (1958–60), 238, 240; Bulaq, 241; City of the Dead, 253n.66; and Comité pour la Conservation des Monuments Arabes, 43; Coptic Museum, 44; Heliopolis, 237; Helwan urgent housing project, 239; Imbābah "Workers' City," 240; Madinar al-Awqaf (Engineers' City), 240; Masaakin el-Qadima (urgent housing), 240; Midan Tahrir, 239; Mosque-Madrasa of Amir Khayrbak, 241; Mugamma, 239; Nasr City (Madinet Nasr, Victory City), 240; National Theatre and City of the Arts, 240; Nile Hilton (1953–59), 238, 240; Old Cairo (Fustat, founded 641), 241, 242; Radio and Television Center in, 239; School of Architecture in, 208; Zamalek, 237
Cambridge, Massachusetts, 21, 87
Cambridge University, Charterhouse and Pembroke College, 42
Canada, 143
Cansever, Turgut, 124
Carnegie, Mrs. Andrew (Louise), 48
Casablanca, Morocco, 226
Caudill, Rowlett & Scott (CRS), 232
Cegizkan, Ali, 133
Celebration, Florida, 54
Chadirji, Rifat, 23, 86, 91, 101, 109; and Tobacco Monopoly offices (1966), 92
Chandigarh, India, 99
Church, Frederick Edwin, 41
climate, 18, 21, 22, 68, 69, 70–72, 87, 88, 108, 125, 128, 221, 226, 230, 239, 258–59
coffee houses, 103
Cohen, Abner, 190, 196
Cold War, 108, 116, 118, 119, 239
Colonial Williamsburg (Virginia), 54
Committee for the Conservation of Monuments of Arab Art, 9
Congrès International d'Architecture Moderne (CIAM), 226
Coste, Pascale, 7, 8
Creswell, Keppel A. C., 10, 11, 32n.11
Crimea, 30n.3
"Cromer System," 47
Ctesiphon, 14, 92
cultural memory, 30
culture of fear, 190, 193

Dahan, Gabriel, 194, 195
Dalokay, Vedat, 36n.47; and Kocatepe Mosque in Ankara (1957), 127
Dammon, Saudi Arabia, 231
Dannat, Trevor, 232
Darwish, Mahmud, 202, 203, 204, 206
Datsun, 234
Dayr Yasin, 201
Decemviri, 43
decolonization, 23
democracy, 128–33, 163, 171, 173, 264
Derviş, Rıza, 122
Dhahran, Saudi Arabia, 231–32; airport at, 233
Di Fausto, Florentano, 61, 72, 73, 74; 'Ain el-Fras Hotel design, Ghadames (1935), 73, 74, 75; Tripoli madrasa proposal, 73
Difesa della Razza (journal), 74
disposable architecture, 142
Diyala River (Iraq), 100
Dogon huts (Mali), 223
Doha, Qatar, 264
Doxiades, Constantinos, 17, 28, 97–102, 105–6, 108–11, 110, 226, 231
Doxiadis Associates, 98–111

Dubai, Saudi Arabia, 264
dynapolis, 99, 106, 107

Echochard, Michel, 226
eclecticism, 14, 28, 73
Edinburgh, Scotland, 52
Egli, Ernst, 15, 34n.32
Egypt, 5, 9, 10, 13, 14, 22–23, 31, 40, 48, 97, 208, 236–37, 243, 256, 258–60; Infitah policy, 223, 240; Socialist architecture in, 259
Ekistics, 99, 106, 107
El-Khoury, Pierre, 228
El-Wakil, Abdelwahed, 234
Eldem, Sedad Hakkı, 16, 20, 29, 119, 121, 122, 125, 127, 133
Elon, Amos, 169
Emlak Bank, 128
Erol, Nevzat, and Istanbul City Hall (1953), 127
Ersin, Neja, apartment block (Ankara), 134
Eshkol, Levi, 140, 142, 143
Ethiopia, 71
European Union, 6, 136n.6
Exhibition of Rationalist Architecture (1928), 69

Faluja, Iraq, 188
Farouk (King), 237
Farsi, Sheik Mohammed Said, 234
Fathy, Hassan, 22, 91, 107, 234, 237, 259–60
Faysal (or Faisal) (King of Saudia Arabia) 83, 84, 231–32
Faysal II (King), 89
Ferguson, James, 11
Ferrara, Italy, 55
Finland, 143
Finley, John H., 42, 52
Finsbury, England, 10
Firdawsi's grave, 10
Fletcher, Bannister, *The Tree of Architecture* (1896), 11, 12

Florence, Italy, 74
Foroughi, Mohsen, 14
France, 154, 226
Fu'ad (King), 10
Fulbright grants, 123
Fuller, R. Buckminster, 161, 164, 167

Gabr, Ali Labib, 260
"Garden of Eden" theme park, Baghdad, 88, 89
Garnier, Tony, and Cité Industrielle, 102
Geddes, Patrick, 51–52
George V (King of England), 48
Gérôme, Jean-Léon, 13
Ghadames: Hotel 'Ain el-Fras, 75; Oasis, 73; Piazza of the Large Mulberry, 73
Gibberd, Frederick, 130
Giovannoni, Gustavo, 64
globalization, 135, 136, 221–54 passim, 255–66
Godard, André, 10, 14
Goldhagen, Sarah, 120
Gorst, Sir Eldon, 43
Greece, 244
green space, 51, 88–89, 102, 103, 106, 152, 160n.19, 178, 179, 207
Gropius, Walter, 82, 92, 125; and civic center plan (Talahassee, Florida), 88; and University of Baghdad campus, 87, 90, 101, 221, 222, 222
Gutbrod, Rolf, 232

Hadad, Michael, 200
Haifa, Israel, 206
Hajj Terminal, 232, 236
Hall, Stuart, 136
Halprin, Lawrence, 164
Hamdi, Osman, 9
Hamid, Abdul (Sultan), 51
Hanci, Abdurrahman, 124
Hanna, Hanna Abu, 202, 203, 205, 206
Hashimshoni, Avia, 168
Hashimshoni, Zion, 168

Hassan, Faiq, 85
Haussmann, Georges E. Baron, 173
Hegel, Georg W. F., 55
Hellmuth, Obata & Kassabaum (HOK), 232
Herzfeld, Ernst, 8, 10
Herzl, Theodor, 153, 154, 155
Hijazi, Ibrahim, 206
Hindieh, Maurice, 226
historical justice, 187
historic preservation, 10, 45–48, 51, 53, 54, 62, 74, 91, 161, 163, 168, 171, 179, 222–26, 234, 242, 262
Hittites, 34n.33
Hobsbawm, Eric, 31
Houston, Texas, 240
Howe, Fisher, 50
Hunt, Mrs. Holman, 48
Husayn, Faysal ibn (King), 81, 83, 84, 90, 93
Hussein, Saddam, 83, 115n.39
Hussein, Sherif (King), 43

Ibrahim, Saad, 240
Idumea, 40
immigration, 6, 29, 139–40, *141*, 142–60
Imperial Ottoman Bank, 48
India, 7, 24
International Bank for Reconstruction and Development, 98
International modernism, 3, 16, 17, 30, 91, 116–19, 121–28, 133–36, 161, 167, 169–71, 174, 221–25, 228, 229, 237, 239, 242–44, 256, 259, 263; and developmental modernism, 163, 169, 178, 180, 181; and functionalist modernism, 168, 226; and "Ornamented Modern," 2; and situated modernism, 163, 169, 180
Iran, 5, 6, 9, 10, 13, 14, 24, 261
Iran Society for National Heritage, 9
Iraq, 5, 7, 14, 21, 22, 24, 27, 81–96, 257, 259; British occupation of, 5, 82, 100; and Department of Antiquities, 86;
and Hashemite monarchy, 81, 83, 90, 97, 100, 109
Iraq Consult, 23
Iraq Development Board (IDB), 22, 28, 29, 84, 86–88, 90, 93, 97–100
Iraqi Petroleum Company (IPC), 82, 84
Iraq war, vii, 93, 257; and reconstruction, 111; and sectarian divisions, 106; and tribal divisions, 106, 107
Irving & Jones, 229
Isa, Fathi Uthman, 203
Isaiah (biblical prophet), 173
Islamabad, Pakistan, and Mosque of Shah Faisal, 36n.47
Islamic revival, 6
Israel, 6, 27, 29, 106, 139–60 passim, 161–85 passim, 186–217 passim, 223, 225, 240, 261; American influence, 164; Beit Yosef settlement, *156*; Bet Lid prison, 202; border police, 194, 195; Histadrut labor union, 150; Housing Ministry, 149, 152; Islamic Movement of Israel, 211; and Israel Defense Force, 187; Jewish Agency's Settlement Department, 140, 145; Knesset (Israeli Parliament), 140, 152, 199; Lifta, *162*; Little Triangle, 188, 189, *189*, 190; military laws, 202; Million Plan, 155; New Town program, 148, 149, 150, 152; and 1956 Sinai Campaign, 187; and 1967 War, 161, 174, 239; Planning Department, 148; Public Committee, 195, 196; Rashish Committee, 198; Salo Hershman, Gilo, *162*; Shekem, Israeli army caterers, 198; Shikum Ovdim (Workers' Housing), 150; transit towns (*ma'abaras*), 139–60
Istanbul, Turkey, 5, 6, 8, 116; airport, 128; Anadolu Club Building on Büyükada, Prince Island, 124, *125*; Ataköy Cooperative Development, 128, *131*; Bosporus, 119; Çınar Hotel, 128; City Hall (1953), 127, 128, *129*;

Index 297

Istanbul, Turkey *(continued)*
    Fine Arts Academy, 13; Florya motel and beach facilities, 121; Hilton Hotel (1955), 20, 24, 29, 119–23, *120*, 124, 125–28, *126*, 130, 134, *136*; Hyatt Regency Hotel, *135*, 136; Imperial Ottoman Museum, 9; Lawyers' Cooperative apartments, Mecidiyeköy, 130, *131*; suburb of Yeşilköy, 130, *132*; Suleymaniyye Mosque complex, 9; Villa on Büyükada, Prince Island, 122
Istfahan (Isfahan), Iran, 236
Italian colonialism, 61–78; and Fascist imperial politics, 74

Jacobs, Jane, 223
Jaffa, Israel, 44
Jaljulya, Israel, 190, 191, 197
Jameson, Frederic, 118
Jansen, Hermann, 15
Japan, 143, 225
Jawdat, Ellen, 21
Jawdat, Nizar Ali, 21, 87
Jeddah, Saudi Arabia, 43, 231, 232, 234
Jerusalem, Israel, 27, 28, 29, 39, 40, 41–60, 161–66, *166*, 167–74, *175*, 176–85; 1968 Jerusalem Masterplan, 164, 165, 168–71, *169*, *172*, 176, 180, 181; Al-Haram al-Sharif, 39; Anglo-Egyptian Bank, 48; Armenian Convent, 46; Central Boulevard design, 172, 173; ceramic street sign, *49*, *50*; Church of Calvary, 40; Church of the Holy Sepulchre, 39, 40, 42; Citadel, 51; clock tower, 46, 51, *52*; Damascus Gate, 44, 51, 178; Dome of the Rock, 39, 48, 49, 56; Gethsemane, 54; Hass promenade, 179; Hebrew Union College campus, 179; Herod's Gate, 51; Inner Loop design, 171; Jaffa Gate, 51–52, *52*, *53*; Jerusalem Committee, 161, 163–69, 173, 174, 176–81; Mamluk fountains, 39; Mammila complex, 179; Mt. Herzl, 173; Mt. Scopus, 172–73; Mount of Olives, 39, 44; Municipal Ecology Section, 178; Quarries of Solomon, 44; St. Stephen's Gate, 51; Sherover promenade, 179; Solomon's Temple, 54, 56; Subcommittee for Town Planning, 164; Tyropean Valley, 51; Walls of Süleyman the Magnificent, 39, 41, 46, 51, 54, 55; Western Wall, 173; Yad Vashem Museum to Holocaust Victims, 187
Jerusalem Post, 165
Jewish Colonization Society of Vienna, 45
Jewish National Fund, 45
Johnson, Philip, 164
Johnson Institute (Sweden), 87
Jordan, 161, 173, 188, 189; Amman, 173
Jubran, Salim, 202
Judea, Israel, 44, 45

Kacel, Ela, 130
Kaempfer, Engelbert, 7
Kafr Qasim, Israel, 186–217 passim; and 1956 massacre at, 29, 187, 193, 206, 207, 211, 212; archives, 207; cemetery, 191, *192*, 199, 200, 204; community center, 207–8, *209*, *210*, *211*; monuments, *201*, 202, 206–7, *208*; museum, 207, 212
Kahn, Louis, 145, *147*, 161, 164, *167*, 169, 170, 171, 176, 178
Kaiser Wilhelm II, 32n.12, 46, 51
Karim, Sayed (or Sayyid), 231, 232, 237
Karkur, Israel, 151
Karradah, Iraq, 100
Katsav, Moshe, 207
Kerry, John, 92
Keun & Loeb, Messrs. *See* Kühn, Loeb & Co.
Keynbes, J. M., 43
Khairallah, Samir, 228, 229
Khalifeh, Marcel, 203
Khan, Fazlur, 232, 236
Khan, Riza (also Pahlavi, Riza Shah), 5, 9, 10, 11

298   Index

Khayat, Shlomo, 208, 211
Khomeini, Ahmad, 25
Khomeini, Ayatollah, 24; tomb of, 24, 25
Kiev, Ukraine, 48
King Faisal University (Damman), 232
King Saud University (near Riyadh), 232, 233
Kirkuk, Iraq, housing projects, 98
Kitchener, Lord Horatio, 43
Kollek, Teddy, 161, 163–69, 167, 177, 178, 179, 180–81
Korean War, 116, 119
Kortan, Enis, 123
Kufic calligraphy, 91
Kühn, Loeb & Co. (Abraham Kühn and Solomon Loeb), 48
Kurdani, Israel, 151
Kutcher, Arthur, 165
Kuwait, 5

labor therapy, 153, 154
Lamartine, Alphonse de, 39
Larco, Sebastiano, 69
Lasdun, Denys, 171
Lavon, Pinhas, 140
Lawrence, T. E. (Thomas Edward; "Lawrence of Arabia"), 43
Lebanon, 5, 223, 225–26, 243; and Department of Antiquities, 230; French Mandate period, 225–26, 230; and Ministry of Tourism, 230
Le Corbusier, 87, 90, 101, 124, 130, 226
Legault, Rejean, 120
Leon, Edwin de, 41
Leptis Magna (Libya): Hotel at the Excavations of, 69, 70, 70, 74; Oasis of Al-Khums, 70
Lerner, Daniel, 117, 118, 133
Levant, 121, 229
Lever House (New York), 124
Lewis, Bernard, 117, 177
Libya, 27, 28, 31, 61–78; Jabal Nafusah region, 74, 75; Office of Indigenous Applied Arts, 62; Troglodyte houses, 74
Limongelli, Alessandro, 66
Lindstroem, Sune, 232
local materials, 21, 45, 108, 125
London, England, 8, 10, 40, 95n.20, 264
Los Angeles, California, 240
Luxor, Egypt, 237, 259

ma'abara, 142–43, 145, 149, 150–55, 157, 158
Macfarlane, P. W., 98, 111n.4
Maclean, Sir William, 46
Makiya, Kanan, 92
Makiya, Muhammad, 86, 101, 109; and 1963 Khulafa Mosque, 90; and 1965 Mosul Museum of Antiquities, 91; and 1967 Baghdad Ministry of Foreign Affairs, 91
Malinki, Shmuel, 194, 195, 197
Mamluk period, 13, 260
Manchester, England, 48
Marefat, Mina, 88
Marshall Plan, 5, 98, 118, 119
martyrs, 191, 206, 207
Masa'ud, Ali al-Maligi, 240
Mashrabiyya, 125
Masri, Aziz el, 43
Mata, Arturo Soria y, 102
McDonald & Yakeley, 232
McLaren, Brian, 28, 61–78, 290
McMahon, Sir Henry, 43
McMillen, Louis, 87
Mecca, 5, 231, 232, 234
Medieval revivals, 13, 33–34n.28, 49, 86, 88, 89, 91, 242, 243, 259, 265
Medieval sites, 100, 240, 241
Medina, 5, 232
memorial rituals, 187, 188, 191, 193, 194, 196, 198, 200, 202, 204, 205, 212
memorialization, 30, 188, 193, 199, 203, 206, 207, 212
Menderes, Adnan, 127
Mesopotamian heritage, 82, 83, 89, 157

Index   299

Middle East, map of, 2
Mies van der Rohe, Ludwig, Farnsworth House, 123
Milner, Lord Alfred, 48
Minoprio & Spencely, 98
Mitchell, Timothy, 222, 223, 261
Mitchell, W. J. T., 174, 179
Moemem, Galal, 239
Mond, Sir Alfred, 48
Moneo, Rafael, 230
Money, Sir Arthur, 46
Monk, Daniel, 56, 174
monuments, 3, 8–10, 188, 190, 194–96, 200, 201, 206, 211, 212, 225, 236; proposed for Deir Yassin massacre, 187; Holocaust memorials and, 187; Land Day massacre, 186
Morocco, 31, 62, 63, 223, 229, 244
Morris, Benny, 188, 190
Morris, William, 46
Mosul, Iraq, 91, 98
Moustapha, Ahmed Farid, 232
Mshatta Palace façade, 8, 9, 32n.12
Mughal India, 236
Mumford, Lewis, 161, 164, 173
Munich (Germany) Exhibition of Islamic Art (1910), 8
Munir, Hisham, 86
Museum of Arab Art (Cairo), 9
Museum of Islamic Art (Istanbul), 9
Mussayib, Iraq, housing projects, 98

Nakhleh, Yusuf, 200
Napoleon, Bonaparte, 7, 30n.3, 154
Nasiriyyah, Saudi Arabia, 230
Nasser, Ali, 259
Nasser, Colonel Gamal Abdel, 97, 225, 237, 239, 240, 242, 258
national identity, 13–17, 260–62
nationalism, 8, 11, 23, 24, 27, 28, 31n.6, 31n.10, 32n.13, 36n.48, 82, 83, 91, 98, 100, 109, 117–22 passim, 136, 139, 148, 152, 153, 158, 163, 170, 176, 177, 179, 193, 212, 237, 255, 257, 258, 264

Nazareth, Israel, 202; Mary's Well plaza in, 200
Neema, Pierre, 229
Nervi, Pier Luigi, 127
Neutra, Richard, 122
New Gourna, Egypt, 23, 224, 237, 259, 260
New York, NY, 26, 32n.12
New York Globe, 53
New York Times, 107
Niemeyer, Oscar, 127, 229
Noguchi, Isamu, 164
Nooradin, Hoshia, 86
North Atlantic Treaty Organization (NATO), 118, 137n.6
Northcliffe, Lord Alfred, 41, 48
Nouvel, Jean, 26
Nubia, 40, 258

Ofer, Shalom, 195
oil, 5, 31, 47, 82, 84, 97, 225; and OPEC, 223, 231, 232
Olearius, Adam, 7
Omar, Ramzy, 259
Onat, Emin, 122
Orientalism (or Orientalist), 3, 6–8, 29, 30n.1, 32n.13, 35n.43, 89, 107, 108, 125, 133, 163, 171, 173–74, 177–78, 180, 198, 221, 223, 225, 236, 262
Otto, Frei, 232
Ottoman architecture, 13, 125, 127, 174
Ottoman period, 4, 5, 7, 13, 81, 82, 84, 100, 117, 236
Oxford University (England), 47

Paestum, Italy, 40
Pahlavi, Riza Shah. *See* Khan, Riza
Pahlavi dynasty, 10, 32n.16
Palestine, 29, 30, 47, 140, 153, 154, 155, 174, 176, 186–217 passim, 223; amd Mandate Palestine, 5, 6, 27, 56, 173–74; American Red Cross in, 42
Pan-Arab nation, 82, 83, 225, 237
Paris, France, 86, 226, 264; and École des

300   Index

Beaux-Arts, 13, 14, 208; and Institut du Monde Arabe (1988), 26
Pasargade, Iran, Achaemenid palace in, 3in.11
Pellegrini, Giovanni, 71, 72
Perkins, G. Holmes, 123
Persia, Iran, 88, 89, 92
Pevsner, Nikolaus, 164
Pharaonic period in Egypt, 7, 8, 237, 240, 260
photographic aesthetic, 68
Piacentini, Marcello, 64
Piccinato, Luigi, 128
Pierpont Morgan, John Pierpont and John Pierpont Jr., 48
pilgrimage, 25, 28, 41, 42, 52, 55, 178
poetry, 170, 176, 187; Iraqi, 86, 89, 95n.17; Palestinian, 199, 200, 201–6, 212, 213n.5
Polish soldier-artists, 85
Ponti, Gio, 87
Pope, Arthur Upham, 10, 11
populist architecture, 25, 26, 31n.10
postcolonial identity, 4, 27, 31, 81, 98, 111, 120, 133, 170, 223, 237, 255, 256, 257, 259, 261, 263, 264
prefabricated architecture, 143, 144, 145, 154, 230, 232
Progressive Architecture (journal), 17
Pro-Jerusalem Society, 46, 48, 51, 53, 56
Pro-Palestine Society, 48

Qajar period, 5, 10, 13, 33n.27
Qalansuwa, Israel, 188
Qaqun, Israel, 188
Qasem, General Abd al-Karim, 90
Qasr al-Hajj mosque (Libya), 68
Qassim, Abdul Karim, 24
Qawar, Jamal, 200

Rabegh, 43
racist discourse, 61, 71, 74, 76, 243
Ramleh, Israel, 195
Ranger, Terrence, 31

Rava, Carlo Enrico, 61, 66, 67, 68, 69, 70, 71, 72, 74
Rava, Maurizio, 66, 67
Ravenna, Italy, 55
Rhodes, 73
Riad, Mahmoud, 240
Ricard, Prosper, 63
Richmond, Ernest, 46, 48
Riyadh, Saudi Arabia, 30, 231; Paolo Ghera's Central Market, 232; conference center, 232; King Faisal Foundation, 232; Masmak Castle, 236; Qasr el-Hokm palace and government district, 230, 235, 236; WAISIA, 232
Riyadh University, 232
Robert Matthew Johnson Marshall and Partners (RMJM), 232, 234
Roberts, David, 40
Romanelli, Pietro, 65, 67
Roman influence, 11, 63, 65, 67, 68, 70, 221
Rome, Italy, 40, 44, 86. *See also* Exhibition of Rationalist Architecture (1928)
Rosh ha-Ayin, Israel, 195
Rostow, W. W., 222
Roth, Alfred, 226
Ruppin, Arthur, 45
Rusafa, Iraq, 84, 100
Russia, Czarist rule in, 97
Russian constructivism, 68

Saarinen, Eero, 123
Sadat, Anwar, 223, 240, 242
Safide, Moshe, 164
Said, Edward, 30n.1, 177, 178, 180, 185n.48, 245n.6
St. Petersburg, Russia, 264
Salim, Jewad, 85, 86
Salter, Lord Arthur, 22
Samarra, Iraq, 7, 92
Samuel, Herbert, 47–48
San Juan, Puerto Rico: Caribe Hilton Hotel, 124; La Concha Hotel, 127

Index 301

Sarre, Friedrich, 8
Sarsur, Fatimah Salih, 195
Sarsur, Hamdelelullah, 198
Sarsur, Ibrahim, 197, 198, 199, 207, 211, 212
Sasanian period, 10, 13, 14, 92
Saud, Abdul Aziz al ("Ibn Saud"), 230, 232
Saudi Arabia, 5, 223, 230–36, 243
Scarin, Emilio, 74
Schumpter, Joseph, 225
Schweid, Yoseph, 168, 176
Sert, Josep Lluis (or José Luis), 21, 95n.24, 125, 221, 222
Seville, Spain, 236
Shadmi, Issachar, 194
Shalom, Mordechai Ish, 168
Sharett, Moshe, 188
Shebib, Naoum, 239
Shehab, Fuad (president of Lebanon), 229
Shi'as, 106, 114n.38
Shibab, Fuad, 225
Shiber, Saba George, 228
Shihab government, 230
Sikh Regiment, 51st, 48
Siloah, Israel, 52
Siroux, Maxime, 14
Skidmore, Owings and Merrill (SOM), 20, 119, 121, 123, 124, 130, 232, 236
Solomon (King), 44
Stein, Joseph, 125
Stoddard, John, 41
Stone, Edward Durrell, 125, 229
Storrs, Rev. John, 42
Storrs, Ronald, 42, 43, 44–45, 46, 51, 53, 54, 55, 56
Strachey, Lytton, 43
social engineering, 106
Soviet Linear Cities (1930s), 102
Soviet Union, 6, 119, 240
Sudan, 257
Suez Canal, 5, 237, 239

Süleyman the Magnificent, 39
Sumerian forms, 86
Susa, Iran, 31n.10
Sweden, 143
Syria, 5, 7, 40, 48, 226

Tabet, Antoine, 226
Taliesen West (Phoenix, AZ), 89
Tallin, Estonia, 87
Tange, Kenzo, 232
teahouses, 105
Team X (Ten), 170
Technion City, Israel, 168
Tehran, Iran, 6, 7, 25; Academy of Arts and Sciences, 33n.25; Iran Bastan Museum, 14, 15; Iranian Senate Building, 14; museum in, 34n.29; tomb of Ayatollah Khomeini, 24, 25, 36n.47
Tehrani, Mohammad, 25
Tehran University, Faculty of Technology, 14, 16
Tel Aviv (or Tel-Aviv), Israel, 148
Tel Yeruham, Israel, 151
Tennyson, Charles, 43
Texier, Charles, 7
Thebes, Egypt, 55
Tigris River, 84, 87, 100, 102
Tira, Israel, 151, 188
Titus (Roman emperor), 54
Tod, General James, 7
Tokay, Enver, 124
Torro, Ferrer, and Torregrosa: Caribe Hilton Hotel, San Juan (Puerto Rico), 124; La Concha Hotel, 127
tourism, 4, 8, 28, 41, 48, 51–52, 54, 63, 68, 70, 73, 125, 127, 207, 223, 228, 230, 240–41
Tripoli, Libya, 65, 66, 71; ancient castle, 62, 66; Corso Vittorio Emanuele III display, 63, 64; house photographed by Giovanni Pellegrini, 72; International and Permanent Fair, 229; Madrasa proposal for, 73; Oasis, 66,

68, 69; Piazza Italia, 66, 67; Qaramanli house, 65, 65; walls of, 62, 66
Tripolitania, 63
Tubi, Tawfiq, 199, 200
Tunisia, 62, 63
Turkey, 4, 5, 6, 15, 24; Americanization of, 29, 116–38 passim; Chamber of Architects, 123; Democrat Party (DP), 116–20, 122, 127, 134, 135; Kemalist revolution, 118; Ministry of Education, 122; Ministry of Transportation, 122; Republican Peoples' Party (RPP), 116; Turkish Pension Funds, 119
Tyrwhitt, Jaqueline, 113n.25

Ukhadir, Palace, 92
Ummayad period, 7
UNESCO, and plan for medieval Cairo, 242
United Kingdom, 81
United Nations, 18, 129, 188; Blueprint for Peace (1951), 18, 19; UNDP, 231; Relief and Work Agency (UNRWA), 190; Secretariat Building, 18, 119
United States, 6, 11, 24, 116–38, 143, 188, 240, 243; and CIA, 239; Economic Cooperation Administration, 119; as empire, 264; Information Services agency (USIS), Istanbul, 129; oil-related investments in the Middle East, 225; Operations Mission, 226; navy, 230; Pax Americana, 223; State Department, 23, 230
Universal Declaration of Human Rights (1948), 18
universal humanity, 18
University of Florence, 74
University of Pennsylvania, 123
University of Southern California, 95n.20
Upper-Yokneam, Israel, 142
urban planning and urbanism, 4, 82, 88–89, 97–115 passim, 122, 163, 165, 167, 168, 170, 171, 178–81, 222, 223, 225, 236, 240, 256–60, 262–64

Van Eyck, Aldo, 170
Venice, Italy, 55
vernacular architecture, 22, 55, 70, 72, 83, 91, 92, 134, 136, 171, 221, 223, 234–37, 240, 243, 256, 260
vernacular motifs, 23, 229, 234, 260
Vienna, Austria, 8
Volpi, Giuseppe, 62, 63, 65, 66

Wadi 'Ara, Israel, 188
Wahabi fundamentalism, 231
Waziriyah (Iraq), 100
Welfare Party (Refa Partesi) (Turkey), 25
Wogenscky, André, 226
World War I, 5, 10, 24, 32n.11, 41, 43, 53, 81, 84
World War II, 17, 18, 20, 23–24, 84, 85, 103, 116–17, 120, 124, 133, 161, 163, 170, 221, 223, 225, 230, 236, 242, 258
Wright, Frank Lloyd, 82, 87, 90, 92, 93, 111; Baghdad Theater and Opera house, 88, 89, 101; German publication of Illinois prairie houses, 17; plan for Baghdad, 88, 89; plan for Baghdad art gallery, 88–89, 93

Yamasaki, Minoru, 123, 231
Yokneam, Israel, 142, 143, *143*, 144, *144*, 146, 150, *151*, 152
Young, James, 187

Zaharoff, Sir Basil, 48
Zayyad, Tawfiq, 200, 202
Zevi, Bruno, 161, 164, 172, 176
Zionism, 45, 139, 148, 152–55, 157, 158, 163, 165, 168, 174, 176
Zionist Commission, 48
Zubaida, Sami, 81

www.ingramcontent.com/pod-product-compliance
Lightning Source LLC
Chambersburg PA
CBHW030608230426
43661CB00053B/1896